Ink-Stained Hollywood

The publisher and the University of California Press Foundation gratefully acknowledge the generous support of the Kenneth Turan and Patricia Williams Endowment Fund in American Film.

Ink-Stained Hollywood

The Triumph of American Cinema's Trade Press

Eric Hoyt

UNIVERSITY OF CALIFORNIA PRESS

University of California Press

Oakland, California

Suggested citation: Hoyt, E. *Ink-Stained Hollywood: The Triumph of American Cinema's Trade Press*. Oakland: University of California Press, 2022. DOI: https://doi.org/10.1525/luminos.122

Library of Congress Cataloging-in-Publication Data

Names: Hoyt, Eric, author.
Title: Ink-stained Hollywood : the triumph of American cinema's trade press / Eric Hoyt.
Description: Oakland, California : University of California Press, [2022] | Includes bibliographical references and index.
Identifiers: LCCN 2021040705 (print) | LCCN 2021040706 (ebook) | ISBN 9780520383692 (paperback) | ISBN 9780520383708 (ebook)
Subjects: LCSH: Journalism and motion pictures. | Motion picture industry—California—Los Angeles—History—20th century.
Classification: LCC PN1993.5.U65 H79 2022 (print) | LCC PN1993.5.U65 (ebook) | DDC 791.4305—dc23
LC record available at https://lccn.loc.gov/2021040705
LC ebook record available at https://lccn.loc.gov/2021040706

31   30   29   28   27   26   25   24   23   22
10   9   8   7   6   5   4   3   2   1

For Esme, Arli, Liam, and Emily

CONTENTS

LIST OF TABLES

ACKNOWLEDGMENTS

This book developed over many years, with the help of many people, organizations, and institutions. I will never be able to adequately thank them all. What follows represents my best attempt.

The research and writing of *Ink-Stained Hollywood* has been inextricably linked to my role in leading the Media History Digital Library (MHDL). Thank you to the MHDL's founding director, David Pierce, for his vision and tenacity in building this project. I have been honored to be part of it. I am grateful to David for teaching me so much and for trusting me to lead the MHDL forward.

To build this collection, we borrowed and scanned books, magazines, and trade papers from a number of leading film heritage institutions, including the Library of Congress Motion Picture, Broadcasting, and Recorded Sound Division; Museum of Modern Art Library; Academy of Motion Picture Arts and Sciences' Margaret Herrick Library; University of Maryland, College Park; Berkeley Art Museum and Pacific Film Archive; Prelinger Library; and Wisconsin Center for Film and Theater Research. The contributions of private collectors, particularly Karl Thiede, Eileen Bowser, and Richard Koszarski, were also vital. Thank you to all these institutions and individuals for generously lending the MHDL your materials—many of which are analyzed in this book. My deep thanks also extend to the Internet Archive, which served as a vendor for most of the scanning and continues to host and preserve the MHDL's digital files.

The MHDL's operations have been financially supported by the contributions of many organizations and individuals, including the Mary Pickford Foundation, California Digital Library, Columbia University Library, Domitor, University of Zurich, Matthew and Natalie Bernstein, Q. David Bowers, Stephen P. Jarchow, Jeff Joseph, Charlie Keil, John McElwee, Russell Merritt, Northwestern University in

Qatar Library, Richard Scheckman, David Sorochty, David Stenn, University of South Carolina, University of St. Andrews Library and Centre for Film Studies, and an anonymous donor in memory of Carolyn Hauer. Grant funding from the American Council of Learned Societies, Institute of Museum and Library Services, National Endowment for the Humanities, and Social Sciences and Humanities Research Council of Canada has enabled significant enhancements to the MHDL's collections, capabilities, and platforms. Without the support of these sponsors, neither the MHDL nor this book would exist.

In addition to scanning and funding, the MHDL has depended on the hard work of a brilliant team of people. Carl Hagenmaier and Wendy Hagenmaier were instrumental in the development of the Lantern search engine. Thanks also go to Edward Betts, Andy Myers, Joseph Pomp, and Anne Helen Petersen for their contributions to Lantern's success. Charles Acland, Kevin Ponto, and Alex Peer were vital collaborators on the Arclight app. Robert Farr was crucial in formulating and implementing a social media strategy. Keeping our servers and database going would have been impossible without the dedication and expertise of Peter Sengstock and Samuel Hansen.

Over the past nine years, I have benefited enormously from the graduate students at the University of Wisconsin–Madison who have supported the MHDL and my work on this book. No amount of thanks will ever be sufficient for Derek Long, Kit Hughes, and Tony Tran, who, from 2013 to 2017, collaborated with me on the completion of Lantern, the development of the Arclight app, and the coauthorship of several research publications (sections from one of which, "*Variety's* Transformations," is adapted from and reproduced in this book). My thanks also go to JJ Bersch, Matt St. John, Maureen Mauk, Caroline Meikle, Jacob Mertens, Connor Perkins, and Olivia Johnston Riley for their work in digitizing some of the sources that are discussed in this book (and are now available on the MHDL). Laurel Gildersleeve, Caroline Leader, and Austin Morris kindly visited out-of-town archival collections on my behalf when I was not able to travel in person. Last, but not least, thank you to Lesley Stevenson, who was absolutely clutch when it came time to prepare the final book manuscript. I am so lucky to have been able to work with all of you.

In UW-Madison's Department of Communication Arts, I am fortunate to work with an extraordinary group of colleagues. I would like to thank the Media and Cultural Studies and Film faculty and academic staff—Jonathan Gray, Michele Hilmes, Derek Johnson, Lori Kido Lopez, Jason Kido Lopez, Jeremy Morris, Jennifer Hyland Wang, David Bordwell, Kelley Conway, Lisa Ellis, Aaron Greer, Erik Gunneson, Lea Jacobs, Vance Kepley, Darshana Mini, J. J. Murphy, Ben Singer, Jeff Smith, and Kristin Thompson—for the intellectual and creative community that makes this work possible (and fun). My thanks also go to the Wisconsin Center for Film and Theater Research team, Mary Huelsbeck and Amanda Smith, for their collaboration and all they have taught me in our work together.

This book and the MHDL have further benefited from substantial institutional support. Support for this research was provided by the University of Wisconsin–Madison Office of the Vice Chancellor for Research and Graduate Education, with funding from the Wisconsin Alumni Research Foundation. Trips to visit archives, time to think and write, and the open access publishing subvention were all made possible thanks to this support. UW-Madison's College of Letters and Science and the generous research endowment from Kelly and Kimberly Kahl supported the completion of this book and the expansion of the MHDL. Thank you as well to my friends at the UW Libraries and Wisconsin Historical Society for all the guidance they have offered over the years.

Beyond Madison, I am fortunate to belong to an international community of scholars who work in the domains of media history and the digital humanities. For their insights and words of encouragement at key moments during the research and writing process, I would like to thank Richard Abel, Robert C. Allen, Kaveh Askari, Cari Beauchamp, Daniel Biltereyst, Emily Carman, Michael Cowan, James Crawford, Darrell Davis, Mary Desjardins, Tom Doherty, Allyson Nadia Field, Barbara Flueckiger, Kate Fortmueller, Jane M. Gaines, Philippa Gates, Daniela Treveri Gennari, Catherine Grant, Malte Hagener, Laura Horak, Richard B. Jewell, Charlie Keil, Tom Kemper, Shawna Kidman, Elana Levine, Richard Maltby, Luci Marzola, Paul McDonald, Tamar Jeffers McDonald, Denise McKenna, Philippe Meers, Cynthia B. Meyers, Paul S. Moore, Rielle Navitski, Julia Noordegraaf, Jan Olsson, Clara Pafort-Overduin, Louis Pelletier, Wyatt Phillips, Dana Polan, Nicolas Poppe, Thomas Schatz, Laura Isabel Serna, Josh Shepperd, Katherine Spring, Shelley Stamp, Deb Verhoeven, Patrick Vonderau, Gregory Waller, Kristen Warner, Haidee Wasson, Jessica L. Whitehead, Mark Williams, Chris Yogerst, and Emilie Yueh-Yu Yeh. Thanks especially to Scott Curtis, Priya Jaikumar, and Ellen Seiter for their mentorship and support, which has spanned almost every phase of my career.

I am also grateful to have had opportunities to share earlier iterations of this research at a number of institutions and events. The feedback helped me sharpen this project, and the trips were an absolute blast. Thank you to my hosts at Carnegie Mellon University; Concordia University; Ghent University; New York University; Stockholm University; University of California, Los Angeles; University of Pennsylvania; University of Toronto; University of Wisconsin–Milwaukee; University of Zurich; and Wilfrid Laurier University. Thanks also to the History of Moviegoing, Exhibition and Reception (HoMER) and Society for Cinema and Media Studies (SCMS) for supporting my work and bringing together such wonderful scholarly communities.

Selections of the research and prose included in this book were first published elsewhere. Thank you to the publishers—and, most of all, to my coauthors—for permitting me to revise and reuse the material. Here is the list of credits (in order of appearance):

- Eric Hoyt, Derek Long, Anthony Tran, and Kit Hughes, "*Variety*'s Transformations: Digitizing and Analyzing a Canonical Trade Paper," *Film History* 27, no. 4 (2015): 76–105.
- Eric Hoyt, "Exhibitors, Technology, and Industrial Journalism in the 1910s and 1920s," *Velvet Light Trap* 76 (Fall 2015): 49–53. Copyright © 2015 by the University of Texas Press. All rights reserved.
- Eric Hoyt, "Arclights and Zoom Lenses: Searching for Influential Exhibitors in Film History's Big Data," in *The Routledge Companion to New Cinema History*, ed. Daniel Biltereyst, Richard Maltby, and Philippe Meers (New York: Routledge, 2019), 83–95.
- Eric Hoyt, "The Trade Papers and Cultures of 1920s Hollywood," in *Resetting the Scene: Classical Hollywood Revisited*, ed. Philippa Gates and Katherine Spring (Detroit: Wayne State University Press, 2021): 267–79.

Some of the best research shared in the abovementioned presentations and publications (and now in this book) emerged from archival sources outside of the Media History Digital Library. For opening up their collections to me, I would like to thank the Alliance for Audited Media; John F. Kennedy Presidential Library and Museum; Superior Court of California, County of Los Angeles's Archives and Records Center; National Archives and Records Administration, College Park; National Archives and Records Administration, San Francisco; New York County Clerk Records Center; and Wisconsin Historical Society, Madison. Thanks to Scott Taylor at Georgetown University Library's Booth Family Center for Special Collections for invaluable help with both the early and final stages of this project. And this project would have been impossible without the collections and staff of the Academy of Motion Picture Arts and Sciences' Margaret Herrick Library. Big thanks go to the Herrick team, past and present, who helped me: Val Almendarez, Sandra Archer, Barbara Hall, Kristine Krueger, Jenny Romero, Faye Thompson, and Lea Whittington.

I am privileged to be able to work again with the University of California Press. Thank you to my editor, Raina Polivka, for making the entire review, revision, and production process such a pleasure, even as we both had to adapt to the insanity of trying to work and parent kids during a pandemic. Thank you to Madison Wetzell, Francisco Reinking, Joe Abbott, and Joan D. Shapiro for their skill in moving the book through the production process. Thanks also to editors Mary Francis and Sara Cohen for their guidance and support at other key junctures during this book's long development.

The book you are reading is substantially improved over earlier manuscript drafts thanks to the insightful feedback of peer reviewers. I wish to extend my sincere thanks to Peter Decherney, Kathryn Fuller-Seeley, Ross Melnick, Eric Smoodin, and an anonymous reader of an earlier draft for their thoughtful reviews and for helping me strengthen this project. Thank you!

Finally, I would like to thank my family for their love and support over the long period of this project's research and writing. Thank you to my parents, Elizabeth and Christopher Hoyt, and in-laws, Debby and Carl Hagenmaier, for their encouragement, even with something that might feel as quirky as old movie magazines. Thanks also to my brother William, sister Whitney, and wider family: Rob, Hannah, Wendy, Alex, Dave, Becky, Will, Doug, and Barbara.

Most of all, I wish to thank the four immediate family members who shared the same home/office/schoolhouse with me as I finished this book during the COVID-19 pandemic. This was an unimaginably hard year in so many ways. But we made it through together. Thank you to Esme, Arli, and Liam for your inspiring curiosity, creativity, and resilience. And thank you, Emily, for your love, mindfulness, and partnership.

Thank you for giving me the time to finish this book . . . and for the interruptions, too.

Introduction

DELIVERING THE TRADES

This book contains many stories, some shared for the first time, almost all concerning people long gone. So, let me begin with a more recent story from my own life. Without this experience, I can say with confidence that the book you are reading would not exist.

Before I ever pursued academia—a career path that would lead me to teaching students, poking around archives, and digitizing millions of pages of old movie magazines—I pushed around a mail cart at 7 a.m. every day, delivering copies of *Daily Variety* and *Hollywood Reporter*. It was 2005, and my first job out of college was working in the mailroom of a large Hollywood talent agency. There wasn't time to read the trades on my delivery runs. So, when most of the office cleared out for lunch, I would pull crumpled trade papers out of the recycling bins. I devoured them like the free donuts laid out every Friday morning.

I read the trades for news and information. As an agent trainee, I was expected to have a sense of "who's who" and where industry players fit within Hollywood's hierarchy. But I also read the trade papers with a critical eye. I learned this practice from the people around me. Talent agents dismissed certain stories as puff, desperate attempts to put a positive spin on a string of flops. At the same time, however, those same agents invested a tremendous amount of meaning in the trades. A tirade ensued, for instance, when a young agent was omitted from a list of up-and-coming movers-and-shakers. As I came to understand, the trade papers communicated information, but they did much more, playing important gatekeeping and scorekeeping functions within the industry's culture.

Fast-forward a decade. Now working at the University of Wisconsin–Madison, I was far from the talent agency mailroom in Beverly Hills. Yet I was more immersed than ever in Hollywood trade papers. Through a mixture of good timing, great collaborators, and a whole lot of grunt work, I was playing a leading role in the open access digitization of historic sources for film and broadcasting history. As codirector of the Media History Digital Library (MHDL), I worked closely with the project's founder, David Pierce, on making millions of pages of out-of-copyright trade papers openly accessible online. To build this collection, we collaborated with a number of leading film heritage institutions, including the Library of Congress, Museum of Modern Art, and the Academy's Margaret Herrick Library, as well as private collectors, such as Karl Thiede, Eileen Bowser, and Richard Koszarski. Thanks to their generosity and the support of sponsors, we were making decades of *Film Daily, Motion Picture News, Moving Picture World, Motion Picture Herald*, and *Variety* freely available for users all over the world to search, read, and download. We were also scanning many fascinating yet lesser-known publications, such as *Film Spectator, Film Mercury*, and *Cine-Mundial*.[1]

All of these publications (and more) now pop up when researchers run keyword searches in Lantern—the search platform for the MHDL that my team and I developed. Much of my subsequent work became driven by a new question: how could I help users interpret and utilize these historic sources they were encountering online? How could I provide new contexts for the otherwise decontextualized snippets that they scrolled through on the Lantern results page? This line of inquiry led to the creation of publication descriptions within Lantern, experimentation with computational research methods, and the publication of several research articles.[2] I became part of a community of film and media historians curious about movie magazines and trade papers, a scholarly community that took the sources used by others in the field as our own objects of study.[3] But this work also brought me back to memories of the talent agency—back to being twenty-two years old, dressed for work in a baggy, hand-me-down suit, reading the trade papers, and observing the ways that the people around me read them. The Hollywood trade papers actively participated in the creation and maintenance of industry cultures and communities, not merely as vehicles for disseminating the news. Interpreting the trade papers requires understanding the constituents of the industry and their norms, fears, and aspirations at particular moments in time.

A new research question emerged from so much scanning, coding, reading, and thinking about the trades: why were there so many publications covering the same industry? The movie business was an outlier. Between 1915 and 1950, no American industry had more trade papers devoted to it than the movie business. During this period, the American film industry consistently had a dozen or more national trade papers reporting on and influencing its actions. Additionally, many more regional trade papers profiled film production, distribution, and exhibition. As I came to discover, many executives, workers, and publishers within the film industry a century ago were asking my same question—*why so many trade papers?* They viewed the number of papers, as well as the unruliness of some in particular, as industry problems. They wanted to find a solution. In 1930, *Exhibitors Herald* publisher Martin Quigley forged a collaboration with the Hollywood studios with the goal of eliminating all the competing trade papers. But the plan ultimately failed. *Ink-Stained Hollywood* is the story of why this and numerous other attempts at consolidation flopped.

Ink-Stained Hollywood examines the film industry trades' most heterogeneous and tumultuous period—from the early feature film era in the mid-1910s to the vertically integrated studio system, strained by the Great Depression, of the mid-1930s. By chronicling the histories of well-known trade papers (such as *Variety* and *Motion Picture Herald*) alongside many important yet forgotten publications (such as *Film Spectator, Film Mercury*, and *Camera!*), my book challenges the established canon of film periodicals and offers new frames for interpreting them as sources. I explore the communities of exhibitors and creative workers that constituted key groups of subscribers, and I argue that a heterogeneous trade press triumphed by appealing to readers' specific sensibilities, values, and fears. I also argue that we are best served by taking a broad view, analyzing the trade papers in relation to one another and to other players within the film industry's ecosystem rather than looking exclusively at individual trade papers in isolation. By taking this broad view, we can see how the trade papers were frequently in tension with the norms of industrial journalism, as well as in tension with one another and sectors of the film industry.

There is a great deal of ground to cover. But before this cart can leave the mailroom, there are more letters and parcels that need to be brought aboard. In the remainder of this introduction, I seek to accomplish this onboarding, surveying the fields and scholarly literature in which the book makes its contributions, the theoretical frameworks that inform my analysis, the sources and methods used to gather evidence, and some key background history about the entertainment trade press.

SCHOLARLY FIELDS, LITERATURE, AND CONTRIBUTIONS

Ink-Stained Hollywood draws on and contributes to two growing subfields and modes of cinema and media studies: new cinema history and media industry studies. Significantly, both of these subfields define themselves less in terms of periodization or national cinemas (though there is certainly a great deal of scholarship in both areas on American cinema during the period covered in this book) and more in terms of approaches to studying film and media and their relationships to the economy, society, and culture. New cinema history has emphasized the value of investigating cinema's connection to society, as well as its meaning in the lives of the people who have participated in its exhibition, circulation, and reception.[4] In the introduction to the edited collection *Looking Past the Screen*, film historian Eric Smoodin referred to this basic approach, with its emphasis on nonfilmic primary sources, as "film scholarship without films," a description that fits this book as well.[5] Similarly, media industry studies has sought to bring together aspects of political economy and cultural studies for a more nuanced understanding of how media institutions operate, how individuals exercise agency within larger systems, and what the consequences are for our larger culture.[6] Both new cinema history and media industry studies have embraced mixed-methods toolkits, including welding together techniques from the humanities and social sciences, an approach that animates my own research, with its blend of archival research and quantitative content analysis.

As this project draws from new cinema history and media industry studies, I also hope to contribute something to both fields by enriching our understanding of Hollywood trade papers. New cinema history scholars frequently footnote the trade papers as evidence without critically interrogating their editorial frameworks. Media industries scholars, in contrast, are more likely to analyze the trades' discourse, but it is often at a general level that doesn't take into account the unique histories of particular papers or their specific functions. This book seeks to constructively address these gaps in a manner that will assist other researchers as they search and interpret the trades.

In writing this book, I am also pleased to be part of a community investigating the history of the Hollywood studio system from new vantage points. The history of Hollywood might seem well-worn owing to the foundational scholarship by Tino Balio, Douglas Gomery, Richard B. Jewell, David Bordwell, Kristin Thompson, and Janet Staiger, among others.[7] But by asking new questions and utilizing previously ignored sources, a new generation of film historians, including Kia Afra, Erin Hill, Peter Labuza, Derek Long, Luci Marzola, Miriam Petty, Paul Monticone, and Chris Yogerst, have nuanced our knowledge of the Hollywood industry and deepened our understanding of its meanings for film workers and audiences.[8] *Ink-Stained Hollywood* joins this cohort of historical research into Hollywood, and I hope it will become a valuable secondary source for the next generation of researchers who reinvent the field yet again.

Additionally, *Ink-Stained Hollywood* draws from the history of American journalism. Books and manuals from the 1910s and 1920s on the field of "industrial journalism" were important sources for my understanding of the norms and aspirations for this larger field. Histories of American journalism by Carolyn Marvin, Michael Schudson, and Gerald J. Baldasty provided helpful models for my investigation of changes in journalism over time and for analyzing the assumptions of editors, writers, and readers.[9] And studies of cinema's relationship to newspapers by Richard Abel, Anna Everett, Paul Moore, and Jan Olsson were especially valuable as models for bringing together these scholarly domains.[10] Because trade papers are less frequently studied in histories of journalism than are newspapers and magazines, I hope that *Ink-Stained Hollywood* provides a useful model for future research in this space. As will become clear in the chapters that follow, the extent to which the motion picture industry adhered to or defied the wider norms of industrial journalism became a source of conflict and debate.

This book also seeks to contribute more specifically to our knowledge of entertainment industry periodicals. Whereas Hollywood fan magazines have received a significant amount of attention over the last two decades, Hollywood's trade press remains underscrutinized.[11] Moreover, the scholarship that does exist tends to focus on individual trade papers rather than analyzing them in relation to one another. Kathryn Fuller-Seeley, Richard L. Stromgren, and Gregory A. Waller, for example, have all published high-caliber essays that focus on specific writers or sections of a trade paper. The 1985 reference guide *International Film, Radio, and Television Journals*, edited by Anthony Slide, also made a valuable contribution by offering brief descriptions of dozens of film periodicals, including some of the trade papers discussed in this book.[12] I am pleased to build on these earlier works and put the various trade papers into conversation with one another and the broader industry they participated in and served.

Variety is, by far, the entertainment trade paper that has received the most attention from scholars and nonacademic writers alike. Dayton Stoddart's *Lord Broadway: Variety's Sime* (1941) and Peter Besas's *Inside "Variety"* (2000) are two books devoted exclusively to *Variety's* history.[13] Both books contain valuable details about the paper's operations (and some very amusing anecdotes). But they also have their blind spots, especially in tracking *Variety's* changing relationship with the film industry. By using quantitative research methods, I present evidence that challenges Stoddart's and Besas's claim that *Variety's* film reporting increased following a growth in film advertising. In fact, the inverse was true. Only after devoting substantial resources to covering the film industry did *Variety* reap the benefits of increases in film advertising.

In reviewing the available literature, it should also be noted that the sons of two important trade paper editors have published biographies of their fathers. Martin S. Quigley's *Martin J. Quigley and the Glory Days of American Film, 1915–1965* discusses Quigley's career as the editor of *Motion Picture Herald* and an author of the Production Code.[14] More recently, W. R. Wilkerson III published *Hollywood Godfather: The Life and Crimes of Billy Wilkerson* (2018), a biography of his father, the founder of the *Hollywood Reporter*.[15] Both authors provide valuable biographical details about their fathers' early lives. My research questions, analytical framework, and use of sources are all quite different from Quigley's and Wilkerson's, resulting in different emphases and interpretations.

THEORETICAL FRAMEWORKS

The most important theoretical framework at play in this book comes from the fields of communication studies and journalism. In his landmark "Cultural Approach to Communication," James W. Carey contrasts two frameworks for understanding communication: the transmission view and the ritual view. "If one examines a newspaper under a transmission view of communication, one sees the medium as an instrument for disseminating news and knowledge," writes Carey. In contrast, a ritual view of communication will understand "newspaper reading less as sending or gaining information and more as attending mass, a situation in which nothing new is learned but in which a particular view of the world is portrayed and confirmed." As Carey points out, "a ritual view does not exclude the processes of information transmission or attitude change," but it insists that these occur within a broader cultural framework.[16]

The ritual view of communication captures what I observed at the talent agency: the trade papers delivered news, yes, but it was always embedded and interpreted within a particular community and culture (in this case, show business). Carey's model also fits the arguments and debates at play within early 1920s trade papers claiming to represent the interests of independent exhibitors, such as *Harrison's Reports* and *Exhibitors Herald*. The expansiveness and flexibility of Carey's model make it well suited for studying trade papers and the show business community. In conceptualizing communication, Carey defines communication as "a symbolic process whereby reality is produced, maintained, repaired, and transformed."[17] What is remarkable is how consistent this view is with the entertainment industry's own thinking. "Perception is reality" has become a commonplace adage in today's Hollywood, and many of the historic trade papers' best customers were companies and individual workers attempting to mold and elevate their perceptions within the industry.

Carey's ritual view of communication also resonates with the work of media industries studies scholar John Thornton Caldwell. "Perception is reality" is an example of what Caldwell calls "industry self-theorizing"—the way that film and television workers make sense of their culture and world.[18] In his influential book *Production Cultures*, Caldwell argues that film and television "do not simply produce mass or popular culture . . . but rather film/TV production communities themselves are cultural expressions and entities involving all of the symbolic processes and collective practices that other cultures use: to forge consensus and order, to perpetuate themselves and their interests, and to interpret the media *as* audience members."[19] As will become clear in the chapters that follow, the history of the film industry's trade press includes attempts to forge consensus and order, as well as pushback from communities that define themselves in opposition to other players within the industry.

In its emphasis on mass communication and community formation, Carey's theoretical framework also evokes Benedict Anderson's better-known conceptualization of "imagined communities." In his analysis of nineteenth-century newspapers and the rise of nationalism, Anderson argues that "the convergence of capitalism and print technology on the fatal diversity of human language created the possibility of a new form of imagined community, which in its basic morphology set the stage for the modern nation." Anderson defines the nation as "an imagined political community—and imagined as both inherently limited and sovereign."[20] In applying this concept to trade papers and the film industry, we can substitute an "imagined business community" for "imagined political community." If, however, we consider *political* less as referring to governance and more as method (i.e., to "play politics"), then the motion picture industry was certainly both an imagined business and political community.

The theories of Carey, Caldwell, and Anderson inform my conception of film industry trade papers and the functions they fulfill within the culture of show business. Even so, I have chosen not to fill the rest of the book with lengthy quotations from these authors. This is partly for the sake of readability. It's also a deliberate decision; I want my uses of quotation marks to, as much as possible, elevate the voices of historical actors and lesser-known contemporary scholars. Yet it's a reflection of something else, too: none of the theories of communication and culture can effectively explain historical change. Carey's ritual view of communication can help us understand why, at particular moments in time, various constituencies within the industry supported certain publications—the papers that, for instance, affirmed their worldviews as independent exhibitors or screenwriters within the studio system. But the theories don't explain why so many trade papers sprang into being between the mid-1910s and early 1920s and why particular publications transformed considerably over time (e.g., *Variety, Exhibitors Herald, Reel Journal*) while others remained relatively consistent (e.g., *Harrison's Reports*). Addressing these changes and continuities requires the historiographic work of identifying and weighing of causal factors. And the identifying of causal factors, in turn, depends on the selection and interpretation of sources.

SOURCES AND METHODS

Film scholars have long utilized trade papers as historical sources, and, unsurprisingly, the trades remain important sources for my own project investigating their history. But there are many different ways of going about reading and analyzing these texts, especially after they are digitized. There are also many other primary sources—such as circulation auditing records, archival lawsuits, and individual manuscript collections—that can shed light on aspects of the trade papers, including details that the editors were not keen to share about themselves in print. Identifying, locating, and integrating these sources have been among the major tasks of this project.

My most important sources in writing this book have been *Motion Picture News, Moving Picture World, Variety,* and the film industry's dozens of other trade publications. Although I discuss some trade papers that have not been scanned (and some that are not known to be physically available anywhere), most of the publications that I analyze are freely available—either in part or in their entirety—through the Media History Digital Library. Because they exist as digital files, I have been able to embed hyperlinks in my notes. Readers of the online edition can click through to see the relevant pages I am quoting or citing as evidence. But digital access meant much more for my research process. Early on, I applied computational methods, such as topic modeling and scaled entity search, to the periodicals as a way to look at them in new ways and see what patterns the computer might notice that I did not. The experience helped me get to know these publications better (especially calling my attention to sections that I tended to skip over), though, for the sake of readability, I have left the lengthy descriptions of the processes and results out of the historical narrative that follows. I also became a super-user of Lantern, the search engine I developed for the MHDL's collections, as a way to quickly test out hunches, chase new leads, and then follow more new leads from there (a process that film historian Gregory Waller usefully refers to as "search and re-search" and that many readers have no doubt undertaken themselves, possibly even leading them to the discovery of this very book).[21]

One useful method for studying periodicals in comparison to one another and individually, as a particular publication changes over time, is quantitative content analysis. By randomly sampling issues from a given year and assigning every page to a category (e.g., advertisement, editorial, news, etc.), a researcher can identify large-scale patterns that might be missed through close reading alone. As a method, quantitative content analysis does not require digital access; it can be done using microfilm or print originals. But the process is vastly accelerated in the digital realm thanks to the speed at which issues can be accessed and analyzed. With the help of outstanding research assistants, I was able to generate quantitative content analyses for eight trade papers: *Variety, Motion Picture News, Moving Picture World, Motography, Exhibitor's Trade Review, Film Daily, Motion Picture Daily*, and *Exhibitors Herald / Motion Picture Herald*. In all eight cases, we used a random number generator to select six issues per year—advancing every year for some publications, every two years for others—to analyze for their content.

The most in-depth and detailed content analysis was performed on *Variety*. Derek Long, Kit Hughes, Tony Tran, and I tracked the number of pages dedicated to various entertainment forms (e.g., vaudeville, burlesque, legitimate theater, motion pictures), both in news/editorial coverage and paid advertisements.[22] The results were illuminating and surprising (see fig. 1). Through our content analysis, we discovered that the importance of the film industry to *Variety* did not grow linearly over the paper's first four decades. Instead, this was a relationship of fits and starts—the contribution of film to *Variety*'s financial health declined during the period of 1908 to 1912, rose during the period of 1914 to 1918, fell again during the period of 1920 to 1922, grew once more and peaked during the years of 1929 and 1930, then declined again in the early 1930s. As these results show, the increasing importance of film to *Variety* cannot be understood as simply the reflection of the industry's growth. Fully explaining *Variety*'s transformations requires scrutinizing the paper's internal strategies alongside external shifts taking place within the media industries.

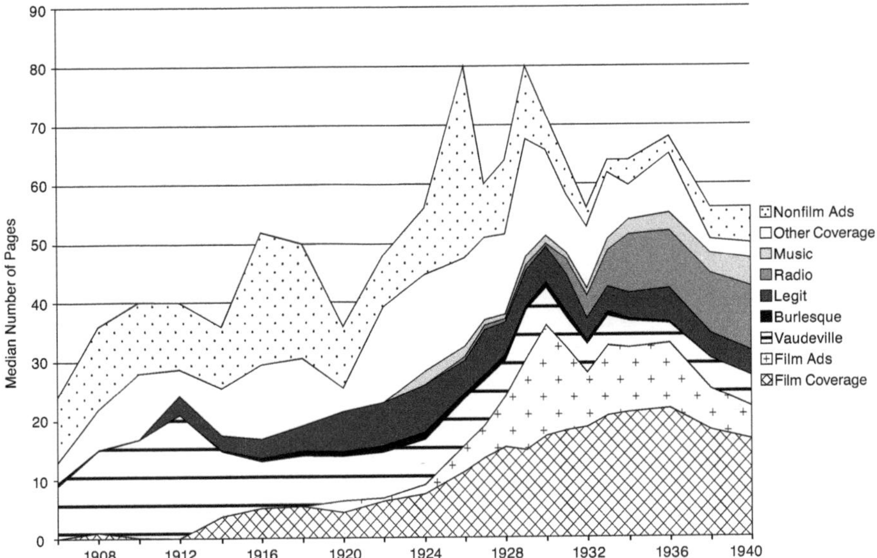

FIGURE 1. Visualization of content distribution of *Variety*, 1906–40. *Source:* Six trade paper issues analyzed per year, selected using a random number generator. Graphic by Lesley Stevenson.

For the other seven trade papers (which all primarily addressed themselves to motion picture exhibitors), we used a more simplified version of content analysis. For each sampled issue, we categorized pages as either (A) news/editorial or (B) advertising, counted the pages in each category, and generated averages and medians for purposes of comparison and change over time. Here, too, the results were revealing. The tremendous growth of advertising in *Motion Picture News* in the mid-1910s, and the equally clear decline in the 1920s, points toward important developments in the history of the US film industry and its press, as discussed in chapters 1, 2, and 5 (fig. 2). Similarly, the results of the content analyses of *Moving Picture World, Motography, Exhibitors Trade Review*, and *Exhibitors Herald / Motion Picture Herald* help to contextualize my discussions of those trade papers.

For all my uses of computational methods, keyword searches, and quantitative content analysis, though, much of what fills this book comes from closely reading the trade papers and other primary sources that shed light on them. The editorial temperaments and distinguishing styles of the trades most fully come to life from closely reading them, issue after issue. I hope that when readers encounter the voices of Franchon Royer, Tamar Lane, and Welford Beaton in chapter 4, they come across as a welcome change of tone from the earlier perspectives, just as they proved to be during the course of my own research.

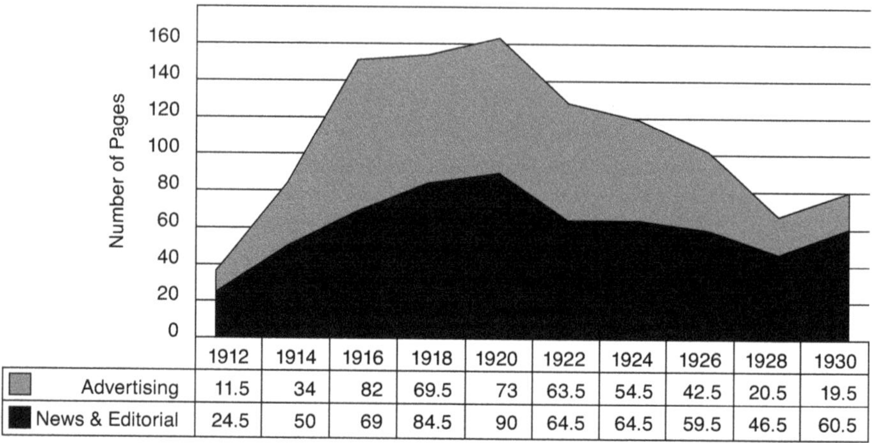

	1912	1914	1916	1918	1920	1922	1924	1926	1928	1930
Advertising	11.5	34	82	69.5	73	63.5	54.5	42.5	20.5	19.5
News & Editorial	24.5	50	69	84.5	90	64.5	64.5	59.5	46.5	60.5

FIGURE 2. Median pages per issue by type in *Motion Picture News*, 1912–30. *Source*: Six trade paper issues analyzed per year, selected using a random number generator. Graphic by Lesley Stevenson.

I also benefited a great deal from being able to access and closely read unpublished archival manuscript collections. Georgetown University Library possesses the papers of *Motion Picture Herald*'s publisher and editor in chief, Martin Quigley, and editor Terry Ramsaye. The Quigley papers provided key sources for understanding the publisher's perspectives and attempts at consolidating the industry's trade press, even as the majority of the archived materials—focused on his role in the Production Code and his relationships with Catholic leaders and organizations—suggest what Quigley and his family came to see as his greatest legacy. While no other trade paper publishers left their papers to an archive or collecting institution, I was able to find traces of their activities in the manuscript collections of other prominent figures within the film industry during this period, including Harry Aitken, Irving Thalberg, Edwin Loeb, and Joseph Kennedy.

My best archival sources came from the courts. Nearly all of the trade paper publishers, including Quigley, were repeatedly sued and also sued others. This litigation generated documents that are now stored in county court record centers in Los Angeles and New York, as well as National Archives repositories in San Francisco and Washington, DC. Courtroom transcripts were available in some cases, along with contracts, letters, memos, and other documents that were gathered during the proceedings and submitted to the courts as evidence. Archival court documents contain evidence and insights about the publishers' internal operations that one cannot glean simply from reading the magazines or the existing secondary literature about them. They also inherently center on conflicts, allowing us to observe tensions at play within the film industry and its press. The conflicts, involving libel, plagiarism, and tax evasion, also make for interesting stories.

One final group of primary sources has been invaluable for my research: the manuals, guidebooks, and auditing records generated by the larger field of industrial journalism. As chapter 1 discusses at length, industrial journalism underwent a period of transformation and expansion in the early twentieth century. With the field's emphases on integrity and "quality circulation," the top trade papers in most industries employed the services of the Audit Bureau of Circulations (ABC) to verify their subscription lists to advertisers. The total circulation number for each publication was generally reported in annual directories, such as *N. W. Ayer & Son's* (see fig. 8 in the next chapter for a graph of early trade paper circulations). But more granular information about the categories of subscribers, as well as the regions in which they lived, was also generated in the audits and saved by the ABC (now the Alliance for Audited Media, headquartered in Arlington Heights, Illinois). The audit reports were an outgrowth of the new standards that had developed within industrial journalism, standards that were articulated in lectures, manuals, and guidebooks. As we will see, the turn-of-the-century entertainment industry did not fit neatly within this journalistic field's categories, nor did most of its papers play by the rules.

HISTORICAL SCOPE AND BACKGROUND

This book focuses on the American film industry's trade press across the two-decade period of 1915 to 1935. Nonspecialist readers may read that line and wonder, "That's all?" Meanwhile, historians of silent feature and early sound film eras may wonder how I can possibly do justice to all the developments, transitions, and tumult during this period. I sympathize with both viewpoints, especially that of the silent film historians. Trying to describe and contextualize the institutions, changes, and complexities of the film industry during this period has been one of the biggest challenges of writing this book.

As I hope to make clear, there is a rationale for this particular structure and periodization. The book starts with a transformation within the film industry's trade press, along with the increase of trade papers becoming identified as an industry problem. The story moves forward with the introduction of yet more voices within the trade press, the construction of new industry communities, and the demarcation of new battle lines. The book ends in the mid-1930s following the unsuccessful takeover and concentration of the industry press. By that point, the marketplace was shared by several different publications that would continue to compete and stay in business for decades to follow.

To be sure, the history of entertainment trade papers did not begin in the year 1915. And while it's beyond the scope of this book to fully fill in that history (dissertation project, anyone?), some background history is important for understanding the developments and debates that took place in the mid-1910s and beyond. Moreover, it's productive to defamiliarize ourselves a bit with the very term *trade paper*.

By the rubric of early twentieth-century industrial journalism, the two trades, *Hollywood Reporter* and *Daily Variety*, that I delivered to desks around the talent agency would have been considered "class journals" and not trade papers at all.

In the 1923 textbook *Industrial Publishing*, Horace M. Swetland wrote that "the basic purpose of Industrial Journalism is to assist in the production and distribution of commodities." Swetland and other proponents of industrial journalism generally distinguished between three types of industrial periodicals: technical, class, and trade.[23] Technical journals, according to Swetland, were "those serving production."[24] The *Journal of the Society of Motion Picture Engineers* and *American Cinematographer*, for instance, exemplified technical journals that centered on motion picture production. These journals emerged from craft and technical organizations that formed within the film industry. Publishing a journal was a means of disseminating technical knowledge, legitimizing the organization, and policing the boundaries between insiders and outsiders.[25] They are not covered in this book because they did not compete against the class journals and trades to become part of the perceived industry problem of too many trade papers. The film industry's technical journals remain valuable sources for film history, however, and they can tell much about technological innovations within the industry and the communities that participated in them.

The second category was the trade paper. Although the term eventually became expansive enough to include *Variety* (which came to refer to itself as a trade), *trade paper*, as defined by Swetland, was something more specific: a periodical focused on the distribution and merchandising sides of an industry. These were the publications that connected manufacturers with the industry's jobbers and retailers. The *Dry Goods Economist*, for example, informed its readership about fabrics and other goods for sale, changing trends in women's fashion, the threat of taxes and other policies, and the commodity markets for cotton and wool. In the case of the film industry, the retailers were exhibitors. Exhibitors needed to know about new products for sale/rental (films), but they also turned to trade papers in the 1910s and 1920s for the latest news about censorship legislation, exhibitor organizational activities, and theater designs.

The third category of publication, according to Swetland, was also the most amorphous: class publications. Typically, class publications spoke to a profession at large. *Variety*, *Billboard*, the *New York Clipper*, and the *New York Dramatic Mirror* were all publications that Swetland would have viewed as "class papers," addressed to entertainment professionals. Although the papers differed in terms of their emphases and editorial voices, they shared certain characteristics. They carried news items related to the theater (a popular new play in London, for instance), and they reviewed productions and new acts (taste, then as now, mattered to creative professionals). Additionally, all of these papers contained classified advertising sections—*Billboard*'s was especially large—that connected managers with performers, performers with hotel rooms, and even the occasional theater for sale with a prospective buyer.

Motion pictures first emerged, in ink, within the pages of these American theatrical "class" papers of the late nineteenth and early twentieth centuries. The *New York Clipper* (est. 1853) and the *New York Dramatic Mirror* (est. 1879), followed soon after by *Billboard* (est. 1896) and *New York Morning Telegraph* (est. 1897), opened their pages to advertisements from motion picture services and reports on exhibitions at vaudeville houses, fairgrounds, and other performance venues. These papers cast attention on motion pictures—and sought the advertising patronage of their manufacturers and distributors—during the vitascope's "novelty phase" of 1896 to 1897, the rise of story film in 1903, the nickelodeon boom of 1905 and 1906, and the decade (and beyond) after the American film industry had four trade papers dedicated exclusively to it. To understand the theatrical papers, we need to take stock of the performance industries they covered, industries that underwent tremendous growth and transformation from 1880 to 1905, along with the growth of American journalism and publishing during this same period. Theatrical trade papers piggybacked and thrived off the industries they covered, but they operated and competed within the publishing industry and, more specifically, the sphere of industrial journalism.

By analyzing the performance industries alongside the field of industrial journalism, we can see numerous similarities that unite the *New York Dramatic Mirror*, founded in 1879, with other trade papers launched that same year, such as *Pottery and Glassware Reporter, Western Undertaker,* and *Butcher's Advocate and Market Journal.*[26] All these trade publications aggregated and delivered timely information to their industries. They all depended on the growth of the railroad. Their advertising pages became virtual marketplaces for buyers and sellers to meet, and their editorial columns offered prescriptions for industry improvement. Perhaps most basically, they legitimized their respective industries and professions, much like the small western town that, after a printer published its first newsletter, felt validated as a community on the map.

But for all the similarities across the publications devoted to theater, butchery, and other industries, there were also important differences. Some of the differences were tied to the particular structures of the industries. Other differences were cultural, rooted in the values and identities of the industry's participants. The culture of show people was especially strong. Show people cared about making a living, but they also participated in a community that cared about taste, status, and applause (ideally, from both the public and their peers). They cared about belonging, and this required recognizing that others did not belong. Their ability to understand the Broadway slang that appeared in print and to identify the targets of satirical attacks marked them as insiders. The theatrical trade papers were community gatekeepers. And, as legitimate theater and vaudeville became entangled, they turned increasingly into community ushers—assigning players, writers, managers, vendors, and performance forms to their place within a shifting hierarchy.

The American performance forms of theater, vaudeville (fig. 3), and lectures experienced a period of dramatic growth and transformation in the decade leading up to the large-scale debut of motion pictures in the US in 1896 and 1897. Many of the causes for these transformations can be traced back to changing social conditions of the audience, especially the growing population in American cities and the demand by workers and inhabitants of those cities for leisure time and recreation.[27] Additionally, a robust transportation infrastructure supported new forms of industrialized entertainment: national rail lines transported traveling showmen and acting troupes into the city; municipal streetcar networks enabled residents to congregate in central districts for work, shopping, and pleasure. Legitimate theater and vaudeville were especially important for the theatrical trade press, and I will limit my discussion here to them. But fairs, parks, and lectures were also intertwined with the nascent motion picture industry and covered in the theatrical press. In all four cases, the content of the performance mattered less than its exhibition context. As social historian David Nasaw has argued, the same act (and, later, film) could move across the different forms and mean something different in each space, depending on the site of its presentation and the demographics of the audience.[28]

The highest form in the pecking order of American performance arts—and the form of greatest importance to the theatrical trade press prior to the 1890s—was the "legitimate" theater (with that adjective, *legitimate*, signifying much). Even within the legit theater world, not all performers were equal; actors fell into hierarchies based on the roles they played and where they played them. Stars, who would headline a play, enjoyed top-tier status. Stars were followed in the hierarchy by leads, then character actors, then supernumeraries and chorus girls. Similarly, the type of company an actor worked for connoted status. According to theater historian Benjamin McArthur, itinerant repertory companies sat at the bottom, followed by local stock companies, which declined in numbers during the 1870s. The same performance unit that displaced the stock company also rose to occupy the top of the theater world's hierarchy: the touring combination company, which McArthur defines as "theatrical companies that performed a single play for a season on a pre-arranged tour."[29] Although the combination system sent actors out on the road, it also demanded a hub for actors, managers, and booking agents to come together. By the time the *New York Dramatic Mirror* launched in 1879, New York City, which already possessed more theaters than any other American city, had become precisely this hub for producing and planning combination tours.[30] New York–based theatrical trade papers thus attached themselves to America's theater capital and its central command center for the planning of touring shows.

FIGURE 3. The outdoor stage for Oscar John Schendel's "All Star Vaudeville, Big Three-Ringed Circus, and Mammoth Menagerie" (1901), representative of the growth and enmeshment of performance forms at the turn of the twentieth century. Schendel would have likely subscribed to *The Billboard* and *New York Clipper*. Photograph courtesy of the Wisconsin Historical Society.

An especially important development in the theater industry coincided with the appearance of motion pictures in the theatrical trade press. In 1896, the two biggest booking agencies, led by partners Charles Frohman & Al Hayman and Abe Erlanger & Marcus Klaw, joined with theater owners Samuel Nixon and J. Frederick Zimmerman to monopolize theater bookings in the US. The Theatrical Syndicate, as it became known, had the power of Frohman's prolific producing company behind it, and the syndicate either owned or partially owned thirty-three first-class theaters in major cities. Even more importantly, they managed the bookings for more than five hundred theaters, many of them the only theaters in small-to-midsized cities that a combination company needed to play in order to make a tour break even and keep the company in the black.[31] Some theater managers welcomed the Theatrical Syndicate for the greater efficiency and stability that it brought (broken contracts were all too common in the preceding years, as evident in reports of touring companies failing to show up as promised or, alternatively, arriving to find another troupe performing in their place). As a monopoly, though, the syndicate undermined free competition and reduced the bargaining power of both individual theaters and the touring actors. With its tremendous market power and polarizing effect within the theatrical world, the Theatrical Syndicate foreshadowed similar developments that would come in the vaudeville and motion picture industries.

Vaudeville proved especially important in trends within the theatrical press that would later extend into covering the film industry. Vaudeville's popularity increased dramatically from 1880 to 1900. The essential structure of a vaudeville show remained consistent across the period: a performance comprising several discrete acts, which might include comedy, dance, music, acrobatics, or drama, that were united on the same bill. But much that surrounded that basic structure changed. B. F. Keith and his manager (and future business partner) Edward Albee implemented several important innovations that expanded vaudeville's appeal to a much larger audience and enabled new economies of scale. Beginning in 1880 with his Dime Museum in Boston, Keith found ways to appeal to middle-class, female, and family audiences who never would have stepped into a saloon for a variety performance. Keith, along with other similarly minded vaudeville managers, forbade the sale and consumption of alcohol, ejected disrespectful male patrons, censored off-color material from acts, kept the interior as clean as possible, and advertised in newspapers and other respectable forums. Albee would later describe the three C's on which his empire with Keith was built: "cleanliness, comfort, and courtesy."[32]

If one could add a fourth C, then it would be "continuous." Beginning around 1885, Keith theaters turned into repeating loops of performances. Families, shoppers, and other audience members could purchase a ticket anytime between 10:30 a.m. to 10:30 p.m. and step into a show. They knew it was time to leave when the same juggler or singer they had seen when they first walked in was back onstage performing his same act again.[33] Later, one-reel pictures would be included as acts within the program of many vaudeville shows.[34] Continuous vaudeville increased seat turnover and ticket sales. Keith and Albee reinvested the increased revenue from continuous vaudeville by booking better acts and acquiring and building better theaters. They developed a network of vaudeville theaters in the eastern US among which performers would move and tour, complemented by the Orpheum's network of theaters that dominated the West and Midwest. With the exception of major stars, vaudeville performers had very little power within the system, and they correctly perceived that Keith and Albee wanted to chip away at what little agency they did have.

The founding of *Variety* in December 1905 occurred during a period of escalating tension between vaudeville management and labor. In its debut issue (see fig. 4), *Variety* emphasized that it was to be "an artist's paper" and "'ALL THE NEWS ALL THE TIME' and 'ABSOLUTELY FAIR' [were] the watchwords."[35] *Variety*'s emphasis on fairness, artists, and the separation between editorializing and advertising were intended to distinguish it from the theatrical trade papers (especially the *New York Clipper* and the *New York Morning Telegraph*), which

FIGURE 4. Cover of the debut issue of *Variety*, Dec. 16, 1905. The cover emphasizes the paper's initial focus on "vaudeville, circus, parks, burlesque, minstrels, [and] fairs" and introduces its iconic and long-lasting waving V logo. Courtesy of the Media History Digital Library.

it implied were management-oriented organs for their advertisers. Throughout its first year in print, *Variety* largely followed its stated mandate. One example occurred in the summer of 1906, when Keith and Albee merged the Western Vaudeville Association and the BF Keith Booking Agency to create the United Booking Office (UBO). It was a key moment in the consolidation of the vaudeville industry, coinciding with the expansion of theaters controlled by Keith and Albee to roughly 130. Additionally, the UBO continued the controversial practice of charging artists a 5 percent booking fee.

The *New York Clipper* praised Keith, saying he was a man of "courage, determination, [and] inflexible purpose" to have built "this great superstructure of vaudeville."[36] In contrast, *Variety* analyzed what the consolidation and new booking agency would mean for performers. The paper cynically remarked on the intent behind the name *United Booking Office:* "The Keith executives think that the name of 'Keith' left off the title would in a measure remove the red flag from the artists' sight."[37] And in his editorials, *Variety* publisher and editor Sime Silverman kept raising the red flag again and again, arguing for the need for vaudeville artists to organize and stand up to Keith and Albee before it was too late.[38] *Variety*'s relationship with the most aggressive vaudeville labor union, the White Rats, ultimately proved to be complicated and fraught, as I will discuss in chapter 2. But the stances it took in its first year—emphasizing its independence and allegiance to artists— became important frames for the way members of the vaudeville industry perceived *Variety* in relation to the more established *Clipper* and *Morning Telegraph.*

Variety's launch in December 1905 also coincided with the growth of stand-alone movie theaters in the US.[39] The success of early storefront theaters that showed continuous film programs bred thousands of imitators. Between 1905 and 1908, an estimated eight thousand nickelodeons (fig. 5) sprang up across the US.[40] No fewer than four national trade papers emerged during this same period to try to serve them and capitalize on the growing industry. The first US film trade paper, *Views and Films Index*, debuted in April 1906. Nickelodeon exhibitors were imagined as the core readership of the paper. The advertising base was the film manufacturers, distribution services, and theater equipment dealers who needed to reach them. *Views and Films Index* lamented in its first issue of April 1906 that "exhibitors and showmen have sought for years and still seek for their trade news in theatrical newspapers." *Views and Films Index* professed not to be "a hybrid publication," promising to "make a specialty of the trade and not to mix it up with a thousand theatrical details which have nothing to do with our business."[41] Despite these bold declarations, however, most of the basic practices of *Views and Films Index* and the other early exhibitor-oriented trade papers, as well as many of the structures and forms they published week after week, were inherited from the theatrical trade papers. This tension between the categories of a "class" and "trade" paper never went away. No matter how hard the new papers scrubbed, the greasepaint never fully came off.

In March 1907, a second and more influential exhibitor-oriented trade paper entered the marketplace. The new paper, *Moving Picture World*, was edited by Alfred H. Saunders, who had previously worked for *Views and Films Index*. The business operations of *Moving Picture World* were run by J. P. Chalmers Jr., who pushed out Saunders a year later and took over editorial control. *Moving Picture World* quickly surpassed *Views and Films Index* in all departments, providing

FIGURE 5. The Comet Theatre, a New York nickelodeon, ca. 1910. The Comet's managers would have been among the target readers of the first motion picture trade papers, including *Views and Film Index, Moving Picture World,* and *Nickelodeon.* Photograph courtesy of Wisconsin Center for Film and Theater Research.

superior news coverage, more thorough film reviews, and excellent projection guidance through the columns of F. H. Richardson. In 1908, Richardson began his "Lessons for Operators" column, and two years later, he began editing a section of *Moving Picture World* called the "Trouble Department" (later retitled "Projection Department"), encouraging readers to write in with questions about projection and theater operation.[42] Through detailed descriptions and visual aids, Richardson explained the workings of carbon arc lamps and program boards to operators in St. Louis and Salt Lake City. Despite the highly technical discussions, Richardson sought to maintain a clear, straightforward, and unpretentious voice in his writing. He also fostered a sense of community—referring to letter writers as "friend," "neighbor," and "brother."

In 1908, however, the rise of the Motion Picture Patents Company (MPPC, also referred to as "the Trust") fundamentally changed the industry's structure. These changes have been chronicled at length elsewhere, and I will discuss some of them in chapter 1. For our immediate purposes, the most important legacy of the MPPC was that it became a polarizing force—much like legitimate theater's Theatrical Syndicate and vaudeville's UBO that preceded it—that changed the perceptions of the trade press. Trade papers were expected to take a stand. *Views and Films Index* became the most adamantly pro-MPPC publication, and by 1910, it was most likely financed by MPPC member companies. On the other end of the spectrum, *Moving Picture News*, founded in 1908 by Alfred Saunders after his split with Chalmers, was highly critical of the MPPC and came to define itself as the "official organ of the independent manufacturers."[43] Within this polarizing environment, Chalmers's *Moving Picture World* tried to emphasize its editorial independence, though it was generally supportive of the MPPC. In 1911, *Moving Picture World* acquired *Views and Film Index*, a purchase that increased the perception within the industry that it was on the side of Thomas Edison and the Trust.

This backstory is important because it sets the stage for what came next and the book that will follow. The decline of the MPPC and rise of the feature film created a robust marketplace in which *Moving Picture World* and *Moving Picture News* would thrive under new management (J. P. Chalmers Jr. died in an accident at an exhibitors' convention in 1912; Alfred Saunders sold *Moving Picture News* the next year). The new editors, W. Stephen Bush at *Moving Picture World* and William A. Johnston at the retitled *Motion Picture News*, emphasized their editorial independence and took on prominent leadership roles within the wider industry. In the case of *Motion Picture News*, Johnston imported the new reforms and formal standards from industrial journalism in an effort to improve the perception of the trade press and his paper in particular. But the threat of oligopolistic industry power—so central to the late nineteenth- and early twentieth-century industries of legitimate theater, vaudeville, and motion pictures—never went away. Traveling actors and independent exhibitors, who suffered under unequitable power structures, were quick to perceive bias in the pages of the trade papers. In the end, giving voice to their anger proved to be an easier task for the trade papers than persuading readers of their editorial independence and neutrality.

BOOK STRUCTURE AND CHAPTER DESCRIPTIONS

Just as trade papers have certain standardized conventions, so, too, do academic books. One such convention is that the introduction provides chapter summaries of the book that follows. If you like this convention, then read on. If not, and if you enjoy a story with some surprises, then you may want to skip ahead to chapter 1.

The book begins, *in situ*, with the film industry's trade papers selling historic amounts of advertising and taking on prominent leadership roles within industry-wide trade organizations. In "Remaking Film Journalism in the Mid-1910s," I analyze how the rise of the feature film, the power vacuum that formed from the decline of the MPPC, and the industry's need to organize to oppose censorship all offered new opportunities for the trade press. The two most successful editors, W. Stephen Bush (*Moving Picture World*) and William A. Johnston (*Motion Picture News*), seized on these conditions and transformed themselves into influential industry figures. I argue that William A. Johnston left an especially important legacy. Although he invented very little himself, his importation of practices and ideals from the growing field of industrial journalism changed the film industry's trade press. Data aggregation and market reports, a separate magazine for theater equipment, and an emphasis on circulation quality rather than quantity all became integral parts of the motion picture trade press for the next century. But Johnston proved unwilling to follow the calls of industrial journalism to stop printing publicity announcements for advertisers. His continuation of this practice—which grew in parallel to his booming pages of advertising—earned him enemies, particularly among small exhibitors and rival trade paper editors. In 1916, the perception among exhibitors that Johnston represented the interests of manufacturers, not theater owners, only increased. This set the stage for the creation of *Exhibitor's Trade Review* and what *Variety* would describe as "the war of the motion picture trade journals."

Chapter 2, "Trade Papers at War," chronicles those bitter conflicts that played out among the entertainment industry's publishers as World War I raged in Europe. In late 1916, *Exhibitor's Trade Review* debuted and immediately became a lightning rod of controversy. The paper was founded by W. Stephen Bush and Lee A. Ochs, president of the Motion Picture Exhibitors League of America (MPELA). *Exhibitor's Trade Review* claimed to represent only the interests of the American exhibitor. When *Motion Picture News* challenged the truthfulness of this claim, *Exhibitor's Trade Review* published a vicious personal attack on its editor, William A. Johnston. The papers rapidly began to fight one another—and members of the industry they claimed to serve—in a series of libel lawsuits: *Motion Picture News* sued *Exhibitor's Trade Review*; *Exhibitor's Trade Review* sued *Variety* and an exhibitor; a theater chain sued *Moving Picture World*; and the White Rats actors' union sued *Variety*, which was also under investigation by the Federal Trade Commission. Drawing from archival court case documents and the trade papers themselves, I argue that trade publishers strategically filed, provoked, and defended libel lawsuits in an effort to enhance, rather than merely protect, their reputations and credibility. At the end of 1917, William A. Johnston called for the industry to eliminate all but two papers. There were too many trade papers, he argued, and most of the industry agreed. Attempts to consolidate the film industry trade press became a major theme over the next twelve years.

The trade press war of 1917 did not have the desired outcome of putting any of the existing trade papers out of business. On the contrary, the number of film industry publications nearly doubled over the next five years. Chapter 3, "The Independent Exhibitor's Pal: Localizing, Specializing, and Expanding the Exhibitor Paper," explores how the new papers differentiated themselves from incumbents and gained credibility through strategies of specialization and localization. In short, they succeeded by tailoring themselves to particular cultures and communities within the industry. The chapter begins by exploring a cluster of regional exhibitor papers that attached themselves to distribution exchange hubs across the country. For example, Kansas City's *Reel Journal*, founded in 1920, tracked censorship regulations, tax proposals, and other issues of interest to local exhibitors and fostered a sense of community and shared interests between southwestern exhibitors and the Kansas City–based distribution exchanges that served them. The chapter also explores another distinctive paper for exhibitors: *Harrison's Reports*. Founded in 1919 by former *Motion Picture News* reviewer P. S. Harrison, *Harrison's Reports* addressed the critiques of the trade press head-on and became "a reviewing service free from the influence of film advertising." Exhibitors paid several times the subscription rate of the other trades to read this four-page weekly newsletter that rejected the standard business model of trade papers. Finally, the chapter profiles Martin Quigley's *Exhibitors Herald*, which began in 1915 as a local exhibitors' paper in Chicago but grew in the early 1920s into a powerful national trade paper.

Chapter 4, "Coastlander Reading: The Cultures and Trade Papers of 1920s Los Angeles," shifts focus to map out the overall landscape of 1920s Hollywood and the film industry trade papers that sprang up to serve it. *Camera!, Film Mercury*, and *Film Spectator* all spoke to Los Angeles–based communities of creative workers, as well as many readers who wanted to break in to the industry. These and other LA-based trade papers sought to speak to a creative community that prioritized taste, along with gossip, gatekeeping, scorekeeping, and self-publicity. In their addresses to a distinctive creative community, the Los Angeles papers borrowed from the conventions and structures of New York–based vaudeville papers. Meanwhile, *Variety* used the 1920s to pivot from being primarily a vaudeville publication to one focused on motion pictures. *Variety*'s 1923 acquisition of *The Clipper* and the 1925 opening of an LA office, headed by a former *Clipper* writer, were especially important for the pivot. But the paper's reputation for independence, scorekeeping, and distinctive use of language proved to be the most significant strengths of all.

Chapter 5, "Chicago Takes New York: The Consolidation of the Nationals," explores the vertical integration and mergers-and-acquisitions environment of the Hollywood studio system during the mid to late 1920s. The decade was a period of decline for the three national trade papers analyzed in the first two chapters: *Moving Picture World, Motion Picture News*, and *Exhibitor's Trade Review*. All three papers were acquired by *Exhibitors Herald*'s Martin Quigley, who forged an alliance with the major Hollywood studios. In the battle lines being drawn, Quigley stood with Motion Picture Producers and Distributors of America (MPPDA) head Will Hays against the Brookhart Bill and went on to play a key role in addressing Hollywood's censorship problems through the creation of the Production Code. While these steps placed Quigley in Hays's favor, they alienated many of the nation's independent exhibitors who had previously admired Quigley and supported *Exhibitors Herald*. They also exposed rifts between the producers based in LA and the home-office executives based in New York. The chapter culminates in 1930, with the studios financing Quigley's purchase of two rival papers and the creation of *Motion Picture Herald, Motion Picture Daily*, and *Hollywood Herald*. More than any other moment, it seemed as though the film industry finally had a plan to solve the problem of too many trade papers.

The plan failed. Chapter 6, "The Great Diffusion: Hollywood's Reporters, Exhibitor Backlash, and Quigley's Failed Monopoly," chronicles how a group of rival trade papers outmaneuvered Quigley and attracted reader loyalty (and wealthy industry patrons) during the height of the Great Depression. I look especially closely at Quigley's most hated rival, *Variety*, as well as the paper that *Variety* took to court for stealing its news, *Hollywood Reporter* (founded in 1930). The *Hollywood Reporter*'s Billy Wilkerson understood the importance of social relationships in Hollywood, and he shrewdly supported creative labor over management during the banking crisis of 1933. In contrast, Quigley's LA-based paper, *Hollywood Herald*, took the side of the major film corporations, and it went out of business before the end of the year (just weeks before the debut of *Daily Variety*). Independent exhibitors also perceived Quigley as a sellout and mouthpiece for the studios. New trade papers, such as *Showmen's Round Table* and *Independent Exhibitors Film Bulletin*, as well as increasingly powerful regional papers, such as *Boxoffice* and *The Exhibitor*, competed for the loyalty of alienated exhibitors and found a stable advertising base through the output of Poverty Row studios. By 1934, more film trade papers existed than in the years leading up to the formation of *Motion Picture Herald*. Remarkably, most of these papers remained in publication through the early to mid-1960s.

THE END OF THE BEGINNING

This book concludes during the decade that many readers might consider the beginning: the emergence of the *Hollywood Reporter* and *Daily Variety*, the two daily trade papers best known within the entertainment industry. The old publishers of *Hollywood Reporter* would certainly have viewed the paper's launch in 1930 as the right place to begin this story. In one of its anniversary numbers, *Hollywood Reporter* boasted, "No one had ever published a trade paper from Hollywood before."[44] This statement would be true if it weren't for *Camera!*, *Film Mercury*, *Film Spectator*, and at least a half dozen other LA trade papers that preceded *Hollywood Reporter*. Nor was *Hollywood Reporter* the first to publish celebratory anniversary issues and encourage advertisers to purchase space for its birthday presents; the strong-arm sales tactics of special issues were already well established among the trades.

When I delivered *Hollywood Reporter* and *Daily Variety* to the desks of talent agents in Beverly Hills, I remember feeling, at times, a sense of continuity with the Golden Age of Hollywood. I can still see some of those continuities, but I now see more clearly the complexities, differences, tensions. I hope that this book helps others see them as well.

More could be said here, but my cart is feeling very full. It's time to leave the mailroom and make our first stop.

1

———

Remaking Film Journalism
in the Mid-1910s

Two images can serve as an entry point for understanding the transformation of the motion picture industry and its trade press during the mid-1910s. The first image gives us a quantitative view of the transformation; the second, a qualitative view.

The first image (fig. 6) graphs the median page length of a weekly issue of the three most prominent film trade papers of the period: *Moving Picture World, Motion Picture News,* and *Motography.*[1] Absent from the graph are five theatrical papers that during the 1910s increasingly covered film: *Billboard, Morning Telegraph, New York Clipper, New York Dramatic Mirror,* and *Variety.* Similarly, the weekly film review magazine *Wid's* and Chicago-based *Exhibitors Herald* (both founded in 1915) are not represented in the image. As far as quantitative measures go, however, the growth in the sheer number of trade papers was less significant than the growth in their size.[2] The graph quantifies what any number of silent film historians have felt in their hands and backs: *Moving Picture World* had grown heavy by 1916.

Even more dramatic than the growth of *Moving Picture World* was that of *Motion Picture News*—a publication that ballooned from a mere 36 pages per issue in 1912 to 84 pages in 1914 and to 151 pages in 1916. The statistical content analysis of these papers shows that the growth of news and editorial content in both *News* and *World* closely mirrored increases in advertising pages. The rise of the feature film contributed to this growth of the papers. Manufacturers and distributors needed to differentiate their programs of feature films and, in some cases, individual productions from those of the competition. The trade press offered feature manufacturers and distributors a vehicle to achieve this. The relatively small page growth of *Motography,* however, demonstrates that we cannot assume that the trade press

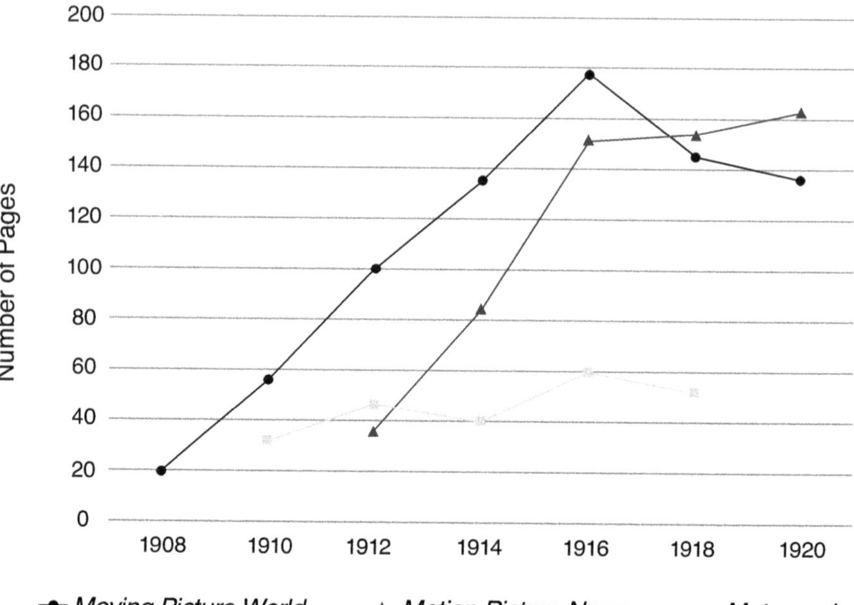

FIGURE 6. Median total pages per issue of *Moving Picture World*, *Motion Picture News*, and *Motography*. *Source:* Six issues analyzed per year for each trade paper, selected using a random number generator. Graphic by Lesley Stevenson.

merely reflected the rising and falling prosperity of the film marketplace. Despite achieving the highest estimated circulation of any film trade paper of the 1910s, the Chicago-based *Motography* failed to leverage these subscribers toward increased advertising.[3] Therefore, any convincing explanation for the growth of *Moving Picture World* and *Motion Picture News* must account for how and why these two papers were the most effective at participating in and capitalizing on the film industry's changes.

The second image (fig. 7) provides one piece of this explanation, revealing the leadership roles that *News* and *World* had assumed within the film industry by the mid-1910s. The photograph was taken in October 1915 at the board of directors meeting of the Motion Picture Board of Trade. Established the previous month to combat the threat of censorship laws, the Board of Trade was the first significant industry trade organization to form in the wake of the collapse of the Motion Picture Patents Company (MPPC) in 1915.[4] The Board of Trade's founding directors included two trade paper editors, both of whom appear in the photograph. W. Stephen Bush (a columnist and editor of *Moving Picture World*) stands second from the left, wearing a light-gray suit. William A. Johnston (publisher and editor of *Motion Picture News*) stands ninth from the left, between the bearded Ohio exhibitor Max Stearn and the ambitious young showman Samuel "Roxy" Rothafel, whose publicity savvy exceeded even that of Johnston's.[5]

FIGURE 7. Photograph from the first meeting of the board of directors of the Motion Picture Board of Trade in October 1915. W. Stephen Bush *(Moving Picture World)* is second from the left; William A. Johnston *(Motion Picture News)* is ninth from the left. *Source:* "Men Who Head the Motion Picture Board of Trade," *Moving Picture World,* Oct. 30, 1915, 802, http://lantern .mediahist.org/catalog/moviwor26chal_0826.

The photograph offers a window into a time when, for a brief moment at least, trade paper editors occupied formal leadership roles within the film industry. The MPPC (or the "Trust") never would have admitted a trade publisher to its board of directors—it financed one trade paper *(Film Views and Index)* and fought others *(Moving Picture News* and *Motography).* Similarly, the Motion Picture Producers and Distributors of America (MPPDA), established in 1922, did not allow publishers or editors to be official members. Although, as we will see, Martin Quigley came to play an influential role within the MPPDA, he and his fellow trade press editors were not official members, much less directors. In 1915, however, the Board of Trade recognized trade paper publishers as one of six membership classes allowed in the organization (the other five classes were manufacturers; equipment and film suppliers; exchange operators; exhibitors; and a miscellaneous class of actors, directors, writers, and employees). This was the sign of a heterogeneous trade organization, to be sure. But it was also a sign of the important role the trade press was playing in public relations and the restructuring of the industry, including the formation of the very trade organization depicted in the photo. After receiving his appointment to the board of directors of the Board of Trade, William A. Johnston wrote, "MOTION PICTURE NEWS takes a natural pride in the final accomplishment of the body. The very name, 'Board of Trade,' was first mentioned by this publication."[6]

This chapter explores the industrial contexts and publisher maneuverings that allowed *Motion Picture News* and *Moving Picture World* to achieve so much success and influence in the mid-1910s. Specifically, the ascent of these trade papers depended on three interrelated developments in the US motion picture industry: the fall of the MPPC, the rise of the feature film, and the threat of censorship policies. These changes created the need for articulate industry leaders, new cooperative organizations, and larger advertising budgets. At this same moment, important changes were under way in the American publishing industry. In the early to mid-1910s, the field known as "industrial journalism" was formalizing its standards of practice and arguing for its importance to the American economy. William A. Johnston had a background in industrial journalism and advertising. His meteoric rise came from his skillful application of the practices of industrial journalism to the motion picture industry. In the process, he gained powerful allies and more enemies than he could count.

FILM INDUSTRY TRANSFORMATION

Only a few years before the taking of the Board of Trade photograph, a very different trade organization dominated the editorial columns of the film industry trade press. The Motion Picture Patents Company framed the discourse of the American film industry, forcing the trade papers to take sides—either for the MPPC, against it, or somewhere in the middle. The trade paper battles over the MPPC and the Independents reached their height in 1910. The hostility expressed in ink reflected and exacerbated the tensions within the industry following the MPPC's aggressive takeover of fifty-eight exchanges across the country, a maneuver that formed the basis of the MPPC's distribution arm, the General Film Company (GFC).[7] In this climate, the wishy-washy editorial positions of previous years gave way to condemnations and expressions of outrage.

By the dawn of 1913, however, the situation had changed significantly. The MPPC was in decline—the result of internal conflicts, ineffective and expensive patent litigation, and inflexible production and distribution strategies.[8] Independent manufacturers and distributors were effectively competing against this organization and its members. *Moving Picture World*, which had acquired the MPPC-backed *Film Index* in 1911, offered listings and reviews of both MPPC and Independent films and commented that both had a legitimate place within the industry. Even more telling, *Moving Picture News*, which had described itself in 1911 as the "official organ of the independent manufacturers and the N.I.M.P.A.," now included advertisements, listings, and news stories about MPPC manufacturers and their films.[9] Two years before the US Supreme Court ruled that the MPPC was in violation of the Sherman Antitrust Act, the trade press was already presenting a view of the industry in which the distinction between Trust and Independent meant less than the distinction of product quality of the leading manufacturers. Some of these leading manufacturers were MPPC members (Vitagraph and Biograph); others were Independents (Famous Players and Universal). All of them needed to persuade exhibitors to book their films.

A second key industry change in the mid-1910s—and very much related to the MPPC's waning power—was the rise of the feature film.[10] The number of feature films in the American marketplace skyrocketed in the 1910s, from only eight in 1912 to an estimated 835 in 1916.[11] The producers and distributors of these films utilized a business strategy of product differentiation; they distinguished their films from the films of competitors based on screen stories, production values, and, especially, the casting of stars. Some of the MPPC manufacturers produced feature films, but their distributor, the GFC, was poorly equipped for the exploitation of features. The GFC rented films to exhibitors for single days and charged them on a per-foot-of-film basis. Many exhibitors liked the price stability and daily program changes. But the Independent manufacturers and their distributors, especially Paramount, found exhibitors willing to accept a different model—longer runs and pricing based on a film's quality or star power, not a flat per-foot basis. Independent manufacturers could invest more in feature productions because their distribution and rental model enabled them to profit more from a successful film.[12]

The film industry trade papers were beneficiaries of the feature's rise. The growth in feature films closely correlates with the swelling of *Moving Picture World*'s and *Motion Picture News*' pages in the mid-1910s (see fig. 8). The trade papers offered a way for feature distributors to differentiate their products and promote them to exhibitors. A colorful two-page advertisement, a positive review, and an exciting news story about the making of the film could help craft the perception that a feature film was, indeed, something special. Even if an exhibitor had already signed on to a feature program—thus becoming contractually obligated to accept a whole slate of films—distributors knew that if exhibitors believed in a movie, they promoted it more to their clientele, resulting in a larger box-office gross.[13] The production of short films in 1916 also remained strong: 4,115 shorts, which required some promotion to exhibitors.[14] The coexistence of features and shorts was a boon to the trade papers' advertising departments. Much like the late-1920s transition to sound—in which distributors simultaneously promoted silent and sound films to exhibitors—the rise of the feature and continued production of shorts effectively created two marketplaces for film buying. The trade papers most effective at connecting buyers to sellers stood to gain handsomely in this environment.

The rise of the feature film also encouraged the theatrical trade papers to devote more coverage to film. *Billboard* and *New York Dramatic Mirror* were the leaders in this respect. Both papers established film sections in 1908, and these sections more than doubled in size from 1912 to 1916. The best-remembered theatrical paper to cover film, *Variety*, lagged in comparison. As a data visualization of *Variety*'s shifting content coverage illustrates, the publication actually decreased its attention to film in 1910 and 1912 compared to 1908 (see fig. 1). It was not until the rise of the multireel feature film in 1913 and 1914 that *Variety* established a film news and reviews section and increased its film coverage again. *Variety* was the indisputable king of vaudeville papers in the 1910s, but it did not really become a leading film-oriented trade paper until the mid to late 1920s (a topic I explore in depth in chapter 4).

Feature films brought more money and significance to the film and theatrical trade papers, but they had the opposite effect for thousands of small movie theaters. In his essay on the crisis of the small exhibitor, Ben Singer describes the "painful transition for many rank-and-file exhibitors" during the mid to late teens: "With their small capacities, low admissions, humble trappings, and modest socioeconomic demographics, many small theaters had great difficulty affording the expensive feature services."[15] *Moving Picture World, Motion Picture News*, and *Motography* had to walk a fine line with this group of exhibitors, who were avid readers of the papers. The trade papers framed any criticism of the industry and its films as constructive; they wanted to improve the industry. Similarly, they praised the construction of new, bigger, and better theaters. Small exhibitors reading these papers took offense at the implicit suggestion that the industry's improvement and welfare meant the ruination of their personal businesses. The growing resentment and suspicion felt by these exhibitors exploded during the trade press war discussed in the next chapter.

With the MPPC's decline and the feature film's rise, new fault lines were forming in the film industry, between manufacturer-distributors and exhibitors, as well as among exhibitors themselves. Yet the common threat of censorship laws required coordination across the different branches of the industry. Chicago passed the nation's first motion picture censorship statute in 1907, but these laws really started to catch on across the country in the early 1910s. Between 1911 and 1913, Pennsylvania, Ohio, and Kansas all enacted censorship laws that prohibited the exhibition of films deemed "immoral," "indecent," "obscene," or likely to inspire crime.[16] These laws added new expenses to the business of film distribution. In addition to requiring that certain films be altered before being shown, the censor boards raised revenue by charging fees to distributors, an expenditure that became known as a "censorship tax." In 1915, the US Supreme Court famously upheld the constitutionality of Ohio's censorship law, declaring that films were a "business pure and simple" and need not be afforded the First Amendment rights of free speech. *Mutual v. Ohio* enabled the continuation and expansion of state and municipal movie censorship laws across the United States for the next four decades.[17] Even more common than censorship boards in the early to mid-1910s were state and municipal laws prohibiting the Sunday screening of motion pictures. The genesis of such bills came from politicians and religious leaders—some of whom perceived the movies as immoral, others of whom more pragmatically calculated that church attendance went up when there were no public amusements with which to compete.[18]

Manufacturers, distributors, and exhibitors all agreed that censorship laws and Sunday ordinances posed threats, but they disagreed about what should be done about them. If they did nothing, their businesses would suffer. If their response was too aggressive, they risked alienating community leaders and inviting harsher restrictions. In this context, trade papers became important sites for debating strategies, tracking policy developments, and affirming the anger of exhibitors. *Moving Picture World, Motography*, and *Motion Picture News* gave significant news coverage to censorship policies being drafted across the country and the efforts of local exhibitors to curb such measures. A common refrain among the trade papers called for collective action. Choosing the right strategy was important, but it could only succeed if sufficient numbers within the industry backed it and worked in concert. This growing belief led to the 1915 establishment of the Motion Picture Board of Trade, an organization composed of manufacturers, exchanges, exhibitors, and trade paper editors that "Declare[d] War on Enemies of [the] Industry."[19]

The leading trade paper editors became some of the industry's most important voices on such matters. Among exhibitors, no trade paper columnist carried more influence than W. Stephen Bush. Bush had earned the respect of exhibitors through his *Moving Picture World* columns, which advocated for exhibitors to hold a status and influence within the industry on par with the manufacturers. He also published film reviews that panned movies he considered bad for exhibitors, the advancement of film art, and/or the industry as a whole. Unlike William A. Johnston, his chief rival editor, Bush had an intimate understanding of exhibition. Beginning in 1908 (and perhaps earlier), he had traveled across the eastern United States, presenting lectures to accompany films and slideshows.[20] Midsized and small movie houses were not abstract concepts to Bush; they were real spaces, owned and run by real people whom he had met. He understood his audience of readers very well. He also understood their resentments. For too long, he argued, the exhibitors had been treated as a "janitor"; exhibitors needed to seize their proper place as leaders of the industry.[21] To borrow a phrase from twenty-first-century politics, W. Stephen Bush knew how to fire up his base. Exhibitors turned to his columns to have their worldviews confirmed and resentments validated just as much as, if not more than, to be educated or persuaded about some particular point.

Bush's substantial writing on censorship began with advocating for a "Modern Sunday"—one that could satisfy the desires of community leaders and exhibitors alike. In a series of 1912 columns, Bush advocated for rewriting Sunday laws so that they legalized movie exhibition on three conditions: "(I) The religious or educational character or tendency of the picture, (II) The explanatory lecture, which is allowed on Sunday everywhere under the present laws and which gives the Sunday exhibition a dignity of its own, and (III) The limitation of time, setting a certain hour on Sunday for the beginning of motion picture exhibitions."[22] Bush went on to state that "educational character or tendency" should be understood broadly, and clearly *Moving Picture World*'s advertisers agreed (Universal promoted certain films as being "Fine for your Sunday show" and "A 'Jim Dandy' for the Sunday program").[23] As censorship laws and Sunday restrictions only grew in subsequent years, however, Bush's stance became increasingly militant and uncompromising.

Film historian Richard L. Stromgren observes, "From 1913 until the end of his association with *Moving Picture World* in 1916, Bush's focus on issues narrowed continually until he was, by the last year, writing about virtually nothing but censorship."[24] In his increasingly hardened stance in 1915 and 1916, Bush forcefully argued against legal censorship of any form. This stood in contrast to others who argued that state laws were preferable to city laws or that a federal law, the Smith-Hughes Bill, would be better than a patchwork of state laws.[25]

On the matter of censorship, Bush was the trade press's most significant inward-facing or industry-facing columnist, especially when it came to the exhibitor community. But the most powerful trade press publishers and editors are also outward facing: they speak to the public, government, and other groups on behalf of the industry. In this public-facing role of the editor, Bush was second in importance to William A. Johnston of *Motion Picture News*. In 1914 and 1915, Johnston had emerged as the film industry trade press's most capable diplomat. His effectiveness at speaking to those outside the film industry may have stemmed from the fact that, until 1913, he was fully outside of the industry himself. The tool kit he brought with him came from a field that was on the rise: industrial journalism.

THE FORMALIZATION OF INDUSTRIAL JOURNALISM

To fully understand the dramatic growth of the motion picture trade press in the 1910s, one must look beyond the film industry. The trade papers may have covered the movie business, but they engaged directly and competed in the business of publishing.

At the same moment that the film industry was trying to reorganize itself in the mid-1910s, the field of publishing known as "industrial journalism" was enjoying a triumphant moment—the result of several years' worth of coordination, government lobbying, public relations, and policy drafting.

If censorship was the key policy issue for film distributors and exhibitors, then postal rates were the key policy issue for trade publishers. In 1907, the trade papers used their own trade organization—the Federation of Trade Press Associations of the United States—to lobby for the second-class mailing privilege to apply to a broader array of trade publications.[26] Charles T. Root, publisher of the important American retail trade paper the *Dry Goods Economist* and a leader of the lobbying efforts, remarked that the second-class postal law was one of "the two principal foundation stones on which all our periodical publications are built. . . . Without the cheap, efficient, and prompt distribution granted to papers by this postal law, the dissemination of the business press would probably never have reached its large and influential proportions."[27] The savings were enormous: publishers paid a penny per pound to mail their periodicals second-class, even though the actual cost of delivery borne by the Post Office came out to somewhere between five to eight cents per pound.[28]

Congress had created this generous foundation stone with the Post Office Act of 1792. The US Post Office offered subsidies that charged a lower postage rate to recipients of magazines and newspapers than recipients of letters (eventually, senders were charged instead of recipients owing to the difficulty of collecting payment).[29] The postal subsidies may have been idealistically borne from the vision of encouraging citizens to read and participate in their democracy, but the generous second-class subsidies lasted well into the twentieth century thanks to political forces. Publishers lobbied Congress to maintain and expand the subsidies, and more than a few politicians understood that cheap postage and a grateful press helped them to spread their message, win elections, and stay in office. Nevertheless, as the subsidies grew increasingly expensive for the federal government, and as more and more publications applied for second-class mailing status, the Post Office undertook several attempts to distinguish between which periodicals did and did not merit the privilege. In 1879, the Post Office imposed content guidelines, disallowing the postal subsidy for publications chiefly focused on advertising rather than news and commentary. As the attorney for the Post Office argued, "the government should not carry at a loss to itself publications which are simply private advertising schemes."[30]

The restriction against "private advertising schemes" receiving the second-class mailing subsidy was one of the greatest gifts that American trade publishers ever received. If corporations could have obtained the subsidy for their house organs and advertising circulars, then they might have concentrated their spending and outreach efforts there. Instead, advertising in a trade paper became a more cost-effective way to reach readers. And as US trade papers gained readership and stature in the late nineteenth and early twentieth centuries, this became an instance of path dependency—an initial decision and advantage influencing the future course of decisions. Some companies, both within the film industry and outside it, published their own organs and circulars. Yet these always came as supplements, not substitutes, to their purchases of advertising in the trade press.

For Charles T. Root, advertising represented the second "principal foundation stone" of trade publishing, and, to mix metaphors, "the cord on which pretty much all publishing is strung."[31] Even with the benefit of cheap postage, the cost of producing a trade paper far exceeded the revenue obtained from subscriptions. Typically, subscriptions generated between only 10 to 20 percent of a publication's revenue. In many ways, paid subscriptions were more important as evidence that the right readership wanted to receive the paper than they were as a source of income. Within this environment, trade papers had to walk a certain tightrope: they had to stay friendly enough to the advertisers of the industry to retain their business, but they also had to appeal enough to readers to keep their subscriptions.

The film and theatrical trade papers had heaped accusations of advertiser bias on one another during the height of the MPPC conflicts. And for decades preceding that moment, similar suspicions had cast a negative light on the trade papers of larger American industries. As Horace M. Swetland, president of the Federation of Trade Press Associations of the United States in the early 1910s, remarked, "The early history of Industrial Journalism was besmirched with the trade 'write-up,' the 'puff,'—and an attempt to cater to personal pride and prejudice of the advertiser. It has out-lived this degrading and debasing period, and stands to-day, clean and wholesome in its advocacy of what it believes to be for the best interests of its readers."[32] By casting the age of the "puff" as part of industrial journalism's early history, Swetland presented the modern era as one governed by higher levels of professional standards. Under Swetland's presidency, the federation pursued a campaign designed to legitimize the profession and formalize standards of practice.

In 1913, the federation took a major step at codifying industrial journalism's standards of practice and improving its image by adopting a "Declaration of Trade Press Principles." Because most of these principles were evoked, followed, or violated by the film industry trade papers over the next few years, the ten-point declaration merits full reproduction here:

1. We believe the basic principle on which every trade paper should build is SERVICE—service to readers and service to advertisers, in a way to promote the welfare of the general public.
2. We believe in TRUTH as applied to the editorial, news, and advertising columns.
3. We believe in the utmost frankness regarding circulation.
4. We believe the highest efficiency of the Business Press of America can be secured through CIRCULATIONS OF QUALITY rather than of Quantity—that character, and not mere numbers, should be the criterion by which the value of a publication should be judged.
5. We believe in Cooperation with all those movements in the advertising, printing, publishing, and merchandising fields which make for business and social betterment.
6. We believe that the best interests of manufacturers, the Business Press and consumers can be advanced through a greater interchange of facts regarding merchandise and merchandising and to this end invite cooperation by manufacturers and consumers.
7. We believe that the logical medium to carry the message of the manufacturer directly to the distributer [*sic*] and the user is the Business Press.
8. We believe that while many advertising campaigns may profitably employ newspapers, magazines, outdoor display, etc., no well-rounded campaign seeking to interest the consumer or user is complete without the Business Press.
9. We believe in cooperating with all interests which are engaged in creative advertising work.
10. We believe that business papers can best serve their trades, industries or professions by being leaders of thought; by keeping their editorial columns

independent of the counting-room, unbiased and unafraid; by keeping their news columns free from paid reading notices and puffery of all kinds; by refusing to print any advertisement which is misleading or which does not measure up to the highest standards of business integrity.[33]

The tenth and final point is especially noteworthy. It announces the high ambition of trade paper editors: "being leaders of thought," leading an industry by leading its press. In a 1915 lecture to New York University journalism students, trade publisher E. A. Simmons made the point even more emphatically: "the success of any trade, technical, or class journal lies in the determination to make a paper that will not follow, but will lead the industry to which it is devoted—that will be a motor, not a trailer."[34] This was the goal that William A. Johnston was striving to achieve. In the course of doing so, he loudly embraced these ten trade press declarations, even as he became the film industry's most notorious printer of "puffery."

WILLIAM A. JOHNSTON AND THE TRADE'S QUALITY CIRCULATION

When William Allen Johnston launched *Exhibitors' Times* in May 1913, he was not an expert on motion pictures. The young industry already had a small stable of self-proclaimed experts, most of whom had worked in some capacity for *Moving Picture World*. Thomas Bedding, Louis Reeves Harrison, F. H. Richardson, Epes Winthrop Sargent, Alfred H. Saunders, and the abovementioned W. Stephen Bush all had experience writing about motion pictures and, in some cases, working in production and exhibition. Johnston lacked this intimate understanding of the film medium, yet he possessed an expertise that proved even more valuable: he understood journalism and advertising as businesses. Johnston took the framework he had learned in journalism and applied it to motion pictures—an industry that seemed chaotic yet full of promise, an industry in need of a professionally conducted trade paper to lead it.

For the first year, Johnston focused on the business and advertising sides of trade publishing, leaving the editorial page to Thomas Bedding. In the first issue of *Exhibitors' Times*, Johnston wrote a column restating familiar platitudes: the influence of the motion picture was "probably as great as, if not greater, than words from the pulpit, the newspaper, and stage"; and in light of this huge responsibility, nothing would "appear in the pages of THE EXHIBITORS' TIMES which does not tend toward the propagation of good pictures."[35] But for the next several months, it was Bedding's voice that spoke for *Exhibitors' Times*. To call Thomas Bedding arrogant would be like calling Thomas Edison litigious—true statements, yes, but they don't capture the extreme lengths to which each man went. Although Bedding addressed various industry issues in his "Right off the Reel" column, his writing always seemed to wind its way back to the topic of his own greatness. Bedding frequently reminded readers that he was a Fellow of the Royal Photographic Society and had participated in the growth of motion pictures since 1896.[36] In 1912, merely one year before taking the helm of *Exhibitors' Times*, Bedding proclaimed that he was "predestined to edit 'The Implet.'" Despite being the house organ for Carl Laemmle's Imp Film Company, *The Implet*, Bedding promised, would "address all exhibitors, manufacturers, and the general public throughout the world" and "be different from anything and everything else."[37] In actuality, *The Implet* lasted only a few months before transforming into the more straightforward exhibitor-oriented house organ *Universal Weekly*. His lack of modesty aside, Bedding did have strengths as an editor, and his greatest attribute was his understanding of England's film market. At their best, his columns and the correspondences he published offered interesting comparative analyses of the American and English film marketplaces that most other American trade papers lacked.[38]

Although Johnston mostly stayed away from Bedding's editorial page, the publisher's hand very much guided the rest of the makeup of *Exhibitors' Times*. Johnston emphasized that *Exhibitors' Times* operated "solely in the interests of Motion Picture Exhibitors," following the example of the *Dry Goods Economist*—the US's leading retail-oriented trade paper—which had a policy of service to its readers above all else.[39] Every week, the thirty-two-page weekly paper included an "Operators Forum" (*operator* was the contemporary term for a projectionist) and a number of separate departments designed to inform the exhibitor and uplift the field of exhibition as a whole. There were departments devoted to "Theatre and Construction," "Music and the Picture," "Advertising the Picture," and "Appearance and Manners," which offered suggestions on how theater ushers should dress and stand. In addition to these departments, *Exhibitors' Times* covered exhibitor gatherings and solicited letters and correspondences from leading industry figures, including manufacturers.

One section that was missing from *Exhibitors' Times* was film reviews. This is somewhat surprising considering *Exhibitors' Times*' stated emphasis on providing a service to exhibitors and, especially, in light of the fact that *Moving Picture World*, *Motography*, *Billboard*, and *New York Dramatic Mirror* all published sections of film reviews. Instead, the titles of films only appeared within one of three places: (1) the listing of release dates printed at the back of the paper (standard practice among all the industry's trade papers); (2) an occasional news story announcing the production or release of a quality film (the Famous Players adaptation of *Tess of the D'Urbervilles*, for example)[40]; or (3) an advertisement (the amount of advertising was modest—no more than six pages, typically, per issue—and included equipment advertisements along with those promoting films and distribution services). Overall, *Exhibitors' Times* was the expression of a publisher who was more focused on an industry's ideals and macrolevel structure than the nitty-gritty realities of day-to-day management. The abstract notion of making "better pictures" mattered more than evaluating individual films. Similarly, theater construction and usher etiquette received more attention than the question of how a small exhibitor could balance mortgage payments, labor costs, and film rental fees and still stay in business. Focusing on high-level issues of industry improvement also allowed Johnston to keep his hands clean of the partisan fighting that had earlier engulfed the trade papers. Johnston repeatedly emphasized that *"The Exhibitors' Times* is an independent journal . . . and that it is not connected, directly or indirectly, with any commercial enterprise whatever."[41]

A mere five months after founding *Exhibitors' Times*, Johnston acquired *Moving Picture News*. He merged the papers under a new title: *Motion Picture News* (Bedding and Johnston "endeavored to familiarize the public with the correct nomenclature of the subject—'motion' pictures not 'moving' pictures").[42] The deal, completed in September 1913, proved transformative both for Johnston and the film trades. In his 1914 book, *Theatre of Science*, Robert Grau marveled that "the rapid growth of the new publication, under the editorship of William A. Johnston, formerly publisher and founder of 'The Exhibitors' Times,' has been unprecedented in the trade-journal field. . . . 'The Motion Picture News' is and will remain absolutely non-partisan in every sense. It is utterly free from control."[43] Although Johnston deliberately distanced *Motion Picture News* from the partisan reputation of *Moving Picture News*, he gained two important assets from the acquisition: exhibitor subscriptions and advertising contracts. In 1912, *Moving Picture News* claimed a circulation of ten thousand and included a dozen pages of advertising in the typical issue—numbers that dwarfed *Exhibitor's Times*. Johnston quickly embarked on a campaign to retain and increase *Moving Picture News'* base of advertisers. He also became the paper's dominant editorial voice. Thomas Bedding left *Motion Picture News* in October 1913, and it is unclear whether his exit was voluntary. What is clear is that the merger of the two journals led to a merger in Johnston's titles: he became the publisher *and* editor of *Motion Picture News*.

Although Johnston reiterated that *Motion Picture News* was published in the interests of exhibitors, he used his columns to speak to manufacturers and a larger imagined community of the motion picture industry. Significantly, he sought to enhance the legitimacy of his paper and himself by educating the motion picture industry about the best practices of industrial journalism. In one November 1913 column, entitled "Advertising Is an Economy," Johnston explained the logic for advertising in a professionally conducted trade paper. "You have alternatives," Johnston explained:

> You can send out your own printed matter: letters, booklets and the like; or you can even publish your own medium to carry your advertising.
>
> You can do this: And it isn't economical—not as economical as it is to take advantage of an established journal which goes through the mails cheaply and never into the waste-paper basket.
>
> You want to reach 10,000 people, let us say. Very well, the mailing then of a letter will cost you in postage $200.00 alone. You can have a magazine or newspaper carry this same message for you for a few dollars per ten thousand circulation.

As for your own publication you not only bear its heavy publishing charges, and Uncle Sam very properly calls your medium an advertising house-organ and charges you high mailing rates. All of which is frightfully expensive.

Again, it is certainly more convincing to the buyer to have your message given him through a disinterested medium, a medium he knows and believes in, and to which he pays a yearly subscription price for authoritative information about his business.[44]

Johnston was educating the film industry about the second-class postal subsidies that made trade papers a bargain compared to a house organ. But his references to "a disinterested medium, a medium [the buyer] knows and believes in," are also telling. Johnston understood the importance of perception to his brand—especially the perception that *Motion Picture News* would be unbiased by the very advertisers he was courting.

In the same November 1913 column, Johnston attempted to attract advertisers that had already paid for space in *Moving Picture World, Billboard*, and other publications. He emphasized that "duplication should not be avoided. This is an accepted fact today. . . . Duplication—letting several mediums tell your message—is impressive, and the basic force of advertising is to impress your buyer. It doesn't cost any more. A judicious division of large and small space will stretch your appropriation through several mediums just as long as in judicious space in one."[45] Four years later, after *Motion Picture News* had outpaced all its rivals in advertising growth, Johnston argued the exact opposite point—for the end of duplication in advertising and the elimination of all but two trade papers.[46]

In 1914, Johnston disrupted the status quo of American cinema's trade press—and dramatically increased his advertising revenue—by redefining the industry's understanding of circulation. The third and fourth "Declarations of Trade Press Principles" had emphasized circulation, particularly the importance of accurately reporting the paper's readership and the principle of "CIRCULATIONS OF QUALITY rather than of Quantity—that character, and not mere numbers, should be the criterion by which the value of a publication should be judged."[47] These principles were firmly established among the trade papers covering American iron, dry goods, and shipping, but the film and theatrical papers had essentially ignored them. Prior to 1914, the film and theatrical trade papers had competed for the crown of quantity and the highest circulation. The paper Johnston had acquired, *Moving Picture News*, bragged in 1911 that it offered "guaranteed larger circulation than any other trade paper."[48] *Billboard, Moving Picture World,* and *Motography* all made similar claims.[49] To boost their circulations, these trade papers tried to recruit any and all possible subscribers and, additionally, distributed their paper to newsstands. Unlike the leading trade journals of other industries, these motion picture and theatrical trade papers did not employ the services of an outside firm to audit their circulation and subscriber list. They reported their

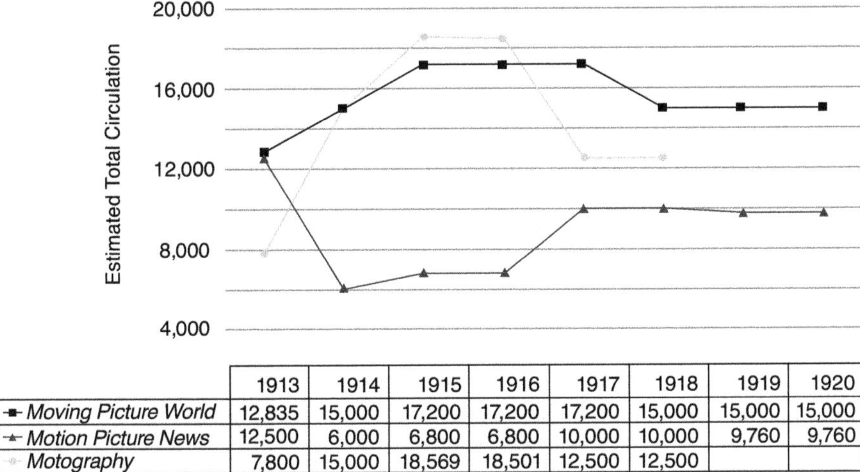

	1913	1914	1915	1916	1917	1918	1919	1920
Moving Picture World	12,835	15,000	17,200	17,200	17,200	15,000	15,000	15,000
Motion Picture News	12,500	6,000	6,800	6,800	10,000	10,000	9,760	9,760
Motography	7,800	15,000	18,569	18,501	12,500	12,500		

FIGURE 8. Circulation estimates for *Moving Picture World*, *Motion Picture News*, and *Motography*, 1913–20. Source: *N. W. Ayer & Son's American Newspaper Annual and Directory*, Library of Congress Digital Collections, https://lccn.loc.gov/sn91012092.

circulations each year to the advertising bureaus, and most readers and advertisers knew they needed to take the numbers with a grain of salt.

Johnston wanted to steer his publication, and the motion picture industry as a whole, in a different direction. He refused to allow *Motion Picture News* to be sold on stands. He claimed to only pursue subscriptions of the "purchasing exhibitors" who were valuable to manufacturer and equipment advertisers (he estimated the number was seven thousand, far lower, he noted, than the guesses of eighteen thousand theaters, which, he said, "the trade itself has found and knows to be incorrect"). He promised to be more truthful and transparent with advertisers about who was receiving their messages. Any dollar an advertiser spent reaching someone outside the industry, someone who couldn't purchase his wares, was a waste of money.[50] As a result of these new policies, *Motion Picture News'* reported circulation fell by half from 1912 to 1914 (see fig. 8). But this steep drop in circulation should not be interpreted as a failure. After all, *News'* advertising sales were skyrocketing across this same period (see fig. 2). Instead, Johnston had redefined in the minds of his advertisers what circulation meant to a trade paper. He had shifted the standards of American cinema's trade press toward the professional standards of industrial journalism, which valued "CIRCULATIONS OF QUALITY rather than of Quantity."[51] In fact, this became the new slogan for *Motion Picture News*. Beginning in September 1914, the phrase "HAS THE QUALITY CIRCULATION OF THE TRADE" appeared in all caps immediately underneath the title of *Motion Picture News* (see fig. 9).[52] Johnston had imposed the standards of industrial journalism on the film industry and, in the process, increased

FIGURE 9. Beginning on September 26, 1914, *Motion Picture News* printed on its cover: "Has the Quality Circulation of the Trade." *Source: Motion Picture News,* Sept. 26, 1914, cover, https://lantern.mediahist.org/catalog/motionpicturenew101unse_0969.

advertising sales and enhanced his legitimacy among the industry's leading manufacturers, distributors, and suppliers.

Two months later, in November 1914, Johnston borrowed further from the playbook of industrial journalism, launching a separate magazine called *Accessory News* (fig. 10). *Accessory News* appeared within *Motion Picture News* and focused on "Construction, Equipment, Operation."[53] But by listing *Accessory News* as a separate magazine, Johnston was able to charge premium advertising rates to the manufacturers of projectors, chairs, and other theater supplies who wanted their products to appear in the section that would be most closely read by potential buyers. Before Johnston, film trade papers had edited projection and equipment sections for the benefit of the reader. The leading section, F. H. Richardson's "Projection Department" in *Moving Picture World*, encouraged readers to write in with questions about projector and theater operation.[54] And, in 1910, *Moving Picture World* aggregated numerous columns by Richardson and published them in book form as *Motion Picture Handbook: A Guide for Managers and Operators of Motion Picture Theatres*.[55] Richardson's "Projection Department" and *Handbook* organized information for the benefit of the reader. In so doing, Richardson and *Moving Picture World* were embracing one of the ideals of industrial journalism: putting the subscriber's interests first.[56] But Johnston went a step further with *Accessory News*: he organized readers for the benefit of the advertiser. Johnston did not invent this model himself (*Accessory News* essentially imitated the *Store Equipment* magazine within the *Dry Goods Economist*).[57] He was, however, the first to successfully import it into the film industry, where others would reuse it—most notably, Martin J. Quigley in the "Better Theatres" section of *Exhibitors Herald*.

Johnston's most significant accomplishment of 1914—and the one that may have been most responsible for attracting more manufacturers and distributors to purchase advertising—was the "Review of Film Trade Conditions of America," a special issue of *Motion Picture News* published in the summer. The leading trade papers of other American industries had long compiled data on the industry and shared it through special issues and annuals. Johnston brought this practice to the film industry with a new level of detail and thoroughness. The information was collected, he claimed, by ninety-seven field correspondents dispersed across the US, Canada, and England. The correspondents were told to investigate their territories and report on a series of questions:

- What is the approximate number of theatres compared with last year?
- How are the small houses being affected by the new and larger theatres?
- How many theatres are being remodeled and improved and in what ways?
- What types of features are in demand?
- How does the single-reel program compare in popularity with multiple-reel subjects?
- Are audiences changing, and how?[58]

Construction,
Equipment,
Operation

Accessory News

Everything for
the Modern
Picture Theatre

Tel. 7650 Bryant

NO. 220 WEST FORTY-SECOND STREET

New York City

Volume X

NOVEMBER 14, 1914

Number 19

What "Accessory News" Means

THIS is the day of the modern picture theatre, finely and fully equipped, and efficiently run.

Which, briefly, is the reason why we have added "Accessory News" to MOTION PICTURE NEWS.

* * *

WE have been planning "Accessory News" for some time.

It has seemed to us that such matters as theatre construction, equipment and operation are important enough to demand a new magazine devoted wholly to this field.

We have felt that they deserved more than a mere department and much more than casual editorial interest— that they should, by no means, be pushed out of sight by the mass of film news, reviews and advertising.

* * *

SO we hit upon the idea of "Accessory News."

It is not separate from MOTION PICTURE NEWS, but it is, nevertheless, a magazine within itself.

It has its own manager and its own separate staff of writers.

It has its own cover or title page in color and in every way is made to stand out prominently and distinctly as it should.

* * *

IT is the writer's opinion that "Accessory News" will grow till it rivals—and perhaps outdoes—that part of MOTION PICTURE NEWS which is devoted to pictures and picture making.

The making of pictures is of the utmost importance. But so also is the showing of pictures. The latter problem, however, has fallen far short of the attention it deserves.

* * *

A MAKER of screens has shouted insistently, for the past several years, that what the exhibitor is really retailing to the public is *picture light*.

So he is.

He doesn't merely retail pictures. The best pictures ever produced are of little use to him—they will not gain and hold patronage—unless they are well projected on the screen and well reflected from that screen.

* * *

IN other words, the successful exhibitor is the man who also sells good picture light.

He must sell other things, too, beside pictures.

He must sell an attractive and comfortable interior, which means a great many things, such as ventilation, pleasing lights and decorations, comfortable chairs, excellent music, courtesy from employees—service and efficiency *all along the line*.

And to bring his patrons in, he *must have* an attractive lobby.

THE lack of all this may have been well enough in the days when theatres were only converted shops, when exhibitors were merely speculators with a new and untried amusement; but today these elements of theatre service and efficiency are *necessities*.

The public has been educated up to well-shown as well as well-produced pictures.

They *demand* a pleasing environment. Among the exhibitors of the country, a stern survival of the fittest is in progress of which the mismanaged, poorly-equipped theatre is fast dying and by which the modern picture theatre finely and fully equipped is becoming more and more of a big and important institution.

* * *

AGAIN, there is the growing importance of motion picture technique.

All the faults of projection today are charged upon the projection machine and the screen.

These important facts are not taken into account: that we have no standardized methods of film perforation, camera work, developing and printing, etc.

Until we achieve this standardization, we shall not have perfect picture light.

* * *

THEN, too, among other things, is the question of furnishing and equipment contributing to the comfort of patrons. The right kind of seating has a great deal to do with attendance, and its importance has commanded the attention of manufacturers.

It has been a long way from the crude chairs of the "store shows" to the luxurious upholstered seats of the present motion picture theatre.

* * *

PROPER decoration is now recognized as a big asset in a theatre's popularity. The highest skill is employed in rendering the walls and ceilings pleasing to the most critical eye.

The best carpets and draperies, formerly used only in the more pretentious places of amusement, now grace the temples of the new art.

The demand for furnishings of this character from motion picture theatres has considerably augmented the business of firms in this line, and called upon the services of experts who make a specialty of estimating on the outfitting of photo play houses.

* * *

"ACCESSORY NEWS" aims to take up all these important matters—competently and continuously— for the benefit of the progressive exhibitors and operators, for the prospective theatre builder—and for the betterment, we trust, of the problem of picture exhibition.

WILLIAM A. JOHNSTON.

FIGURE 10. The premiere of "Accessory News," in William A. Johnston's *Motion Picture News*, Nov. 14, 1914, 71, https://lantern.mediahist.org/catalog/motionpicturenew102unse_0489.

Motion Picture News organized market reports by region, with separate headings for Canada, New England, the East, Capitol area, the Southeast, Central states, and the West. Further subheadings reported on the conditions of specific cities. There was "Demand for Genuine Features in Springfield [Illinois]," but Cincinnati was a "Town Too 'Cheap' for Features."[59] As a preface to the collection of reports, Johnston wrote a one-and-a-half-page summary, synthesizing what he considered to be the key points about contemporary market conditions.[60]

Johnston claimed the special issue was the first of its kind and "of practical value to the exhibitor and to the manufacturer and distributor of films and of theatre equipment and supplies."[61] In reality, though, the market reports were far more valuable to manufacturers, distributors, and equipment suppliers than to exhibitors, who were the customers that the reports were studying. In other words, *Motion Picture News* claimed to be published in the interest of exhibitors, but its most ambitious issue was servicing manufacturers, distributors, and suppliers. Johnston claimed that one of the lessons of the report was that "manufacturers should study local conditions." No film company currently had a system for gathering and analyzing data in a reliable, timely, and comprehensive manner. The implicit suggestion, rendered explicitly in subsequent editorials and special market report issues, was that *Motion Picture News* was the best source available for delivering this vital information.[62]

Under Johnston's leadership, the volume of advertising in *Motion Picture News* boomed. We can page through *Motion Picture News* and read Johnston's many self-promotional remarks, explaining why manufacturers and distributors should buy space in his paper. What we don't have evidence for—and thus requires some speculation—are the behind-the-scenes maneuverings of Johnston as he sought out the business of Universal, Mutual, Paramount, and the nation's other leading manufacturers and distributors. In an article he wrote more than a decade later, in 1926, Johnston remarked about the importance of the distribution sales chiefs based in New York City who determine "the nature of the advertising to be used, the expenditures, and where the advertising is to be placed," both in the trade papers and in the popular press.[63] Although we lack archival memos and restaurant receipts, we can certainly imagine Johnston, who was also based in New York City, visiting with the top distribution executives in 1914 and 1915, offering advice based on his market research and persuading them why they should buy more space in *Motion Picture News*. Johnston seems to have been especially effective at ingratiating himself with Carl Laemmle, the head of Universal. Johnston publicized Laemmle, whose name appears frequently in *Motion Picture News*. Laemmle returned the favor, purchasing considerable advertising and inviting Johnston to attend the March 1915 opening of Universal City in Southern California.[64]

If there was one section of his paper that Johnston cared even more about than the advertising pages, it was his editorial column. Although Johnston had known little about the film industry in early 1913, he spent much of 1914 and 1915 trying to prove that he was its preeminent thought leader. Like W. Stephen Bush and the other trade columnists, he frequently focused in his columns on the threats posed by censorship bills. Johnston wrote about censorship in *Motion Picture News*, but he also sought a larger stage, publishing articles in popular newspapers and magazines defending the motion picture. In the battle against censorship policies, Johnston became one of the industry's leading diplomats, capable of forcefully arguing against such legislation while retaining a respectful tone.

The most prominent theme of Johnston's editorials across the mid-1910s was the film industry's inefficiency. Writing in an analytical style, Johnston surveyed the industry's "considerable disorder" and offered prescriptions.[65] In 1914, Johnston argued for the importation of tested management and merchandising techniques from other industries. "Often it is argued that this is an amusement business and so cannot be ruled economically and methodically. Which is *wrong*," wrote Johnston. "Business executives, trained to other and older—if not greater—industries, are entering the ranks here and there and are making themselves felt in no uncertain way. They are patiently introducing system and sense and impatiently crowding out loose action and talk—jealousies, temperament, gossip, exaggeration, *gambling*."[66] Johnston had modeled *Motion Picture News* on the leading trade papers of American retail. In his columns, he sought to reshape the motion picture industry so that it more closely resembled the orderly convergence of supply and demand that one found in paint shops and grocery stores.

Johnston argued that the intense competitiveness and uncertainties of the exhibition marketplace were slowing the industry's progress. In 1915, he argued against the daily change model of the shorts program. Instead, the industry should embrace the motto, "FEWER PICTURES—BETTER PICTURES—LONGER RUNS."[67] He was essentially advocating for the feature film distribution model that would catapult Adolph Zukor's Famous Players and Paramount to the forefront of the industry. He also spoke out in support of mergers and consolidations, which he believed would create greater efficiencies and avoid the escalation of a dog-eat-dog, "survival of the fittest" marketplace.[68] In these columns, Johnston argued that these changes would benefit exhibitors. But the smaller exhibitors who could not afford feature films (or simply did not want them) and who depended on booking programs of short films would have been justified if they felt more threatened than protected by Johnston's plans.

Some exhibitors also doubted the integrity of the film reviews published in *Motion Picture News*. They recognized an inherent tension between pleasing the advertiser and serving the exhibitor. Prior to Johnston's acquisition of the paper in 1913, *Moving Picture News* did not have a review section at all. Instead, there was a list of "Manufacturers' Synopses of Films."[69] Johnston had turned a transparent system (reprinting synopses prepared by manufacturers) into something much more murky and opaque (printing reviews trying to balance the exhibitor's and advertiser's interests). Film historian Alan Gevinson has called the reviews the "worst part" of the publication: "In most cases reviewers merely retold the plot and either waxed enthusiastically about the production or tactfully avoided any negative judgment."[70] Although *Motion Picture News* was developing the reputation as the most manufacturer-friendly paper, the reviews in *Moving Picture World* and *Motography* largely followed the same approach. In contrast, *Variety* tore apart weak films, but it had little in the way of film advertising in the mid-1910s and therefore fewer advertisers it needed to worry about offending.

Exhibitors needed reliable information about upcoming films, but they could not fully trust the reviews published in their trade papers. In response, exhibitors sought out alternatives and exercised critical reading practices. In 1915, two new publications that specialized in offering independent reviews sprang into existence. Wid Gunning's journal, *Wid's*, is best remembered as the industry's first daily paper and the basis for *Film Daily*. But *Wid's* originated as a weekly reviewing service for exhibitors.[71] Similarly, B. P. Fineman launched *Exhibitor's Film Review Service* for the "purpose of supplying exhibitors with unbiased, impartial, conscientious, and thoroughly dependable reviews."[72] Because they lacked the advertising revenue of *News* and *World*, both magazines charged substantially higher subscription prices than the leading weekly trade papers. Clearly, though, some exhibitors considered the service worth the price. Neither *Exhibitor's Film Review Service* nor this iteration of *Wid's* lasted beyond the decade. But a film reviewer for *Motion Picture News* named P. S. Harrison would soon break free from Johnston and launch his own magazine that, for forty years, delivered reviews to exhibitors that were "free from the influence of film advertising."[73]

NEWS, PUFF, AND INDUSTRY DISCORD

Motion Picture News published special issues, equipment sections, editorials, reviews, and lots of advertising. But what about the more routine news gathering and reporting of the paper? When we think of news, we tend to think of a reporter, notepad in hand, breaking a story, asking different sides to comment, typing it all up under deadline. But the reporter model was not common in industrial journalism in the 1910s. Instead, *Motion Picture News* generated a great deal of news content from the same network of field correspondents who contributed to the market reports. The correspondents mailed, telegraphed, or hand delivered their news to a midlevel editor. An exhibitor correspondent in Cleveland, for example, might have news to share about an upcoming convention. If the editor chose to use the item, he would edit it and, frequently, rewrite it in the process. The result was the collage of news items that one finds in these papers. Many individual events are described, but they are presented in clipped fashion rather than as part of a synthetic, coherent whole. In many ways, this further enhanced the importance of

Johnston's editorial page, which became the site for drawing broad generalizations from the multitude of smaller industry news items.

In generating news, *Motion Picture News'* office managers in Chicago (Theodore S. Mead) and Los Angeles (J. C. Jessen) also played important roles. They needed to keep their relationships strong with correspondents and sources in their territories. But they also had to be jacks-of-all-trades—paying solicitation calls to advertisers, finding new subscribers, collecting money from advertisers, and reporting on local events. In a sign that some things about Los Angeles culture never change, Jessen posed for a photograph next to his automobile. The image was printed in a 1916 issue of *News* with the caption, "The Los Angeles Manager of Motion Picture News and His Traveling 'Office.'"[74] Jessen and Mead both compiled two- to four-page sections of news content each week focused on developments in their cities.

Johnston proudly called attention to his network of correspondents and office managers based in Chicago and Los Angeles. But his paper's fastest growing supply of news items came from sources he was more reluctant to acknowledge: publicists and advertisers. Ironically, despite all his rhetoric about "quality circulation" and improving the professional conduct of trade papers, Johnston became the film industry trade press's worst violator of publishing press releases as news. To be clear, all of the film industry trade papers engaged in this practice. But *Motion Picture News* became the most visible offender, especially in 1916, as the advertising pages swelled and a growing number of exhibitors perceived Johnston as a mouthpiece for the manufacturers.

The Federation of Trade Publishers Associations of the United States had been trying to discourage its members from publishing publicity items. The federation believed that valuable news could come from advertisers, but editors needed to sift between items of genuine news value and those intended simply for private promotion and gain. The following litmus test was put forward: "If the publicity sought is in the nature of a social service, for the good of the general public or the trade as a whole, and not to boost some private enterprise, or for personal gain, then it is all right to print it. Otherwise, it should be paid for at regular space rates."[75] Most of the news items in *Motion Picture News* concerning the activities of manufacturers and distributors failed to meet this standard.

The testimonies of industry insiders and a close reading of the trade papers both suggest that there was a well-understood *quid pro quo* agreement at play. Leander Richardson, publicity director of World Film Corporation and formerly the editor of the *Morning Telegraph*, confronted Johnston on the matter:

> Probably you have noticed, Mr. Johnston, that the reading pages of the motion picture trade papers are loaded with press matter from the various manufacturers, closely balancing the volume of their advertising. That is to say, the company carrying two pages of paid space gets at least twice as much free notice in the reading part of the paper as the company buying a single page. The corporation carrying ten pages

of advertising receives fully ten times as much reading matter as the one that runs a single page—and so on. This is the fact.[76]

If you read an issue of *Motion Picture News* from 1915 or 1916, you can quickly reverse engineer the *quid pro quo* described by Richardson. Start at the front of the magazine. After turning the cover, you will find thirty-six pages of advertising—all of them full-page ads, often laid out in two- or four-page spreads, promoting the feature releases of Paramount, VLSE, Mutual, Metro, Triangle, and other leading distributors. Turn past the two editorial pages and you will get into the forty- to fifty-page news section, which will include a couple of full-page original articles but mostly a mixture of news items supplied by correspondents and publicists. Like a child playing a matching game, one can spot the publicity pieces—"Essanay in Throes of Moving into New Quarters," for example, or "Mutual Cameraman Gets Striking European Scenes"—then flip through the advertisements that appear in the front and find those same companies.[77] If you don't find the company's advertisements in the front section (which permitted four-color printing), then keep looking through the additional black-and-white ads in the middle and back of the paper until you find the company.

Exhibitors in the 1910s were very much playing this very game—cross-referencing ads, reviews, and news for signs of bias. These exhibitors engaged in what media scholar John Caldwell has called a *critical industrial practice*—applying an interpretive scheme within a particular industry context as part of one's work.[78] Writing nine decades before Caldwell, W. Stephen Bush understood this on some level, observing that exhibitors "are watching the motion picture journals more or less critically."[79] Readers might scan a film review, then check the advertising pages to gauge the likelihood of bias. Importantly, the trade paper's reputation influenced how exhibitors interpreted what they read. Was a trade paper credible and independent, or did it kowtow to the demands of advertisers? As the new year of 1916 dawned, the exhibitor perception was increasingly that a new rift was forming between them and manufacturers. They brought their critical eyes to bear on the Board of Trade updates and manufacturer announcements that William A. Johnston called "news."

In the spring of 1916, some exhibitors found new reasons to be suspicious of the Board of Trade and *Motion Picture News*. Johnston frequently reminded readers that he was a director of the Board of Trade, and he insisted that the board represented all branches of the industry.[80] The New York branch of the Motion Picture Exhibitors League disagreed. In March 1916, the league's members voted overwhelmingly to pull out of the ambitious May convention that the Board of Trade was planning for New York City's Madison Square Garden.[81] Much of the dispute came down to money. Like a trade paper, a trade convention made money from charging manufacturers, distributors, and equipment suppliers for space (in this case, the space of a booth on the convention floor rather than the space on a page). The Board of Trade offered the exhibitors 25 percent of the convention's net profits, an amount that they considered insultingly low. The New York Exhibitors League perceived the board as attempting to take over the yearly convention it hosted, which financially supported its state organization.

Ultimately, the board and exhibitors decided to each hold their own conventions, the Exhibitors League of New York's running from May 1–6, 1916, and the Board of Trade's from May 6–13.[82] Johnston characterized the whole situation as a "regrettable misunderstanding," and the Board of Trade tried to offer the reassurance that it "seeks harmony with exhibitors." But irreparable damage had already been done. One manufacturer, Metro, quit the Board of Trade over the incident. In a maneuver apparently calculated to curry favor with exhibitors, Metro claimed it would not belong to an organization that employed a policy intended to "throttle the exhibitor."[83] Because Famous Players and its distributor, Paramount, had never agreed to join the Board of Trade, Metro's quitting meant that the board lacked two of the industry's most important manufacturer-distributors.[84]

An ambitious New York City exhibitor also used the controversy to rise in prominence within the industry. Lee A. Ochs was a Brooklyn theater owner and president of the New York Exhibitors League. In March 1916, he and Samuel Rothafel had been two of only five New York exhibitors to vote in favor of the joint trade convention with the Board of Trade, losing to 185 against it.[85] Two months later, Ochs became the most vocal exhibitor in the country to denounce the Board of Trade. He characterized the board as unrepresentative of exhibitors and, what's more, as "a rank failure in the fight against censorship."[86] Because of the controversy and the withdrawal of support from Famous Players, Metro, and the leading exhibitor organizations, the Board of Trade dissolved itself in June 1916. The following month, exhibitors gathered in Chicago from across the country and voted Ochs president of the Motion Picture Exhibitors League of America (MPELA). He would lead the national organization to which his New York branch belonged. Ochs also became a director of the National Association of the Motion Picture Industry (NAMPI), an organization launched within weeks after the Board of Trade's dissolution, which promised to be more inclusive of exhibitors.[87]

At a dinner hosted in New York on the eve of the Chicago convention, W. Stephen Bush was one of several prominent industry figures to speak in favor of electing Ochs to the MPELA presidency. According to *Motography*, Bush "spoke of his friendship for Mr. Ochs and that gentleman's splendid qualifications."[88] Bush also supported Ochs in his *Moving Picture World* columns, much more so than he ever publicly supported the Board of Trade. Bush commented that "the idea of giving the exhibitors a representation of two on a board of directors of ten was among the causes fatal to the Board of Trade."[89] In that same August 12, 1916, issue, Bush unleashed a thinly veiled attack on the trade paper editor who had occupied one of those ten board of directors seats. "The race for publicity in the motion picture journals begins to resemble a speed contest in a psychopathic ward," wrote Bush. "There is nothing that provokes and irritates the average reader more than piles upon piles of puffing. . . . It is only the paper with either no circulation at all or with a pitiably small circulation which can afford to open its news and editorial columns to every demand of the publicity man and press agent."[90] Bush's reference to "piles of puffing" and "a pitiably small circulation" were digs at Johnston's *Motion Picture News*, which had fewer subscribers than *Moving Picture World* and *Motography* but more advertiser-planted news pieces.

William A. Johnston, for his part, gave it right back to his critics. "You, as a producer, would scarcely admit to yourself that a competitor's product were better because it had been made longer," he wrote, addressing his advertisers, in reference to Bush's longer running *Moving Picture World*.[91] Amid his success in growing *Motion Picture News*' advertising pages, Johnston's typical analytical editorial style gave way at times to a more petulant and cavalier tone, particularly in his discussions of exhibition. At the height of the Board of Trade Convention controversy in April 1916, Johnston wrote, "Thanks! To the New York exhibitor who cancelled his subscription to MOTION PICTURE NEWS both by telephone and letter—so great was his anxiety to be sure that his cancellation was known—we return thanks."[92] As for the accusations of puff, Johnston framed the matter differently. "The advertisers, by custom, expect editorial notice." As long as the news items had some value to the reader, Johnston had no objection to the custom.[93]

Johnston's defense of publishing large quantities of publicity matter as news content did not placate his enemies. To them, the ocean of press notices in *Motion Picture News* only confirmed Johnston's obsequious personality and lack of integrity. Additionally, in their eyes, his emphasis on "quality circulation" reflected his arrogance and bias in favor of manufacturers and distributors instead of exhibitors. Johnston's appeal to industry custom would have also failed to meet the standards of the Federation of Trade Press Associations. The whole point of Horace Swetland's decrying "the 'puff'" was that the American trade press needed to move beyond this custom because "the editorial department of a proper industrial publication is absolutely divorced from its advertising department. In many cases it does not know the names of its important advertisers."[94] Clearly, Johnston was playing by a different rulebook.

In fairness to Johnston, though, most of the leading trade papers also failed to live up to these standards. What's more, they had something that Johnston did not: a near monopoly over their respective industry's trade publishing. In contrast, the film industry trade papers suffered from what Martin Quigley later called "diffusion." If advertising dollars were diffused across a dozen papers, then it meant none of them could afford a large staff of reporters and editors. As a result, Johnston had to operate in somewhat slapdash fashion—focusing on selling ads and writing attention-grabbing editorials, hastily piecing together the "news" from whatever correspondence he received that week from readers, exhibitor organizations, and advertisers. Furthermore, the importance of staying in the good graces of the US Post Office should not be overlooked. Because the Post Office demanded a significant amount of nonadvertising content to obtain the second-class subsidy, his advertisers were doing him (and themselves) a favor by supplying news content. The goal of stopping the diffusion, consolidating the film trade papers into one, and producing a new type of business publication would come to define the industry's next fifteen years.

CONCLUSION

The time was ripe in the mid-1910s for the film industry trade papers to grow in size and importance. The rise of the feature film, the power vacuum that formed from the decline of the MPPC, and the industry's need to organize in opposition to censorship all offered new opportunities for the trade press. The most successful editors, William A. Johnston and W. Stephen Bush, seized on these conditions and transformed themselves into influential industry figures. They were active participants and leaders within the motion picture industry, not merely chroniclers of it.

William A. Johnston and his *Motion Picture News* left an especially influential mark. Although he invented very little himself, his importation of practices and ideals from the growing field of industrial journalism changed the film industry's trade press. Data aggregation and market reports, a separate magazine for theater equipment, and an emphasis on circulation quality rather than quantity all became integral parts of the motion picture trade press for the next century. Johnston, however, proved unwilling to follow the calls of industrial journalism to stop printing publicity announcements for advertisers. His continuation of this practice—which grew at a parallel pace to his booming pages of advertising—earned him enemies, particularly among small exhibitors and the trade paper editor who understood them and spoke to them directly. When the Board of Trade came under fire and collapsed in spring 1916, the perception among small exhibitors that Johnston represented the interests of manufacturers, and not theater owners, only increased.

As Johnston's competitor, *Moving Picture World*, reported on these strains within the industry and advocated for the leadership role of exhibitors, internal strains were occurring at the paper's offices. W. Stephen Bush was *Moving Picture World*'s most famous columnist and one of the paper's editors. But unlike Johnston, he did not manage the publishing side of the paper or retain a major ownership stake in it. Since the death of *Moving Picture World*'s cofounder, J. P. Chalmers, in 1912, the paper had been owned and published by Chalmers's father and brother. These two men were the primary beneficiaries of Bush's tireless activities as a film reviewer, censorship watchdog, and exhibitor advocate. And, ultimately, it was the Chalmers clan, not Bush, who controlled the paper's direction.

What if Bush could edit and own a large stake in a new trade journal, one unquestionably devoted to the American exhibitor? It is unclear who first hatched the idea. But what is clear is that by the fall of 1916 Bush was plotting with MPELA president Lee A. Ochs and Merritt Crawford, former assistant editor of *Motion Picture News*, to launch a new trade paper. The new publication, *Exhibitor's Trade Review*, prompted, in the words of *Variety*, "the war of the motion picture trade journals"—with libel lawsuits, accusations of blackmail, and a growing perception that the trade press had become an industry problem.[95]

2

———

Trade Papers at War

The first glimmer of the controversy and scandal that *Exhibitor's Trade Review* would unleash occurred in the fall of 1916, a few weeks before the paper's debut. The New York City branch of the Motion Picture Exhibitors League of America (MPELA) had gathered to address accusations leveled by two of its members against the national organization's recently elected president, Lee A. Ochs. The New York City exhibitors, Maurice Fleischman and Charles Goldreyer, owned theaters that competed against those run by Ochs. They accused Ochs of using his office as MPELA president to pressure Metro, Paramount, World, Pathé, and Mutual to cancel their distribution service with their movie houses and favor Ochs's own theaters instead. Fleischman and Goldreyer sent their letter of grievances to the executive board of MPELA and *Variety*, which reprinted it in its October 27, 1916, issue.[1]

New York City exhibitors gathered for a hearing to address the charges. According to *Moving Picture World*, "Ochs was in attendance, and for probably half the four and a half hour session was in the witness chair."[2] The hearing was supposed to focus on the specific allegations of official misconduct published in *Variety*. Tobias A. Keppler, however, attorney for Fleischman and Goldreyer, kept turning the line of questions toward *Exhibitor's Trade Review*. Keppler pressed Ochs to open the books of the new trade paper and turn over a list of its stockholders. Previously, Ochs promised that *Exhibitor's Trade Review* would be the official paper of the MPELA and wholly owned by exhibitors. Keppler was now challenging Ochs to prove that no manufacturer or distributor owned a financial interest in the paper. Ochs and his attorney kept evading the question. They claimed that they could not share the books because their associate who kept them was busy playing golf that afternoon and his office was closed. Next, they refused to turn over the books on the grounds that the current inquiry was unrelated to *Exhibitor's Trade Review*. Finally, an exasperated Ochs asked, "If the gentlemen feels the *Exhibitor's Trade Review* is so important, why doesn't he try to get it into court?"

"I'll make an offer to Mr. Ochs right now," Keppler responded. "A libel suit can be preferred. If Mr. Ochs will serve us today, Saturday, we will serve an answer Monday and we will consent to go to trial Wednesday morning. If Mr. Ochs wants to get a trial we'll go Wednesday morning."[3]

Two weeks later, Keppler and Ochs went head-to-head again at an MPELA branch meeting. *Moving Picture World* reported:

> Keppler repeated his offer of two weeks ago to go to immediate trial of the libel suit of Ochs vs. Fleischman & Goldreyer. He said he had not yet seen a complaint. Mr. Goldsmith [Ochs's attorney] said he had it in his pocket.
>
> "Then we can go to trial tomorrow," said Mr. Keppler. "There we can force witnesses to testify. We will be dee-lighted to meet this issue if you will give us our day in court."
>
> "You annoy me," said Mr. Goldsmith. He did not accept the challenge, however.[4]

These heated exchanges at the MPELA branch meetings foreshadowed the larger fights involving *Exhibitor's Trade Review* that would soon follow. They also established the venue and tactics of the fights. Libel courts would become a battleground for industry reputations. Within this battleground, someone could claim to be injured and sue the publisher that defamed him. This remains the conventional relationship between libel lawsuits and reputation—the legal action serving as a means for a plaintiff to restore and improve his or her standing within a given community. Yet, as Keppler realized, something could be gained by being the defendant. Keppler was inviting a libel lawsuit, not trying to avoid one. Draw your opponent into the ring, expose him as a hypocrite, and walk away with your own reputation enhanced. The trade papers, like any number of lawyers and exhibitors, wanted to be perceived as strong, independent, and unafraid of a fight. *Exhibitor's Trade Review* and *Variety* would both attempt to enhance their reputations as the defendants of libel lawsuits, though their effectiveness varied significantly.

This chapter explores the libel lawsuits and related conflicts of *Exhibitor's Trade Review* and *Variety* in depth. *Exhibitor's Trade Review* became embroiled in a multifront war against the industry's establishment by defaming *Motion Picture News* editor William A. Johnston and attacking Universal Film Manufacturing. The fallout from these feuds disgraced *Exhibitor's Trade Review*'s leaders and left a lasting rift among American exhibitor organizations. *Variety* fared better in playing the roles of defendant and fearless, independent trade publication. Lee A. Ochs ultimately took Keppler's bait and sued *Variety*, Fleischman, and Goldreyer for libel (Ochs appears to have lost).[5] But the far more significant libel lawsuit came from vaudeville actor Edward Clark, who was also a leader of the White Rats actors' union. Clark's lawsuit against *Variety* was one fight within a much larger vaudeville labor conflict, which resulted in a strike, blacklist, and Federal Trade Commission (FTC) investigation into *Variety* and the big-time vaudeville managers.

Sandwiched in between my case studies of *Exhibitor's Trade Review* and *Variety*, I address the other developments occurring at this historical moment, the most important of which was the First World War. Not everything that occurred in the trade papers from 1916 to 1918 involved fighting. I also use this chapter to discuss three constructive changes made by motion picture trade papers. The innovation of a daily trade paper, *Wid's*, and publication of yearbooks and annuals helped to solve the industry's information management problems. Additionally, *Motography*'s popular section of exhibitor-written reviews, "What the Picture Did for Me," offered a solution to the perceived bias among the large trade paper's staff reviewers. All of these changes proved influential in the years ahead.

The metaphor of war for these conflicts among the trade papers may sound hyperbolic in light of an actual, devastating war occurring in Europe at this same time. And, yes, the war metaphor for the trade press is hyperbolic, perhaps even offensively so. But this was the motion picture industry and trade papers' own metaphor and hyperbole. "The war of the motion picture trade journals goes merrily on and there are libel suits galore," wrote *Variety* in March 1917.[6] The war was a brief one—the US's entrance into World War I in April 1917 had a humbling effect—but it left lasting impressions on the industry. The resulting rifts in the ranks of exhibitors lasted for decades. Additionally, exhibitors, manufacturers, and distributors all came to regard the status quo of the trade press as an industry problem, one that needed to be solved through the consolidation and elimination of papers. Because of these lasting consequences and what the conflicts can tell us about reputations within the culture of show business, the trade press libel war of 1917 demands our attention.

LIBEL, BLACKMAIL, AND REPUTATION—THE FIRST YEAR OF *EXHIBITOR'S TRADE REVIEW*

For a trade paper that generated so much controversy, the first issue of *Exhibitor's Trade Review*, published on December 9, 1916, looked fairly conventional. It contained exhibitor correspondences, reviews, and advertisements from manufacturers and distributors (though noticeably fewer than *Moving Picture World* or *Motion Picture News*). The editorial pages proclaimed the paper's devotion to the exhibitor and included an announcement that W. Stephen Bush would, beginning the next week, serve as the paper's first editor in chief. The announcement stated Bush was "known throughout the industry as 'THE EXHIBITOR'S BEST FRIEND,' the man who fought censorship to a standstill, the man who consistently advocated the cause of organization, the man who championed the cause of Sunday opening and who has always battled for exhibitor's rights."[7] The editorial pages also addressed the initial criticisms that had been leveled at *Exhibitor's Trade Review*. Toward the end of a column most likely written by managing publisher Merritt Crawford, *Exhibitor's Trade Review* turned the criticism back against the rival trade papers: "Unlike a certain other journalist in this industry, whose polished periods and inspired utterances have often thrilled even as they have uplifted exhibitors and producers alike, the editors of EXHIBITOR'S TRADE REVIEW never hope to produce a 'Perfect Product.' This is only possible for one editor in the industry and—he is not on the staff of this paper."[8]

The "certain other journalist in this industry" was William A. Johnston, editor of *Motion Picture News*. Or was it? By keeping the remark somewhat vague, *Exhibitor's Trade Review* was protecting itself against accusations of libel. For libel to occur, the injured party must be identifiable in the publication. Johnston followed the same strategy in his own paper. Just two months earlier, *Motion Picture News* referred to "an editorial writer whose temperament, apparently, is exceedingly bilious. He barks at us constantly. He worries excessively—over our circulation, our editorial and reviewing policy, our advertising—over everything in fact we do. There are times when we gravely question his sincerity as well as his knowledge of the methods of better-class journalism."[9] The bilious, barking editorial writer would seem to be W. Stephen Bush, who was then still affiliated with *Moving Picture World*. But again, the reference is purposely ambiguous. In both of these examples, the lack of clarity guards against a potential libel lawsuit. At the same time, however, each encourages the reader to make a guess—reinforcing the trade papers' community gatekeeping function. Show business remains divided between insiders (who can get a reference or, at the very least, make an educated guess) and outsiders (who won't get it at all).

A victim of libel must be identifiable, but a perpetrating publisher also needed to meet the legal criteria of being "a malicious publication" that exposed a person to "hatred, contempt, ridicule, or obloquy." Nowhere in New York's legal definition was it stipulated that a libelous claim had to be a lie. Indeed, a libel could be true; a statement merely needed to defame someone and damage his reputation. But a libel could be justified if "the matter charged as libelous is true, and was published with good motives and for justifiable ends" and excused "when it is honestly made in the belief of its truth and upon reasonable grounds for this belief, and consists of fair comments upon the conduct of a person in respect to public affairs."[10] To return to the chapter's opening incident, Keppler knew that his clients had libeled Lee A. Ochs. But he welcomed the chance to prove in court that their libel was justified based on the truth: that Ochs had inappropriately used his office as MPELA president. The film trade papers had generally been less bold. They avoided making attacks on their competitors completely identifiable and, when they did, they made sure they had solid libel defenses based on evidence and the principle of "fair comment."

Over the next few weeks, though, a combination of internal and external forces changed the dynamics at *Exhibitor's Trade Review*. Internally, the new paper was in financial trouble. To pay the high salaries promised to Crawford and Bush and stay afloat, the paper needed to immediately attract advertisers and subscribers. When

Exhibitor's Trade Review sent a solicitation letter to members of the newly formed trade organization National Association of the Motion Picture Industry (NAMPI) on December 23, 1916, the publishers included financial details that revealed the paper's survival depended on overnight success. *Exhibitor's Trade Review* wrote that "the officers of this company estimate that with 75 pages of advertising at $75 a page and a circulation of 10,000, the expenses of the paper are assured, and that any sums realized over and above this amount will be profit to be divided as above set forth" (the first $50,000 in profits divided among the paper's stockholders; the next $50,000 divided among advertisers; and any profits beyond $100,000 divided 50/50 between stockholders and advertisers).[11] An estimate of seventy-five advertising pages per issue was aggressive, to say the least. In 1916, *Moving Picture World* and *Motion Picture News* both had a median of eighty-two pages of advertising per issue—a record high for both papers. To merely break even, *Exhibitor's Trade Review* would need to equal the best year in advertising that its two strongest competitors had ever achieved.

Moreover, the paper's value to its advertisers depended on its circulation, and ten thousand subscribers was an ambitious target—higher than the estimated 1916 circulation of *Motion Picture News* (6,800), though lower than the circulations of *Moving Picture World* (17,200) and *Motography* (18,501).[12] The actual circulations of all of these publications probably fell below their estimates, but regardless of the actual numbers, none of them achieved a circulation of ten thousand overnight. Yet this was exactly what *Exhibitor's Trade Review* was proposing to do and needed to do to stay solvent. To sell more subscriptions, Bush went on tour across America. He called his trip a "service tour"; he offered to speak to local exhibitor organizations and help them address their local problems.[13] The overriding goal, though, was subscribers, and they did not come cheaply. According to *Variety*, Bush's travel costs amounted to $12 for every $1 subscription that he sold.[14]

In the midst of all this, William A. Johnston kept gloating in the pages of *Motion Picture News*. Johnston had relished the hearings that placed Ochs in the hot seat, declaring, "Lee Ochs' Trial Is a Thrilling Affair."[15] Moreover, he was winning the advertising game, hands down. The 1916 Christmas issue of *Motion Picture News* ran more than two hundred pages. For *Exhibitor's Trade Review*, the yuletide was less bright; its first Christmas annual ran only seventy-eight pages, fewer than its debut issue just three weeks earlier. In the editorial columns of *Motion Picture News'* Christmas issue, Johnston thumbed his nose at Ochs and his new publication. Just the previous week, Johnston had categorized the MPELA as a "pitiful failure," utterly incapable of rising above petty politics to serve the exhibitors it claimed to support.[16] Picking up this same thread in the holiday issue, Johnston said that what "we would like for Christmas" is "an exhibitors organization," and he endorsed Ochs's rival Sam Trigger for the presidency of the New York branch of the MPELA.[17] Johnston also used the opportunity to announce his New Year's resolution: "We shall get out this year more than ever before a—*service* paper. Service to the exhibitor. . . . This policy we shall pursue in an utterly impersonal, independent manner. We are tied to no one, no branch, no organization of the industry. We are unbiased."[18] The message was clear: the independent, unbiased *Motion Picture News* served exhibitors better than the partisan trade paper of the MPELA.

Across two incendiary issues—published on January 27 and February 3, 1917—*Exhibitor's Trade Review* went on the attack and ridiculed Johnston as a hypocrite. First, in an editorial entitled "Sweet William and Dear Old Frank," *Exhibitor's Trade Review* called out Johnston by name and referred to him as "Sweet William, the pink cheeked editor of the quality (oy, oy) circulation trade paper."[19] The following week, *Exhibitor's Trade Review* published an even more scathing attack on Johnston. In a piece entitled "Motion Picture Exhibitors League of America vs. William A. Johnston," *Exhibitor's Trade Review* wrote:

> The impudence and arrogance of Johnston and his manufacturers' organ in coolly declaring that we have "ceased to recognize" Ochs as President of the Exhibitors' League should not be allowed to pass unchallenged by that body, or by any of its State branches and locals.
>
> The fact that Lee A. Ochs happens to be the man attacked by our perfumed pen-pusher has nothing to do with the matter. It might just as well have been anyone else—so long as it wasn't an advertiser. Needless to say, Sweet William would not "cease to recognize" Carl Laemmle as President of the Universal Film Manufacturing Company, for instance, no matter what Mr. Laemmle did. But, except for advertisers, William is perfectly neutral. He doesn't care who he ceases to recognize—as long as he doesn't lose any advertising by it.
>
> The point is this: That Johnston has been meddling in matters that do not concern him, and he should be promptly, severely and permanently put in place.[20]

Ochs, Bush, and Crawford understood that perceptions mattered in the film industry. In these two editorials, they simultaneously assaulted Johnston's reputation while bolstering their own credibility as strong and fearless publishers. But they had also crossed a line—issuing personal attacks that abandoned the typical caution exercised by trade papers.

The ink had barely had time to dry on *Exhibitor's Trade Review*'s editorial page before Johnston and his attorney were in court. On February 13, 1917, Johnston filed a libel complaint against *Exhibitor's Trade Review*, demanding $100,000 for the damage done to his reputation. Johnston's complaint called particular attention to phrases loaded with gender and sexual innuendo, such as "Sweet William, the pink cheeked editor," "the sweet-scented one," "perfumed pen-pusher," and "keyed in the high falsetto that tickles Sweet William's left ear." Johnston's attorney argued that the innuendo was "intend[ed] to ridicule the plaintiff, and place him in an odious position by likening him to an effeminate, vulgar and immodest man."[21]

How did readers interpret the characterization of Johnston? Historian George Chauncey has demonstrated that the category of the "fairy," an effeminate man who had sex with other men, existed in early twentieth-century American

FIGURE 11. A dramatic staging of a courtroom scene in *Back of the Main* (1917), a Triangle film in circulation during the same period of William A. Johnston's libel lawsuit. Photograph courtesy of the Wisconsin Center for Film and Theater Research.

culture.[22] *Exhibitor's Trade Review*'s editorials can certainly be interpreted as personal attacks on Johnston's sexuality (the "effeminate, vulgar and immodest man" conjured in his complaint). But the complaint also emphasized that *Exhibitor's Trade Review* was "likening" Johnston to this man. The editorials operated, in other words, on the level of metaphor: *Motion Picture News* was an effeminate, weak, and unscrupulous trade paper that lied to exhibitors and kowtowed to the demands of manufacturers. In contrast, *Exhibitor's Trade Review* attempted to represent itself as possessing stereotypically masculine qualities: strong, resolute, unafraid of a fight. The author of the incendiary editorials, Merritt Crawford, had served in the Spanish-American War and would soon become appointed a captain in New York's State Regiment.[23] He regarded himself as an emblem of masculine strength, even as his enemies portrayed him as a fat windbag (*Motion Picture News* had written the previous year that the "floor sagg[ed] in where Merritt Crawford stood" during an exhibitor event).[24] Regardless of whether readers interpreted the columns literally or metaphorically, however, Johnston could convincingly claim that his reputation had been damaged.

Faced with the lawsuit, *Exhibitor's Trade Review* dug in its heels even more. The goal all along, after all, was to win a battle of perception; the worst move in such a situation would be to back down. Because the libel complaint included interpretations for the innuendo, *Exhibitor's Trade Review* deemed it "the best humorous and original reading since the days of Artemis Ward and Josh Billings."[25] After Johnston filed additional libel lawsuits against Crawford and Lesley Mason, another former *Motion Picture News* junior editor who had gone to the new paper, *Exhibitor's Trade Review* continued to exhibit a cavalier attitude about the whole affair.[26] *Exhibitor's Trade Review* reprinted the new complaint against Mason "in the hope that it will charm our readers as it has delighted us."[27] Publicly, *Exhibitor's*

Trade Review acted completely unshaken by the affair and portrayed Johnston as a thin-skinned coward.

In their legal papers, though, *Exhibitor's Trade Review* took a far more cautious tone. The paper's lawyers argued the columns were "fair comment," downplaying the harsh language used in the editorials. They also attempted to introduce a novel defense: "It is important to note that this action differs materially from the ordinary action or libel, in that in effect this is an action by one editor against another editor."[28] Ultimately, the New York City judge hearing the case was not persuaded, finding "the publication in suit is libelous, as involving a personal attack upon the plaintiff beyond the scope of fair criticism directed to his work as editor."[29] On June 15, 1917, the judge issued a summary judgment in favor of Johnston. *Exhibitor's Trade Review* lost its appeal, and it is unclear how much the paper paid out to Johnston in damages (though we can be sure it was less than the $175,000 Johnston had cumulatively sought).[30]

Despite losing the libel suit against Johnston, *Exhibitor's Trade Review* had succeeded in publicly humiliating its most loathed rival and portraying itself as strong and fearless. At this same moment, however, a far greater scandal was bringing down the paper that Ochs, Bush, and Crawford were trying to build up. In the same January 27, 1917, issue that ridiculed "Sweet William, the pink cheeked editor," *Exhibitor's Trade Review* had issued a public attack on a more dangerous enemy: the Universal Film Manufacturing Company. In an open letter, Lee A. Ochs charged Universal with spreading "CONTEMPTIBLE LIBEL" about the exhibitors of America. The inflammatory statement in question had been published two years earlier in the *Universal Weekly*. Universal president Carl Laemmle had written that he "discovered that at least half and maybe sixty percent [of exhibitors], want the pictures to be 'risque' which is a French way of saying 'smutty.'" Advocates of censorship had seized on Laemmle's remarks, reproducing them widely. *Exhibitor's Trade Review* wanted to make it clear to exhibitors that their reputations had been smeared by Laemmle. Universal was to blame for the growth of censorship laws. Ochs was pursuing this "libel" in the court of community opinion rather than any legal court; he encouraged exhibitors to demand the ouster of Universal executive Pat Powers from NAMPI's recently formed committee addressing censorship. Ochs also used the opportunity to trumpet the greatness of *Exhibitor's Trade Review* and insult his competitors. Writing in eye-grabbing CAPS, Ochs remarked: "I CONFESS WITH SHAME THAT THERE HAS NOT BEEN, UP TO THIS MOMENT, ENOUGH COURAGE AND INDEPEDENCE IN MOTION PICTURE JOURNALISM TO SPEAK THE PLAIN TRUTH IN THIS MATTER. ON THE CONTRARY, EVERY MOTION PICTURE TRADE PUBLICATION HAS CONCEALED THE FACTS IN THE CRAVEN FEAR OF LOSING A PAGE OR TWO OF ADVERTISING."[31] Like its attack against Johnston, *Exhibitor's Trade Review* was attempting to enhance its own reputation as a strong, independently minded voice for the exhibitor as it tore apart the reputations of its enemies.

Just days before the publication of Ochs's open letter, however, Universal advertising executive Bob Cochrane presented a different set of "FACTS" to the motion picture industry. And Cochrane's facts were very much related to the issue of trade paper advertising. Cochrane wrote his account as a two-page "statement" that he intended for wide distribution. Because it offers a rare primary source account of the trade press from the perspective of a film executive, Cochrane's statement merits reproduction at length. Here is the story, as Cochrane tells it:

> On Wednesday, Jan. 17th, Mr. Lee Ochs called at my offices and solicited advertising from the Universal Film Mfg. Co. for the Exhibitors' Trade Review, in which Mr. Ochs has a proprietary interest.
>
> After listening to all that Mr. Ochs had to say, I called his attention to the fact that he had not given me any reason why the Universal Company should advertise in his publication. I likewise called his attention to the fact that unless he wanted the Universal Company to pay his publication some money for either charity or blackmail, there was nothing for our company to gain by advertising in his columns. He denied that he wanted either charity or blackmail.
>
> He then asked me if I did not believe in reciprocity to the extent of giving advertising to the Exhibitors' Trade Review (Mr. Ochs' paper) because exhibitors pay money to the Universal Company for film rental. I replied that every exhibitor who paid money to us got full value for it; and that whenever he did not get full value, he transferred his business to some of our competitors; that I would not buy advertising space on any but business grounds; and that if we could not hold the exhibitors' business on the merit of our film we surely would not try to hold it by advertising in Mr. Ochs' publication.
>
> This was on Wednesday January 17th.
>
> On Thursday, January 18th Mr. Ochs wrote a scurrilous letter to various trade papers, making a bitter attack on the Universal Company as a whole and on the officers in particular.
>
> From various sources the Universal Company has heard that if it did not support the Exhibitors' Trade Review, scores or even hundreds of exhibitors would cancel their orders with Universal exchanges. I have forgotten how many thousands of dollars per week was to be taken from us. This has been threatened ever since the Exhibitors' Trade Review (Mr. Ochs' paper) first entered the field of trade papers.
>
> The Universal Company does not believe that the Exhibitors' Trade Review is owned by exhibitors. Neither does it believe that the exhibitors of this country would approve of the methods used by Mr. Ochs to compel the Universal, and other companies, to buy advertising space in his paper.
>
> Mr. Ochs, however, endeavors in every way to make it appear the exhibitors of the country either own his paper or are backing it. For example, the letter in which he attacks the Universal was written on stationery bearing the imprint of the Exhibitors' League of America but was mailed in an envelope bearing the imprint of Exhibitors' Trade Review.
>
> In his letter he rakes up an editorial which was published in the Universal's own weekly publication a year or more ago. It was an article on smutty pictures and was a part of a series of articles, the intention of which was to bring forth from exhibitors

a storm of protest against such pictures. It accomplished its end, but ever since then it has been used by pro-censors as an argument for censorship. To do this they resorted to the old trick of quoting only extracts from the series, instead of the whole. Before the articles were published in our house organ, we showed them in proof form to Mr. Stephen Bush, then employed on Moving Picture World and now working for the Exhibitors' Trade Review and explained the campaign to him. Mr. Bush instantly saw what the plan was and called it a good thing. I feel confident that Mr. Bush will bear me out in this statement, regardless of the fact that he is interested in the Exhibitors' Trade Review at the present time.

Kindly remember, Mr. Ochs' remarkable letter was written the day after the Universal refused to advertise in his paper.[32]

Cochrane's story was immediately picked up by the other motion picture and theatrical trade papers. Ochs had attempted to bait the fellow trade papers with his letter dredging up Laemmle's comments on "smutty" pictures. But his efforts backfired. Now, Ochs's letter became evidence in a much more sensational story— one about a self-righteous exhibitor and trade paper publisher who was actually a hypocritical, corrupt blackmailer. *Billboard, New York Clipper, Variety*, and *Moving Picture World* all covered the Ochs-Universal feud.[33] As we might expect, *Motion Picture News'* coverage of the scandal was especially rich in schadenfreude. Johnston's paper covered the play-by-play of the feud throughout the month of February 1917. It was "Time for House Cleaning," wrote Johnston, who demanded the ouster of Ochs from the presidency of the MPELA.[34] Interestingly, Johnston gave far less attention in his paper's columns to his ongoing libel suit against *Exhibitor's Trade Review*, perhaps wagering that the Universal scandal would do far more damage to the reputation of *Exhibitor's Trade Review* than his personal dispute possibly could.

The Ochs-Universal feud damaged *Exhibitor's Trade Review* irreparably. Ochs and Bush had spent the previous year attacking *Motion Picture News* for allowing advertisers to dictate news, editorial, and review content. *Exhibitor's Trade Review*, it turned out, was just as advertiser-oriented, though in a far more destructive and nasty manner: pay us or else. Many exhibitors were outraged by Ochs's behavior and the thought that his trade paper spoke for them. When the Universal scandal hit, Bush was on his "service tour," attempting to sell new subscriptions. Although his columns don't directly say it, he must have had exhibitors confront him. Why should they subscribe to a paper that practiced extortion? Why should they have to pay for a paper published by their dues-collecting national organization? Why would Bush go into business with a scoundrel like Ochs? What does seep through in Bush's columns is a humbling. Bush promised, "*Exhibitor's Trade Review* eliminated all waste from its columns. The paper has been made to order for the exhibitor and meets his practical needs."[35]

Meanwhile, in New York City, Ochs and Crawford continued to fight with any and all perceived enemies. They tried to frame the conflict as being about a trade paper's right to free speech, an extension of the battle against screen censorship.[36]

Increasingly, they saw themselves as the victims. In a March 1917 editorial titled "Warfare Below the Belt," *Exhibitor's Trade Review* alleged that unnamed trade papers had conspired to push it out of business by (1) pressuring its engraver to drop the paper as a client; (2) convincing its printer that it wasn't creditworthy; and (3) persuading the US Post Office to deny *Exhibitor's Trade Review* second-class mail status.[37] Ochs and Crawford refused to quit without more of a fight.

Nor did Ochs go gentle from his post as MPELA president. When the national MPELA convention met in Chicago in the summer of 1917, Ochs rigged the election to ensure he remained the organization's head.[38] Ochs's election scandal—combined with the controversies involving *Exhibitor's Trade Review* and other allegations of abuse of power—had a lasting detrimental effect on exhibitor trade organizations. In 1918, the American Exhibitors Association (AEA) formed in opposition to Ochs's MPELA. As Deron Overpeck relates in his excellent history of exhibitor trade organizations, Ochs's leadership caused "ruptures in the exhibition ranks that would shape the national trade association from 1920 until 1947." During those years, the leading manufacturer-distributors acquired their own theaters, building the vertically integrated corporations that we now recognize as the Hollywood studios. Too much time that exhibitors could have used to act in unison was instead squandered on internal fighting.[39]

As for *Exhibitor's Trade Review*, its founders lasted barely a year. They had lost the feud against Universal and run out of money. Merritt Crawford and Stephen Bush both left in March 1918. *Variety* reported that Bush still had four years on contract, at a salary of $6,500 per year plus expenses.[40] Ochs left the paper the following month to head United Picture Theaters of America, which was to be another lightning rod of controversy and source of more libel lawsuits.[41] With the founders ousted, and their high salaries cleared from the books, a new owner stepped into the picture—A. B. Swetland.[42] Swetland was the brother of Horace Swetland, the president of the Federation of Trade Press Associations of the United States, and the man who, in 1923, literally wrote the book about trade publishing.[43] The Swetlands' company, Class Journal Publications, controlled trade publications such as *Iron Age, Motor Age, Distributing and Warehousing*, and the flagship American retail paper *Dry Goods Economist*.[44] The establishment was attempting to take over the film industry's trade press.

NEWS, COMMERCE, AND INNOVATION DURING WARTIME

The motion picture trade papers did more from 1916 to 1918 besides fight among themselves. Some of the most lasting changes made by the trade press were constructive rather than destructive in nature. Before turning toward the vaudeville industry and *Variety*'s legal battles, we should take stock of the other developments taking place simultaneously within the journals, industry, and nation.

FIGURE 12. Motion picture superstar Charles Chaplin speaks to a large crowd at a New York rally for War Bonds in 1918. Photograph courtesy of the Motion Picture Academy of Arts and Sciences, Margaret Herrick Library.

The major event—and one that seemed to briefly quiet the bickering editors—was the US's entrance into World War I. On April 2, 1917, President Woodrow Wilson called on the US Congress to declare war against Germany, officially involving the nation in the war that had been ravaging Europe for the previous three years. In her history of the US film industry during World War I, Leslie Midkiff DeBauche describes how members of the industry followed a path of "practical patriotism," seeking to do their part for the war effort while continuing to maintain, and ideally grow, their businesses. "Cooperation with the government's efforts on the home-front cast both national and local members of the film industry in a favorable light," writes DeBauche. "It offered local film exhibitors the opportunity to validate their businesses within their communities, and it offered the film industry at the national level the chance to garner good publicity and so enhance its image."[45] The trade papers document these industry activities on the local level (stories of Kentucky exhibitors using slides to encourage military enlistment and enrollment in the Red Cross) and national stage (coordinated efforts between NAMPI and the Treasury Department to sell Liberty Loans, including personal appearance tours by Mary Pickford, William S. Hart, and other stars).[46]

The war influenced the trade papers' discussions of other policy matters, including taxation. Shortly before the US entrance into World War I, NAMPI proved it was more effective than its predecessor, the Board of Trade, when it brought different wings of the industry together to defeat New York's proposed admissions tax.[47] Wars are expensive, though, and the government needed to finance US participation in World War I. To achieve this, Congress passed the War Revenue Act of 1917, which among other measures included a 10 percent admissions tax on theaters.[48] Exhibitors knew it would look bad if they publicly opposed the tax, but they used the trade press to debate the fairness of the tax falling on them and strategies for passing it on to their theater patrons.[49] Discussions of tax policy would play out extensively in the pages of the film industry trade papers for the next century, especially following the increase of income tax rates in the early 1930s.[50]

The trades also covered the global influenza pandemic of 1918, which caused major disruptions to the film industry and bears many similarities to the COVID-19 pandemic of 2020. The conditions of World War I—overcrowded military camps, mass movements of people across the country and world—accelerated the spread of this vicious strain of influenza, which produced deadly cases of pneumonia at such alarming rates that many at the time believed they were living through a return of the plague. During the spring of 1918, major influenza outbreaks spread in Philadelphia, Boston, and other eastern American cities. The flu then struck again with even greater force during the winter of 1918–19.[51] Recognizing that movie theaters were ideal sites for the virus to spread and find new hosts, many municipalities ordered theaters to temporarily close.[52] Theaters that remained open played to smaller crowds. The trade papers reported on the public health crisis while generally maintaining an upbeat attitude, projecting confidence that things would soon get better. The dissonance between the trade papers' functions as industry boosters and conveyors of the news was especially evident in the juxtaposition of "situation improving" reports and the obituaries of members of the industry community who had died of pneumonia. In some cases, these notices appeared within pages of each other.[53]

The trade papers covered other industry developments during this period that had little directly to do with the war or pandemic. The editorial pages of *Moving Picture World, Motion Picture News, Motography*, and *Exhibitors Herald* all took stands opposing the advance deposit system—the prepayments manufacturer-distributors demanded from exhibitors and then used to finance new productions.[54] But the trade papers and their exhibitors came down more unevenly on the new distribution policy of "open booking"—a term used to describe a variety of distribution practices but especially the renting of films to exhibitors on a one-off basis rather than as part of programs.[55] Larger exhibitors tended to like the selectivity and star power that open booking allowed. Smaller and midsized exhibitors wanted the features of stars available for open booking, but they often could not afford the higher rental fees and preferred the earlier model of renting a year's worth of films from a distributor for the bulk of their bookings. Moreover, selling pictures one at a time was an inherently less efficient system than selling programs of forty or fifty pictures.[56] Beyond the higher transaction cost of renting a single picture, every feature distributed under the booking system needed to be advertised to exhibitors. The trade papers benefited from the enhanced need to advertise and differentiate individual productions, even as their editors paid lip service to exhibitor complaints that theaters were being asked to bear too much of the growing expenses from the open booking system.

But the most successful film trade papers of the period did not simply sit back and wait for advertising dollars to roll in, nor did they extort manufacturers to advertise. Instead, the most successful papers were entrepreneurial problem-solvers. They identified industry problems, including some of their own making, and found constructive solutions that could make them money. The biggest problem they constructively addressed between 1916 and 1918 was the management of information. How could exhibitors and other industry readers efficiently pick out the important bits of information from the advertising-and-puff-loaded 180-page issues of *Moving Picture World* and *Motion Picture News* that landed at their doors with a thud every week? How, too, could they return to back issues and reports that they later realized they needed? The motion picture trade press devised two methods for helping the industry organize and access its data. The first was a daily trade paper, the second yearbooks and trade directories.

Wid Gunning had launched a weekly film review publication in 1915, but over the next two years, he tweaked the format of his sheet. He kept the emphasis on reviews, publishing appraisals of the latest films in a Sunday issue running eight to sixteen pages. But Gunning and Jack Alicoate, his managing editor, began publishing brief four-page issues throughout the week. The paper, *Wid's Film and Film Folks*, contained short announcements and news stories. Borrowing a technique from the theatrical trade papers, it also published cards of "Prominent Film Folk." Directors, writers, and other production personnel paid *Wid's* to "keep [their] name before the right people" and act as their answering service. Whereas William A. Johnston continually boasted about the growing size of his weekly paper, *Motion Picture News*, Gunning and Alicoate understood that brevity and speed could be equally powerful assets. "WID'S DAILY IS READ NOT SKIMMED," explained the paper in July 1918, shortly after changing its title to *Wid's Daily*.[57] In 1922, the paper would change its title again to the one that stuck for the next five decades: *Film Daily*. Film historian Douglas Gomery has likened *Film Daily* to "a headline service, a *USA Today* for the film business."[58] In the context of solving an information management problem, we can understand Gomery's characterization less as a pejorative than as a statement of *Wid's Daily*'s strategic advantage: it condensed information into brief, digestible segments and distributed these segments more quickly than its competitors.

Wid's Daily also became a leader in the publication of industry yearbooks, though, like so many other developments, Johnston's *Motion Picture News* was the first to bring this trade publishing practice to the film industry. Johnston published *Motion Picture News'* first *Studio Directory* in January 1916 and the first *Trade Annual* in July 1917. *Wid's* caught up with its first yearbook at the end of 1918.[59] Elegantly bound and hundreds of pages long, industry yearbooks may seem like the polar opposite of a slim daily trade sheet. But they represented two sides of the same information management coin. By aggregating and organizing data about theaters, manufacturers, and industry personnel, the yearbooks offered an efficient system for industry participants to retrieve information. They were also advertising bonanzas. The publishers encouraged manufacturers, distributors, theaters, equipment suppliers, and individual industry workers to purchase half-page or full-page advertisements. The value gained by the advertiser was not the immediate sale of a product. Instead, the yearbooks offered advertisers something more amorphous yet enormously important in show business—the opportunity to position oneself as an insider and a legitimate member of the industry community (a topic explored more in this chapter in relation to *Variety*).

The daily trade paper and annual directories found success not just within the immediate industry but also among the growing number of newspapers and magazines that covered the movies for a much wider readership. As film historian Richard Abel has shown, newspapers across the US expanded their coverage of the movie industry during the early to mid-1910s.[60] There was a push and pull in the flow of news. Motion picture manufacturers and distributors *pushed* advertising and publicity items to newspapers across the country. Their publicity departments sent out mass mailings, for example, promoting the production of a star's new films. Yet there was also a *pull* factor: local readers were interested in movie news, and newspapers sought out and reprinted the stories they thought would most appeal to their readers. Some newspaper editors preferred reprinting stories from the motion picture trade papers over publishing the publicity stories received by mail. The news published in trade papers had undergone some minimal level of vetting, and an editor could more efficiently comb through and pluck out the items of interest from a four-page issue of *Wid's* than a stack of letters. Additionally, as newspaper and magazine editors prepared stories for print, the annuals served as indispensable reference books, containing biographical details of players and personnel and information about the industry's performance from the previous year.

One of the magazines most excerpted and reprinted by newspapers and magazines during the mid-1910s was *Motography*.[61] In 1914, *Motography's* "Gallery of Picture Players," "Brevities of the Business" page, and Mabel Condon's profiles of movie stars were well suited for general interest newspapers. Indeed, Robert Grau praised the Chicago-based paper, claiming "no more readable and informing periodical dealing with the industry from all angles is to be found anywhere." Yet *Motography's* breadth was also its problem. The paper lacked focus as a trade publication. One of Condon's star profiles might appear next to a report about a Cincinnati exhibitor convention. While the paper was more readable for the movie fan, it was inessential to the nation's leading manufacturers, distributors, and exhibitors. As noted in the previous chapter, *Motography* trailed far behind *Moving Picture World* and *Motion Picture News* in advertising sales.

In 1915 and 1916, *Motography* tried to revamp its format and become more exhibitor-oriented. The paper continued to struggle to find a niche until it found a creative solution to a long-standing problem. How could exhibitors trust that trade paper reviewers were being truthful? How could they be sure reviewers were not going soft on the films of advertisers? On October 7, 1916, *Motography* published a half-page column titled "'Reviews' by Exhibitors." The word *reviews* appeared in quotation marks to emphasize the novelty, even humor, of allowing exhibitors to pass judgment. Six exhibitors, five from Chicago and one from northwest Indiana, shared their personal experience playing movies to their patrons. George H. Moore of Chicago's Orpheum offered the following appraisal of Lois Weber and Phillips Smalley's *Saving the Family Name:* "While it is a fair picture it is nothing for one to lose one's mind over. We have been having a fair crowd all day." Meanwhile, Moore had clearly lost his mind over Theda Bara, reporting that the Fox star's latest picture, *Her Double Life,* "played to capacity houses all day long." The appeal of these "reviews" lay in their plain language, business-oriented perspective, and attribution to a member of the exhibitor community. They were also models of brevity. Louis Feuillade's *Fantomas* serial has generated hundreds of pages of critical writing over the past century, but George Madison of the Kozy told his fellow exhibitors everything they needed to know in nine words: "It's a great picture. It made money for me."[62]

One week later, *Motography* repeated the section with a new title, "What the Picture Did for Me," and promised "Actual Criticism of Films by Exhibitors, from a Business Standpoint."[63] This new section quickly snowballed into the most successful department in the history of *Motography.* By April 1917, six months after its launch, "What the Picture Did for Me" occupied four full pages at the front of the paper. Roughly half of the reviews still came from Illinois exhibitors, but theater managers from across the country also wrote in. *Exhibitor's Trade Review* imitated the department with its similarly titled section, "How Did That Picture Go at Your Theatre?"[64] But *Motography* warned its readers not to accept any knockoff: "'What the Picture Did for Me' was the first department of its kind in any trade paper, and exhibitors say it is the best trade paper feature there is."[65] *Motography* had found a solution to the perceived bias of trade paper reviews by having exhibitors write reviews themselves. And in doing so, the paper united a supportive, trustworthy community of exhibitors at the same moment the MPELA was polarizing theater owners and the industry. When *Exhibitors Herald* purchased *Motography* in 1918, the "What the Picture Did for Me" department and its passionate community of writers and readers were some of the most valuable assets that *Herald* publisher Martin Quigley acquired.[66]

The motion picture journals were not the only trade papers experimenting with a daily edition at this time. In December 1916, *Variety* began publishing a daily bulletin every day except Sunday and Friday (the day it published the weekly edition).[67] The vaudeville industry was in a state of crisis with a labor strike waiting in the wings. *Variety*'s bulletin disseminated the latest news quickly, but it also reinforced its reputation as the leading vaudeville paper. As we will see, *Variety* was simultaneously a reporter of the crisis, its scorekeeper, and one of its leading players.

VARIETY, THE WHITE RATS, AND PERFORMING INDEPENDENCE

The news that *Variety* expected to publish in its daily bulletin that winter was that the White Rats actors had gone on strike. Although the union had insufficient numbers to shut down the US vaudeville industry, the White Rats' strike and the managers' retaliatory threat of a blacklist had polarized the vaudeville community. The full history of the vaudeville wars is beyond the scope of this book, and readers should turn to the detailed research of Arthur Frank Wertheim for a complete account.[68] Yet understanding *Variety*'s role in the conflict is important for two reasons. First, and most important, the White Rats strike was a key moment in the formation of *Variety*'s reputation as an independent paper that claimed allegiance to no single constituency or industry. *Variety*'s reputation became a key asset that it leveraged toward expanding its presence in the film industry in the 1920s (a transformation discussed in chapter 4). Second, the White Rats' allegations that actors felt compelled to purchase self-promotional ads in *Variety* foreshadowed what was to become a booming business for the motion picture trade papers. Like the budding genre of film yearbooks and studio annuals, *Variety* became a space in which industry players sought to shape perceptions of themselves and prove that they belonged to the show business community.

Variety's relationship with vaudeville labor in general and the White Rats in particular was a complicated one. As discussed in my introduction, *Variety* used its first editorial column in 1905 to articulate its values: it was to be "an artist's paper," and "'ALL THE NEWS ALL THE TIME' and 'ABSOLUTELY FAIR' [were] the watchwords."[69] *Variety*'s emphasis on fairness, artists, and the separation between editorial and advertising were intended to distinguish it from the theatrical trade papers (especially *New York Clipper* and *New York Morning Telegraph*), which it implied were management-oriented and organs for their advertisers. Throughout its first year in print, *Variety* largely followed its stated mandate. One example occurred in the summer of 1906 when B. F. Keith and his general manager, Edward Albee, merged the Western Vaudeville Association and the BF Keith Booking Agency to create the United Booking Office (UBO). It was a key moment in the consolidation of the vaudeville industry, coinciding with the expansion of theaters controlled by Keith and Albee to roughly 130. Additionally, the UBO continued the controversial practice of charging artists a 5 percent booking fee. The *New York Clipper* praised Keith, saying he was a man of "courage, determination, [and] inflexible purpose" to have built "this great superstructure of vaudeville."[70] In contrast, *Variety* analyzed what the consolidation and new booking agency would mean for performers. The paper cynically remarked on the intent behind the name United Booking Office: "The Keith executives think that the name of 'Keith' left off the title would in a measure remove the red flag from the artists' sight."[71] And in his editorials, *Variety* publisher and editor Sime Silverman kept raising the red flag again and again, arguing for the need for vaudeville artists to organize and stand up to Keith and Albee before it was too late.[72]

For someone supportive of artists' rights, though, Silverman had an ambivalent and frequently antagonistic relationship with the leading vaudeville union—the White Rats. The White Rats had formed in 1900 as a union for white male vaudeville performers under the leadership of George Fuller Golden. The name derived from the British actors' union the Water Rats and the backward spelling of the word *Star*.[73] *Variety*'s earliest mention of the White Rats occurred in the paper's second issue, published December 23, 1905. Silverman editorialized that "the White Rats, with an hysterical head and no definite aim or stability, won a great victory—which they immediately afterward lost. A new organization, if formed, should be framed up on enduring lines and officered by some cool headed man rather than a glowing enthusiast."[74] Silverman's enthusiasm for the White Rats ebbed and flowed over the next few years, but it took a decisive turn toward the negative in 1910 and 1911 during Harry Mountford's leadership of the organization. An English actor and labor organizer, Mountford joined the executive board of the White Rats and pushed the organization toward a more aggressive course of action against managers. Mountford affiliated the union with the American Federation of Labor, expanded the membership to an all-time high of twenty-five hundred, lobbied for the state of New York to regulate booking fees, and demanded the vaudeville managers agree to a closed shop. Keith, Albee, and the other vaudeville managers vehemently opposed all of these measures.[75] Mountford also began an official journal for the White Rats, *The Player*, which he promised would be clean of the promanager propaganda that filled other theatrical trade papers.

Silverman wanted better conditions for vaudeville artists, but he objected to Mountford's militant tactics. "He has brought the managers to believe that actors are their enemies. . . . He has brought the actor before the public as an agitator," wrote Silverman in January 1911. Silverman wanted a more conciliatory approach; in fact, his journal depended on it. *Variety* spoke to managers and artists as part of a broad community and sold considerable advertising to both parties. Silverman regarded *Variety* as occupying a middle ground of fairness between the White Rats' sheet, *The Player*, and the trade papers biased toward the managers, such as *Clipper* and *Morning Telegraph*. To Mountford, though, it must have seemed like Silverman wanted to have it both ways—better conditions for the actor without enduring the labor struggle needed to achieve them. Mountford escalated the fight with Silverman when he remarked that actors were being "held up" by *Variety* to purchase advertising. Silverman exploded, calling Mountford a liar and a fool. "We did not gamble on our future and our time for five years to establish a journal under a new policy to have an Englishman (who may yet be unnaturalized for all we know) come along in an attempt to undo what we had done," wrote Silverman.[76] In this column and many others, *Variety* brought up Mountford's English origins to attack him. *Variety* was playing its gatekeeping function. The paper depicted Mountford as an outsider who needed to be expelled from American vaudeville.

Later that same year, in 1911, Silverman obtained his wish. The White Rats' board pushed out Mountford for being too militant and uncompromising. *Variety*'s relationship with the White Rats and vaudeville artists improved with Mountford out of the picture. Meanwhile, *Variety*'s relationship with the managers worsened. Silverman openly criticized the UBO and mocked its head, Albee. In response, Albee implemented a blacklist against music publishers and vaudevillians who advertised in *Variety*.[77] The feud lasted for roughly two years, until August 1914, when *Variety* and UBO reached a détente.[78] Midway through the feud, in November 1913, the White Rats ceased publication of *The Player* and began publishing a four-page section, "White Rats News," in *Variety*. Silverman explained to readers that "White Rats News" was editorially separate from *Variety*, but its inclusion represented an alliance with the post-Mountford Rats.[79]

Unfortunately for the White Rats' members, *Variety*'s support did little to materially improve their lot. Without the "agitator" Mountford at the helm, the White Rats organization weakened, and conditions for artists only became worse. Vaudeville artists still had major grievances with management: a broad "cancelation clause" in their contracts that made it easy for managers to fire them; the expense of railway transportation from one city to another (they, not the managers, paid for their tickets); the 5 percent commission fees to their agents and the UBO's booking office; and, excepting the biggest stars, salaries that remained flat or declined during the 1910s. It continued to be a hard life, with many nights spent in freezing cold dressing rooms and filthy flophouses, conditions that bred tuberculosis and other illnesses.[80] In October 1915, the White Rats invited Mountford to return, and he leapt at the opportunity to reignite American vaudeville's labor movement.

Tensions between labor and management quickly escalated again.[81] In June 1916, White Rats performers joined a strike in Oklahoma that members of fellow AFL (American Federation of Labor) union, IATSE (International Alliance of Theatrical Stage Employees), had called against theater management. The prospect of a wider White Rats strike felt imminent. In the fall of 1916, the Vaudeville Managers' Protective Association (VMPA), a trade organization that counted the Keith-Albee and Orpheum chains as its leading members, cancelled the engagements of White Rats actors and blacklisted them from their theaters.[82] Soon after, *Variety* began publishing its daily bulletins, which tracked who was blacklisted, how the White Rats responded, and what the developments meant for nonunion performers. In February 1917, the much-anticipated strike began. White Rats members picketed theaters in Boston, Chicago, East St. Louis, and New York that refused to sign closed shop agreements. They formed picket lines and, when non-striking actors crossed the lines to perform, they hurled fruit and eggs at the scabs. The strike lasted until the US declared war on Germany on April 6, 1917, an event that prompted the AFL to call on its unions to halt all strikes.[83]

All the theatrical trade papers lined up in opposition to Mountford before, during, and after the strike.[84] *Variety* stated emphatically that it was "against Mountford."[85] If any reader had missed this point in a column, he or she would have surely gotten it from one of *Variety*'s full-page cartoons, illustrated by Edward Marshall. "The Moth and the Flame," a cartoon published in December 1916 before the strike, portrayed "Mountfordism" as a candle and "strike" as its flame. Gullible performers were the moths flocking to the light, unaware they were being led to their ruin (see fig. 13). A second cartoon, published during the strike in March 1917, offered a peek inside Mountford's famously high forehead (fig. 14). According to Marshall and *Variety*, Mountford's mind was filled with his luxurious lifestyle, lies, and Hun-like leadership techniques—all at the expense of doing anything for the benefit of the actor.

In retaliation for these and other slights, Mountford sought to damage *Variety*. He chose the law as his venue. Mountford asked the recently formed Federal Trade Commission (FTC), established in 1914, to investigate a monopoly conspiracy carried out by the UBO, VMPA, and *Variety*. He is probably also the reason why Edward Clark, a member of the White Rats, sued *Variety* for libel. Clark was among the leaders of the White Rats and helped organize a ball to raise funds to support the strike. In a March 23 column, *Variety* reported: "Eddie Clark, who is connected with 'You're in Love,' at the Casino, is said to have reserved two boxes for members of that company for the White Rats' ball last Friday night, then sent each member a bill for the proportionate share of the cost. The last reports were the principals had refused to be held up."[86] A few weeks later, Clark filed a libel suit against *Variety*, claiming $25,000 in damages. He insisted that he bought and gave away tickets for the ball, never insisting that his cast members pay.[87] It's unclear whether or not it was intentional, but the libelous phrase was identical to the one that had infuriated Sime Silverman six years earlier: actors were being "held up."

Faced with Clark's libel complaint, Silverman had several options about how to respond. He could defend his remarks as "fair comment" or minimize them by arguing that readers interpreted them in jest (they appeared as part of a column called "The Funny Side"). He could also issue a retraction or even, simply, an apology. Instead, *Variety* went on the counterattack. In a June 2, 1917, news item entitled "Eddie Clark Feels 'Damaged,'" *Variety* ridiculed Clark and his lawsuit:

Edward Clark as the complaint describes the defendant, was born Issy or Isadore Balty. He is a Hebrew and has been in show business for a number of years, going on the stage from the race tracks. When known as Issy Balty, the present "Clark" was a frequenter of the tracks throughout the country and it is said that it was his experiences on those tracks that assisted him to a stage debut where he did a race track tout in vaudeville.

Under the name of Edward Clark he also has an action pending against the United Booking Offices and associates, alleging he has been prevented from appearing in vaudeville through a conspiracy, although in the Marinelli suit, Clark, when

VAUDEVILLE

"THE MOTH AND THE FLAME"

FIGURE 13. Edward Marshall's anti-Mountford illustration, "The Moth and the Flame," appeared in *Variety* on the eve of the White Rats strike in December 1916. *Source:* Edward Marshall, "The Moth and the Flame," *Variety,* Dec. 29, 1916, 7, https://lantern.mediahist.org/catalog/variety45-1916-12_0344.

testifying, was obliged to admit that his acts were "shown" in U.B.O. houses but could not secure bookings.

Nourishing his grievances against vaudeville managers who did not think his act was suitable to their stages, Clark joined the White Rats. During the recent White Rats strike he was one of the organization's principal agitators. It was during the

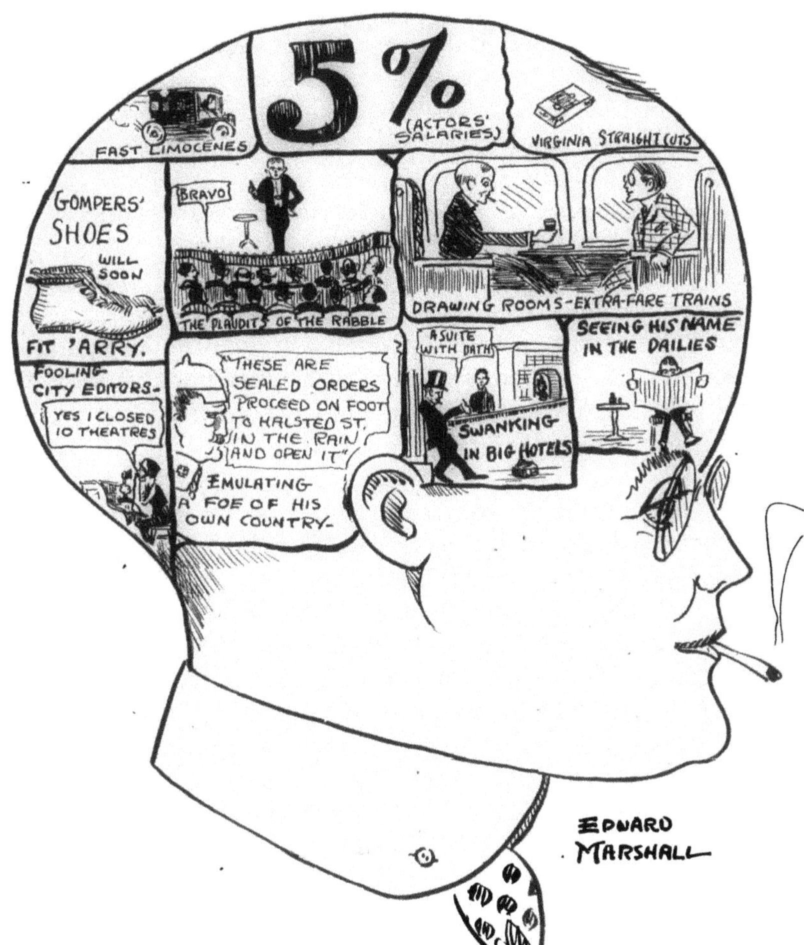

"THE MIND OF MOUNTFORD" (Nothing in it for the actor)

FIGURE 14. *Variety* published this satirical cartoon by Edward Marshall during the White Rats' strike in March 1917. The cartoon illustrated "The Mind of Mountford," emphasizing there was "Nothing in it for the actor." *Source:* Edward Marshall, "The Mind of Mountford," *Variety*, March 30, 1917, 5, https://lantern.mediahist.org/catalog/variety46-1917-03_0252.

White Rat troubles that the order held the ball for which Clark swears he bought some tickets and gave them away.[88]

It was a nasty piece of writing that was designed to humiliate Clark, the very definition of libel. *Variety* was flexing its strength to the vaudeville community: you go after us; we go after you. In the process, *Variety* had published a new libel that dwarfed the original. Clark and his lawyer filed a second libel complaint that included the references to racetracks, the Marinelli lawsuit, and inability to book performances with UBO theaters.[89] *Variety*'s lawyers responded that the piece was published "without malice, but in the spirit of good-natured ridicule." Furthermore, *Variety* argued to the court that it had the facts on its side: Clark was Jewish (as was Silverman), and he was known to frequent racetracks.[90]

The lawsuit remained tied up in the New York county court system for the next two and a half years. Ultimately, in January 1920, the two parties reached a settlement. *Variety* agreed to pay Clark $600, plus legal expenses. The paper also agreed to publish a retraction on the cover of its next issue.[91] In a story headlined "Clark Suits Settled," *Variety* acknowledged: "Subsequent developments proved that both articles were founded on misinformation and untrue. Clark did not ask his guests at the White Rats Ball to reimburse him, nor did he testify in the Marinelli suit as reported."[92] By this point, however, *Variety* had already won in the court of industry perception. Silverman used his position as a libel defendant to project his independence, fearlessness, and appetite for a fight.

Silverman was able to further advance the perception of *Variety* as strong and independent when *Variety* became a defendant in a larger legal case related to the White Rats. During the period of escalating tension that led up to the 1917 strike, Mountford and lawyers for the White Rats had argued that the actions of the big-time vaudeville managers violated the Sherman Antitrust Act. When the FTC issued its formal compliant in the spring of 1918, *Variety* was listed as one of the defendants. The FTC reproduced the same argument that Mountford made in 1911: *Variety* disseminated the managers' "propaganda" to vaudeville artists; in the return, the managers and their organizations "require that actors patronize the advertising columns of the publication to such an extent that in holiday numbers and special issues of 'Variety' it contains approximately two hundred pages of advertising by actors and their 'personal representatives' which is paid for at the rate of approximately $125 per page."[93] *Variety* denied the allegations and, what's more, distanced itself from the managers during the legal proceedings. The archival court records reveal that the VMPA, UBO, and other defendant companies were all represented by the same attorneys and filed joint briefs. *Variety*, however, insisted on its own defense. Silverman incurred higher legal costs to make it clear that he and his journal were independent of the VMPA, UBO, and the managers. The case resulted in hearings over a period of several months in 1919. As Wertheim describes: "The case revolved around a key question: Were performances by vaudevillians interstate commerce as interpreted in the antitrust laws?" Ultimately, the commissioners ruled the performances were a form of labor, not commodities, and therefore not subject to antitrust regulation.[94]

The FTC's distinction between labor and commodities in vaudeville was highly problematic. Vaudeville managers packaged acts like commodities, arranging a program of ten or eleven acts like a stack of blocks. One act might even be a motion picture, which was a commodity according to the FTC. More relevant for this study, *Variety* and the other theatrical trade papers encouraged performers to promote themselves like commodities. The ads they purchased frequently appeared on the same page as advertisements for furniture, pianos, and lights. And, much like those other commodities for sale, the performers needed to distinguish their product benefits and uniqueness of their acts. Unlike a chair or piano, however, these actors also needed to prove they were members of an entertainment community. An advertisement in *Variety*, vaudeville's gatekeeper with its reputation for taste and independence, was a mark of belonging. Based on my reading of the archival FTC documents, I do not think that *Variety* participated in the conspiracy alleged by Mountford—which is to say, I do not think *Variety* agreed to do favors for the managers in exchange for having managers demand their performers take out ads in *Variety*. What is indisputable, though, is that actors felt pressure to advertise in *Variety*. Some of this pressure may have come from managers, but more of it came from their industry environment, which was extremely competitive and valued visibility and community membership.

Although studying vaudeville's industrial history may seem like a digression from the motion picture trade press, it is important for understanding the development of the Hollywood studio system, the migration of theatrical trade press practices to film, and *Variety*'s 1920s transformation into the film industry's leading class journal. Two of the heads of major Hollywood studios, Marcus Loew and William Fox, owned small-time vaudeville theaters (which, unlike the big-time vaudeville of Keith and Albee, devoted as much as half their programs to motion pictures).[95] Other studio moguls imitated the vaudeville industry's consolidation and management techniques and eventually acquired the big-time theaters to exhibit their motion pictures. Similarly, motion picture trade papers adopted practices from the theatrical trade press—evident in *Motion Picture News Studio Directory*'s and *Wid's Daily*'s emphasis on selling advertisements directly to actors, directors, writers, and other film production personnel. As for *Variety*, the paper emerged from the vaudeville wars with its reputation for strength and independence enhanced. And it was this reputation, more than any other asset, that it would leverage toward becoming a leading voice within the motion picture industry.

CONCLUSION: THE PROBLEM OF TOO MANY TRADE PAPERS

The trade paper war of 1917 was both climax and prologue. The fight between *Exhibitor's Trade Review* and *Motion Picture News*, as well as the fight between *Variety* and the White Rats, punctuated long stretches of growing animosity. But the trade paper war is more significant to study for the new conflicts it established, conflicts that continued for the next fifteen years. Despite the trade papers' constructive solutions to some of the industry's information management problems, *Wid's Daily* and the annuals were, at the end of the day, more publications claiming to serve the film industry, asking for subscriptions and advertisements. To a growing number of industry insiders, trade papers themselves were the problem. "Buying space in publications of various sorts simply to avoid incurring the enmity of such publications has been one of the worst and most costly evils we have all had to contend with," wrote a Universal executive during the Ochs feud.[96] The industry suffered from too many trade papers chasing after the same purse of advertising dollars.

The last trade paper fight of 1917 directly addressed the problem of too many trade papers. In a December 1917 column, *Motion Picture News'* William A. Johnston argued the industry needed to eliminate waste and eradicate all but two trade papers. "Once [*sic*] is enough to reach properly and completely the purchasing power of the field, but two are necessary to preserve a desirable balance of competition," wrote Johnston. "All advertising expenditure outside of two papers is waste pure and senseless. There is absolutely no excuse for the good natured maintenance of a dozen papers WHERE ONLY ONE CAN BE READ, and the proposition stands right up to the manufacturer and distributor for instant action."[97] Presumably, Johnston thought that his paper should be one of the two permitted to survive in the industry's new, efficient era.

Variety pounced on Johnston and his comments. In an editorial entitled "Which Two?," *Variety* criticized Johnston for his apparent interest in only the advertising function of the trade press; there was no mention of how many papers were needed to communicate the news to the various constituencies of the film industry. *Variety* also used the editorial as an opportunity to call out—and, in some cases, insult—the other film and theatrical trade papers, most of which it found preferable to the *News*. *Variety* reserved its harshest assessment for its most direct competitors, trade papers that covered film alongside theater and vaudeville. *Dramatic Mirror* was "once theatrical paper, now haphazarding it"; the *Morning Telegraph* "published reams of the picture press agents' press publicity piffle without wasting the time to edit it"; and *Billboard* "threw away its chance some years ago to be the leading film sheet, as it has thrown away its chance to become even a theatrical medium."[98] *Variety* was willing to burn the other film and theatrical trade papers, but it was circumspect about its own role within this environment. "*Variety*, not professing to be a film trade publication, may discuss 'The News' statement calmly and impartially," wrote the paper. *Variety's* comments were accurate on a purely quantitative basis; the paper in 1916 and 1918 devoted roughly three times the amount of space to vaudeville as it did to film. Despite the claim of not being a film trade paper, though, the primary takeaway from the editorial was the reassertion of *Variety's* authority among the increasingly crowded entertainment industry press.

Two weeks later, in its December 28 edition, *Variety* published an even more forceful critique of Johnston's call for only two papers. This time, the remarks were those of Leander Richardson, who had been Sime Silverman's boss years earlier at the *Morning Telegraph*. In the time since then, Richardson had left his post as an editor to work for the publicity department of World Film Corporation (W. Stephen Bush and Merritt Crawford both made similar transitions to film company publicity departments after leaving *Exhibitor's Trade Review*, and the revolving door continued for decades that followed). In the pages of *Variety*, Richardson proposed his own solution:

> What we really need in the motion picture business is ONE trade paper, not two.
>
> Look over the other industries—iron, for example. Take a good look.
>
> You will find one real trade paper to every real trade. Where there are others, they merely feed on the crumbs from the rich man's table; and this is precisely as it should be, and as it will be when the motion picture business becomes more tangible and less sensitive to ghosts.
>
> And, as a parting thought, Mr. Johnston, the one paper that will survive in the motion picture industry will be a paper of character, that does not spend its entire force upon its one or two editorial pages; that does not split itself up into a few cut-and-dried departments; that does not give up its columns to the drivel of incompetent boosters; that does not go drilling along a fixed course of so-much-for-so-much; that plunges out to find the real news of the industry—that, in a word, has something behind it which means more than getting to press.[99]

Nowhere in the piece did Richardson reference *Variety* or Silverman by name. And *Variety* did not prioritize motion pictures over vaudeville until 1926, by which point the vaudeville industry's profitability had declined significantly.[100] But Silverman and his allies may have already been aware that *Variety*'s reputation for independence—hard-earned through libel lawsuits and public feuds—could serve its efforts to become a leader in the film industry.

Meanwhile, the idea of "ONE trade paper" representing the film industry seized the imaginations of several ambitious publishers. After acquiring control of *Exhibitor's Trade Review*, the Swetlands named their new holding corporation "United Motion Picture Publications," a sign of their intent to consolidate the film industry's trade publications in the same manner they had done for the automotive and iron industries.[101] But the Swetlands would have to compete for the crown against William A. Johnston *(Motion Picture News)*, the Chalmers family *(Moving Picture World)*, and an outspoken young Chicago publisher, Martin Quigley *(Exhibitors Herald)*. For the next twelve years, the dream of consolidation and control animated the actions of the film industry trade papers, as well as, more famously, the film manufacturers and distributors that they chronicled.

Yet a fallacy inhered in Richardson's proposal, a fallacy that continually pushed the dream of "ONE trade paper" out of reach. For one trade paper to represent the motion picture industry, there needed to be consensus about what the industry was and what it should be. No such consensus was reachable. Exhibitors resented manufacturers and distributors, who, in turn, distrusted exhibitors. And within the ranks of exhibitors, the conflicts between factions only grew across the following two decades. As the national exhibitor organization splintered, local exhibitor organizations and the regional trade papers that spoke to them only became more important. Additionally, the writers, directors, producers, and actors living and working in Southern California came increasingly to regard themselves as belonging to their own community. This production community was distinct from the cluster of industry executives in New York, and each community found publications that served its needs. The trade paper war of 1917 was an explosion of long-simmering tensions, enhancing and damaging industry reputations in the process. Ironically, though, it did not have the effect of putting any trade papers out of business. In fact, the opposite occurred. As we will see in the next two chapters, the number of film industry trade papers doubled over the next five years.

3

The Independent Exhibitor's Pal

*Localizing, Specializing, and Expanding
the Exhibitor Paper*

A few blocks north of Union Station and just a few blocks south of the heart of downtown Kansas City, Missouri, sits a cluster of small brick buildings known as Film Row (fig. 15). In the early 1920s, the nearly twenty buildings in Film Row were constructed to be single-use and low to the ground, just in case of a fire. Their occupants, besides the flammable nitrate reels and stacks of posters and promotional materials, were the men and women who managed film exchanges. Some exchanges were states' rights distributors—a form of distribution in which a company acquired the exclusive rights to rent a film or group of films to theaters in a particular region, sometimes limited to a single state though generally a bit larger (e.g., Kansas and Missouri). Other exchanges were part of national distribution networks. Paramount, Pathé, and a growing number of other national distributors needed a means of contracting with exhibitors, controlling print circulation, and collecting rental revenue. Local exchanges provided the vital, if costly, nodes of this distribution infrastructure. Whereas Kansas City's film exchanges had previously leased space in downtown offices, the Film Row development of the early 1920s marked a big step forward—both for protecting public safety and creating an industrial hub where buyers and sellers, competitors and collaborators all came together.

Ben Shlyen came of age in this rapidly changing ecosystem. In 1916 or 1917, Standard Film Co., a Kansas City states' rights outfit, hired Shlyen as a high school student to help with shipping, then promoted him to writing advertising literature when the copywriter on staff went to fight in World War I. Shlyen developed an intimate understanding for Kansas City's exchanges and the theaters they served, and he saw that there might be an opportunity for a young go-getter like himself. In 1919, at the age of eighteen, Shlyen pitched his idea for a regional film trade paper to local exchanges and prominent exhibitors. In January 1920, Shlyen

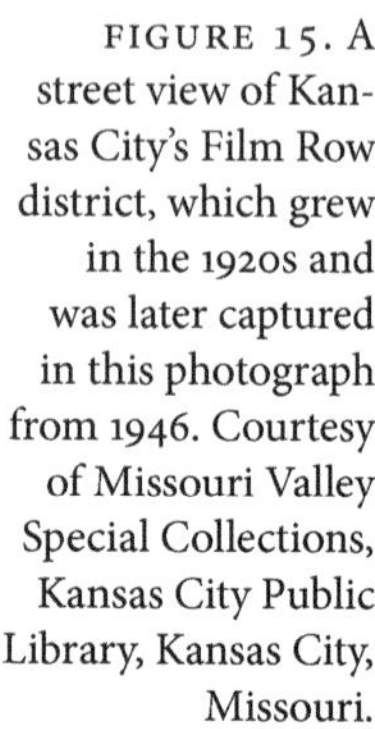

FIGURE 15. A street view of Kansas City's Film Row district, which grew in the 1920s and was later captured in this photograph from 1946. Courtesy of Missouri Valley Special Collections, Kansas City Public Library, Kansas City, Missouri.

published the first issue of the *Reel Journal*, a mere four pages long.[1] The paper grew during the 1920s, nearly in parallel to the developing Film Row district (where Shlyen had his office), and it ultimately expanded well beyond Kansas City to become the most widely read exhibitor trade paper of all time: *Boxoffice*. In January 1920, though, Shlyen was just another young entrepreneur attracted by the potential to connect buyers and sellers, the low barrier to entry of publishing a newsletter, and, perhaps on some level, the allure of motion pictures.

This chapter explores alternatives to the national film trade papers that developed from the mid-1910s through the early 1920s. As *Moving Picture World*, *Motion Picture News*, and *Exhibitor's Trade Review* continued printing and squabbling in New York City, numerous localized and specialized exhibitor publications sprouted up in places such as Philadelphia and Minneapolis, in addition to Kansas City. These regional papers began by serving specific business needs; however, the most successful ones expanded and endured because of their ability to speak to communities of exhibitors and, in some cases, negotiate with major industry players behind the scenes.

To appreciate both the similarities and differences of these localized publications, this chapter is organized across three sections and utilizes both a survey and case study approach. The first section surveys regional exhibitor papers, including *Reel Journal*, that essentially attached themselves to nearby distribution networks and exchange offices. Looking at several different publications is a necessity in this case; our access to the early issues of these journals is largely limited to scattered issues here and there. The second section profiles a different type of specialized exhibitor paper. Founded in Philadelphia in 1919, *Harrison's Reports* issued weekly reviews to exhibitors that were "free from the influence of film advertising." P. S. Harrison's fiery editorial page, which called attention to the plight of independent exhibitors, also offers a useful prism into understanding how the major developments in the US film industry in the early 1920s were understood and interpreted by the exhibitor community. Third and finally, this chapter explores the early history of Martin J. Quigley's *Exhibitors Herald*, which began as a regional trade paper in Chicago and grew into a paper of national statute and circulation.

Before analyzing any of these publications, though, we need to briefly examine the business environment facing exhibitors, particularly exhibitors operating low-capacity theaters in small or midsized towns. These were the readers that regional trade papers, *Harrison's Reports*, and *Exhibitors Herald* claimed to serve and, sometimes, did.

CHANGES IN FILM DISTRIBUTION AND EXHIBITION, 1919 TO 1923

As small exhibitors gained more reading options than ever before in the late 1910s, their overall leverage within the industry was eroding. Small exhibitors faced interrelated pressures from competing theaters, higher film rental costs, and conditions mandated by distributors. In larger and midsized cities, for example, theaters that had succeeded during the Motion Picture Patents Company (MPPC) era—those generally seating two hundred to four hundred patrons and changing programs of short films daily—found it more difficult to compete against the bigger and better theaters, seating one thousand people or more, that were being built just blocks away. Features cost exhibitors more to rent than programs of short films, and the audience turned over more slowly.[2] Small theaters could sell fewer tickets than large theaters in a given day but still had to pay high rental costs (that is, if they could obtain the desirable feature films at all). In 1919, for example, the small Empress Theatre in Toledo, Ohio, was pushed out of business by four nearby competing theaters that offered more desirable films and the amenities that audiences increasingly expected theaters to provide.[3] The larger theaters often charged more for tickets, but they did not necessarily have to charge a lot more because their higher seating capacities could translate into greater overall revenue.

Not all small exhibitors, though, found themselves competing against shiny new theaters. Hundreds of small towns across the US were serviced by a single screen (fig. 16). These exhibitors still had competition, arriving in the form of baseball games, bad weather, the traveling circus, and other local events or circumstances. Additionally, the market power they gained from possessing a movie monopoly in a town of two thousand people was very limited. Distributors wanted to waste as little time as possible negotiating with them. Small exhibitors operated on an entirely different tier within the industry than the large urban exhibitors and chains that in the late 1910s bound together to form First National and the United Picture Theaters of America. Although these consortiums promoted the idea that they would give exhibitors the types of films they wanted and at a better price, the reality is that they were controlled by powerful exhibitors and/or get-rich-quick

FIGURE 16. View of the Opera House in Traer, Iowa, which had a population of 1,329 in 1920. The Traer Opera House typified the sort of small-town, independent theater that regional exhibitor papers claimed to represent. Courtesy of the Wisconsin Historical Society.

opportunists. When these consortiums approached small-town exhibitors, it was not for their advice about what type of film to produce or acquire; it was for their money. In some cases, the solicitations arrived not for the films themselves but for dodgy shares of stock that would confer some preferred status for booking.[4]

From the perspective of the larger distributors—especially the distributors with production capabilities, such as Paramount, Metro, and Pathé—the goal was to maximize the industry's gross revenue and, more important, the share of that revenue that went back into their pockets. In the mid to late 1920s, the pursuit of this goal would lead the major producer-distributors toward a frenzied spree of theater buying. But, in the late 1910s and early 1920s, the movement of producer-distributors into exhibition was still quite modest. Just consider Paramount, generally cited as the leader of Hollywood's vertically integrated model. From 1918 to 1924, Paramount used Wall Street financing to acquire ownership stakes in fifty-one theaters and grow its total consolidated assets to $49,018,000. In the following six years (1925 to 1931), however, Paramount partially or fully acquired ownership in 762 theaters and grew its total assets to $306,269,000.[5] At the dawn of the 1920s, exhibitor trade organizations were nervously anticipating the incursion of distributors into theater ownership, and many independent exhibitors loudly protested.[6] But the reality of this taking major effect was still a few years away.

Instead, the more immediate battles that exhibitors were fighting against the producer-distributors in 1920 were the conditions and policies that the latter group were implementing to make their businesses more profitable and predictable. After experimenting with the "open booking" of features on a one-off basis in the late 1910s, Paramount and the other major producer-distributors largely returned to the practice of block booking—compelling exhibitors to enter into contracts for entire slates of films.[7] For the producer-distributors, block booking mitigated the financial risk associated with any single picture and lowered the transaction costs of selling those pictures. For independent exhibitors, however, block booking took away their ability to select only the pictures they wanted and to negotiate over specific price points. Rather than refusing outright to enter into block booking contracts, a different pattern emerged—exhibitors signed contracts, then refused to follow through on their stipulated terms. Some exhibitors strategically over-booked film programs in order to deprive their competitors of access to product. In other cases, exhibitors ignored their contracts because they did not think their patrons would like a film, or they realized they could substitute a different film at a better price. In 1920 and 1921, more than a third of all movies contracted for in the US were never shown or paid for.[8] Some exhibitors used the reviews they read in *Harrison's Reports* as their guides to decide which movies to keep and which to ditch. The block booking practices and forceful negotiation tactics of Paramount led independent exhibitors and their trade organizations to complain to the FTC about unfair competition. In 1921, the FTC began what would become a six-year investigation and, ultimately, unsuccessful legal case against the studio.[9]

The studios, for their part, argued that exhibitors were themselves to blame for many of the policies that they did not like. One of the few archival collections left by an independent exhibitor of this era offers a striking portrait both of exhibitor malfeasance and of a bitter and hateful person. Thomas Watson owned the Superba Theater in Freeport, Illinois. In the early 1920s, he found himself in competition with a larger theater in his same town and the subject of complaints from Chicago-based film exchanges.[10] Watson routinely booked pictures that he never played (his papers are rich in notices asking him why he had not scheduled a film's play-date yet).[11] He would also book films at a certain price, then complain about the films' quality and demand either a lower rental fee or threaten to pay nothing at all.[12] Most egregiously of all from the distributors' perspective, he engaged in the illegal business of subrenting (or "bicycling") films to exhibitors in nearby towns. Watson received repeated complaints from exchanges, many of which he ignored. In other cases, he wrote back defiant and sometimes racist letters, referring to exchange operators with an anti-Semitic slur.[13] Watson's racist beliefs and activities appear to have run deep. His archival collections include Ku Klux Klan memorabilia—a point that requires calling out in order to resist the tendency to view the Thomas Watsons of the industry as noble underdogs fighting against the giant studios, and, more broadly, to remind us that some local exhibitors participated in their communities through hate, exclusions, and support of violence against Black and Jewish people as much as they did through welcoming and inclusive behaviors.[14]

To more efficiently deal with exhibitors like Watson, national distributors and their trade organization, the National Association of the Motion Picture Industry (NAMPI), encouraged exchanges across the country to create FILM Clubs (the acronym stood for Film Industry Local Managers). The FILM Clubs participated in the city planning of film row developments and engaged in public outreach activities—arranging special screenings for war veterans, for example, or organizing an athletic field day.[15] The FILM Clubs' most important function, however, was to monitor and discipline unruly exhibitors. Like a group of landlords gathering together to compare notes about bad tenants, FILM Clubs could blacklist exhibitors from renting films.[16] More important, FILM Clubs implemented arbitration systems, which represented a much cheaper and more efficient tactic for handling disputes than filing lawsuits.[17] Thomas Watson behaved badly toward the exchanges, in part, because he knew he could get away with it. He was sued on only a few occasions; most distributors did not bother to sue him to claim the $20 or $30 rental fee they were owed. Additionally, there was enough competition among exchanges—including the many states' rights distributors operating in the early 1920s—that he kept receiving sales calls about booking films even when some Chicago exchanges were furious with him. In 1922, Chicago's FILM Club became the Board of Trade, which comprised half of exchanges, half of exhibitors, and existed primarily to arbitrate disputes initiated by the exchanges.

When the leading producer-distributors formed the Motion Picture Producers and Distributors Association (MPPDA) and appointed Will Hays as its chairman in January 1922, the new trade group inherited and improved on the arbitration systems already in place with FILM Clubs and Boards of Trade.[18] One of the MPPDA's first major accomplishments came in the drafting of the standard exhibition contract in 1923. The MPPDA's creation has been frequently discussed in film histories as a response to the 1921 scandals involving Roscoe "Fatty" Arbuckle and William Desmond Taylor. But as Richard Maltby has argued, based on his close examination and digital curation of the MPPDA's papers, the organization was also designed to address "the extreme contractual instability of the film industry."[19] The standard exhibition contract streamlined both the sales process for exchanges and the arbitration process when particular deals went bad.

In this context of mutual animosity, exhibitors found a coterie of new publications pitched to them. Some of these publications tried to soften industry tensions; others were eager to amplify them. All of them offered exhibitors a guide of sorts for interpreting the changing motion picture industry and their roles within it.

REGIONAL TRADE PUBLICATIONS

By the time Ben Shlyen's *Reel Journal* celebrated its first birthday in 1921, it was one of at least twenty regional trade publications serving the exhibitors of an exchange territory. Table 1 provides a list of all the regional trade papers that we know,

TABLE 1. Regional Exhibitor Trade Papers, 1921

Title	City of Publication	Circulation	Frequency	AFP Member?
New England Exhibitor	Boston, MA	1,271	Weekly	Yes
Motion Picture Journal	New York, NY	1,600	Semi-monthly	Yes
The Exhibitor	Philadelphia, PA	1,200	Semi-monthly (later changed to weekly)	Yes
Canadian Moving Picture Digest	Toronto, Canada	2,000	unknown	Yes
Moving Picture Bulletin	Pittsburgh, PA	1,600	Weekly	Yes
Interstate Film News	Cleveland, OH	1,600	Weekly	Yes
Michigan Film Review	Detroit, MI	1,000	unknown	Yes
Reel Facts	Cincinnati, OH	1,500	Weekly	Yes
Weekly Film Review	Atlanta, GA	1,212	Weekly	Yes
Southern Picture News	Atlanta, GA	unknown	Weekly	No
Exhibitors Herald	Chicago, IL	8,000	Weekly	No
Amusements	Minneapolis, MN	3,127	Weekly	Yes
Reel Journal	Kansas City, MO	2,000	Weekly	Yes
Movie Age	Omaha, NE	unknown	unknown	No
Motion Picture Journal	Dallas, TX	1,500	Weekly	Yes
Oklahoma Film News	Oklahoma City, OK	unknown	Weekly	No
Rocky Mountain Screen News	Denver, CO	1,000	Semi-monthly	Yes
*Motion Picture Weekly**	Los Angeles, CA	unknown	unknown	No
Motion Picture Bulletin	Los Angeles, CA	700	Weekly	Yes
*Pacific Coast Independent Exhibitor**	San Francisco, CA	unknown	Unknown	No

SOURCES: "The Fourteen Points of Successful Advertising" [Advertisement for Associated Film Press], *Moving Picture World,* May 14, 1921, 178, https://lantern.mediahist.org/catalog/movpicwor501movi_0238; *N. W. Ayer & Son's American Newspaper Annual and Directory,* Library of Congress Digital Collections, https://lccn.loc.gov/sn91012092.

NOTE: Papers are listed geographically from East to West.

* Indicates a degree of uncertainty regarding whether the trade paper was operating in 1921; these may have gone out of business by then or may have not yet officially started.

with a degree of confidence, existed in 1921. Some of these publications existed for a very short time. More regional papers were introduced later, and there were probably some others in 1921 that we just don't know about. Still, this table provides a snapshot of the exchange cities (ordered geographically, east to west) that supported these publications and the circulation of readers (nearly all of whom were exhibitors) that these papers reached. A snapshot taken just three years earlier, in 1918, would have looked very different, probably featuring only three publications: Minneapolis's *Amusements* (est. 1914), Philadelphia's *The Exhibitor* (founded in 1917 or 1918), and Chicago's *Exhibitors Herald* (est. 1915, but, as detailed below, moved beyond the Chicago exchange market by 1918).

What explains the dramatic increase of regional trade papers over the period from the end of World War I to 1921? One answer is that entrepreneurial publishers identified a promising market with a low barrier to entry. The first two decades of the twentieth century witnessed the diffusion of inexpensive and user-friendly duplication technologies, which were marketed especially to businesses for internal communications. These developments pressured printers to lower the rates they charged clients and created new possibilities for self-publishing newsletters in small batches.[20] "It is frequently said, facetiously, that anybody with a typewriter and four weeks' credit can start a trade paper in the motion picture business," quipped the general manager of a leading paper more than a decade later.[21] After inexpensive regional trade papers proved successful in Minneapolis, Chicago, and Philadelphia, the model caught on elsewhere.

The growth of states' rights feature film distribution during and after World War I was also crucial in building an advertising base for local publishers. The *Reel Journal* and other regional papers depended on ad revenue from businesses that needed to target their message to a narrower audience than the readership of *Motion Picture News* and the other national trade papers. The theater seating supplier in Cincinnati and the states' rights distributor that controlled the Texas and Louisiana rights to a group of feature films could both spend their advertising dollars more efficiently by placing ads in papers that reached only exhibitors in their areas. The regional trade papers also sought the patronage of the national distributors with exchanges in their cities (for example, the Metro exchange located within Kansas City's Film Row). But not all of the national distributors permitted their local exchanges to buy ads; the advertising budgets were controlled by the New York home offices. As a result, states' rights distributors were the best customers of the regional trade papers in the late 1910s and early 1920s.

In addition to the states' rights marketplace, regional trade papers glommed onto exhibitor trade organizations. During the Lee Ochs scandals of the late 1910s, the national exhibitor organizations were a dysfunctional mess. The situation improved around 1920 as Sydney S. Cohen led the formation of the Motion Picture Theater Owners Association (MPTOA).[22] But local exhibitor organizations, like the Miami Valley Exhibitors' League, still offered the potential for a cohesive community that was absent on the national level. Although it could be difficult to get competing exhibitors to cooperate, the common threats they faced—particularly in terms of state censorship laws and increasing film rental prices—could bind them together.[23] Although it's always dangerous as a historian to label anything as the "first," the *N. W. Ayer & Son's Newspaper Annual and Directory*, along with multiple accounts from trade papers, suggest that the earliest regional exhibitor paper hails from Minnesota. In 1914, Minneapolis exchange operator Tom Hamlin founded *Amusements: The Motion Picture Exhibitors Weekly Trade Journal*.[24] The sole issue of this trade paper's early run that I have been able to locate was published on August 10, 1916, and contained approximately six pages of news and editorial content and ten pages of advertising—half of which was taken out by states' rights distributors based in Minneapolis.[25] Beyond simply providing a medium for local exchanges to advertise, however, *Amusements* shared reports from the Northwest Exhibitors' Association and attempted to build a sense of community among the local exchange managers and exhibitors. One of its initiatives in this regard was organizing a golf tournament for local exchange managers and exhibitors, a practice that Omaha's *Movie Age* would later implement as well.[26] The golf tournaments and other local film industry events suggest that regional trade papers attempted to play a role in mediating and repairing frictions between exhibitors and exchanges.

Other early regionals to emerge, both in 1915, were *Exhibitors Herald* and *Canadian Moving Picture Digest*. Despite Canada's national autonomy and its massive size geographically, the *Canadian Moving Picture Digest* had a readership size and business model (based in the exchange city of Toronto) that was comparable to regional papers such as *Amusements* and *Reel Journal*. Additionally, the US film industry conceived of its "domestic" film market as including Canada—a categorization that persists in the reporting of box-office grosses today. Nevertheless, *Canadian Moving Picture Digest* had a unique editorial voice that distinguished it from other regionals and insisted on Canada's separateness. From 1918 to 1954, Ray Lewis served as *Canadian Moving Picture Digest*'s editor. Ray Lewis was a woman, and she endured a great deal of misogyny and belittlement from her male peers (including *Variety*'s Sime Silverman, who called her "the girl friend in Canada").[27] As Jessica L. Whitehead, Louis Pelletier, and Paul S. Moore argue in their excellent book chapter on Lewis, she was highly effective at "commanding her editorial pulpit to become a leading opinion maker in Canadian distribution and exhibition."[28] Even though her paper depended on the advertising of US companies, she was not afraid to bite the hand, serving as a "tireless advocate for making the Canadian film industry independent from the United States."[29]

After *Amusements, Exhibitors Herald,* and *Canadian Moving Picture Digest*, the next regional exhibitor paper noted in the *N. W. Ayer & Son's* directory is *The Exhibitor* (fig. 17), which David Barrist began publishing in Philadelphia either in 1917 (according to *Ayer*) or 1918 (according to a self-congratulatory issue *of The Exhibitor* published in 1939).[30] As table 1 illustrates, no fewer than fourteen additional trade papers, including *Reel Journal*, sprouted up in important exchange cities between 1919 and 1922. Some cities and territories even had competing regional papers. Atlanta, for example, was a hub for film distribution across seven southern states: Alabama, Florida, Georgia, Mississippi, North Carolina, South Carolina, and Tennessee. For at least a couple of years, two regional trade papers based in Atlanta claimed to serve exhibitors across those states—Nat L. Royster's *Southern*

Picture News (founded in 1920) and Anna Eugene Aiken's *Weekly Film Review* (which was most likely established that same year). Similarly, Art Meyer's *Motion Picture Bulletin* and Cecil A. James's *Motion Picture Weekly* claimed to represent the exhibitors of California and Arizona.

In 1920, Tom Hamlin attempted to bring both greater organization and profitability to the growing number of "regionals," as they became known within the industry. Hamlin had left Minneapolis and *Amusements* around 1918 to move to New York City and take a job reviewing films for the elite national trade paper *Motion Picture News*. But in 1920, he left *Motion Picture News* to found a new regional paper, *Motion Picture Journal*, which sought to appeal to the exchanges and exhibitors of New York and Northern New Jersey.[31] The decision to start a new publication in a market already oversaturated by trade papers might seem odd, but Hamlin planned to leverage *Motion Picture Journal* toward the larger and more lucrative business of running an advertising agency. In 1920, he persuaded eleven other regional papers, including his former Twin Cities sheet, *Amusements*, into becoming clients of the Associated Film Press (AFP).[32] Much like the agencies that represented local newspapers and, later, broadcasting stations, Hamlin's Associated Film Press leveraged its proximity to the headquarters of the major film corporations in New York to try to persuade those companies to buy ads in some or all of the regional papers.[33] When Metro or Pathé placed an ad in Cleveland's *Interstate Film News* or Denver's *Rocky Mountain Screen News* through Hamlin, his office took a fee. To streamline operations, Hamlin mandated that all AFP member papers conform to the same publishing size: nine inches by twelve. The same ad could easily be placed in anywhere between one to a dozen papers.

Regional papers seemed to welcome the arrangement with Hamlin and Associated Film Press. It is easy to understand why. The regional papers were successful at selling ads to states' rights distributors and local equipment suppliers. But when it came to the major film corporations, it was the New York City distribution headquarters, not the local exchanges, that controlled large advertising budgets. Hamlin funneled advertising revenue to the regionals from New York, while the papers could continue selling ads to their more reliable base of local customers. Hamlin's client list grew over the following years, reaching eighteen trade papers in January 1923. Yet focusing on total numbers alone does not capture the rapid churn within the marketplace. Regionals ceased publication or left AFP nearly as quickly as they sprouted up. For example, three of AFP's twelve clients in December 1920—*Allied Amusements Bulletin* (Chicago), *Screencraft* (New Orleans), and *Southern Picture News* (Atlanta)—were no longer being promoted to advertisers just a few months later. The May 1921 list of clients shows a net increase of two (fourteen regionals, by that point), but the fact that five new papers were added and three departed over such a short period suggests that the low entry and exit barriers of regional publishing led to a revolving door of players.[34]

The most successful regional trade papers—the ones that had the most staying power—were led by dedicated editors who fostered the sense of a local community. These editors, like *Reel Journal*'s Ben Shlyen and *The Exhibitor*'s David

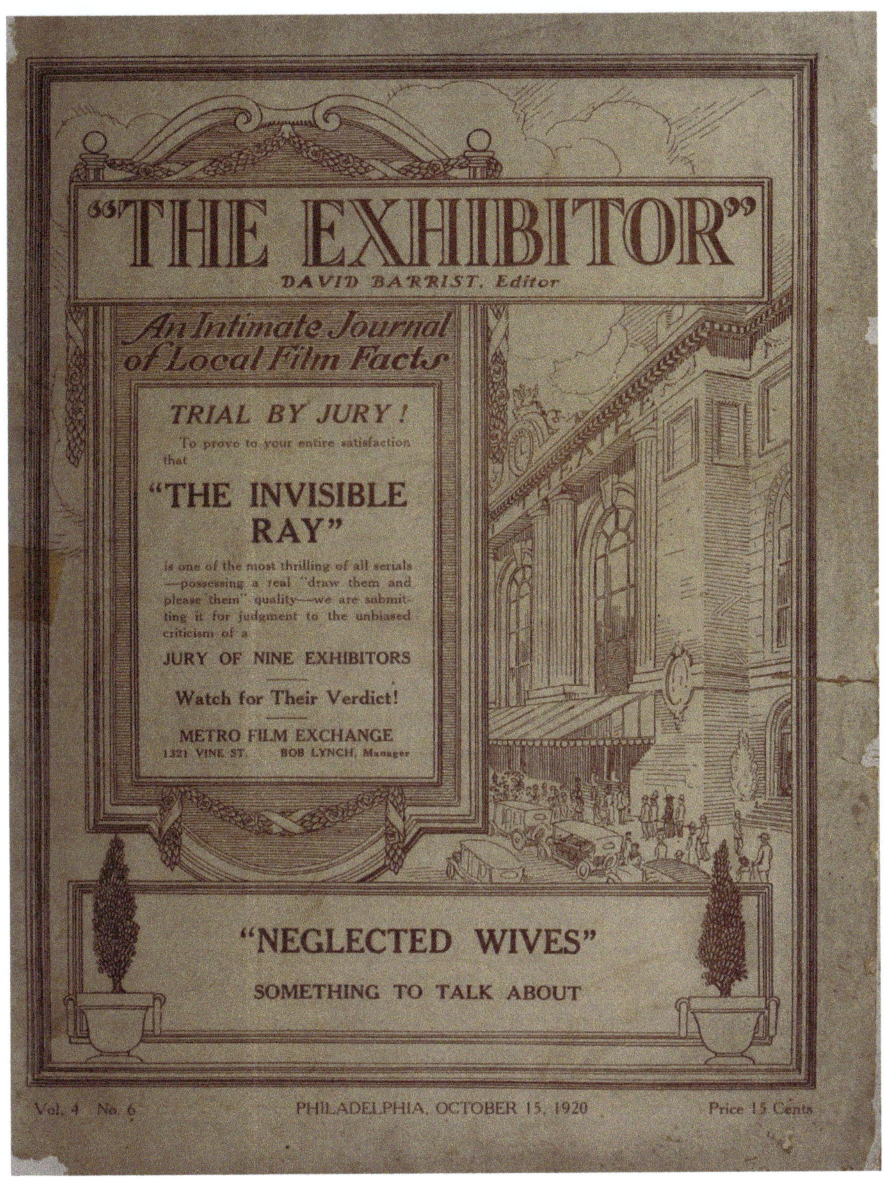

FIGURE 17. Philadelphia's regional exhibitor paper, *The Exhibitor*: "An Intimate Journal of Local Film Facts." *Source: The Exhibitor,* Oct. 15, 1920, https://lantern.mediahist.org/catalog /exhibitoroctober00exhi_0001.

Barrist, actively participated in their local film rows and avoided, as much as possible, the perception that they preferred certain exhibitors or exchanges over others. Through their editorial pages, the events they hosted, news coverage of local theater openings and exhibitor meetings, and advertisements listing local exchange staffers by name, the regional trade papers sought to construct a sense of the local film industry as a coherent community. The papers acknowledged exhibitor grievances but maintained an optimistic vision of industry cooperation and community. If everyone in the local industry could just come together and play fairly—whether in golf or film rental contracts—then everything would work out okay. When conflicts emerged, these papers and their editors preferred to perceive themselves as mediators rather than partisans for one side or the other (the positions that the New York trade papers occupied during most of the MPPC years and during the Ochs controversy).

The emphasis on community extended into how the regional papers conceived of the role of the movie theater within a small town or neighborhood. "The exhibitor of any community should rank his influence with that of his newspaper editor," argued *Reel Journal*'s Ben Shlyen, who encouraged theater managers to participate in local civic organizations and perform public service.[35] When *The Exhibitor* profiled a new neighborhood theater in Collingswood, New Jersey, the paper noted how the opening ceremony brought together representatives of the Philadelphia film exchanges, some of whom sent flowers in advance, as well as important civic leaders. Collingswood's mayor addressed the event's attendees and "was enthusiastic in his promise to give the theatre the support of the community."[36] By calling for greater community engagement and celebrating instances of it, the regional trade papers were following a familiar script. In numerous *Moving Picture World* editorials from 1913 to 1916, W. Stephen Bush had observed that one of the best defenses against adverse censorship and tax policies was for exhibitors to be involved in local governance and positively contribute to their communities. When they served their communities by hosting fundraisers and special screenings for children, in other words, exhibitors were also serving their own best interests and those of the film industry at large.

During the 1920s and beyond, the idealization of the small-town theater and its importance to the community became ingrained in the trade discourse. In his essay "Imagining and Promoting the Small-Town Theater," Gregory A. Waller identifies different flavors of this discourse. His analysis focuses on the year 1930, but it is quite applicable to the early 1920s as well. Popular magazines, such as the *Saturday Evening Post*, often framed the local picture show as "an inviting, accessible, hometown gathering place run by an enterprising, neighborly showman. Thus understood, the movie theater becomes a site where community was constituted and reaffirmed in the pre–World War II era, a testament to the resilience of the local within a marketplace of commodified mass entertainment." The trade papers Waller surveyed maintain this ideal, emphasizing the theater's active civic participation: "the picture show—especially at the small-town theater—works in concert with schools, seeks out the advice of churches and women's clubs, and vigilantly pays heed to public opinion."[37] Paying heed to local public opinion was often invoked as safety measure against the threat of legally imposed censorship.

These ideals played another important strategic function, too. As the 1920s continued and theater chains acquired thousands of independent theaters and smaller chains, the ideal of the local exhibitor as community leader gave a powerful rhetorical stance to those small-town and neighborhood theater owners who wanted to see more government intervention—not in the form of new censorship laws but in antitrust legislation and unfair competition enforcement.

By and large, the editors of the regional trade papers did not advocate for government intervention into the industry's ownership and trade practices. Yet local conflicts did erupt that challenged the illusion of the exhibitor-exchange community. In one notable example, a Los Angeles–based paper launched its first issue by taking a shot at a powerful local exchange. The cover of *Motion Picture Weekly*'s first issue, dated November 1, 1919, featured a portrait of Michael M. Gore, surrounded by hand-drawn shapes and slightly skewed photos of five of his seven Los Angeles theaters. The twenty-page issue included a brief complimentary profile of Gore titled "From Newsboy to Exhibitor," but, more important, it contained a full-page advertisement taken out by the showman in the form of an "open letter to exhibitors, producers, and exchange-men."[38] Gore wrote the following:

> I feel it my duty to the Motion Picture Industry, with which I have been identified for many years, to relate an unhappy, unjustifiable, unethical, and unjust transaction practiced upon me by WALTER RAND, Branch Manager of UNITED ARTISTS CORPORATION Exchange located at Los Angeles.
>
> I went to the offices of the United Artists Corporation to book the picture "Broken Blossoms" and entered into a contract with WALTER RAND, Branch Manager, to pay the sum of two hundred and twenty-five dollars for the said picture to run at the Casino, Rosebud, and Savoy Theatres on Central Avenue, Los Angeles. WALTER RAND booked me the picture, furnished me with matter which to advertising the picture and accepted my check for $225.00 payment in advance. The following day I paid to said corporation $11.25 war tax on said picture.
>
> A few days ago while I was in the office of SELECT PICTURES, booking some pictures, WALTER RAND entered and handed me the two checks I had given in payment for "Broken Blossoms" and the war tax. I said, "What does this mean?" and he replied, "I had the chance to sell the picture for $25.00 more than you paid so I took more money." I called his attention to the contract he made with me and he said, "Contracts mean nothing to me, I am out to get the most money."
>
> The fact has developed that WALTER RAND, after selling me the picture "Broken Blossoms," obtained an offer of $25.00 more than I had paid from another exhibitor, and without consulting or informing me, tore up my contract and entered into a new one with the other exhibitor.
>
> ARE CONTRACTS MADE BETWEEN EXCHANGE MEN AND EXHIBITORS MERE SCRAPS OF PAPER TO BE TORN UP AT THE WILL OF THE EXCHANGE MEN?

I believe the trend of the Motion Picture Industry is toward a more stable and firmer business foundation than the "policy" pursued by WALTER RAND.

I do not believe WALTER RAND'S above-mentioned conduct is the ethical ideal of business methods entertained by the four great artists comprising the UNITED ARTISTS CORPORATION.

It is unbelievable and unthinkable that the four great artists who are associated in the UNITED ARTISTS CORPORATION sanction, or will EVER endorse or EVER PERMIT, such methods to be used in the sale of their pictures as used by WALTER RAND.

The letter continues for another four paragraphs, hammering WALTER RAND (always in caps) for his lack of integrity.[39] Gore sought to publicly shame WALTER RAND and tarnish his reputation both in the exhibitor community and the larger Los Angeles production community. Indeed, by mentioning the four great artists (D. W. Griffith, Mary Pickford, Douglas Fairbanks, and Charles Chaplin), who had founded United Artists just nine months earlier in 1919, Gore emphasized the chasm between the ideals expressed in their press releases and the realities of business negotiations between exchanges and exhibitors.

After the publication of Gore's open letter, the Los Angeles Theater Owners' Association took up the matter, threatening to withhold all future bookings from United Artists until the company fired Rand.[40] United Artists seems to have essentially called their bluff, keeping Rand on staff and continuing to rent films to exhibitors in Southern California. One year later, United Artists promoted Rand to western district manager, a position that placed him in supervision of the Los Angeles, San Francisco, Seattle, and Denver exchanges. As he monitored branch managers, he no doubt kept an eye on rental contracts, making sure his subordinates, like him, got the most money possible.[41]

The dispute received only a small amount of coverage in the national trade press, appearing as brief news items in *Wid's Daily*. But one newsletter made it the topic of a full-page editorial. In a piece entitled "Are Your Film Contracts Just So Many Scraps of Paper?," P. S. Harrison described Gore's *Motion Picture Weekly* open letter to the subscribers of *Harrison's Reports*. The story confirmed Harrison's worldview of how film producer-distributors abused the exhibitor. Harrison concluded the editorial by reiterating the same argument he had been making for months: "This condition will not change until you organize." He warned they should not organize with the producer-distributors, who seek to further "their own pocket-books, but with men who breathe the same air as you do; who feel the same heartthrobs you do; who fight the same battles you do—EXHIBITORS."[42]

FREE OF ADVERTISING INFLUENCE— HARRISON'S REPORTS

Like so many developments in the film industry's trade press, the origins of *Harrison's Reports* can be traced back to *Motion Picture News*. In March 1918, *Motion Picture News* announced "a radical step in review service," offering readers "the crisp, terse appraisals that you would give to a fellow exhibitor asking your opinion of a picture you had just viewed."[43] *Motion Picture News* already had a lengthy section of film reviews, as well as a recently added department entitled "Exhibitors' Own Box Office Reports," which included brief accounts akin to those in *Motography*'s "What the Picture Did for Me" (e.g., "Good show, star not very popular") but strove for greater comprehensiveness by analyzing how the film performed in different regions. The section offered four columns—East, North, South, West—and listed the film's performance there as "Poor," "Average," "Big," or "Extra." Yet both the film reviews and box-office reports had their limitations. Although Johnston did not admit it in his columns, he probably knew that many exhibitors perceived *Motion Picture News*' reviewers as too soft on the films of his advertisers or, at the very least, out of touch with their immediate business needs. The "Exhibitors' Own Box Office Reports" department offered the perspectives of exhibitors; however, the perspectives could be inconsistent and inevitably arrived weeks, if not months, after a film's release. Johnston imagined a new film review section that would deliver "exhibitor to exhibitor reviews" ahead of the films' release dates and in a clear, consistent, and trusted voice. He also proposed that the section would benefit producers by contributing to the production of higher grossing films. The service "will indicate definitely the kind of pictures wanted and the elements in them which are not wanted."[44]

The person Johnston selected for the job was Peter S. Harrison, who had entered the film industry in 1907 as an exhibitor in California. At some point, Harrison segued into distribution—operating exchanges that served California and the Pacific Northwest.[45] But it was his experience as an exhibitor, not an exchange-man, that Harrison continually brought up in his writing over the next four decades. His having been a showman was what gave his reviews their authority.

Motion Picture News promised that Harrison's reviews would be "based solely on the entertaining qualities of the picture" and written in a "concise, readable manner, shorn of all adjectives and confusing verbiage."[46] Yet, from the beginning, Harrison's taste and writing style never fit neatly within this promised framework. Adjectives abound in his writing (e.g., "a corking good picture"), and Harrison evaluated entertaining qualities based on an implicit hierarchy. He offered his greatest praise to films that had a morally uplifting story, leaving a "lump in your throat" (a favorite expression of his), without being maudlin or overly sad. In one of his first reviews, he lamented that Vitagraph's *The Desired Woman* (1918) was "an excellent picture—spoiled by the death of a little child," a plot point that he was sure would send audiences "from the theatre downcast."[47] One year later, he criticized D. W. Griffith's *Broken Blossoms* (1919), the source of Michael Gore's dispute with United Artists and a film that many critics regarded as a masterpiece, for making spectators feel more "gloomy and depressed" than "an hour and a half spent in a grave yard among skull and cross bones."[48]

Harrison's reviewing style stayed quite consistent across *Motion Picture News* and the first few years of *Harrison's Reports*. His review of *Anne of Green Gables* (1919) is emblematic of his style and the type of films he wanted producers to make:

> You owe it to your patrons, as well as to yourself and the profession in general, to show in your theatre pictures of this character. "Ann of Green Gables" is one of the cleanest, sweetest, most human pictures the screen can boast of. It is the personification of all that is pure and simple in life. It is one of those pictures that sink deep. Laughs and tears mingle in the situations, making the spectator sympathise intensely with the joys and sorrows, hopes despairs, pleasures and afflictions of characters.[49]

For Harrison, calling a picture "one of the cleanest" was high praise. Harrison scorned movies that he regarded as prurient, immoral, or likely to offend audiences. "No matter how strong or interesting an attraction may be, unless the entertainment is free from suggestiveness, it is not in keeping with the wants of the great majority of the picture-goers nowadays," Harrison wrote in a review of William S. Hart's *Selfish Yates* (1918), which contained a scene that suggests a woman was sexually assaulted.[50] As Harrison continued to review films month after month, his distaste for films he considered prurient grew into a full-blown critique of the industry: out-of-touch producers made these films, exhibitors were required by contract to show them, and, as a result, audiences stopped frequenting the movies, and reformers proposed censorship regulations.

In July 1919, Harrison left *Motion Picture News* but took his reviewing section with him. He began his first four-page newsletter with the following announcement:

> TO ALL EXHIBITORS:
>
> Commencing with this number, HARRISON'S EXHIBITOR REVIEWS, which have appeared in Motion Picture News for the past fifteen months, will be published by the undersigned, independently, under the title HARRISON'S REPORTS. THEY WILL BE MAILED TO THE SUBSCRIBERS EVERY SATURDAY, at the yearly subscription of $10.00. Film advertising will UNDER NO CIRCUMSTANCES be accepted, this to remain the permanent policy of the service."[51]

As noted in chapter 1, *Harrison's Reports* was not the first film review service for exhibitors. B. P. Fineman's *Exhibitor's Film Review Service* and the first iteration of *Wid's* both made a go of this format in 1915. But Harrison quickly differentiated his publication from those earlier efforts and the film industry's national and regional trade papers. Fineman and Wid Gunning had regarded the limited advertising their reviewing papers received as an unfortunate problem, something that had to be offset by higher subscription prices. Harrison transformed this liability into an asset. He was emphatic that he would never accept advertising, and this meant he was "absolutely under no obligation to anyone except you—the subscribing exhibitor." Beginning in January 1921 and continuing until its final issue in 1962, the phrase "free from the influence of film advertising" appeared prominently in every issue of *Harrison's Reports*, just below the title heading.

The circumstances surrounding Harrison's departure from *Motion Picture News* are unclear. It's certainly tempting to imagine a dramatic confrontation: Harrison sits at his desk as William A. Johnston, looking over his shoulder, asks Harrison to soften the tone of his review of the latest Paramount release; Harrison tightens his fist, cracking a pencil in half, and stands up to tell Johnston he's had enough and that he's going to start his own advertising-free film review service. But the little evidence we have suggests a different story, one far more amicable. Harrison went to great lengths in his first newsletter to thank Johnston for "his unfailing courtesy and generous support . . . rendering pleasant a connection that will always be cherished."[52] Harrison also used *Motion Picture News* to promote his new venture, placing advertisements throughout the summer of 1919. Johnston, for his part, gave Harrison the same courtesy he gave to other advertisers; he even ran a puff piece about his former employee entitled "Harrison Starts Well on Review Project."[53] So why did Harrison leave *Motion Picture News?* The most likely explanation involves some combination of desires—to make more money, gain greater recognition, exercise more autonomy, and fill a need within the exhibition community.

The length, style, and point of view of Harrison's reviews remained quite consistent as he transitioned from *Motion Picture News* to his own newsletter. But the context surrounding the reviews changed a great deal. Harrison added an editorial page that gave him a platform to address industry developments beyond the evaluation of specific films. Harrison's editorials, by and large, can be distilled into a three-part structure. First, identify a problem facing exhibitors: a lack of good pictures, rising rental prices, new censorship policies, or even dishonest exchangemen who rip up their contracts. Second, express outrage and lay the blame of the problem squarely at the feet of producers and distributors. And, third, propose greater exhibitor organization as the solution to the problem.[54] In the case of censorship, for example, Harrison blamed producers, some of whom he called out by name (William Fox, Ivan Abramson, and Lewis Selznick), for creating the "vile sort" of pictures that invited the attention of reformers, who had recently achieved a huge victory in the federal prohibition of alcohol sales. "But you will never succeed in altering this condition unless you organize," wrote Harrison.[55]

As a small-business owner, Harrison faced two practical challenges from which Johnston had sheltered him at *Motion Picture News*. First, and most obviously, he had to persuade exhibitors who only paid $3.00 per year for *Moving Picture World* or *Motion Picture News* that his service was sufficiently valuable for them to spend an extra $10.00 per year. Second, he needed to maintain the same level of access to advance screenings of new films that he had previously enjoyed while working for an editor who maintained excellent relationships with most of the industry's key players. The closer he came to solving the first challenge, the more the second one grew as a problem.

These challenges, developments, and conflicts played out in Harrison's editorials, which addressed readers as part of a community, one united with him in a common set of interests. Harrison liked to quote letters and cables from exhibitors to show how a subscription more than paid for itself. In the typical letter, an exhibitor explains that he was getting ready to book some film for a particular price; then he reads the latest issue of *Harrison's Reports* and realizes that either the film was dreadful or that he was on the brink of overpaying. He thanks Harrison for helping him avoid this costly mistake.[56]

But the exhibitor testimonials intended to justify the cost of subscribing to *Harrison's Reports* also demonstrated why several producer-distributors were keen to keep P. S. Harrison away from reviewing their films. Harrison was bad for their bottom lines. At various points in 1920 and 1921, Metro, Associated Producers, and Vitagraph all banned Harrison from attending their preview screenings.[57] An outraged Harrison called on his community of exhibitor readers to write letters to the companies and demand they welcome him into the screenings. "Write the letter at once. Let the blow come sledge-hammer like," implored Harrison, who encouraged exhibitors to tell Metro that they were prepared to boycott booking any of the company's new pictures until he was allowed to review them in advance alongside other members of the press.[58] In all of these cases, Harrison's strategy of having his readers apply pressure to the distributors was successful. The distributors caved and, begrudgingly, began inviting Harrison to press screenings.[59] Harrison thanked his community of readers for their "loyal support." He was especially touched that the Illinois exhibitors passed a resolution at their convention championing his cause.[60] Within two years of starting his paper, Harrison had found a way not simply to bring together a community of exhibitors but to harness and direct their anger toward objectives that he felt served both his paper and readers well.

Behind the scenes, however, Harrison's relationship with his exhibitor readers was becoming more conflicted than the vision of community that he publicly projected. In a remarkable two-page editorial entitled "Is the Game Worth the Struggle?," Harrison directed his anger and frustration toward the exhibitor. "Your interests are at stake. Your very existence is threatened," he wrote in April 1921. "You are slowly but surely being forced out of business, by the big interests on the one hand, and by the self-styled reformers on the other. And who is to blame? Yourselves alone! For you will not take effective measures to stave off the impending catastrophe." Harrison's angry editorial grew increasingly desperate as he told exhibitors about his own frustrating experience working with them:

> Having frequently rejected all overtures that might in any way hinder me from loyally serving their interests, I placed my faith entirely upon their common sense. I even refrained from accepting film advertising to cover the cost of publication, so as to preserve absolute independence.
>
> But what has been the response?
>
> Nothing less than a disappointment! For near the end of a two-year faithful service, I find myself face to face with the same problems as do the few self-sacrificing workers in the [exhibitor] organization—lack of appreciation and ingratitude. So after the [*sic*] studying the situation over I have come to the conclusion that the exhibitor himself is responsible for whatever may befall him—he is worthy of his fate.

Let each exhibitor judge his own conscience and judge if this is not the unvarnished, though bitter, truth! Who is responsible for the exacting conditions imposed by producer-distributors? Deposits, C.O.D.'s, full payment in advance, F.I.L.M. Clubs, and other such impositions have been due to the unwillingness, or at least to the neglect, of the main body of exhibitors to live up to obligations of business ethics. If pictures are booked [but] are not played, or paid for; if bills are not met at their maturity, and responses to courteous letters are not sent giving a reason for the delay, it is only natural that the creditors should take their measures to protect their interests; and as these measures are applied to all indiscriminately, the good exhibitors are thus made to suffer along with the bad ones.

Take my own case for example: I have on my books today thousands of dollars due on ordered subscriptions and renewals. Some of these exhibitor-debtors have been sent as high as six bills and three courteous letters to remind them that their subscriptions have been long past due; but in the majority of cases no reply has come forth. . . .

Is the yearly subscription too much? In order to put out these REPORTS I work no less than twelve hours out of each twenty-four, seven days a week. I have no Sundays, no Holidays. I work just as hard (harder in fact), as I would for an individual. And my exclusive services could not be acquired for less than ten thousand dollars a year. Is ten dollars for this amount of work too much? If I save an exhibitor from booking a harmful, or worthless picture even once a year, is it not worth the trivial sum this Service costs?

It often looks to me that honesty pays the poorest dividends, indeed. My experience in this work has been extremely disappointing.[61]

Harrison's editorial was a rare expression of personal anguish. He harnessed the rage he usually reserved for producers, distributors, and racy pictures and poured it out upon his core constituency. Rather than uniting the exhibitors together as a community through shared victimhood, he bound together exhibitors as the dupes responsible for their own poor state of affairs.

Across the next several issues, Harrison indicated that he was pleased with the editorial's reception. More exhibitors paid him the money they had promised. And they encouraged other exhibitors they knew to become new subscribers and pay their bills promptly. He reprinted a handful of the letters he received, including one from an exhibitor who fully accepted the flogging he had endured. "You are *absolutely right*. We are digging our own graves. . . . For heavens sake, Harrison, don't give up!"[62] Perhaps encouraged by the outpouring of support, Harrison continued to push forward and turned his editorial cannons back on more familiar targets, the producers and distributors.

In the coming years, Harrison's enemies would give him a nickname: "Pete the Poisoner" or "Poison Pete Harrison." Harrison's reviews could poison the independent exhibitor market for any picture that he panned. And his editorials that denounced the industry's production and distribution practices could be repurposed by moral reformers and legislators, amplifying Harrison's voice beyond the community of exhibitors. From Harrison's perspective, however, it was the major producer-distributors that were doing the poisoning. Hollywood studios wanted exhibitors "to keep on buying blindly this poisonous product without a chance to protect your patrons from it."[63] Harrison was not a poisoner. He saw himself as a toxicologist and watchdog—monitoring the film industry's goods and services, branding the skull and crossbones onto dangerous merchandise, and ringing alarm bells for the good of his public's health.

Over time, Harrison answered the question he had posed in his soul-searching editorial tirade against exhibitors who didn't pay for their subscriptions. He clearly found that the game was worth the struggle. He reviewed more than fifteen thousand more movies in *Harrison's Reports*, carrying on for another forty-one years. He neither accepted advertising nor pulled his punches up through his final issue on September 1, 1962.[64] He refused to quit, and his readers loved him for it.

Exhibitors Herald

Of all the regional trade papers launched between the mid-1910s and early 1920s, none proved more consequential to the American film industry than *Exhibitors Herald*. But when the paper debuted in the summer of 1915, there was little distinctive or noteworthy about it. Originally titled *Exhibitors Film Exchange*, the paper promoted itself to "exhibitors in the states of Illinois, Indiana, Michigan, Wisconsin, and other states dependent on Chicago exchanges for film service."[65] *Exhibitors Film Exchange*'s founding president and editor, James T. Igoe, was primarily self-interested in what the trade paper meant for his core business: printing. Igoe was one-half of Chicago's Cahill-Igoe Company, and he recognized that a trade paper oriented toward the growing film business would be an asset for his press.[66] But after only one month, Igoe handed off the official editorial duties. *Exhibitors Film Exchange*'s fifth issue listed its new editor on the masthead: Martin J. Quigley.[67] It was a quiet introduction to a figure who would go on to leave an enormous imprint on the industry.

When Quigley took the helm of *Exhibitors Film Exchange* in August 1915, he was a newcomer to both the film industry and the city of Chicago. He had grown up in Cleveland, Ohio, and pursued his education across a series of Catholic institutions: first, Niagara University in New York State, then Catholic University in Washington, DC, and finally at Dunwoodie Seminary in New York City. Quigley nearly joined the priesthood, according to his son, but a romantic relationship with his future wife dissuaded him from taking the cloth.[68] Although Quigley did not become a priest, he came away from his training with a deep grasp for how Catholic institutions operated. His ability to speak the language of the church and understand what moved its levers of power became assets for the rest of his career.

In 1910, Quigley took a job at a newspaper in Fremont, Ohio, before moving to work for newspapers in Detroit and, shortly thereafter, in Chicago.[69] He took over editing *Exhibitors Film Exchange* as he was in the process of learning about the motion picture industry and, more simply, about the film medium itself. During his first several months of penning the paper's editorial column, Quigley kept his remarks very generic, rarely discussing individual players within the film industry by name. Even after Quigley changed the paper's name to *Exhibitors Herald* in November 1915, his editorial columns remained detached from any analysis of the industry's inner workings. Instead, he chose, for example, to reflect on why "film play" would be a more dignified name for the medium than "movies."[70] In many ways, Quigley was undergoing the same learning curve that William A. Johnston had completed just two years earlier when he founded *Exhibitors' Times*.

Among the many generic discussions in his columns, however, we can see the emergence of two ideas that would play prominent roles in Quigley's later career. The first was the importance of industry self-regulation and coordination to avoid censorship policies.[71] In making these arguments, Quigley was largely echoing the voices of W. Stephen Bush, William A. Johnston, and, later, P. S. Harrison. Unlike those other figures, however, Quigley would ultimately play a pivotal role in the conception and implementation of Hollywood's self-censorship policy, the Production Code. The second idea—and far more important to the editorial voice and reputation that Quigley cultivated during the late-1910s and 1920s—was the need to deal fairly in business. In only his second month helming the paper, Quigley gently scolded exhibitors who canceled their bookings after entering into contracts and, as a result, drove up rental prices and reduced the film supply for other exhibitors. He asked exhibitors "to be mindful of the golden rule in its business application and deal with exchanges in the manner they would expect to be dealt with."[72] Quigley's criticisms grew more forceful over the coming years, but he always couched them as coming from a forward-thinking and impartial position, designed to improve the industry overall.

If there was one person who helped Quigley find his voice and dig deeper into analyzing the industry's intricacies, it was Lee A. Ochs. In 1916 and throughout 1917, Quigley came to view the president of the Motion Picture Exhibitors League of America (MPELA) and founder of *Exhibitor's Trade Review* as the embodiment of corruption and a scourge to the film industry. To Quigley, Ochs represented the antithesis of fair dealing—an exhibitor who abused his leadership position for his own personal gain and, in the process, made conditions worse for the rest of the nation's exhibitors. "Every exhibitor who supports Mr. Ochs' paper must realize that he is working for the personal gain of some of the league's officers and against the best interests of the league," warned Quigley in a December 2, 1916, editorial, more than a full month before *Exhibitor's Trade Review* libeled William A. Johnston and attempted to extort Universal for advertising revenue.[73] In contrast to Ochs, who saw elected office as a platform to earn more money through his theater business and new trade paper, Quigley presented himself as an independent straight shooter.

The growing tension between the two men exploded in the summer of 1917 when Ochs visited Chicago, Quigley's home turf, for the MPELA convention.[74] After Ochs won reelection to the MPELA's highest office through dubious means, Quigley accused him of rigging the election and praised the exhibitors who quit the MPELA in protest: "The attempt of Mr. Ochs to dominate the convention exclusively for his own interests resulted in the disruption of the Motion Picture Exhibitors League and Mr. Ochs is now a king without a country," he wrote.[75] Quigley lamented that 125 exhibitors had made the journey to Chicago for the convention, "the majority of them expecting to learn something that would assist in bettering their business, and partaking in constructive work for the general advancement of the industry."[76] Exhibitors were denied these services by the MPELA in its summer convention. As the year went on, Quigley reminded exhibitors continually that they would find the honesty, independence, leadership, and community they were looking for in the pages of *Exhibitors Herald*. And while his paper paid particular attention to Chicago and other midwestern markets, Quigley's editorials increasingly spoke to an intended audience of producers, distributors, and exhibitors dispersed across the country.

Exhibitors Herald's acquisition of *Motography* in July 1918 cemented Quigley's leap beyond the status of regional trade paper editor. As we saw in chapter 2, the Chicago-based *Motography* occupied an unusual position among the national trade papers. The name it proposed for the movies—"motography"—had never achieved any staying power, nor had the trade paper's sense of identity. *Motography* changed its format with more frequency than the era's fashions, going from a weekly, to a monthly, to a semimonthly, and finally back to a weekly.[77] Its intended audience had swerved, too, from being a trade paper for exhibitors to more of a general interest film magazine, and back to being exhibitor-oriented, with its popular section "What the Picture Did for Me," established in October 1916. One thread of continuity across all of these iterations was a shortage of advertising revenue. Whereas *Moving Picture World* and *Motion Picture News* were selling sixty to eighty pages of advertising in most issues they published in the late 1910s, *Motography* seldom sold more than a few pages of ads.[78] In an apparent cost-cutting move in April 1918, *Motography* stopped publishing any film reviews other than those penned by theater managers for "What the Picture Did for Me."[79] Two months later, Quigley bought out his Chicago rival and, in July 1918, published the first issue of *Exhibitors Herald and Motography* (the latter part of the title was dropped after a year). It's unclear how much Quigley paid for the publication, but my best guess is that *Motography*'s liabilities had come to far exceed its assets. A willingness to take on debt was likely more important to closing the deal than presenting a large cash offer.

What Quigley gained from the acquisition, beyond a drawer full of promissory notes, were subscriptions and stature. *Motography* had been poor in advertising yet rich in circulation. In 1917 and 1918, *Motography* had self-reported a circulation of 12,500. Even if we accept that this number was probably an exaggeration (no audit was performed to test its veracity), there is no doubt that *Motography*'s subscription base was triple (or more) the circulation of *Exhibitors Herald*. Just as important, those subscribers resided in states beyond simply Illinois, Indiana, Michigan, Wisconsin, and Ohio. Quigley had bought himself a national circulation, and, unlike *Motography*'s editors, he proved capable at translating those subscriptions into ad dollars.

Whereas *Motography* had perceived its Chicago location as a weakness in the competition for national advertising, *Exhibitors Herald* sought to turn it into a strength. "The geographic advantage of publishing in Chicago enables *Exhibitors Herald and Motography* to reach nearly half of the exhibitors of the United States the day following publication," wrote Quigley shortly after acquiring *Motography*.[80] Quigley's son has suggested that his father found other ways to capitalize on his location in one of the nation's largest railroad hubs. Because businessmen generally changed trains in Chicago and experienced long layovers during cross-country trips, "it was relatively easy to arrange a lunch date or other time for interviewing a traveling executive." His son has also described how being based out-of-town was "an advantage in making appointments with company heads and advertising chiefs on his frequent trips to New York. Writing or wiring from Chicago in advance, Quigley found the executives were accommodating to the traveler."[81] The clarity of these geographic divisions and the formality of appointment-making also suited Quigley's preferred style of doing business. He simultaneously valued being closely connected while maintaining clear boundaries.

Beyond the practical considerations of being located in Chicago, Quigley embraced the symbolic value of his midwestern location in his appeal to independent exhibitors. Chicago was "the heart of America."[82] And *Exhibitors Herald* was "The Independent Film Trade Paper" at least in part because it was *not* published in New York City—a hub of greedy film distributors, corrupt exhibitor organization leaders, and smarmy trade paper editors. New York City was out of touch with average American exhibitors, and, when it got in touch, it seemed like it was usually to fleece them. Even the entertainment industry's greatest achievements in New York, like the magnificent Capitol Theatre that opened in 1919 just north of Times Square, inadvertently contributed to the sense of out-of-touchness. The fifty-three-hundred-seat Capitol was located a world away from the concerns of midwestern rural exhibitors, many of whom operated in towns with entire populations that were smaller than that single theater's capacity.[83]

Quigley launched *Exhibitors Herald*'s most important campaign yet to fulfill "its mission as the Independent Trade Paper" during the summer of 1920 when he attacked Paramount's Adolph Zukor for his company's incursions into theater ownership. Across three consecutive issues, Quigley framed the matter at hand in the most dramatic ways possible, outlining Zukor's plans "to shackle the independent exhibitor and producer in the grip of monopoly, reducing them to abject

FIGURE 18. "Stop!," *Exhibitors Herald,* June 12, 1920, 32. https://lantern.mediahist.org/catalog/exhibitorsherald10exhi_0_1072.

commercial slavery or driving them from the business which is now their means of livelihood."[84] Beyond his forceful written critiques, Quigley included political cartoons (which were unusual for the paper) illustrating, for example, the hand of Famous Players–Lasky, adorned in "Wall Street" cufflinks, ripping away an independent exhibitor from his theater (fig. 18). The response of exhibitors was electric.

Quigley had validated their fears and expressed their anger. The Motion Picture Theatre Owners of America passed a resolution at its Cleveland convention that summer, declaring that it "hereby officially express[es] its sincere appreciation to Mr. Quigley for what it justly believes to be the most significant and beneficial act which any trade journal publisher ever has performed in defending the independence of [exhibitors]."[85] A Nebraska theater owner wrote to Quigley, saying that America's independent exhibitors "owe you our moral support and encouragement, that your influence in the cause of justice and fairness may be broadened."[86] Quigley relished receiving these endorsements from the exhibitor community, and he proudly reprinted them in an effort to distinguish his trade paper from others in the field. In the same issue of *Exhibitors Herald* that reprinted the testimonials, Quigley called out the editors of *Motion Picture News, Moving Picture World*, and *Exhibitor's Trade Review* by name, asking them, "IN THE EXHBITORS' FIGHT FOR INDEPENCE—WHERE DO YOU STAND?"[87] The takeaway was clear: Quigley was the only trade paper editor willing to take on Zukor's Paramount, and the nation's independent exhibitors should pledge their loyalty, trust, and subscription dollars to *Exhibitors Herald*.

By the time in 1920 that regional trade papers were springing up in nearly every city with a film row, *Exhibitors Herald* had catapulted itself out of their ranks and become one of the nation's four major weekly trade papers for the film industry. Quigley no longer viewed his competitors as *Michigan Film Review* and *Amusements*; instead, they were *Motion Picture News, Moving Picture World*, and *Exhibitor's Trade Review*. Meanwhile, William A. Johnston refused to acknowledge *Exhibitors Herald* as anything more than a "regional." In April 1921, an incensed Quigley declared that "EXHIBITORS HERALD is The One Really NATIONAL Publication of The Motion Picture Industry. It is Nationwide—East, West, North and South—in CIRCULATION, EDITORIAL VISION, INFLUENCE."[88] He backed up his claim with circulation data, compiled by an unnamed theater canvasser, that showed that if one excluded New York City, then twice as many exhibitors in the state of New York subscribed to *Exhibitors Herald* (457) than to *Motion Picture News* (218), *Moving Picture World* (162), *Exhibitor's Trade Review* (161), or *Wid's* (58).[89] This "comprehensive and definitive data" fit perfectly within the perception that Quigley wanted to craft, the story he wanted to tell. Quigley sought to flip the script: *News, World*, and *Trade Review* were the true regionals since they focused narrowly on the concerns relevant to the industry factions based in Manhattan and Brooklyn. Meanwhile, *Exhibitors Herald* was the true national trade paper, a fact proven by the exhibitors in Buffalo, Rochester, and the rest of New York State who overwhelmingly preferred it over the competition.

Unfortunately for Quigley, his claims about circulation proved to be demonstrably false. He had also made a misstep—picking a fight on quantitative grounds against a trade paper editor who excelled at the art of marshaling data. William A. Johnston went on the counterattack, dismissing the validity of the *Herald's* numbers and pressing Quigley to adopt the professional standards of the field and employ the Audit Bureau of Circulations (ABC).[90] When *Exhibitors Herald* undertook its first ABC audit in 1923, the results showed that it had 5,991 mail subscribers—considerably fewer than *Motion Pictures News'* 9,234 subscribers and *Moving Picture World's* 8,102 subscribers in 1921, the year that Quigley had boasted about his superior circulation. *World* and *News* both had 1,193 subscribers in the state of New York, compared to *Herald's* 540.[91] Even if we accept that a large number of *News* and *World* subscribers were based in New York City, it is nearly impossible for Quigley's math to add up. Quigley would have been on firmer ground to make the claim that his paper had the most subscribers in the Midwest. Because the ABC tracked subscriptions by region, we can go back to the historic reports—now on microfilm—and see that the twelve midwestern and plains states (Ohio, Indiana, Illinois, Michigan, Wisconsin, Minnesota, Iowa, Missouri, North Dakota, South Dakota, Nebraska, and Kansas) accounted for 3,306 of *Exhibitors Herald's* subscriptions, roughly 55 percent of its paid circulation. The ABC report suggests that *Exhibitors Herald*, in the early 1920s, occupied a middle ground between being a super-regional and a national trade paper comparable in reach to *Moving Picture World* and *Motion Picture News*.

The same year as its underwhelming circulation audit, however, *Exhibitors Herald* flexed the loyalty, passion, and influence of its readers. The idea for the "Herald Only" Club first emerged from Ohio exhibitor George Rea, who in May 1923 complained that exhibitors were reporting on movies in a variety of trade papers instead of exclusively in *Exhibitors Herald*. Rea emphatically declared: "I, for one, am going to report my pictures exclusively to the *Herald's* 'What the Picture Did for Me' department and nowhere else. Let's keep our reports where we know they'll be taken care of by a paper that knows how and isn't afraid."[92] Quigley coined the term "'Herald Only' Club" and, week by week, tracked the movement's growth (see fig. 19). Although the idea had originally formulated around exclusively *writing* to *Exhibitors Herald*, the club was soon framed as being equally about exclusively *reading* the *Herald*. "It is the only paper I take now and I find it covers everything," wrote a small-town Oklahoma exhibitor in one of many such testimonials published in regard to the "Herald Only" Club.[93]

Alongside such testimonials, the growing roster of "Herald Only" Club members was frequently published. The December 8, 1923, issue of *Exhibitors Herald* listed seventy-seven club members. They came from thirty different states, and three managed theaters in Canada.[94] It is worth noting, however, that almost exactly half the members (thirty-eight of seventy-seven) managed theaters in one of six midwestern states: Illinois, Indiana, Iowa, Michigan, Nebraska, and Ohio.[95] Four "Herald Only" members came from the state of New York, but their theaters were all located in small towns more than one hundred miles away from the island of Manhattan. These details suggest that even as *Exhibitors Herald* expanded its distribution beyond the Chicago exchange region, its core constituency of exhibitor readers remained centered in the Midwest, especially in small towns. In her

FIGURE 19. Portraits of the "Herald Only" Club's most prolific correspondents, including Idaho exhibitor Philip Rand (lower right), who penned hundreds of "What the Picture Did for Me" reviews. *Source: Exhibitors Herald,* "'Herald Only' Club Album," Oct. 6, 1923, 73, https://lantern.mediahist.org/catalog/exhibitorsherald17exhi_0181.

book chapter, "'What the Picture Did for Me': Small-Town Exhibitors' Strategies for Surviving the Great Depression," film historian Kathryn Fuller-Seeley argues that "the overwhelming majority of the column's contributors were independent theater owners who operated 200- to 500-seat houses in towns of 5,000 or fewer people. Most of these small-town exhibitors were in the Midwest, Plains, and Mountain states."[96] An examination of the "Herald Only" Club list reveals that the demographic trends that Fuller-Seeley identifies for mid-1930s "What the Picture Did for Me" contributors also holds true for the early to mid-1920s.

Philip Rand owned the Rex Theater in Salmon, Idaho, a rural town with a population of 1,311 in 1920. Rand was also an obsessive reviewer of films. His name appears on 531 pages of *Exhibitors Herald* scanned by the Media History Digital Library (MHDL), nearly 70 percent more than the next most prolific "Herald Only" Club member.[97] True to his word, Rand confined his reviews to the *Herald's* "What the Picture Did for Me" section and did not publish in competing trade papers. In late 1923, Rand's writing earned him a trip to Los Angeles, which he reported on in the Christmas issue of *Exhibitors Herald*. When Rand visited the Metro set, he had his photo taken with actress Viola Dana, who appears dressed as a nun as Rand smiles ear to ear and holds an issue of *Exhibitors Herald*. Rand began the article by gently mocking both himself and "Follywood," but he concluded on an earnest note: "To say that I am surprised is to put it mildly. I am overwhelmed with the high moral tone of the people, their unfailing kindness and the seriousness of their work. I will venture an opinion that no other industry in America has as fine a lot of men and women as the picture industry at Hollywood."[98] The box-office revenue that Rand's rural theater generated for the Hollywood studios was completely insignificant to their bottom lines. Rand's writing, however, was meaningful to thousands of exhibitors who read *Exhibitors Herald* and rented films. A Hollywood publicist seems to have recognized this and arranged a tour for him accordingly.

Exhibitors Herald had facilitated the growth of a virtual community of exhibitors. It was an exhibitor community connected through shared circumstances rather than by the particular exchanges they used or the state they lived in. And it was a community that had its own star system. For the loyal readers of and contributors to the "What the Picture Did for Me" department, an endorsement from Philip Rand meant more than one from Roxy. And, within this community, Martin J. Quigley was a far more trusted and respected figure than William A. Johnston.

Yet Quigley still envied Johnston. He wanted the prominence among industry leaders and the advertising revenue that Johnston enjoyed. In the same May 26, 1923, issue in which the idea for the "Herald Only" Club was first floated, Quigley launched a new section, titled *Better Theatres*, that was more representative of the path that he would take over the next decade in his quest to overtake Johnston. The structure *of Better Theatres* essentially mimicked that of *Motion Picture*

News' Accessory News (which, as noted in chapter 1, had itself imitated the *Store Equipment* section of the *Dry Goods Economist*). These sections were magnets for equipment advertisers. They allowed the trade papers to charge a premium to manufacturers who wanted their products to appear in the section that would be most closely read by buyers.

The title that Quigley chose for the new section was telling. By calling the new section *Better Theatres*, he tied it fundamentally to the goals of uplifting and advancing motion picture presentation. Without the continual improvement of exhibition spaces, he warned, "there certainly must come a disastrous halt in the progress of the motion picture and the film business."[99] But it must have seemed unrealistic, even then, that the passionate small-town theater owners of the "Herald Only" Club could afford the fancy screens, seats, and aisle lights advertised in the pages of *Better Theatres*. And club members based in Elgin, Nebraska; Tripoli, Wisconsin; and other small farming communities would have never had the means to put to use the architectural schematics that *Better Theatres* shared and celebrated. Ironically, just as small-town exhibitors were pledging allegiance to the *Herald*, the *Herald* was subscribing to a philosophy that would serve it well yet leave behind many of those same small-town exhibitors during the transition to sound and the Great Depression. Making the film industry better and more profitable meant accepting that the theaters without the money to improve and upgrade would go out of business. This disconnect between *Exhibitors Herald* and its customer base would ultimately spill into conflict and the entry of new competing papers in the years ahead.

CONCLUSION

"A regional is the independent exhibitor's pal," remarked P. S. Harrison. "He reads it to learn about his fellow exhibitors and their problems."[100] Harrison made this observation in the early 1930s, drawing on nearly fifteen years of reading, competing against, and coexisting alongside regional publications such as *Reel Journal* and *Amusements*. Like Harrison's own *Reports*, regionals sought to build and maintain communities among industry participants. Generally, the community-building work was cordial and constructive, seeking to ease and minimize tensions between distributor and exhibitor, between big exhibitor and little exhibitor. Yet this was not always the case; Ray Lewis and P. S. Harrison both, in their own ways, developed their communities through attacking opponents, policing boundaries, and airing grievances rather than attempts at achieving harmony across the industry. Meanwhile, Martin J. Quigley moved between these approaches of inclusion and exclusion, as the industry itself shifted beneath his feet.

The papers surveyed in this chapter began as alternatives to the leading national exhibitor trade papers. By the mid-1930s, however, they would themselves become the leading national trade papers. Martin J. Quigley, Ben Shlyen, Ray Lewis,

P. S. Harrison, and *The Exhibitor*'s Jay Emanuel (who eventually replaced David Barrist) would all have publishing careers that far outlasted William A. Johnston, W. Stephen Bush, and Merritt Crawford. As the large New York trade papers fought with one another for dominance, their ultimate successors were trying out new strategies and building up reader loyalty in exchange cities across North America.

Innovations in trade paper publishing were also taking place in the capital of film production. The next chapter looks at the explosive growth of film industry trade papers in Los Angeles and the roles they played in the creation of 1920s Hollywood culture.

Coastlander Reading

*The Cultures and Trade Papers
of 1920s Los Angeles*

Franchon Royer, the editor of Los Angeles's first consistently published film industry trade paper, accomplished some of her best reporting at her favorite restaurant. It was April 1921, and she was working on an editorial addressing "Pictures and the Girl Question."[1] The death of actress Virginia Rappe and the subsequent scandal centering on Fatty Arbuckle and Hollywood's immorality that followed were still a few months away. But the film production community had already been mulling over what Hollywood's external image meant in light of the town's internal social, gender, and labor dynamics.[2]

Royer asked her waitress, "How long have you resided in Los Angeles?"

"Oh, about a year, I guess," said the waitress. "Came from Wichita. I thought I'd get into the pictures, but even a pretty blonde ain't got a show. She's lucky if she gets on extra, and you hafta eat."

In her *Camera!* column, Royer then speculated about how the waitress felt about this failure. Was she suffering under the weight of crushed hopes, or "had it merely meant a sporting chance taken, an adventure over?"

"The girls who wait on us over counters, wires, and tables are those who having learned about the law of averages are making the best of it," Royer wrote. While "some impressionable souls" had been led to disillusionment, other women had moved West to escape repressive, dysfunctional, or abusive family situations. No, they had not become the next Mary Pickford. But in many cases, waiting tables in Los Angeles brought far more joy and freedom than the lives they'd known before in Wichita or Grand Rapids.

Franchon Royer surely identified with the waitress. She had grown up in Iowa, and her parents divorced when she was six. In 1918, at the age of sixteen, Royer moved to Los Angeles, briefly studying journalism at the University of Southern

California before deciding to pursue a career as an actress. As film historian Lisle Foote has documented, Royer found unsteady work as an extra and struggled to land roles.[3] Over the next three years, Royer would stop acting, marry *Camera!*'s business manager, and take over the editorial duties of the paper.

All of these twists and turns led Royer to the moment at hand, interviewing the waitress at her favorite restaurant. Then again, she may have invented the whole episode from her typewriter for the purpose of generating a good column. Either way, the column offered a distinctive perspective on Hollywood culture in the early 1920s. Royer insisted on a middle ground between the discourses of Hollywood as a den of sin and as the land of milk and honey. This was *Camera!* at its best—reminding us of the unexpected ways in which human lives become intertwined and transformed within an industry.

This chapter maps out the overall landscape of 1920s Hollywood and the film industry trade papers that sprang up to serve it. Like the previous chapter on specialty exhibitor papers, I survey a range of publications but look especially closely at three publications that played significant roles within the evolving Hollywood industry. *Camera!, Film Mercury*, and *Film Spectator* all spoke to Los Angeles–based communities of creative workers, as well as many readers who wanted to break in. Both on the levels of physical geography and discursive position, the creative communities in Los Angeles were placed at a distance from the communities of New York distribution personnel, independent theater owners, and other industry participants. LA movie people, especially in the late teens and early 1920s, were also a different breed from the nonshow people who had arrived in the Southland years before them and belonged to a different social milieu.[4]

In their address to a distinctive creative community, the Los Angeles papers borrowed from the conventions and structures of New York–based vaudeville papers. One publication, *Inside Facts of Stage and Screen*, modeled itself after *Variety* so closely that it read like a Pacific Coast knockoff of Sime's brand. Meanwhile, *Variety* used the 1920s to pivot from being primarily a vaudeville publication to one focused on motion pictures and radio. These changes came in response to a decline of the market for "straight vaudeville" (meaning vaudeville not staged alongside motion picture presentations). The final section of this chapter explores *Variety*'s transformation in depth. *Variety*'s 1923 acquisition of *New York Clipper* and the 1925 opening of an LA office, headed by a former *Clipper* writer, were especially important for the pivot. But the paper's reputation for its independence, scorekeeping, and distinctive use of language proved to be the most significant strengths of all.

The migration of American motion picture production to Southern California and the construction of permanent studio facilities in and around Los Angeles was largely a movement of the 1910s. But the advent of "Hollywood" as a culture and community—detached from the rest of society within its own "colony" and associated with movies, money, sex, sun, and busloads of aspiring actresses—only truly took form during the 1920s. As film historians have shown, newspapers and fan magazines both played important roles in disseminating the ideas and imagery of what constituted Hollywood. What has received less attention—and occupies this chapter's central focus—is how the industry's Los Angeles trade papers participated in the ways in which movie workers conceived of themselves as belonging to and participating in this community.

EARLY DISPATCHES FROM THE COAST
AND THE EMERGENCE OF CAMERA!

Years before trade papers began emerging on Wilshire, Sunset, and Hollywood Boulevards, *Moving Picture World* and *Motion Picture News* were chronicling Southern California's growing importance for the film industry. *Moving Picture World* and *Motion Picture News* both published news items that they received from correspondents on the Coast. And all the trade papers took note and devoted considerable ink in 1915 when Carl Laemmle opened Universal City in the San Fernando Valley. By the end of that year, *World* and *News* both had Los Angeles offices staffed by LA editors.

In early 1916, *Motion Picture News'* William A. Johnston attempted to harness the advertising potential of the Coast by publishing the first edition of the *Motion Picture Studio Directory*—a special section of *Motion Picture News* that primarily contained information and promotional advertisements for LA actors and production personnel.[5] By the second edition in October 1916, the *Studio Directory* had grown to "over two thousand biographies and many display pages giving correct details and interesting facts about picture people."[6] Johnston initially imagined that his existing readership of exhibitors would be the target audience for the *Studio Directory*. "Exhibitors will find this volume . . . a right hand, permanent guide in preparing their copy for house programs, newspapers and for all theatre publicity," wrote Johnston.[7] By the third edition of the *Directory* in April 1917, though, Johnson emphasized a different constituency—casting directors. "The casting director has been borne constantly in mind in the make-up of these pages," wrote Johnston, who went on to call the *Directory* "an invaluable aid to every Casting Director."[8] The extent to which any Hollywood casting director ever looked at the *Studio Directory* is unknown. But Johnston clearly persuaded a sufficient number of actors that it was worth taking the chance that it might help them achieve their dreams. *Studio Directory* thrived in an industry environment built on aspirations and insecurities, selling advertising space to actors, writers, and other creative workers keen to keep their names and faces in front of an imagined audience of producers and casting directors who flipped through the book.

Although *Motion Picture News* found ways to sell large volumes of ads to Hollywood workers, it did so only on a semiannual basis with the *Studio Directory*. *Camera!*, founded in 1918, earned the distinction of becoming the film industry's first weekly trade paper to consistently publish from Los Angeles. It was a

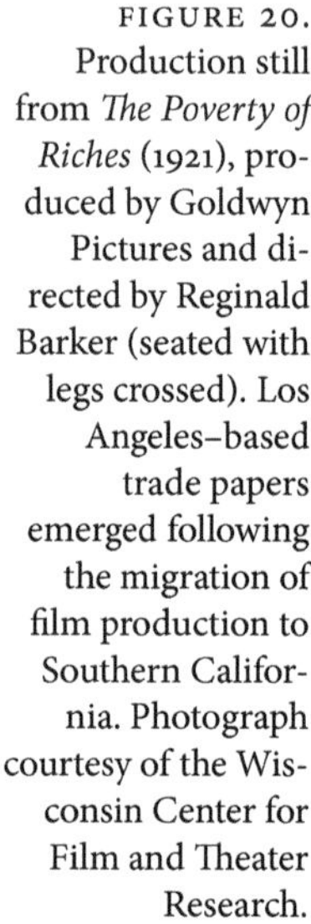

FIGURE 20. Production still from *The Poverty of Riches* (1921), produced by Goldwyn Pictures and directed by Reginald Barker (seated with legs crossed). Los Angeles–based trade papers emerged following the migration of film production to Southern California. Photograph courtesy of the Wisconsin Center for Film and Theater Research.

proof-of-concept that a sufficient advertising base could sustain such a paper. *Camera!* modeled itself on the entertainment industry trade publications published in New York City. The *New York Clipper, New York Dramatic Mirror, Morning Telegraph,* and *Variety* all covered the intertwined industries of legitimate theater, vaudeville, and motion pictures (the Cincinnati-based *Billboard* was also an active participant in these markets). As we have seen in previous chapters, the cost of producing these papers far exceeded the revenue generated through subscriptions. Advertising revenue was essential for the trade papers to exist. Yet advertising posed risks. Selling ads could damage a trade paper's perceived independence and integrity. Of particular relevance to *Camera!*, the practice of cultivating actors as both readers and advertisers had proven controversial within vaudeville. In 1917, the White Rats union of vaudeville performers claimed that its members had been strong-armed by theater managers into purchasing ads within *Variety.*[9] Although *Variety* won the resulting FTC case, the episode (detailed in chapter 2) highlighted the coercive pressures that could be placed on performers—the creation of a pay-to-play system.

Camera!'s success in navigating these tricky waters may have stemmed from the fact that its business manager, Raymond Cannon, was also a working actor. He understood the desires of actors seeking to gain notice, shape their perception, and secure employment. In 1919, a year in which Raymond Cannon was consistently listed as *Camera!*'s business manager, he was also credited as an actor in no fewer than five films, including D. W. Griffith's *True Heart Susie* (1919).[10] We can speculate that working simultaneously toward careers in acting and industrial publishing may have been good for business on both fronts. Being on movie sets and interacting with cast and crew members provided opportunities for Cannon to solicit gossip, news items, and advertisements. Meanwhile, *Camera!* elevated Cannon's own status and visibility within the industry. In the age of the silent movie, it is unlikely that any other character actor of his status possessed such a loud voice.

Camera! provided industry news alongside the advertisements that promoted actors, writers, and directors. The "Pulse of the Industry" section tracked active studio productions, and a column titled "Where to Sell Your Scenario?" pointed aspiring screenwriters toward potential buyers (interestingly, this column was discontinued early; perhaps the industry was already moving toward the "no unsolicited submissions" policy that governs contemporary Hollywood).[11] One consistent theme, across both news items and opinion pieces, was the address toward the film colony as a particular community with shared interests. *Camera!* bristled at the ways that Southern California's elite institutions discriminated against the industry (banning movie people from the Wilshire Country Club, for example).[12] Yet the trade paper also insisted that the movie industry was special; it needed to be treated differently than other commercial enterprises when it came to taxation and other select business matters.[13] Most of all, *Camera!*'s editorials opposed all forms of external regulation. The industry community was in the best position to govern itself.[14]

The author of most of these editorials was twenty-year-old Franchon Royer, the wife of Raymond Cannon. Like her spouse, Royer came to the trade paper from acting. Just a year earlier, in 1919, she had taken out an advertisement in *Camera!* promoting herself as "a versatile ingénue."[15] Over the next three years, Royer would indeed prove herself versatile. Her editorials sometimes performed the voice of the stern trade paper "thought leader," a position that Chicago-based publisher Martin Quigley had come to embrace around the same time. But in her best writing, like the story that opened this chapter, Royer drew from her own experiences to contribute a nuanced understanding of the industry that was missing elsewhere.[16]

Camera! took on an even more forceful approach to its role as an industry gatekeeper under the leadership of Ted Taylor and Ruth Wing (who took the helm in May 1922 and, like Cannon and Royer, were married).[17] Although Taylor and Wing played both editorial roles, it was Taylor who primarily addressed the industry community in *Camera!*'s editorial page. As Peter Lester discusses in his detailed article on this period of *Camera!*'s history, Ted Taylor clashed with certain local businesses, especially fly-by-night acting schools, that he saw as preying on aspiring actors and tarnishing the industry's reputation. As Lester notes, "The 'fake' schools represented a 'safe' enemy to antagonize," since they held little power within the industry and modest advertising budgets. When Taylor used his editorial page to criticize the increasingly "factory-like" approach to film production, however, it was a different story. *Camera!*'s majority owner was now Walter J. Reynolds, who had purchased Raymond Cannon's interest in the paper in 1922. Reynolds was the secretary of the Motion Picture Producers Association (MPPA), an LA trade-based organization and a major booster of both the film industry and city of Los Angeles (these two threads of boosterism intersected in the disappointing Motion Picture Exposition of 1923, a project that Reynolds helped to orchestrate). Reynolds pushed Taylor out of *Camera!* and replaced him with more obedient editors who did not bite the hand that fed them.[18] The episode highlighted the importance of editorial ownership over a Hollywood paper if one was to take shots at the major Hollywood studios—a lesson that Tamar Lane and Welford Beaton would soon put into practice.

FILM MERCURY AND THE INDUSTRY THAT MIGHT HAVE BEEN

A number of small, competing trade papers soon joined *Camera!* on the Coast. Most of them attempted to carve out some sort of niche. *Hollywood Filmograph* (established in 1922) spoke to the community of Hollywood actors, and its editor, Harry Burns, supported Actors' Equity's attempt to gain a foothold on the Coast. Harry Tullar, in contrast, focused his address to exhibitor communities. Tullar promoted his reviews of short films as the distinguishing feature of *Tullar's Weekly* (established in 1922). *Wid's Weekly* (established in 1923) also emphasized reviews, alongside the fiction that Hollywood's elite were all devoted readers of the paper. Editor Wid Gunning, who had previously created the New York–based *Wid's Daily* (which became *Film Daily*), took the hard-sell approach in lecturing aspiring actors and screenwriters on why they should buy ads: "Wid has never claimed or expected that everyone will always agree with his opinions. The important thing from the viewpoint of the advertiser is that every important personage in the film industry—executive, director, author, player, technical artists and theater owners—does read carefully what he has to say. It is your job to sell yourself . . . WHAT'S YOUR NAME WORTH?"[19] Like *Camera!* before it, *Wid's Weekly* conceived of Hollywood as a community invested in taste, exclusivity, and self-promotion.

Tamar Lane's *Film Mercury* (established in 1924) shared many of the features of *Camera!* and its theatrical trade paper predecessors. *Film Mercury* included news items about the studios, reviews of new movies, and editorials addressing industry problems. And it was advertisements purchased by aspiring actors—along with ads for the vendors who serviced them, such as drama teachers and plastic surgeons—that made Lane's publication possible. Yet within this familiar framework, Lane pushed *Film Mercury* in a distinctive, innovative direction. The result may be Hollywood's first and last avant-garde trade paper.

One year before creating *Film Mercury*, Lane had published a scathing book of film criticism. Titled *What's Wrong with the Movies?*, Lane's book provided several answers to this central question, with each chapter offering an indictment of a different sector within the industry. But Lane was able to convey his core thesis in a mere seven words: "The photoplay is an art without artists."[20] The potential of a remarkable art form, in Tamar Lane's estimation, was being utterly squandered. In *Film Mercury*, Lane offered weekly updates on this same general theme. He was aided in this mission by his sister, Anabel Lane, who contributed film reviews to *Film Mercury* and pulled no punches when it came to calling out Hollywood's shortcomings.

The Lanes did not arrive on these views within a vacuum. Their taste sensibility combined two critical frameworks of their day: a Mencken-esque cynicism and modernist theories of film art. Because the combination of these critical frameworks tells us something about 1920s Hollywood culture, each of these traditions merits briefly unpacking. In *The Decline of Sentiment: American Film in the 1920s*, Lea Jacobs details how H. L. Mencken and a coterie of other critics in the late 1910s and 1920s established new values for taste culture and the evaluation of literature, film, and art. Mencken's magazine, *American Mercury*, panned sentimental novels and films, dismissing them with the pejorative label "hokum." As these taste assumptions spread among film critics at other publications, they resulted in the critics imagining American audiences as bifurcated between sophisticated urban viewers and small-town moviegoers who clung to old-fashioned conventions. Jacobs notes the strong degree to which *Variety*'s film reviewers in New York City adopted this disdain for hokum.[21] Tamar Lane, however, embraced the sensibility just as vociferously from his office on Hollywood and Vine:

> The general public has a right to demand hokum entertainment if that is the sort of silent drama it prefers—and judging from the films that are flooding the theatres of the country the public is getting its belly full. To say, however, that every film must be made in accordance with the mentalities of the morons and nit-wits that make up most of our theatre audiences is nonsense. . . . It is quite possible for an institution to be both popular entertainment and art. That is the point being overlooked.[22]

As this passage makes clear, Tamar Lane shared Mencken's contempt for most of the American public, who bore considerable responsibility for "what's wrong with the movies." And Lane's decision to title his magazine *Film Mercury* may have been a nod to Mencken. But what separated the two writers, at least in the way Lane saw it, were their theories about the potential of film as an art form. Mencken primarily concerned himself with writing and language. From *Film Mercury*'s perspective, Mencken had only "contempt for the lowly movie" and "disdain for most of those connected with it."[23] Lane, on the other hand, believed that cinema was "the greatest instrument for stimulating emotion yet born." Few truly great movies had been produced, in Lane's estimation, but there were many films with "scenes which expressed beauty, mood, and imagination," and those scenes held the promise for the brilliant artworks that would one day be made.[24]

Film Mercury participated in a global theorizing of film as a medium and art. Tamar Lane considered his critical peers to be not the other ink-stained trade paper editors in Los Angeles and New York but a group of avant-gardists publishing their ideas of cinema from Europe. In 1928, Tamar Lane promoted his trade paper within the pages of *Close Up*, a film journal that today is far better remembered than *Film Mercury*. An English-language periodical that was published in Switzerland, *Close Up* was a forum for spirited debates about the nature of cinema and manifestos imagining new forms of filmmaking and spectatorship. The magazine published articles by filmmakers such as Sergei Eisenstein and female literary modernists such as H.D. and Gertrude Stein.[25] Tamar Lane contributed to the advertising base of this organ for film theory, purchasing full-page promotions that advised that "Every student of the Silent Drama should read THE FILM MERCURY . . . The most fearless and feared film paper published in America."[26]

Lane's conviction that the Los Angeles film community and European intelligentsia would both find value in *Film Mercury* speaks to a particular moment in Hollywood history—one in which it was possible to believe that a large-scale avant-garde film movement might be commercially viable within the United States. No, Lane did not assume that the nation's "morons and nit-wits" would abandon their appetite for hokum. But he did believe that a more discerning audience existed, and this audience could be further cultivated. How best to serve the audiences of refined taste? Lane advocated for the creation of a parallel system of distribution and exhibition. As the 1920s continued, he praised the development of art house theaters and networks—such as Symon Gould's Little Theatre Movement—even though they never reached the stature and scale that he imagined.[27]

Whereas Lane believed in a division among exhibitors—separating the art theaters from the hokum houses—he was less rigid in his thinking about filmmakers and production personnel. Many directors, screenwriters, and actors had the capacity to create screen art. D. W. Griffith directed the overly sentimental *Orphans of the Storm*, but he had also made *Broken Blossoms*, which Lane considered one of the greatest films ever produced. Lane imagined a system in which the talent, technology, and production resources, all clustered in Los Angeles, would make films to satisfy the discerning theaters and audiences across the country and, more broadly, the world. And, yes, the movie colony would continue making schmaltz and hokum, too. Lane's assumptions about the industry's fluidity seemed viable in the 1920s. In his history of the Los Angeles avant-garde, film historian David James has detailed that "through the 1920s stylistic innovations, production personnel and methods, and career opportunities crossed with no great difficulty between the studios and artisanal practices outside them, between the film industry and the avant-garde."[28] When *Film Mercury* suspended publication in 1931, the Great Depression was at its height, and the resources required to achieve the ideal of a fluid production sector and flourishing art exhibition sector no longer seemed possible. But for a time, industry news, actor self-promotion, and theories of film art could all coexist within the same magazine. The commercial avant-garde had a Hollywood trade paper, even if it never fully materialized within the studio system.

FILM SPECTATOR AND ITS PARTISAN READERS

More Hollywood trade sheets kept cropping up throughout the mid to late 1920s. *Inside Facts of Stage and Screen*, established by Jack Josephs in 1924, wanted to be *Variety* for the West Coast. Visually, *Inside Facts* very much resembled *Variety*, with its large page size and even in its typographical choices. *Inside Facts of Stage and Screen*'s content was also similar (if much briefer), covering vaudeville and legit theater alongside the film industry. Josephs's trade paper gathered much of its "inside facts" about the movies from its office in the Warner Bros. downtown building in Los Angeles (unsurprisingly, Warners featured prominently in its news reporting).[29]

Another paper, *Motion Picture Review*, established in 1925 or 1926, profiled Hollywood film executives like they were movie stars. Irving Thalberg was overrated, according to one of the paper's contributors.[30] *Motion Picture Review* did not last long, but the practice of profiling and assessing the performances of film executives would flourish for decades in the pages of *Hollywood Reporter* and *Daily Variety*.

Two additional short-lived LA papers of the period were initially led by the same person. Fred W. Fox, who had previously worked as *Camera!*'s advertising manager, was the first editor of *Hollywood Topics*. Debuting in October 1926 and published once every two weeks, *Hollywood Topics* attempted a playful, tongue-in-cheek address to the show business community as it presented Hollywood's news. The paper's subheading read, "Hollywood Topics: -cussed and discussed All Over the World."[31] Fox's true talent, though, was in selling ads. *Hollywood Topics* clearly participated in the old quid pro quo arrangement of advertising money for editorial space. Clarence Brown purchased quarter-page ads to keep his name in the press, and *Hollywood Topics* made sure he got his money's worth with puff piece write-ups in multiple issues, tracking his progress across the movies he was making.[32]

Fred W. Fox also sold ads to real estate developers, automobile companies, and other businesses that perceived the film industry as potential customers. Just three years earlier, in 1923, a real estate syndicate with the backing of the *Los Angeles Times* had erected the now-famous "Hollywood" sign, promoting the

FIGURE 21. "Hollywood Knolls" [Advertisement], *Hollywood Topics*, Nov. 3, 1927, 32, https://lantern.mediahist.org/catalog/hollywoodtopicsoo1holl_0070.

Hollywoodland housing development to those driving along LA's Miracle Mile.[33] In the same boosterish spirit, though far less bold and expensive, the Taft Realty Co. purchased full-page ads in *Hollywood Topics* promoting its Hollywood Knolls development.[34] In one of the ads (see fig. 21), a white family overlooks a lush valley—mother standing and holding her child, father sitting and reading the newspaper. The copy of the ad, tailored for the imagined *Hollywood Topics* audience of show people, promised that "an exclusive 'modern art colony' of famous people" was on its way. This enterprise highlights the close relationship between real estate development and the movie industry in 1920s Hollywood.[35] As film historians Denise McKenna and Charlie Keil have shown, this relationship played itself out in various and often unexpected ways, including, in this case, providing an advertising base for a superfluous Hollywood trade paper.

After editing only a handful of issues of *Hollywood Topics*, Fox immediately started a new trade paper in collaboration with Billy Joy. Their new paper, *Hollywood Vagabond*, launched in February 1927. Despite bearing the name "vagabond," the paper was written and organized in a manner that presented itself as the ultimate insider paper, intended only for those fully rooted and immersed in the movie colony. Fox and Joy claimed that their news would be the untarnished dirt on Hollywood, without the massaging or puffery of press agents. Fox once again tapped local real estate developers for advertising support, though *Vagabond* had less advertising pages overall than *Hollywood Topics* and most of the competing LA trade papers. The fact that the annual subscription price was relatively high ($10 compared to $1 to $3 for most of the papers) also suggests that Fox may have overestimated his ability to sell ads in a marketplace of trade papers that had grown so crowded.[36] The defining feature of *Hollywood Vagabond* was intended to be the gossipy, occasionally salacious, style in which it dispensed the insider news of show business. The lead story of *Vagabond*'s debut issue concerned a fight between producer Samuel Goldwyn and actress Belle Bennett, "who was rushed to a sanitarium last week, on the verge of a nervous breakdown."[37] Rather than running away at the sight of a scandal—the approach taken by the Hays Office and many of the industry's power brokers—*Hollywood Vagabond* promised it would seek out and deliver scandalous news to readers. In practice, though, the trade paper quickly took on a more conventional approach to gathering and sharing the industry's news. It's unclear whether *Hollywood Vagabond* survived more than a single year. But the idea that the Hollywood community wanted to seek out and read about scandals, not sweep them away, would live on through manifestations in both the trade press and popular press.

Although *Inside Facts of Stage and Screen, Motion Picture Review, Hollywood Topics*, and *Hollywood Vagabond* all spoke to elements of Hollywood's culture, none of them had a shred of the impact of Welford Beaton's *Film Spectator*. Founded in 1926, *Film Spectator* emerged as a magazine primarily devoted to craft-oriented film criticism. But it exploded in popularity when its editor shifted the paper's incisive criticism away from individual movies and toward the producers, studios, and industry structure that manufactured them. The rise of this particular trade paper can tell us much about Hollywood's culture—which identified as a single community ("picture people") yet bore deep partisan fault lines between management and creative workers.

Film Spectator's founder and editor, Welford Beaton, shared many of Tamar Lane's cinematic tastes. Beaton loved the German Expressionist films that had reached American screens, and he detested stale stories. But Beaton's method of expressing his tastes and observations differed from Lane's. Beaton's prose was loose and conversational. He viewed his magazine as an ongoing conversation with filmmakers who wanted to improve their craft and improve the medium as a whole. He was the hardware store owner, leaning over the counter, offering pointers to the carpenters who came in for supplies.

For the first full year of its publication, Beaton's chief nemesis was the close-up—or, more precisely, the rampant overuse of close-ups. "Close-Ups Spoil a Good Picture" read a February 1927 *Film Spectator* headline, concisely summing up one of his theories of filmmaking.[38] Earlier that same month, he had commented:

> The next time you view a picture note how completely a medium shot presents a scene. Watch how it registers the thoughts of the characters. Notice how clearly you can see the expression on every face on the screen. Then ask the producer of the picture why under the sun he put in so many senseless close-ups. If the direction and editing of a picture be done intelligently there is in no finished production an excuse for more than three or four close-ups. You can measure the degree of the lack of intelligence in a producing organization by the number used in excess of that limit.[39]

In the summer of 1927, however, Beaton transformed the significance of *Film Spectator* when he provided a whole new rationale to "measure the degree of the lack of intelligence in a producing organization." The industry was abuzz over the issue of budgets, with producers insisting that a salary cut was necessary for all writers, directors, and actors. Beaton framed himself as an objective outsider— a "spectator," one might say—to the whole matter. "I must admit that to one like myself, sitting on the sidelines and with no material interests at stake, the whole affair is so amusing that it is difficult to discuss it with so much gravity that the chuckles will not show through," wrote Beaton. Yet he was unequivocal and unrelenting in his placement of blame, decrying how "producers have brought about the present situation."[40] For Beaton, poor management by producers was largely responsible for the poor quality of pictures he reviewed. "The artistic emancipation of the screen waits upon its economic reformation, for perfect examples of screen art can be produced only by following perfect scripts," declared Beaton.[41] He pointed out that film budgets would decline, along with his least favorite type of camera framing, if productions followed the script and avoided filming superfluous shots and scenes: "There is no excuse for taking a long shot, a medium shot and a close-up of the same scene. There is no excuse for taking any scene that does not appear in the finished picture. All these extravagances for which I contend there is no excuse enter into the making of every picture produced in Hollywood. That is the way we make them, because we never have mastered the proper method of making them."[42]

Beaton argued that the producers were wrong, and Hollywood's creative workers were right. Empowering screenwriters, not slashing their salaries, was the key

**Edited by
WELFORD BEATON**

THE 20 Cents
FILM SPECTATOR

Published In Hollywood Every Other Saturday

Vol. 4	Hollywood, California, December 10, 1927	No. 8

Time to give producers a dose of their own medicine

We point out a few ways in which this can be done

The jobless actor and the foreign film market

Why consult producers about standard contracts?

THE CIRCUS	GALLEGHER
JESSE JAMES	THE LOVE MART
FORBIDDEN WOMAN	EAST SIDE, WEST SIDE
BREAKFAST AT SUNRISE	PORT OF MISSING GIRLS
GENTLEMEN PREFER BLONDES	

FIGURE 22. The cover of the December 10, 1927, issue of *Film Spectator* emphasized the paper's antagonistic stance toward producers. https://lantern.mediahist.org/catalog/filmspectator 1920ofilm_0337.

toward improving the film industry. And the best strategy for screenwriters to achieve this new level of power—and then for producers and directors to make those better movies—was for creative workers to organize. "I do not believe in unions, but I do believe in waging a fight with the most potent weapon," wrote Beaton. "Only an organized movement will set matters right; consequently I am glad to see both the actors and writers organizing to present a united front."[43] When the Academy of Motion Pictures Arts and Sciences stepped in to help mediate the contentious salary cut debates, he dismissed the newly formed organization as a "catspaw to pull the producers' chestnuts from the fire."[44]

The response among Hollywood's creative community was electric. *Film Spectator* became essential reading overnight. Screenwriters, actors, directors, and other craftspeople subscribed in droves. Here was a trade paper that validated their resentments and attacked their opponents. *Film Spectator* was only published once every two weeks, so the creative community did not rely on it for the latest breaking news about negotiations with the producers. Instead, they read it to affirm their anger, connect with others in their community, and relish seeing Beaton tear apart their enemies with such forcefulness and wit. Thousands of exhibitors, and most likely a large number of producers and studio executives, also subscribed to follow along.

When *Film Spectator* published its "second birthday" issue in March 1928, Beaton reflected on the unexpected turning point in his journal's young life: "For the first eighteen months apparently I was the only one who took *[Film Spectator]* seriously. Then the salary cut crisis arose, and I wrote an open letter to Jesse Lasky. It acted like an explosion with an element of humor in it. Within thirty days the circulation of The Spectator more than doubled, and it has turned over a couple of times since. I think it now has twice the combined circulation of all the other film papers published in Hollywood."[45]

Beaton credited his success to his policy of "absolute honesty." He believed that "honest opinions in a paper are like honest emotions on the screen."[46] But it requires a viewing audience to observe, interpret, and feel those emotions. And it took a community of creative workers, who felt under attack, to respond to Beaton's opinions and elevate *Film Spectator* into becoming the most important trade paper for the LA film industry of the late 1920s.

VARIETY GOES TO THE MOVIES

Of all the publications discussed in this book, the hardest to place, to generalize about, to fit into a clear category also happens to be the film industry's most famous trade paper: *Variety*. Unlike *Camera!*, *Film Mercury*, and *Film Spectator*, *Variety* was not published in Los Angeles during the 1920s. But *Variety* did make a critical change to its LA office in the mid-1920s and greatly expanded its coverage of film. And in terms of its sensibility and mode of address, *Variety* had far more in common with the LA trade papers than with *Exhibitors Herald* or the New York nationals. For these reasons, it makes more sense to analyze *Variety*'s turn toward the film industry here than in any of the other chapters. Besides, as *Variety* would occasionally quip, we have some extra space here we need to fill.

During the mid-1920s, *Variety* had come to position itself as the film industry's scorekeeper and, more broadly, the most distinctive voice in show business.

Whereas *Motion Picture News* and *Exhibitors Herald* concentrated the voices of their publisher-editors within their editorial pages, *Variety* had come to weave its point of view into nearly every article and story. It was leveraging its distinctive voice—along with the reputation for independence that it had won from drawn-out fights with vaudeville's power players (see chapter 2)—toward greater recognition within the film industry and, important for its bottom line, greater film-related advertising revenue. If the 1920s were the decade that Hollywood became "Hollywood," then they were also the decade that *Variety* became the "*Variety*" that comes to mind for most film historians—a trade paper, written in the lingo of showbiz, with close ties to Hollywood (or the "Coast," "Colony," or "Tinseltown" as it would just as likely be described). How did this come to be?

Variety's embrace of slanguage—and the close association it took on with the paper's brand—followed a more straightforward path than the paper's ever-shifting relationship with the film industry. For this reason, it's worth examining slanguage before exploring the paper's connections to the film industry. As will quickly become clear, however, the two threads were interrelated. Among a crowded field of film industry trade papers, *Variety*'s use of "industry-speak" differentiated it from its competitors and invited readers to imagine themselves as members of a part of the global community of show business.

Variety did not always zowie its readers. "The emergence of slanguage was essentially a phenomenon of the 1920's," notes Peter Besas in *Inside "Variety."* By contrast, "over the first two decades of the paper's existence, slang and abbreviations and acronyms were rarely used," Besas writes.[47] Reading and searching through *Variety* issues of the 1910s confirms Besas's claim that "*Variety*'s prose style was similar to that of other trade publications of the time." Besas credits post–World War I changes in writing culture, the addition of new *Variety* staffers (most importantly Jack Conway, the inventor of "palooka"), and the type of chatter long heard outside of Broadway's stage doors for the rise of *Variety*'s distinctive style.[48] A key moment in forging the link between show business lingo and *Variety*'s brand occurred in 1926 with the publication of an essay by Hugh Kent in *American Mercury*. Kent celebrated the trade paper's use of language, seeing it as an extension of Sime Silverman's editorial independence and street-smarts. "*Variety*'s grammar is barbarous; its style is original and unique and completely independent of any other writing; its phraseology is wild and revolutionary and its diction is the result of miscegenation among shop talk, slang, Broadway colloquialism, sporting neologisms and impatient short-cutting," wrote Kent.[49]

Kent's essay brought *American Mercury* readers into the world of *Variety*, calling attention to how, in *Variety*-speak, a bad act "nosedived" and a great act was an "outstander."[50] Kent and, writing much later, Besas both argue that *Variety* primarily popularized and innovatively reused show business slang rather than inventing terms outright. The data mining research on which I collaborated with Derek Long, Kit Hughes, and Tony Tran reached much the same conclusion.[51] *Annet, extant, legit, copped, fave,* and other terms associated with *Variety* appeared in *New*

York Clipper years before Sime Silverman established the paper. *Variety* appropriated, popularized, and creatively utilized the slang we associate with it. The significance of the slanguage was to build and reinforce an imagined community of show business readers. "Like all jargon, it creates a sense of an 'in-crowd,'" notes linguist David Wilton in his analysis of *Variety*'s slang.[52] Some media depictions of *Variety*, including the film *Yankee Doodle Dandy* (1942), emphasize the translation work required for laypeople to make sense of the trade paper. Yet there is a risk of exaggerating the difficulty of reading *Variety*, misrepresenting this slang-rich English language publication for something written in an alien tongue. The genius of *Variety*'s slanguage was that it was fun to read and that with enough reading, most people could figure it out. For those within the entertainment industry, this reinforced the sense of reading the slang-heavy news as participation in the industry's culture. But, equally important, it created a porous boundary for those outside the industry: a fence to some, a passageway for others. Learning how to read *Variety* could give aspiring actors or writers the sense that they had crossed over and become members of the show business community, even if they had never set foot in Los Angeles or New York.

Ironically, *Variety*'s distinctive, Broadway-infused approach to language was taking off in the early to mid-1920s during the same time that the trade paper's traditional bread and butter—the US vaudeville industry—was in decline. The marketplace for straight vaudeville (that is, vaudeville not staged alongside movie presentations) had shrunk, creating employment challenges for vaudeville performers and managers, as well business challenges for the New York theatrical trade papers that had grown accustomed to their advertising revenue. In 1922, the *New York Dramatic Mirror* changed from a weekly to monthly publication, then ceased publication soon afterward.[53] It appeared as though the country's oldest theatrical trade paper—the *New York Clipper*—would soon follow. Sure enough, in 1923, *Variety* swooped in and acquired the financially imperiled paper. At the time, Sime Silverman assumed that his competitor's biggest asset was the title splashed across its front page. "*Clipper* has a good name, in and out of show business," wrote *Variety*. "It is a better known name as a theatrical paper today than all of the theatrical papers of the world, which of course takes in *Variety*. It is a fact we admit."[54] The announcement reveals that *Variety*'s title and brand had not yet assumed the global status that they would soon enjoy. *Variety* briefly operated both papers as separate entities (*Variety* covering indoor entertainment, *Clipper* covering outdoor) before folding the *Clipper* entirely in 1924, which also happened to be the year that H. L. Mencken and George Jean Nathan founded *American Mercury*.[55]

It was in this context of slanguage innovation and vaudeville's decline that, in the mid-1920s, *Variety* strategically pursued greater advertising from the film industry. *Variety*'s early relationship with film has been so difficult to chronicle, in part, because it does not fit a linear or neat narrative (the paper gave more space to film in 1908 than it did four years later in 1912). Figure 1 in my introduction graphs *Variety*'s pages per category over the period of 1906 to 1940. These findings, gathered through a quantitative content analysis of six issues per year, challenge the standard accounts chronicling *Variety*'s turn toward film.[56] In their books on *Variety*'s history, Peter Besas and Dayton Stoddart have suggested that *Variety*'s film coverage increased following increases in film advertising. As Besas puts it, "Throughout the 1920s, *Variety*'s advertising from the film sector had increased spectacularly, gradually eclipsing that from vaudeville, music, and legit [theater]. . . . [Film's] place grew in importance as advertising from the pictures ballooned."[57] The data reveal, however, that the inverse was true. It was only after devoting substantial resources to covering the film industry that *Variety* reaped the benefits of increases in film advertising. This makes sense given how competitive the landscape for film industry trade papers was throughout the 1920s. As the next chapter will detail, the total number of film companies purchasing advertisements decreased in the 1920s, and those companies that remained periodically cut back on their trade paper advertising expenditures. Within this industry landscape, *Variety* needed to actively pursue strategies to persuade film industry companies and personnel that it deserved their advertising dollars.

Variety took an important step in its pursuit of the film industry in 1925 when it opened a Los Angeles office. Although the paper's New York office was located in proximity to the film industry's chief executives and distribution heads, this decision created stronger ties to the Hollywood production community. This move also proved important because of the staffer selected for the job. "VARIETY'S LOS ANGELES OFFICE. ARTHUR UNGAR in Charge," announced the heading of the LA section edited by Ungar throughout the mid to late 1920s.[58] Arthur Ungar (or "Ung," as he would sign his reviews) spent the first decade of his career as a journeyman through various forms of entertainment, conflict, and reporting. He had studied law and practiced briefly as an attorney. He had worked as a house manager, both at a movie theater and a burlesque show. He fought in the infantry and rode motorcycles during World War I, nearly getting killed in the process. But the job he kept coming back to was as a New York theatrical reporter—working stints at both the *Clipper* and *Variety*, then just *Variety* after Sime Silverman acquired and finally eliminated the rival paper. Jerry Hoffman, who was on staff at the *Clipper* and *Variety* at the same time as Ungar, shared in an oral history interview that Sime Silverman dispatched Ungar to LA in 1925 with a specific mandate. "Ungar had orders to either make the office pay within a year or close it up," remembered Hoffman. "Well, Ungar, as those who've been around know, was a tough, tough guy, who used not a mailed fist but a bare fist. And he made that office pay; he made that office pay."[59]

One of the ways Ungar made it pay was by offering in-depth coverage of LA's vaudeville and theatrical scene. From his LA office, Ung competed with Jack Josephs's *Inside Facts of Stage and Screen* for West Coast theatrical news and advertisements. Yet Ung and his bosses remained mindful that the "inside facts of stage" were less lucrative than those of screen. Vaudeville was in decline nationwide, and the movies represented *Variety*'s most promising area for growth.

With both its New York and Los Angeles offices devoting more energy to covering the movies, *Variety* took a symbolically significant step on May 5, 1926, moving the "Pictures" section to the front of the paper. This meant pushing back the "Vaudeville" section, which had been at the front since the paper's inception, to third position—behind "Pictures" and "Legit" theater. *Variety* explained that the move was due to the decline of "straight vaudeville."[60] Film-related news appeared prominently on most of the front pages the paper published in 1926, too. The typical issue that year contained 11.3 pages of news and editorial coverage related to film and 4.5 pages of film advertising. These marked substantial increases compared to their median numbers in issues of *Variety* in 1922 (which contained 6.25 pages of news and editorial coverage related to film and published a mere half page in film advertising) and 1924 (7.4 pages of film coverage and 1.625 pages of film advertising). When Hugh Kent's essay celebrating *Variety*'s independence, language, and sensibility appeared in *American Mercury* in December 1926, *Variety* still saw itself as a newspaper for the entire show world—but a version of the show world in which movies were now the preeminent business.

Much like a Hollywood studio that would quote a rave review from *Variety* in a film's advertisement, *Variety* immediately put the *American Mercury* essay into service for its own self-promotional purposes. In self-deprecating yet endearing fashion, *Variety* mentioned Hugh Kent's celebration of its "barbarous grammar" with a news story headlined "'American Mercury' Gives Space on Why 'Variety' Is So Terrible."[61] Later in the same issue, *Variety* published a full-page self-advertisement titled, "Why Should You Advertise in Variety?" Here, the quote *Variety* opted to pull from Kent was related not to slang but to global circulation: "No one knows the circulation of Variety, not even the people on its staff, but it's sold all over America and all over Europe," Kent had written. The paper proudly emphasized that "it goes all over the world. Variety has the most influential list of foreign subscribers (prepaid) ever gathered."[62] Yet part of the paper's mystique was that you had to take its word for it. By neither disclosing its circulation nor allowing the Audit Bureau of Circulation to check its records, *Variety* was choosing a path that clearly violated the best practices of industrial journalism (as detailed in chapter 1). But in a magic trick that its reviewers would have applauded as an "outstander," *Variety* turned this potential negative into gold—a competitive advantage, in fact. Keeping the circulation numbers secret became part of *Variety*'s brand. Some potential advertisers were scared away by this practice, but a growing number were willing to take part in the card trick. As advertising in *Variety* became increasingly important to the ways in which film companies branded themselves, the paper's secretive approach to circulation proved highly lucrative. *Variety* charged its advertisers a huge premium—an amount that Martin Quigley later speculated was five times *Motion Picture Herald*'s rates when calculated on the basis of cost per thousand target readers.[63]

In different variations, *Variety* would play this magic trick over and over again. No paper was better at having it both ways—of simultaneously being in and out, of caring deeply and not giving a damn, of having its cake and eating it too. *Variety* would claim not to be a film industry trade paper while simultaneously calling attention to what it perceived as the shortcomings of *Moving Picture World*, *Motion Picture News*, and the industry's other national trade papers. From the standpoint of those established film industry trade papers, *Variety* did not play by the rules, and it was siphoning away advertising dollars that rightfully belonged to its competitors. But there was little they could do to effectively fight back. When *Moving Picture World* and *Exhibitors Herald* complained to film companies and individuals that advertised in *Variety* instead of their papers, the news immediately got back to *Variety*, which was only too happy to publish it as evidence of those trade papers' dubious ethics, desperation, and strong-arm tactics.[64]

Variety also promoted itself—and antagonized its rivals—by claiming that it offered the best film reviews and the most discriminating taste of all the trade papers. In 1927, *Variety* published a "Film Critics' Box Score" that evaluated the film reviewers of the major trade papers for their thoroughness, ability to predict hits and flops, and comparative number of positive and negative reviews.[65] Drawing its inspiration from baseball box scores that offered statistical snapshots of games, *Variety* tabulated the reviews across its own and five other papers and, not surprisingly, found that it was the game's winner. Based on the results (boxes 1 and 2), *Variety* claimed it panned more films than any other paper and was also the best at predicting failure or success. *Variety* was telling the industry that it was the most independent paper, best understood the marketplace, and possessed unparalleled taste.

The box scores were the most blatant expression yet of a role that *Variety* had come to play within the film industry and has never ceased to occupy ever since: scorekeeper. Sime Silverman, Arthur Ungar, and the paper's other leaders understood that show business attracted people who yearned not simply for success but for highly visible success. Most never achieved it. But, along the way, they could feel entertained, jealous, and consoled by reading about the successes and failures (which could be equally if not more visible) of others within the industry. *Variety*'s scorekeeping function also allowed it to dig, with relish, into conflicts within the industry without having to pick a side or attempt to solve the problem. To be sure, there were times when *Variety* picked a side and times when it attempted to solve the film industry's problems. But the default reporting style was to seek out and tell the news—with verve, slang, color, and attention to the winners and losers—in a way that informed, entertained, and made readers feel they were part of a special show business community.

BOX 1. FILM CRITICS' BOX SCORE

Score as of Sept. 5
(including pictures reviewed since June 4, 1927)
Key to abbreviations: PC. (pictures caught); R. (right); W. (wrong); O. (no
opinion expressed); Pc. (percentage)

TRADE PAPERS					
	PC.	R.	W.	O.	Pc.
Variety	66	55	11	..	.833
"Daily Review"	38	28	10	..	.742
"M.P. World"	31	22	7	2	.710
"Film Daily"	46	30	10	6	.652
Reid ("News")	37	24	10	3	.645
"M.P. News" (total)	47	27	16	4	.572

SOURCE: Detail recreated from "Film Critics' Box Score," *Variety*, Sept. 14, 1927, 10, https://lantern.mediahist.org/catalog/variety87-1927-09_0064.

BOX 2. TRADE PAPERS' OPINIONS

(Indicating opinions as expressed without percentages)

	Total.	Good.	Bad.	No Opinion.
Variety	66	45	21	...
"M.P. News"	47	40	3	4
"Film Daily"	46	34	6	6
"Daily Review"	38	31	7	...
"M.P. World"	41	41	4	2

SOURCE: Recreated from "Film Critic's [*sic*] Box Score," *Variety*, Sept. 14, 1927, 10, https://lantern.mediahist.org/catalog/variety87-1927-09_0073.

Variety's timing for its pivot toward film proved prescient. As we will see in the next chapter, the transition to sound in the late 1920s was a period of convergence of different media industries, including music, theater, radio, and film.[66] This convergence worked to the advantage of *Variety*'s titular emphasis. Motion pictures could bring stars, stories, numbers, and songs from across the different fields of American entertainment into a single medium for dissemination to the widest possible audience. *Variety* also benefited from an enlarged marketplace of film rentals. In 1929, film distributors rented sound features, sound shorts, silent features, and silent shorts to exhibitors. More films in the marketplace required more advertising to sell them. During the film industry's transition to sound in 1928 and 1929, *Variety*'s median quantity of film advertising skyrocketed from 1.625 pages per issue in 1924 to 15.5 pages in 1929. Put otherwise, *Variety*'s advertising went from being 12.5 percent film-related in 1924, to 55 percent film-related in 1929, to 75 percent film-related in 1930.

But if *Variety* used the movie industry in the mid to late 1920s for its financial gain, then it's equally true that individuals within the movie industry found ways to use *Variety* for theirs. Since its inception, *Variety*, like the LA trade papers discussed earlier in this chapter, had benefited from the advertising dollars and publicity efforts of actors, who used the paper to promote their careers. Corporations had also attempted to use the trade press to legitimize and promote themselves, but this practice became especially significant during the late 1920s era of Wall Street–financed mergers and acquisitions and sound conversion. No one was more savvy in this regard than Joseph P. Kennedy, who used advertisements and positive news coverage in *Variety* to help him rebrand the companies he controlled (Film Booking Office and, later, Pathé) and then sell them for considerably more than the value of their physical assets.[67] Kennedy used *Variety* to sell himself and his companies, not simply the movies he had a hand in. Sime Silverman would later ask Kennedy to repay the favor when, in 1931, his paper was confronted by the Great Depression and a studio-backed plan to divert advertising away from *Variety*.

CONCLUSION

While the Hollywood studios were engaged in the production of *The Covered Wagon* (1923), *The Big Parade* (1927), and other silent features, the LA trade papers that chronicled those films and studios were participating in the production of Hollywood's cultures and communities. The plural—*cultures* and *communities*—is important here. In the late 1910s and early 1920s, *Camera!* distinguished between LA's community of movie people and the city's elites. But, within only a few years, *Film Mercury* and *Film Spectator* had found new fault lines to conceive of Hollywood—between artists and hokum merchants, between creatives and producers. And all of these trade papers, including *Camera!*, depended on a community of actors, writers, and directors seeking upward mobility within the industry as their advertising base. This was a community premised on aspiration—buying space for their faces and names to appear in front of the influential community that they desperately wanted to join.

The gossip, flair, and bold film criticism in the 1920s LA trade papers and *Variety* make them a pleasure to read today. But these same qualities—along with the sheer number of publications competing for advertising dollars—made them a problem for the major film companies. The next several years would play out in ways that no one at the time could have anticipated. *Exhibitors Herald's* Martin J. Quigley would conspire with the major Hollywood studios to try to take over the LA business paper marketplace. And an upstart daily publication, *Hollywood Reporter*, would outmaneuver Quigley and all the existing LA publications at their own game.

5

—————

Chicago Takes New York

The Consolidation of the Nationals

"MERGERS MAKE GREATNESS!" So proclaimed the cover of the first-ever issue of *Exhibitors Herald and Moving Picture World* (fig. 23). Published on January 7, 1928—deliberately timed to mark the sense of a new beginning—the cover presented an advertisement for Metro-Goldwyn-Mayer, the company that most embodied Hollywood's merger movement. In April 1924, Marcus Loew had consolidated the three production and distribution companies that composed the studio's hyphenated name, Metro-Goldwyn-Mayer (MGM), as a way to stabilize the supply of product into his Loew's Inc. theaters (a chain that had been built, in large part, through other acquisitions and mergers).[1] Over the following three years, MGM had developed a reputation for producing ambitious and prestigious pictures, including *The Big Parade* (1925) and the legendarily expensive *Ben Hur* (1925), as well as cranking out low-budget fare like Tom Mix westerns and the "Our Gang" shorts. The studio's competitors were racing to achieve similar stature through mergers, acquisitions, and vertical integration. To finance these expansions, the major movie companies were partnering with Wall Street investment banks and commercial banks like never before, issuing stocks and bonds amounting to hundreds of millions of dollars.

The consolidation of *Exhibitors Herald and Moving Picture World* was publicly presented as a logical extension of the mergers occurring elsewhere in the motion picture industry and a sign of great things to follow. "The necessity for the building of fewer and stronger units to replace a greater number of lesser strength which has so markedly changed the complexion of the production, distribution and exhibition branches of the industry was bound eventually to have its influence upon the trade paper branch of the industry," reflected Martin Quigley in his first-ever editorial in *Exhibitors Herald and Moving Picture World*.[2] In a canny layout

131

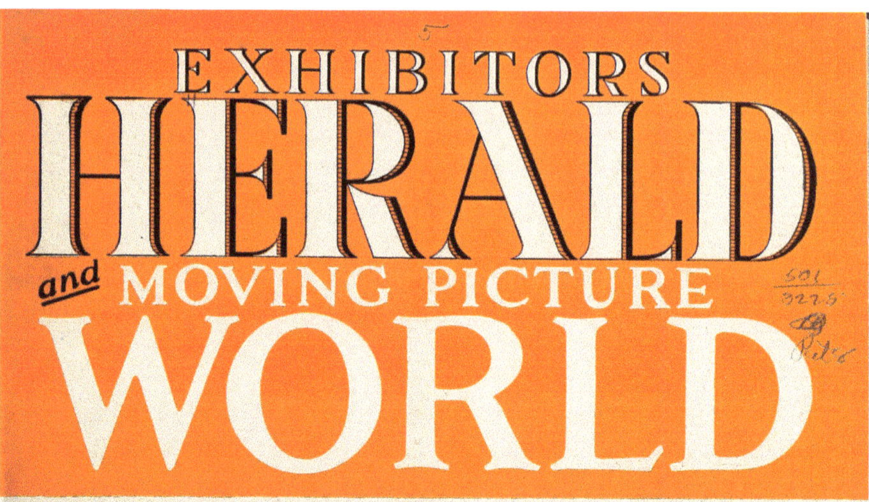

FIGURE 23. Cover of the first issue of *Exhibitors Herald and Moving Picture World*. Source: *Exhibitors Herald and Moving Picture World*, Jan. 7, 1928, 1, http://lantern.mediahist.org/catalog /exhibitorsherald90unse_0007.

choice, Quigley's editorial page was positioned facing the news story "Radio Corp. in Combine with FBO," which announced the Radio Corporation of America's acquisition of a substantial amount of ownership in the Film Booking Office.[3] The page featured a smiling portrait of Joseph Kennedy, FBO's president and the financial wizard who was responsible for that deal and others that would soon result in the formation of a vertically integrated studio, RKO.[4] Quigley was no doubt pleased to have his consolidated journal positioned alongside the mergers engineered by Kennedy and Loew.

The following pages included dozens of congratulatory notes, beginning with one from the head of the trade organization that represented MGM, Paramount, and the other major Hollywood studios. "I hasten to congratulate you on the consummation of the merger of 'Exhibitors Herald' with 'Moving Picture World,'" wrote Will Hays. "I regard this achievement as a great forward step in our industry—one bound to contribute much, indeed, toward the solution of those certain heretofore difficult problems in the business of motion pictures with which you have been so familiar."[5] Martin Quigley had arranged the merger in secrecy, and he was happy for the opportunity to present the consolidated paper and take a bow publicly.

Behind the scenes, however, the business model for the film industry's national trade papers had grown more precarious. A few days after his triumphant first issue, Quigley wrote privately to Hays lamenting that agitation caused by executives at Fox and First National had "led to a reduction by about one half of trade paper advertising. The same number of publications as formerly was used; the lesser publications in the field published practically the same volume of advertising as previously and the curtailment was effected principally through the reduction of advertising in the publications which are acknowledged as the strongest and most serviceable in the field."[6] Quigley singled out *Variety* and *Film Mercury* as two of the irresponsible "lesser publications" contributing to the problem. This state of affairs had made *Moving Picture World* vulnerable for Quigley to takeover. But if left unchecked, it could ruin Quigley's consolidated paper. Whereas Quigley generally supported trimming the salaries of actors, writers, and directors, he was diametrically opposed to cost cutting through any reduction of advertising placed in his paper. He would spend the remainder of the decade and the first year of 1930 attempting to make himself indispensable to the Hollywood studios and persuading them that it was in their interests to support the *Herald* in its pursuit to become the industry's sole trade paper.

Hays, for his part, was waging his own battle against a piece of federal legislation that held the potential to stop the major studios from growing in size and power. The resentments of independent exhibitors toward block booking, arbitration boards, and a system stacked against them had found a champion in Senator Smith W. Brookhart of Iowa. Discussed throughout the early issues of *Exhibitors Herald and Moving Picture World*, the "Brookhart Bill" contained measures designed to stop block booking and vertical integration within the film industry.[7] It was resulting in bad publicity for the Hays office. "We appeal to our patrons to kindly write to your Senator and Representative and ask them to support the Brookhart Anti-Film-Trust Block Booking Bill," read a poster that several Ohio exhibitors displayed in their theaters. "The passage of this bill will permit this and other Independently Owned Theatres to choose from a greater list, the kind of pictures best suited for our audiences. Under existing conditions we are compelled to buy the entire block of pictures and are forced to show some pictures that are not adaptable to our clientele."[8] In both the United States Senate and Cleveland theater lobbies, opponents of the powerful studios were arguing that big business, block booking, and morally questionable movies were all linked, requiring immediate action for the sake of America's audiences and independent theaters. Although the Brookhart Bill ultimately failed, the underlying tensions continued to grow throughout the transition to sound, with risqué Broadway plays being adapted into movies and new financial burdens placed on producers, distributors, and exhibitors.[9]

This chapter explores the consolidation of the national trade papers by analyzing the alliance that formed between Martin Quigley and the major Hollywood studios. These consolidation efforts culminated in 1931 with the launch of *Motion Picture Herald*, *Motion Picture Daily*, and the *Hollywood Herald*. In the battle lines being drawn, Quigley stood with Will Hays against the Brookhart Bill and went on to play a key role in addressing Hollywood's censorship problems through the creation of the Production Code. While these steps placed Quigley in Hays's favor, it alienated many of the nation's independent exhibitors who had previously admired Quigley and supported *Exhibitors Herald*. The creation of the Production Code also exposed rifts between the producers based in Los Angeles and the home office executives based in New York. The closer Quigley came to unifying the film industry's trade press, the more disunity and tensions within the industry became evident.

Before examining how Quigley consolidated the national weekly trade papers, it's important to look at the broader industry contexts in which his actions played out. This was an environment rife with mergers and acquisitions, yes, but it was also a period that saw innovations to film industry's operations and an influx of Wall Street financing, which laid the groundwork for these mergers among film companies. The 1920s were also a period of decline for the three national trade papers discussed earlier in this book that Quigley would come to absorb: *Moving Picture World*, *Motion Picture News*, and *Exhibitor's Trade Review*. The strengthening of the vertically integrated studios, the weakening of the national weekly trade papers, and the pressuring by public groups and federal government set the backdrop for the Chicago publisher—who had nearly become a priest—to dominate his New York rivals.

THE VERTICALLY INTEGRATED STUDIO SYSTEM
TAKES SHAPE

The US film industry's move toward the vertically integrated studio system—with production, distribution, and exhibition dominated by a handful of large corporations—had begun in the mid-1910s as Famous Players–Lasky expanded into distribution and exhibition and, on the flip side, powerful exhibitors bound together to form First National as a distributor of films that they contracted to produce.[10] But a decade later, in the mid-1920s, the push toward vertical integration and industry consolidation accelerated in speed and scale. The transition to sound hastened the pace of expansion, and by the end of the decade, a group of five vertically integrated companies dominated the industry: Famous Players–Lasky/Paramount, Loew's/MGM, Fox, RKO, and Warner Bros. (which acquired First National in 1928). In addition to these "Big Five" companies, there were the "Little Three"—Universal, Columbia, and United Artists—which had significant production and distribution infrastructures but did not own any major theater chains.

The history of how this structure came about is complex, and the very categories "Big Five" and "Little Three" can suggest a false sense of parity across the studios in each group when, in actuality, there were significant differences in the development and strengths of the studios.[11] Fortunately, a recent wave of film history scholarship has added important nuance to our understanding of the period, demonstrating the important roles played by trade organizations and suppliers and revealing how the studios tinkered with the ways in which production, distribution, and exhibition fit together. Kia Afra's research into trade organizations has shown the important role of the Motion Picture Producers and Distributors of America (MPPDA) during this period in confronting censorship and antitrust regulations.[12] The Society of Motion Picture Engineers represented another type of trade organization, one that pursued both innovation and standardization and depended on the contributions of technical vendors and suppliers, such as Eastman Kodak. In tracing the emergence of this technological infrastructure, Luci Marzola has argued that we need to recognize the horizontality of Hollywood's networked companies alongside the more familiar conception of the industry's verticality.[13]

Even our understanding of the vertical integration in the film industry has become enriched from recent scholarship, which draws extensively from primary sources and the film industry's trade papers to explore the relationships across industry sectors. There are no greater emblems of the Hollywood studio system than the grand sound stages on MGM's Culver City lot, the star-studded movies filmed there, and the roaring lion logo that greeted audiences as they began watching those pictures. Yet, as Derek Long has revealed, the huge investments in infrastructure and productions were only possible because of distribution policies that afforded greater predictability, profitability, and control for the studios. The result was "a more rationalized and temporally flexible system": by the mid-1920s, the studios could better plan the number and type of productions that they needed both to satisfy the marketplace and to amortize their overhead costs, while maintaining the flexibility desired to keep successful pictures in the first-run theaters for longer periods and clean up at the box office.[14] Similarly, William Paul has shown the close connection between production planning and exhibition, particularly in terms of first-run engagements and prerelease "specials."[15] As Long and Paul show, the engineers of the studio system depended on theaters and distribution for their thinking as much as they did stars, screen stories, and studio backlots.

In finding better ways to coordinate among themselves and make production, distribution, and exhibition work together seamlessly, the major film companies of the mid-1920s increased their market shares and became masters at creating barriers to entry against new competitors. As we saw in chapter 3, block booking functioned as a barrier to entry against independent producers and distributors, who had a harder time finding screen space because of the play dates that exhibitors had to enter into long in advance. The studios' ownership of first-run theaters was their most important barrier to entry and revenue center. At their peak, the major studios never owned more than 20 percent of US screens. But they made sure that those theaters were the most important screens— concentrating them in downtown locations, charging the highest ticket prices, and granting them first-run status. The first-run theaters played a vital role in the distribution and profitability of a film. Theaters were assigned a particular run (first, second, third, etc.) in a specific geographical zone; each theater could exhibit the film once a predetermined clearance period (perhaps eight to twelve weeks) had passed since another theater in the zone had shown it. This system, known as run-zone-clearance, ensured that the most money possible reached the studios as a film played across the country.[16] But it also meant that the nation's vast majority of non-studio-owned theaters, whose managers made up the principal readership of *Motion Picture News* and *Exhibitors Herald*, found themselves in an increasingly inferior position to compete.

Acquiring and building theaters was an expensive undertaking, and the Big Five studios achieved vertical integration with the backing of Wall Street firms. Through issuing stock and taking on debt, Paramount, for example, financed an expansion that saw its total assets rise from $18,881,000 in 1918 to $306,269,000 in 1929. Meanwhile, Warner Bros. collaborated with Goldman Sachs to provide the capital needed to invest in new sound technologies and acquire Vitagraph, First National, and numerous music publishing companies.[17] "The introduction of sound intensified financial involvement in the film industry," explains media historian Janet Wasko. "As the movies learned how to talk, finance capital's voice became even louder."[18] The important role that Wall Street played in these expansions—and the subsequent bankruptcies during the Depression years—have been well covered by Wasko and Douglas Gomery, among other film historians. But in the above-noted spirit of identifying new complexities about the period to explore, I would like to highlight two points related to the nexus of Hollywood and Wall Street that have tended to go unnoticed.

The first point worth drawing out is the important role that the trade papers played as industry boosters. "The banker is well enough aware today of the greatness and stability of the motion picture as an institution," wrote William A. Johnston

FIGURE 24. A successful example of vertical integration: MGM's *The Big Parade* (1925) attracted large crowds at New York City's grand Astor Theater, which was owned by MGM parent corporation Loews. Photograph courtesy of the Wisconsin Center for Film and Theater Research.

in one of his first *Motion Picture News* editorials of 1926.[19] If bankers were indeed aware of this, though, then it was partly due to the efforts of Johnston and other leading trade paper editors in promoting this view. L. W. Boynton, who edited *Exhibitor's Trade Review* from 1920 to 1923, played an especially significant role. After leaving the paper as part of a controversial ownership change, Boynton wrote an important series of articles for the *Wall Street Journal* in 1924 that analyzed the motion picture industry as an investment opportunity. Citing new efficiencies in production and distribution, Boynton assessed that the movie industry had been "placed on [a] sound business basis" and encouraged the investment community to embrace it. Boynton, Johnston, and other trade paper editors played important roles in communicating advancements in the film industry to Wall Street and shaping the industry's perception in the most favorable way possible.[20]

The second point about Wall Street and the film industry worth drawing out complicates the first point: we should not assume that all bankers and investors were looking to put their money into efficient businesses. Harry Aitken's mismanagement of Triangle in the late 1910s had showed how an irresponsible and unethical movie executive could defraud shareholders out of millions of dollars.[21] Within this context of fraud and mismanagement, the favorable assessments of Boynton and others were clearly important in reassuring Wall Street that the motion picture industry was a solid investment. We also should not overlook, however, the fact that for some bankers and investors, the motion picture industry's inefficiencies were part of what made it attractive. Joseph Kennedy, a young banker at Hayden, Stone & Co., embodied this opportunistic approach. "He had contempt for the business acumen of nearly all the people he encountered in the rapidly expanding film industry and believed he could squeeze more dollars out of their efforts than they even imagined were there," writes RKO historian Richard B. Jewell, before pointing out that "he [Kennedy] was right."[22] In her history of Kennedy's Hollywood years, historian Cari Beauchamp offers a detailed portrait of his financial wizardry. In one of his first film industry forays of the 1920s, Kennedy engineered a scheme to fully control Robertson Cole's New England exchange "by owning over half of the preferred stock, yet he had put in only $5,000 of his own money to create a company with an on-paper value of $300,000."[23] For an active and savvy investor like Kennedy, the trade press was valuable because it enabled him to hype his companies and enhance their perceived value so that he could sell them for a hefty return. During the Great Depression, Kennedy would repay the favor by guaranteeing bank loans to keep the entertainment industry's most famous trade paper afloat.

Within this environment of mergers, vertical integration, and Wall Street financing, the film industry's trade papers attempted to grow and succeed. Some of the more specialized papers reached new heights. *Film Daily* entered into a cooperative news-sharing agreement with three of its international peers: the *Daily Film Renter* (London), *Die Lichtbild-Bühne* (Berlin), and *La Cinématographie française* (Paris).[24] And, in Kansas City, Ben Shlyen expanded the *Reel Journal* in 1927 into seven regional trade papers, eventually forming the basis for *Boxoffice*.[25] But among the weekly national papers—especially the two New York City leaders, *Moving Picture World* and *Motion Picture News*, once powerful enough to earn each of their editors a spot within the executive committee of the film industry's Board of Trade—the mid to late 1920s was overwhelmingly a period of decline.

THE DECLINE OF THE NEW YORK NATIONAL TRADE PAPERS

The 1920s marked a period of contraction and decline for the film industry's nationally distributed, New York–based trade papers. Figure 25 reveals the sharp decrease in advertising pages per issue, especially in *Moving Picture World* and *Motion Picture News*, across most of the decade. The downward trend can be explained in part by the industrial changes discussed above. Consolidated film companies, like MGM, meant there were fewer buyers for ads than before the mergers. Changes in distribution—especially the turn toward block booking, prereleases, and longer runs—also meant there were fewer productions that needed individualized promotion within the trade press. For all of William A. Johnston's talk of rationalizing the industry's trade press, his paper, *Motion Picture News*, and its competitors had thrived in the mid to late 1910s on inefficiencies within the marketplace. Now they had to contend with a new reality: megacompanies that rapidly swerved between sprees of lavish spending and austere cost-cutting measures.

But the industry's movement toward vertical integration cannot by itself fully explain the decline of the national trade papers, nor can it tell us why, improbably,

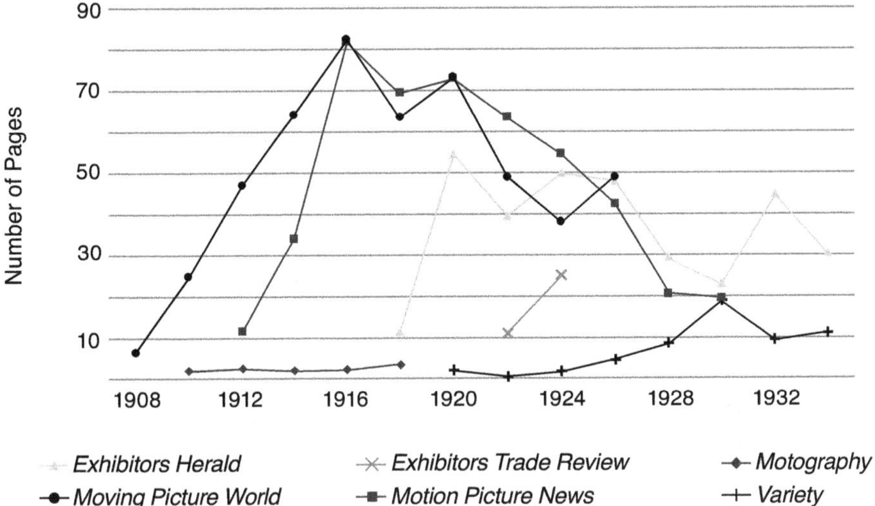

FIGURE 25. Median number of film advertising pages, 1908–34. *Source:* Six issues analyzed per year for each trade paper, selected using a random number generator. Graphic by Lesley Stevenson.

Exhibitors Herald emerged as the survivor and winner. By briefly surveying the four national trade papers that Quigley acquired between 1927 and 1930, we can see how managerial decisions made the publications vulnerable to takeover. Examining these national papers also highlights one of the tensions central to this book: the extent to which the film industry's trade press resisted the logics of other business trade publications even during a period of consolidation in which they would seem to be most similar.

The oldest of the New York trade papers, *Moving Picture World*, was the most emblematic of the downward trend in advertisements and editorial content. As film historian Anne Kail has written, "beginning around the time of Arthur James as editor-in-chief in 1920 and continuing under Robert E. Welsh's and William J. Reilly's editorship, the quality had declined appreciably in terms of writing style, content, and even in terms of the paper stock on which *Moving Picture World* was published. . . . The articles were much shorter and seemed to consist predominantly of studio advertising and planted stories concerning a studio's latest stars and productions."[26] In addition to struggling to publish at the quality that had distinguished *Moving Picture World* during its first decade of existence (1907 to 1917), the Chalmers Publishing Company had difficulties filing its taxes. When Chalmers got into trouble and appealed to the US Board of Tax Appeals, the court rejected the appeal but rendered an opinion that included sobering financial details. The company owned almost no assets aside from its accounts receivable (unpaid advertising invoices, presumably). In 1920, the Chalmers Publishing Company's net income was only $36,000.[27] *Variety* speculated that, during its final year of 1927, *Moving Picture World* was operating at an annual loss of $100,000.[28] Owning and operating the film industry's oldest trade paper had ceased to be a lucrative business.

Still, there were some bright spots for the Chalmers Publishing Company during the 1920s. The Chalmers' Spanish-language offshoot, *Cine-Mundial*, gained traction throughout the decade as it blurred the lines between serving as a trade paper and fan magazine. As film historian Laura Isabel Serna explains, "Far from being a mere translation of its English-language counterpart, *Cine-Mundial* focused on issues that were important to its readers in Latin American [*sic*] and Spain—the representation of Latin Americans on screen, the geo-politics of film distribution, and Hollywood's short foray into Spanish-language film production in the late 1920[s] and early 1930s."[29] While the precise circulation figures for *Cine-Mundial* are unclear, the numbers for *Moving Picture World* remained respectable until the end, never falling below eight thousand subscriptions.[30] The brand name—*Moving Picture World*—was still meaningful to many exhibitors who associated it with the Stephen A. Bush years.

Despite the revolving door of editors in chief, *Moving Picture World*'s "Projection Department" continued forward, year after year, under the supervision of F. H. Richardson. As I noted in my introduction, Richardson's "Projection Department" (which began in 1908 as the column "Lessons to Operators" and expanded in 1910 into a section called "The Trouble Department") encouraged projectionists and theater managers to write in with their questions.[31] Through detailed descriptions and visual aids, Richardson explained the workings of carbon arc lamps and program boards to operators in St. Louis and Salt Lake City. In 1910, Richardson and the Chalmers Company compiled the columns, reorganized them by topic, and added some fresh material to create the first edition of Richardson's *Motion Picture Handbook: A Guide for Managers and Operators of Motion Picture Theatres*.[32] As *Moving Picture World* limped toward the end of its run in 1927, Richardson published his fifth and largest edition yet of the *Handbook*, spanning two bound volumes and more than one thousand pages.[33] The trade papers and movie studios sometimes got into tax trouble for exaggerating the monetary value of "goodwill" in their balance sheets. Over a twenty-year period, however, Richardson and the *Moving Picture World* brand clearly had cultivated goodwill in the eyes of thousands of exhibitors. These strengths, along with a respectable if declining number of subscriptions, were some of the selling points that in late 1927 drove Martin Quigley to purchase *Moving Picture World*.

The strangest trajectory of a film trade paper during the 1920s belonged to *Exhibitor's Trade Review*. After its controversial first year (detailed in chapter 2) and charges that its publishers were unethical, the paper turned a full 180 degrees when it was acquired for $115,000 in 1920 by one of the most important figures in all of trade publishing: Adelbert B. Swetland, the general manager of the Class

Journal Company and the brother of Horace Swetland, the man who literally wrote the book on industrial publishing in 1923.[34] But not everything was as above board as it may have seemed. Adelbert B. Swetland probably assumed that because of his clout and previous success in trade paper publishing, it would be relatively easy to consolidate and dominate the field of film industry trade papers—just as he and his family had done in the automotive and iron industries. But neither the film industry's advertisers nor subscribers got on board for this plan. Meanwhile, Swetland's competitors refused to sell out to the trade paper founded by Lee A. Ochs and now run by a show business outsider.

Swetland might have been just another wealthy outsider who tried to get rich in the movie industry and lost his shirt in the process. But, instead, he found someone else to play that role. James Davis was a twenty-two-year-old college student who possessed a love for the movies and a $30,000 inheritance.[35] Swetland persuaded Davis to invest all of his money in *Exhibitor's Trade Review* and made him feel special by giving him a job as a film reviewer for the publication. Davis claimed that he "trusted Mr. Swetland like a father." Swetland used the young man's investment to cover the operating expenses for *Exhibitor's Trade Review*, avoid borrowing money, and maintain the company's stock valuation while he searched for a buyer. In 1923, Swetland sold the paper to another publisher from outside the film industry, George Williams, for a mere $10,000 in cash (the deal called for a second cash payment and a transfer of stock, but Williams refused to pay any more after getting a closer look at the paper's financial situation). Swetland used the cash and a subsequent legal settlement with Williams to pay himself deferred salary compensation and recoup part of his investment in the paper. Although Swetland lost some money on the enterprise, he was able to soften the blow for himself, according to Davis, by duping the twenty-two-year-old into signing documents that placed him in last position to be paid back. The young film critic's personal wealth was completely wiped out. Davis found some satisfaction when he won a civil lawsuit against Swetland, but, unfortunately for Davis, it was overturned on appeal.[36]

The saga of Swetland's disappointing three-year ownership of *Exhibitor's Trade Review* and the Davis lawsuit is worth recounting for two reasons. First, it highlights the strong degree to which trade publishing within the film industry operated differently from the trade publishing related to other American industries. Based on his previous successes, Swetland assumed that he could be a hands-off owner of *Exhibitor's Trade Review* and that the prestige of his family's name would move the film industry's leaders to embrace him and the paper. He was wrong. William A. Johnston and Martin Quigley found far greater success as hybrid editor-publishers, who imported techniques and features from papers like Swetland's Class Journal Company yet continually found ways to service the film industry's specific needs (including the formation of a Production Code). Second, the story is a small-scale example of the financial manipulations that led to the stock market's crash in October 1929. By 1922, *Exhibitor's Trade Review* had almost no assets (a trait it shared with *Moving Picture World*) and very little profitability. But Swetland utilized a naive investor and confusing contracts to protect his own money and make the company appear healthier than it actually was. The other national trade papers paid scant attention to the *Davis v. Swetland* lawsuit.[37] But the movie industry that they served produced many variations of the underlying archetypes and conflicts during the Depression years: the seemingly kind yet, in fact, ruthless corporate executive who uses his elite position to pull the wool over the eyes of a gullible victim.

During the period following its controversial sale, *Exhibitor's Trade Review*, now edited by William C. Howe, slid further and further into irrelevance. In 1924, the paper looked like it might be turning the corner thanks to a substantial increase in advertisements: roughly twenty-five pages of ads per issue compared to merely eleven pages per issue two years earlier (see fig. 25). Yet these numbers paled in comparison to the advertising sales of the three larger national papers that same year: *Motion Pictures News* (54.5 pages per issue), *Exhibitors Herald* (49.75 pages per issue), and *Moving Picture World* (38 pages per issue). To make matters worse, *Trade Review*'s paid subscriptions fell by 25 percent over the course of that same year, dropping from 5,808 to 4,630.[38] Ultimately, the paper offered its readers very little that they couldn't find someplace else. A growing number of exhibitors felt it wasn't worth the $3 subscription that it cost them per year. In April 1926, the paper changed formats, ceasing its weekly publication and publishing daily as *Exhibitors Daily Review*, which became a direct competitor to *Film Daily*.[39] Two years later, in 1928, *Exhibitors Daily Review* was acquired by an upstart New York–based trade paper and rebranded as *Exhibitors Daily Review and Motion Pictures Today*.[40]

Although *Motion Pictures Today* did not leave much of a long-term impression on the industry, it is worth noting for its head-spinning editorial shifts and its legacy as part of the genetic makeup of two far more significant trade papers: *Motion Picture Daily* and *Hollywood Reporter*. In 1925, *Motion Pictures Today* was founded by Arthur James, who had previously worked as the publicity director for Metro and the editor of *Moving Picture World* (1920–22). For the first year of the paper's existence, James sought to distinguish *Motion Pictures Today* through its acerbic attacks on the powerful producer-distributors, especially Adolph Zukor. Writing in a style that was far more combative than anything he had published on *Moving Picture World*'s editorial page, Arthur James declared that "block booking now stands as the really great evil"[41] and giddily cheered on the Federal Trade Commission in its investigation into Famous Players-Lasky.[42] In a November 1925 editorial, James served up a physiognomic analysis of the mogul:

> Mr. Zukor is small in stature, like the Emperor Napoleon, and the analogy between the two might be carried still further. But Mr. Zukor has not yet met his Waterloo.
>
> The physiognomist would say that there is intellect in that pictured face, cold, crafty, ruthless, cruel. There is boundless ambition, lust of power, a vast determination and LITTLE else.

> Looking at it thoughtfully, one may wonder what manner of the soul the man behind it really has. Study its characteristics one by one and perhaps you will understand why Mr. Zukor has been declared the motivating spirit behind the motion picture "OCTOPUS."[43]

Here and in similar attacks he leveled at Will Hays and the MPPDA, James sought to position himself as strong and brave, unafraid to speak truth to power, willing to take shots at the moguls whom the other trade papers coddled. But this stance proved short-lived. James would soon use his editorials to praise the genius of William Fox and other architects of the Hollywood studio system.[44] When the Presbyterian magazine *The Churchman* attacked Will Hays in 1929, James leapt to the MPPDA president's defense, publishing an op-ed extolling Hays's leadership and taking the ingratiating step of mailing a copy of it to Hays.[45] In assessing Arthur James as a trade paper editor within this larger context, it's hard not to see his fiery editorials at the dawn of *Motion Pictures Today* largely as a posture and a brief blip in his larger career.[46]

Motion Picture News

The most important competitor to *Exhibitors Herald* throughout the 1920s was the trade paper that, a decade earlier, had reinvented film industry journalism: *Motion Picture News*. William A. Johnston remained one of the film industry's preeminent thought leaders. When the *Film Year Book of 1922–1923* included a ranked list of the "twelve men who had accomplished the most for the motion picture industry from an artistic, economic viewpoint," Johnston ranked tenth in votes, just behind Thomas Edison and ahead of Cecil B. DeMille. He was the only editor or publisher on the list.[47] In his weekly editorials, Johnston often wrote in a manner that felt tailored for the ears of his fellow members of the top-twelve list (which also included Adolph Zukor, Samuel L. Rothafel, Mary Pickford, and Will Hays), likely coming across as snooty and condescending to small-town exhibitor readers. Yet Johnston continued to find ways to offer something valuable and distinctive to these exhibitors. Beginning in 1921, *Motion Picture News* began publishing its semiannual *Booking Guide*, which organized information about films (including cast, distributor, plot, length, and which audiences would or wouldn't like it) for fast retrieval.[48] Independent exhibitors appreciated the *Booking Guide* and other services that *Motion Picture News* provided, even if they didn't identify with its editor or feel the communal bond that they did with *Harrison's Reports* or *Exhibitors Herald*.

By the time Quigley had published the first several months' worth of *Exhibitors Herald and Moving Picture World*, however, *Motion Picture News* was in a far more precarious position. The year 1928 proved to be a turning point. *Motion Picture News* had shrunk drastically, down to 67 pages per issue (46.5 pages of news or editorial, 20.5 of advertising) in 1928 compared to 102 pages (42.5 of which were ads) in 1926 and 163 pages (73 ads) back in 1920. The number of subscribers had likely declined, too. We don't know the subscription numbers with any certainty, however, because at some point in the mid-1920s, Johnston dropped out of the Audit Bureau of Circulation (ABC). This was a surprising choice, considering Johnston had argued for the importance of auditing circulation numbers a decade earlier. Did the industry's most data-oriented trade paper editor turn his back on publishing ethics when the data no longer looked favorable? Martin Quigley certainly thought so, and *Exhibitors Herald and Moving Picture World* proudly trumpeted that it was the film industry's only ABC-audited publication.[49]

In an apparent effort to gain more money and resources, Johnston entered into a deal that would tie *Motion Picture News* to the booming stock market. For years, Johnston had been a booster for financing and stock offerings in the film industry. "The appearance of so many motion picture issues on the Stock Exchange marks undoubtedly this industry's outstanding achievement in 1925," Johnston had remarked.[50] In a 1926 editorial, Johnston dismissed fears that Wall Street would take over the film industry and wrest control away from its current leaders. He viewed these fears as ignorant and hysterical: "There won't be any Wall Street control in this business, nor any more Wall Street interference than Wall Street can possibly avoid."[51] In 1928, Johnston put this conviction into action, joining with the publishers of several other periodicals to form the Angus Company. All these publishers, including Johnston, turned over ownership of their papers to Angus and received stock in the new company from its underwriter, Bodell & Co., which also began selling shares of Angus publicly on the New York Stock Exchange.[52] Through this arrangement, Johnston gained access to more cash to operate *Motion Picture News*, and he enjoyed the prospect of watching his shares of Angus increase in value based on the performance of Angus's periodicals and the excitement for investors in his company. Johnston remained the publisher and editor of *Motion Picture News*, as well. What he may not yet have realized was that he had traded away his autonomy. The future of *Motion Picture News* would be determined by what was best for the shareholders of the Angus Company, not what Johnston personally wanted.

Around the same time that the Angus Company was formed, *Motion Picture News* implemented a new department that would have a long-term impact. The idea was to create a "club" where exhibitors could write in, trade ideas, and feel a sense of community. Charles "Chick" Lewis, an exhibitor from New England, founded the club and became its first president. As Lewis told the story a few years later:

> In the month of March or April, 1928, I wrote William A. Johnston and stated that in my opinion the trade papers of that time were without much appeal to the average theatremen. I pointed out that the greatest part of the contents of Motion Pictures News was of more interest to the home office officials than to the theatremen who constituted not less than 90% of the paid circulation. I told him that in my opinion much could be done to make his publication of real interest and value to these many subscribers through the medium of a department or "get-together" section wherein they could meet each week and talk "shop," discussing ways and means of operating their theatres more efficiently, merchandise the pictures and advertise the house in

FIGURE 26. Distinctive typography and a portrait of Charles E. Lewis signaled to readers that they had reached the "Managers' Round Table Club," the most popular section of *Motion Picture News* from 1928 to 1930. *Source: Motion Picture News,* May 17, 1930, https://lantern .mediahist.org/catalog/motionnew41moti_0683.

general. He immediately communicated with me to the effect that after sober reflections he was convinced that what I stated was the truth.[53]

The "Manager's Round Table Club," as it soon became known, was initially pitched toward independent exhibitors in towns containing between ten thousand and thirty thousand residents. In other words, it was intended for a demographic who operated in markets larger than the *Herald*'s "What the Picture Did for Me" contributors (who were primarily from towns with populations under five thousand) yet who still needed to be crafty, scrappy, and creative in order to compete for their customers' attention and stay in business. But *Motion Picture News* quickly encouraged Lewis to expand and include exhibitors in larger towns and cities, too.[54] As a result, the club's members came to include managers in Brooklyn, Toledo, and Denver, as well as smaller town exhibitors. These showmen shared ideas that spanned a wide range of promotional budgets, all the way from elaborate parades to cheap stunts (including free admission to children on their birthday, provided they arrived at the box office with documentation).[55]

Lewis threw himself fully into the task of building up the club's membership. During the summer of 1928, he took a five-week road trip through the states of Ohio, Indiana, Pennsylvania, and New Jersey, enrolling more than fifty new club members in the process.[56] When charter members of the club began sending letters to Lewis, who arranged and edited them in the pages of *Motion Picture News*, it encouraged more exhibitors to sign up as well. The paper as a whole greatly benefited from the new section, which adopted the slogan "Use the NEWS!," a clever way of signaling to exhibitors that they would find material of immediate application and value in *Motion Picture News*. "Manager's Round Table" also gave *Motion Picture News* something that it had never enjoyed before—a passionate, energetic group of exhibitors who directly participated in a community through the paper. William A. Johnston, who for more than a decade had been criticized for being out of step with the experience of independent exhibitors, was given the honorary title of "chairman" of the club.

Over the next two years, the "Manager's Round Table" section grew exponentially. What started as a single-page insert grew to four pages, then to eight pages, and up to sixteen and twenty-four pages in some issues. The popular section was responsible for more than a third of the content in some 1930 issues of *Motion Picture News*, as well as a welcome boost to the paper's subscription base. The many implications and challenges of the transition to sound became a frequent discussion topic for the club, with exhibitors offering one another practical pieces of advice for promoting their installations of the new technology and, in cases where they couldn't afford it, competing with those theaters that could. By mid-1929, the amount of correspondence and editing work had grown so large that Lewis left his theater in Connecticut, moved to New York, and devoted himself full-time to the *News*. Johnston supplied his most important department editor with an office, secretary, and assistant editor. *Motion Picture News* continued to struggle to achieve anywhere close to the level of advertising sales that the paper had enjoyed in the mid to late 1920s, but the paper had achieved a sense of urgency, freshness, and community thanks to "Manager's Round Table."

In September 1929, Johnston seems to have believed that the day-to-day operations of *Motion Picture News* were going well enough to allow him to step away from the role of editor while retaining his title as publisher. To fill his vacated editor-in-chief role, Johnston recruited Maurice "Red" Kann, an energetic and well-liked journeyman in the film industry's trade press who at the time was editing *Film Daily* for publisher Jack Alicoate. "My desk here remains as before," explained Johnston to his readers. "But I shall now have an opportunity to get about more and write for *Motion Picture News* from other sources quite as important as New York City."[57]

None of this was to last.

QUIGLEY, THE MEDIATOR

Ironically, during the same period in the late 1920s when *Motion Picture News* was deepening its engagement with exhibitors, *Exhibitors Herald* was moving in the opposite direction—strengthening its relationships with the major studios and their trade organization, the MPPDA. Martin Quigley had built *Exhibitors Herald* in the mid to late 1910s based on a perception of independence and talking straight to the exhibitor. And, in a series of high-profile issues in the summer of 1920, Quigley had aggressively attacked Zukor's expansion plans for Paramount. Less than a decade later, however, Quigley the independent insurgent was transforming himself into Quigley the industry mediator and unifier. He saw himself as a mediator between the major Hollywood studios and independent exhibitors. He would also become an important mediator between Hollywood and the Catholic Church. From Quigley's perspective, these were important and essential services that he was providing the industry. He believed that serving exhibitors, distributors, and producers did not need to be mutually exclusive. But many of his readers did, and many of the conflicts that followed emerged from that fundamental disagreement and the mistrust it bred. In *Harrison's Reports*, editor P. S. Harrison went so far as to say that "Martin Quigley has forgotten that the independent exhibitors exist."[58]

The transformation of *Exhibitors Herald*'s role and significance within the industry took place over a four-year period, from mid-1927 to mid-1931. Before interrogating the key moments within this change, however, it's useful to assess Quigley's objectives and strategies that drove the actions. "The combination of *Exhibitors Herald* and *Moving Picture World* realizes a goal which myself and my associates have been endeavoring to reach for nearly 13 years," reflected Quigley in the paper's first-ever issue in January 1928. "This goal is a publication commensurate with the requirement of being able to serve effectively and appropriately the entire motion picture industry in all of its branches and in all of its territories."[59] While the ambition of serving all the branches of the industry would come to define the next several years, it was the emphasis on serving *effectively and appropriately* that he emphasized most often in his internal memoranda. Effectiveness was something that Quigley expressed in quantitative terms: better advertising value thanks to wider circulation. But the idea of appropriateness was just as important to him. He had a strong sense of propriety—some things should not appear in print, just as some things did not belong on the screen. *Variety* and *Film Mercury* both violated the aspects of economy and propriety that Quigley held dear. All of these stated goals were built on an unstated goal and assumption: his paper should be granted a monopoly to serve the industry's many branches in an effective and appropriate way.

How did Quigley pull off the deal to acquire *Moving Picture World?* Unfortunately, I have not been able to locate any primary sources to definitively answer this question. But here are a few things that we do know. As I have noted, *Moving Picture World* occupied a vulnerable position throughout most of the 1920s, and it became even weaker as the studios cut back on advertising spending in 1927. The conditions were ripe for Quigley to buy out a competitor. According to Quigley, his negotiations with the Chalmers Company proceeded swiftly and secretly. The announcement came as a surprise to most of the industry, though probably not to Will Hays, whom Quigley thanked in the paper's first issue for his "constructive suggestions and encouragement" that "have had no small influence upon the developments which have led to the consolidation of *Exhibitors Herald* and *Moving Picture World*."[60] The precise figure for the acquisition is unknown, but based on references in court cases over the next several years, it was probably between $75,000 and $150,000. One thing we do know is that Quigley included noncompetition clauses in all of his acquisitions of the era.[61] He wanted to make sure that the publishers he was buying out did not immediately start a new film journal and threaten his business. In the months following its sale of *Moving Picture World*, Chalmers Publishing shifted its attention to a new industry and acquired the *Oriental Rug Magazine*—ironically, reversing the trajectory of Adolph Zukor, Carl Laemmle, and other movie moguls who started as dry goods merchants before venturing into show business.[62] Chalmers Publishing also continued to publish *Cine-Mundial*.

Over the three-year lifespan of *Exhibitors Herald and Moving Picture World*— soon shortened to just *Exhibitors Herald World*—Martin Quigley sought to make both his paper and himself indispensable to the MPPDA and its member companies. The first major battleground was the abovementioned Brookhart Bill. In his editorial page, Quigley opposed the Brookhart Bill for the way it failed to account for the complexities of the film industry and invited the federal government to interfere with private enterprise.[63] On the interrelated matters of distribution policies and screen content, Quigley objected to "outside interference in the internal problems of the business."[64] Quigley also granted ample space in his journal to representatives of the MPPDA to make their case against the bill. The February 25, 1928, issue of *Exhibitors Herald and Moving Picture World* contained a two-page spread that reprinted the legal opinion of the MPPDA's general counsel, C. C. Pettijohn, who deemed any ban on block booking to be illegal for the way it would restrain bargaining between exhibitor and distributor and mandate to distributors who they had to select as their customers.[65] The perspectives of pro-Brookhart exhibitors—of which there were many—found ways to enter the paper, particularly in brief news items reporting on the decisions of exhibitor groups.[66] Supportive references to the Brookhart Bill also popped up in the "What the Picture Did for Me" section. "If the Brookhart bill gets the exhibitor out from under the duds like this one, he will have accomplished something at least," wrote a small-town Indiana exhibitor in his pan of the Pathé-PDC feature, *Angel of Broadway*.[67] Overall, however, the voices of MPPDA leaders who opposed the bill received much greater prominence—and explicit support from Quigley—in *Herald World*.

Although the Brookhart Bill was defeated in March 1928, the tensions between, on the one hand, the major studios and theater circuits, and, on the other, independent exhibitors only deepened over the coming year. The growing dissonance was especially loud in *Exhibitors Herald World* over matters related to the transition to sound film. For example, the first three-quarters of the January 5, 1929, issue contained an assortment of advertisements, reports, and giddy opinions related to what sound films would mean for the year. Quigley was especially adamant about pushing his own neologism, *audiens*, as the term that should be used instead of terms such as *talkies, talking pictures*, or *soundies*.[68] He lost that word-smithing battle, but the overall takeaway from the first fifty-eight pages of the issue was unmistakable: sound films are transforming the industry—for the better. That perspective, however, got flipped in the last several pages of the issue, in "What the Picture Did for Me." Along with the brief exhibitor reviews, the section contained a lengthy piece by the section's editor, J. C. Jenkins. In describing a recent visit to eastern Indiana, Jenkins wrote:

> We have seen more tombstones around theatres the past week than we have ever seen before. Business has been terrible. We have not found a single theatre in all our travels, outside of those in larger cities having sound devices that has anywhere near paid film expenses. . . . Our observations have been that theatres in the smaller towns located within reasonable driving distance of cities having sound equipment are up against a hard proposition, and we can't get away from the conclusion that unless this equipment is placed within reach of these smaller theatres, many of them will be forced to close. We have found many already closed, and more are seriously considering closing. This may be a pessimistic view, but we are reporting conditions just as they exist.[69]

Jenkins was hard-pressed to find any easy solutions. Promotions, advertising, and other forms of "exploitation do not bring the answer," wrote Jenkins, who also commented that, unfortunately, "good pictures do not seem to solve the problem, although it is a great help."[70] As usual, Jenkins also used "His Colyum" (as he called it) to build a sense of community and goodwill among exhibitors, in this case through appealing to the Christmas spirit. But the overall outlook was dire, serving to highlight the differences between the fortunes of the downtown large theaters wired for sound and their small, rural counterparts.

To add insult to injury, Quigley would soon put the entire "What the Picture Did for Me" section out to pasture. As film historian Kathryn Fuller-Seeley has observed, *Exhibitors Herald World* "downsized ['What the Picture Did for Me'] in 1929, thereafter publishing only a few individual exhibitors' reports in the weekly 'Letters to the Editor' column. Although the exact reasons for its diminution remain unknown, it was possibly an indication of the booming film industry's increasingly dismissive attitude toward rural exhibitors."[71] Fuller-Seeley is correct that the major studios and broader, booming industry were dismissive about rural exhibitors. But what is important here is the active choice that Quigley made to join them in this view. The publisher who got his start appealing to independent midwestern exhibitors had made the calculation that they were less important to the future of the film industry and his business than the studios, circuits, and MPPDA.

During this period, some prominent exhibitor leaders criticized Quigley for what they perceived as always taking the side of the MPPDA. In *Harrison's*

Reports, P. S. Harrison charged Quigley with treason, calling him "the most obedient servant of the producers and distributors."[72] Quigley also entered into a feud with Frank Rembusch, the Unaffiliated Independent Motion Picture Exhibitors of America's leader and Indiana exhibitor, who, coincidentally, *Exhibitor's Trade Review* had libeled alongside William Johnston in 1917 (see chapter 2).[73] Rembusch was livid at Quigley's writing, which he viewed as propaganda on behalf of the MPPDA and "just a lot of character assassination and throwing of dung." He went on to say: "Why you love to pick on me is only explained by the fact that you know what Mr. Hays wants to say and probably Pettijohn [the MPPDA general counsel] writes your editorials."[74] In a separate, handwritten note sent to Quigley, Rembusch included a postscript: "Somebody is going to be the 'last of the Mohicans.' *Not me*" (emphasis in original).[75] It was a battle for survival, as Rembusch saw it, and Quigley had clearly picked the side of the MPPDA.

The provenance of the correspondence between Quigley and Rembusch supports the Hoosier exhibitor's claim of a cozy relationship between Quigley and the major studios. The letters were saved in the MPPDA archives because Quigley forwarded them to Hays and Pettijohn. The MPPDA filed away another letter with similar claims from the increasingly powerful Allied States Association of Motion Picture Exhibitors. Sent by Allied's president (and the former FTC commissioner), Abram F. Myers, to the members of his organization, the letter proposed the creation of a monthly twenty-four-page bulletin in response to "the low condition of the trade press. . . . They frankly admit that they dare not pursue a policy favorable to the exhibitors of the country because to do so will deprive them of all producer advertising." Myers envisioned that the bulletin would also play a role in community building, "aid[ing] mightily in knitting together the far flung membership of Allied, now scattered over thirty states."[76] Nothing immediately appears to have come from this proposal, although *Independent Exhibitors Film Bulletin*, founded a few years later in 1934, resembled Myers's plan in many ways.[77]

The relationship between Quigley and the MPPDA was far more dynamic and significant, though, than Harrison, Rembusch, or Myers could have realized. They accused Quigley of being a mouthpiece for the Hays Office. But these roles would soon be flipped, with Quigley coauthoring the document that would become known as the "Hays Code" and profoundly influencing Hollywood's approach to storytelling.

THE CODE AND THE SCOOP

It was through helping the MPPDA address a local matter in Chicago that Quigley got involved in the writing of the Production Code. "Charles C. Pettijohn was working to repeal the city's censorship ordinance by gaining the support of the city's Catholic archbishop, Cardinal George Mundelein," explains film historian Richard Maltby.[78] This campaign placed Quigley in the position of mediator between the MPPDA and the Catholic Church and made the publisher aware, through Pettijohn, that the trade organization was embarking on a rewrite of its rules concerning production.[79] The MPPDA's Studio Relations Committee (SRC) had issued two previous documents concerning the permissible content of movies: "The Formula," passed in 1924, which encouraged producers to send the SRC potentially problematic scripts for review; and the "Don'ts and Be Carefuls," passed in 1927, which distilled the policies of numerous state and municipal censorship boards into eleven prohibitions ("don'ts") and twenty-six areas in which to "be careful."[80] Yet neither of these documents had proven effective at preventing controversial movies from being produced and distributed. Based on a growing amount of negative publicity about immoral pictures—along with economic pressures related to censorship and the transition to sound—Hays instructed a committee of producers, led by Irving Thalberg, to revise the "Don'ts and Be Carefuls."[81]

Quigley shared the view that the industry needed better guidelines and better enforcement. But he believed there was an even bigger problem in the framing of the rules. The "Don'ts and Be Carefuls" were focused on the negative, that which should be avoided. Quigley envisioned a more powerful statement that explicitly affirmed Christian morality, using general principles as a way to address particular instances that would be offensive. To draft the new code, Quigley collaborated with Father Daniel Lord, a priest with an active interest in motion pictures and their influence on public morality (especially in regard to young people). Although he was based in St. Louis, Lord traveled widely and had acted as a consultant on Cecil B. DeMille's feature *The King of Kings* (1927).[82] As they worked on their version of the code in fall 1929 and January 1930, Quigley and Lord kept in close communication with Pettijohn at the MPPDA while simultaneously reporting their activities to Cardinal Mundelein, who told them they were his "contact men" and gave them autonomy on "everything up to the final decision."[83] The goal from the beginning, in other words, was to draft a document that both a Catholic cardinal and the most powerful people in Hollywood would accept. This was an audacious project for a trade paper editor and priest to take on, and it was all the more remarkable for the fact that they succeeded.

In their collaboration on the Code, Quigley and Lord came to resemble a producer-screenwriter team. Quigley was the producer, offering ideas and feedback to Lord, staying in close contact with the power players, and trying to move their project toward a green light from both the church and studios. Meanwhile, Lord was the one responsible for putting pen to paper, writing and rewriting the document that would become the Production Code of 1930. The key negotiations and test occurred in Los Angeles in early 1930. In January of that year, Quigley traveled to California to meet with Hays, who was enthusiastic about the proposed code. Quigley then encouraged Lord to join them on the West Coast so that he could present his document to the producers and address their questions.[84]

FIGURE 27. Martin Quigley stands to address a room of industry leaders in 1935; his frequent ally, MPPDA chief Will Hays, is seated to his left. Photograph courtesy of Georgetown University Library Special Collections.

In a lengthy meeting on February 10, 1930, Lord addressed the producers, imploring them to recognize the influential power of their medium and walking them through the Code's "general principles" and "particular applications" in depth.[85] Quigley was present but mostly silent at the meeting. Among the producers, Irving Thalberg was the chief voice of opposition, advocating for a narrower set of guidelines based on the existing "Don'ts and Be Carefuls."[86] Lord's emphasis on the moral responsibility of film producers and the transformative power of the medium sat uneasy with Thalberg, who viewed the movies as a form of commercial entertainment that simply mirrored public taste and demand. The public influenced movies far more than movies influenced the public, in Thalberg's opinion. Yet it was the charismatic Lord who won the day. After meeting separately to deliberate and make some minor amendments, the producers unanimously voted to accept the Production Code created by Lord and Quigley.[87]

Quigley and Lord kept their names and involvement off the code that was publicly shared. "Formulated by the Association of Motion Picture Producers, Inc. and the Motion Picture Producers & Distributors of America, Inc." was the only attribution of authorship published under the heading "A CODE Regulating Production of Motion Pictures." The agreement was based on three "GENERAL PRINCIPLES":

1. No picture shall be produced which will lower the moral standards of those who see it. Hence the sympathy of the audience should never be thrown to the side of crime, wrong-doing, evil or sin.
2. Correct standards of life, subject only to the requirements of drama and entertainment, shall be presented.

3. Law, natural or human, shall not be ridiculed, nor shall sympathy be created for its violation.

The document moved through twelve sections detailing "particular applications" —the majority of which related to depictions of sex and sexuality in some way (for example, "dancing" was listed as section seven of twelve and forbade "dances suggesting or representing sexual actions or indecent passion"). Other prohibitions included representations of brutal violence, illegal drugs, and the defacement of the American flag.[88]

The origin story of Hollywood's Production Code has been told many times before and with considerably more detail than what I offer in this chapter. Yet it is important to explore again here for what it tells us about the unique position Martin Quigley occupied within the industry during the *Exhibitors Herald World* years. Although many trade paper editors sought to be "thought leaders," no trade paper editor before or since him exerted such influence on film content and industry practice.

By acting as both a leader and intermediary, Quigley had put a Catholic priest at the center of writing new rules that Hollywood agreed to follow. He had offered something valuable to the MPPDA producers and distributors while also, in his view, delivering a win for independent exhibitors, who would become liberated from racy pictures that offended the sensibilities of their communities (and attracted the scissors of censor boards). From his perspective, he was following through on his promise to constructively improve all branches of the film industry. On the train ride back to Chicago, Quigley must have felt a sense of power and triumph.

It was short-lived.

Within a matter of days, Quigley and Lord's sense of victory and accomplishment transformed into feelings of disappointment and betrayal. The first blow came when someone close to the Code leaked it to the New York paper that Quigley most loathed. "Picture 'Don'ts' for '30," announced the February 19, 1930, headline of *Variety*. "Will Hays put the halter around the necks of the members of the Association of Motion Picture Producers at their annual meeting last night (Monday)," *Variety* reported. "Producers and members agreed to abide by his rules and regulations that will govern the industry in such a manner that censorship measures throughout the country will not be required and will probably be abandoned according to his plan."[89] Quigley was furious that *Variety* had scooped him on the biggest story of his career. He was not looking for credit; Quigley and Lord had deliberately left their names off the Production Code to downplay the involvement of the Catholic Church.[90] Nevertheless, the unauthorized leak of a document that he helped bring to life felt like a personal affront. Adding insult to injury, *Variety* had framed the story in terms of "don'ts" rather than a code rooted in decency and morality, and it applied its freewheeling approach to language to describe the MPPDA's action as "Hays put[ting] the halter around the necks."

But Quigley directed his greatest anger toward Hays, whom he felt betrayed him. Hays vigorously denied that he or anyone on his staff had leaked the Code to *Variety*.[91] But Quigley did not believe him, writing to Lord that "Hays continues to lie about the Variety release. He has had no intention of doing anything about it and he has no intention of doing anything about it now. Hays does not even dare speak to Variety about the matter for reasons that both Hays and myself well know."[92] It's unclear what exactly the "reasons" were that Quigley alluded to in his letter. It's possible that he was referring to the fact that many leading film producers and *Variety*'s editor, Sime Silverman, were Jewish. Or it could have been an acknowledgment (and warning) of the increasingly close relationship that *Variety* was enjoying with the Los Angeles production community, a tighter interpersonal bond than either Hays or Quigley enjoyed. In either case, it seems likely that Thalberg or another member of the producers committee was the source of the leak. It was a message to Quigley that he and Lord did not control Hollywood or the producers.

Over the next four year, Quigley grew disillusioned with the lack of Code enforcement. He complained to Hays that "the letter and spirit of the Code" were being violated right and left.[93] No meaningful action came of his complaints. In their correspondences, Quigley and Lord expressed a shared frustration—as did Quigley's friend and fellow Catholic Joseph Breen, who unfurled anti-Semitic insults in his reports on Hollywood and doubted whether Hays had any clout left among studio producers and executives.[94] But while the lack of enforcement for the Code proved disappointing, new opportunities emerged. As the Depression set in, Quigley found the circumstances favorable to complete the consolidation of the trade press and punish his enemies in the process.

SWALLOWING THE NEWS AND FINANCING CONSOLIDATION

Martin Quigley had pursued a strategy of acquiring and absorbing rival trade papers, beginning with *Motography* in 1917 and growing in scale with *Moving Picture World* in 1927. In the months following the adoption of the Code in February 1930, however, he found an ideal set of circumstances for finalizing, in his words, "a motion picture trade press consolidation." Quigley had positioned himself well for this moment, having proven himself a valuable ally to the MPPDA member companies with his roles in drafting the Production Code and opposing the Brookhart Bill and censorship laws. But it was the crash of the stock market in October 1929 and onset of the Great Depression that laid the groundwork for Quigley's market takeover. The Depression resulted in more cost-consciousness for the major motion picture distributors, who were under pressure to deliver results for investors and service debt payments on the huge amounts of money they had borrowed.[95] Previous attempts to consolidate the trade press and concentrate advertising in a single publisher had failed owing to a lack of organization and discipline among the studios. But a plan that could substantially reduce trade paper advertising costs for Paramount, MGM, and the other major companies could no longer be ignored by studio executives facing the prospect of receivership in the near future.

Even more important, Quigley's most formidable competitor, William A. Johnston of *Motion Picture News*, was under pressure from Wall Street in a manner similar to the highly leveraged studios. Two years earlier, in 1928, Johnston had traded away his ownership in *Motion Picture News* for stock in the newly formed Angus Company. Although Johnston served as an executive officer within Angus, the corporation's primary control seems to have resided with Bodell and Co., the bank that had issued its stock offering.[96] With the decline of the stock market, the Angus Company needed to seriously entertain any cash offer to purchase one of its journals. Johnston's ability to say "no" merely on principle had been lost; instead, he had a fiduciary obligation to obtain the best possible purchase offer. Sometime in the summer or fall of 1930, Quigley entered into serious negotiations with Johnston and the Angus Company to acquire *Motion Picture News*. To their credit, the sellers exacted a hefty premium—the purchase price would be $385,000 for a journal with only $40,000 in assets. But the deal came with the same noncompetition provision that Quigley had insisted for the Chalmers Company: Johnston had to sign a contract "agreeing not to engage in similar business for a period of five (5) years."[97] Around this same time, Quigley began negotiating with Arthur James to acquire *Exhibitors Daily Review and Motion Pictures Today* for a significantly lower price than *Motion Picture News*.

To finance the acquisitions of *Motion Picture News* and *Exhibitors Daily Review and Motion Pictures Today*, Quigley turned to the major studios. On October 15, 1930, Quigley sent a letter outlining his plan to Adolph Zukor, the head of Paramount-Publix and a master himself at consolidating and eliminating one's competitors.[98] What was the consolidation plan? Quite simply, the Big Five studios (Paramount, MGM, Warner Bros., Fox, and RKO) would commit in advance to purchasing $100,000 of advertising per year in Quigley's publications. Quigley would then use these guarantees to borrow the money needed to buy out *Motion Picture News* and *Exhibitors Daily Review and Motion Pictures Today*. In return for agreeing to the plan, Quigley promised the studios three things that are especially salient for this study. The first deliverable was economic in nature: "substantial savings to the motion picture advertisers by eliminating duplication in advertising efforts." Quigley estimated savings to the studios of $25,000 to $40,000 per year by concentrating their advertising dollars in one publication

Funneling advertising into just one publisher was the setup for Quigley's second promised deliverable: "Providing for the motion picture industry a publication of outstanding strength, influence and prestige—giving to the motion picture industry a Press comparable in service and personnel potentialities to that offered by the leading journals which serve other industries." This rationale may sound familiar; it was the same basic argument that William A. Johnston had articulated in 1917 when he advocated for only two trade papers to serve the industry. Ironically, it was Quigley's takeover of *Motion Picture News* that was enabling this vision to come to fruition.

Quigley's third proposed deliverable was the one that would wind up costing him the most face. "The plan contemplates the publication of a Hollywood Daily Edition," Quigley told Zukor. "The principal aim in its establishment would be to round out the service of the Press, to give the industry an authoritative voice in Hollywood and to off-set the irresponsible publications now issued there." Quigley did not list the "irresponsible publications" in Los Angeles by name. But readers of chapter 4 will have no problem guessing some of them. *Film Spectator*'s Welford Beaton had angered powerful studio executives by taking the side of labor and creative workers amid the 1927 salary cut debate. Later, in 1929, Beaton raised the ire of Will Hays when he attacked the MPPDA in a widely reprinted speech to the California Federation of Women's Clubs.[99]

Quigley had also expressed disdain on previous occasions for *Film Mercury*. The feeling was mutual; Quigley's editorials and the "What the Picture Did for Me" reviews were favorite punching bags for *Film Mercury*'s editor, Tamar Lane.[100] What remains unclear is the extent to which, in October 1930, W. R. Wilkerson's *Hollywood Reporter* was regarded as a threat. As a daily publication, *Hollywood Reporter* bears the most similarity to the new Hollywood publication that Quigley was proposing. Yet the *Reporter* had only begun publishing a few weeks prior to Quigley's letter to Zukor, suggesting that *Film Mercury, Film Spectator,* and other more established LA publications may have been the primary targets he sought to push aside. In any event, Quigley clearly thought Hollywood would be easy and cheap to win over. As box 3 demonstrates, the estimated budget that Quigley shared with Zukor included only $75,000 annually for the Hollywood daily, far less than the $220,000 budgeted for the New York daily and the $520,000 for the flagship weekly. For a shrewd publisher, this was a major blind spot and misstep.

In the weeks following Quigley's letter, the deal became finalized. The studios appear to have gotten on board, signing the contracts for $100,000 in yearly advertisements that allowed Quigley to finance his acquisitions of *Motion Picture News* and *Exhibitors Daily Review and Motion Pictures Today*. Even though Quigley could contractually block both of their editor-publishers from editing trade papers, he offered them jobs on his new staff. William A. Johnston would serve as the editor of the LA daily, now titled *Hollywood Herald*, with a debut planned for the spring or summer of 1931. Arthur James received a more noticeable demotion. Despite the fact that he had previously edited the publication that was the basis for Quigley's proposed New York daily publication, now titled *Motion Picture Daily*, Quigley gave the job of editor to Maurice "Red" Kann, formerly of *Motion Picture News* and *Film Daily*.[101] James was moved to an associate editor position at *Motion Picture Herald*, reporting to the new editor of the flagship weekly, Terry Ramsaye.[102]

BOX 3. QUIGLEY PUBLISHING'S ESTIMATED ANNUAL REVENUE AND EXPENSE

<u>REVENUE</u>

ADVERTISING

     Five major companies . . . . . . $ 500,000

     Other regular distributors
(based on 1929 expenditures in
  the three publications). 136,000

     Miscellaneous film advertising
(based on 1929 expenditures in the
  three publications). 100,000

     Equipment advertising
(based on 1929 expenditures in the three
publications, less deductions for
duplicating schedules). 198,000

SUBSCRIPTIONS: 70,000

SALES:

  Annual Publication $65,000
  Hollywood Publication
    (Pro. Accounts) . . . .   <u>25,000</u>   90,000

MISCELLANEOUS INCOME: Pro. Advt.,
     Reprints, Inserts, Color Prtg. <u>30,000</u>

                               $1,124,000

<u>EXPENSE</u>

  The cost of publication of the three
papers would, on the basis of present
operating and printing costs, after
allowing for appropriate development,
approximate annually as follows:

    National Weekly........ $520,000
    New York Daily........   220,000
    Hollywood Daily........   75,000
    Annual................   <u>40,000</u>

                                 <u>855,000</u>
                                $269,000

Quigley Publishing's estimated annual revenue and expense from consolidation of trade press through acquiring *Motion Picture News* and *Exhibitors Daily Review and Motion Pictures Today.* October 1930. SOURCE: Recreated from Martin J. Quigley to Adolph Zukor, Oct. 15, 1930, Martin J. Quigley Papers, box 3, folder 16, Georgetown University Library.

As the first editor of *Motion Picture Herald*, Terry Ramsaye brought a combination of prestige and professionalism to the office. Over the previous two decades, Ramsaye had bounced between positions in journalism, film production, and distribution.[103] His biggest accomplishment, however—and what he is best remembered for today—was writing an early history of cinema that wove together colorful anecdotes shared by key figures (especially Thomas Edison) into a dramatic narrative of film's development.[104] The project had started in 1921 as the serialized "Romantic History of the Motion Picture" for the fan magazine *Photoplay*.[105] In 1926, Ramsaye published a revised version of the series in book form as *A Million and One Nights: A History of the Motion Picture*.[106] Ramsaye had distinguished himself by his ability to take other people's stories and tell them well, while simultaneously displaying an ability to manage the minutiae of working for a film exchange or newspaper. Quigley welcomed Ramsaye, with his unique skill set and pedigree, onto *Motion Picture Herald*'s masthead.

With Ramsaye now serving as *Motion Picture Herald*'s editor, Martin Quigley gave himself a promotion, serving as the supervising editor in chief and publisher across all the Quigley publications. Freed from some of the humdrum tasks involved with editing a trade paper week after week, Quigley gained more time to give speeches, take meetings, write to influential people, and perform the role of industry thought leader. Quigley would continue to serve as the key voice in *Motion Picture Herald*'s editorial page, offering a column nearly every week (and frequently reprinting the same pieces in *Motion Picture Daily* and *Hollywood Herald*). Quigley had long wanted to be the voice for the entire industry. Now having dispensed with his biggest rivals, he was in a position to make his voice more loudly heard.

In the final issue of *Exhibitors Herald World* on December 27, 1930, Quigley announced the formation of *Motion Picture Herald*, emphasizing that the new publication "will seek its reward, not in catering to any special interest, but in the satisfaction it shall be able to render to the whole industry." He asserted *Motion Picture Herald*'s independence, insisting that it "shall not deal in either prejudices or favoritism." In the most striking passage of all, he promised to "deal fairly and equitably with every phase and feature of the business from the smallest cross-road exhibition interest to the greatest theatre circuit; from Poverty Row to the greatest studio; from the single-picture state-righter to the greatest distribution system."[107] Like many of Quigley's statements around this time, his attempt at industry unity had a condescending quality, with a "know your place" subtext to the small-time players conjured in his description. Worse yet, the sweeping encompassment of these constituencies ignored the uneven power dynamics that had been central to the Brookhart Bill debates. Did the major distributors "deal fairly and equitably" with small-town exhibitors when they compelled them to book entire slates of pictures, sight unseen, and wait months for their turns to show them? Did the studio-owned theaters "deal fairly and equitably" with the Poverty Row producers who could not get their movies into downtown theaters? Unity, fairness, and equity were not terms that most of *Motion Picture Herald*'s exhibitor readers associated with their chosen industry. If Quigley did not want to address and call out these structural inequalities, those readers would turn to other trade paper editors who would.

CONCLUSION

In 1920, Martin J. Quigley had called out Adolph Zukor's attempts at vertical integration as the greatest threat to the industry, certain to lead to monopolization.[108] A decade later, Quigley requested Zukor's support in granting him just such a monopoly over the film industry's trade press. The irony is remarkable. For P. S. Harrison and many of his independent exhibitor readers, Quigley was a hypocrite and a traitor. Although they would not have had access to the archival letter from Quigley to Zukor, the involvement of the MPPDA in the trade paper consolidations of 1930 was reported on and rumored about following the launch of *Motion Picture Herald*.[109] Exhibitors suspicious of the consolidation would have found just cause even in the new trade paper's title. While *Motion Picture Herald* may have been conceived as a shorthand way of combining *Motion Picture News* and *Exhibitors Herald*, it is telling that *Exhibitors* was one of the words selected to be eliminated in the new title.

From Quigley's perspective, though, he never abandoned those exhibitors. The industry was changing. Rather than fighting that change, he was trying to help it evolve for the better—building better theaters, avoiding government regulation, adopting a Production Code for the creation of more wholesome movies. Harrison had spent years decrying dirty pictures, but what had all of his editorials and reviews ultimately changed? Quigley, however, had brought a priest into a room full of producers and emerged with a document tying movies to Christian morality. Incidentally, that priest, Daniel A. Lord, immediately congratulated Quigley in December 1930 on learning about Quigley's acquisition of two rival trade papers. "I know quite clearly what it means for the future of the Code," wrote Lord, suggesting that Quigley's allies in the Catholic Church perceived the consolidation as a signal of Quigley's increased influence within the film industry and a win for the broader cause of public morality.[110]

Although the consolidation represented a triumph for Quigley, it equally—if not more so—represented the logical conclusion stemming from the decline of the New York trade papers and the increase of efficiencies within the industry. Quigley's plan seemed to have everything going for it. The studios had a strong financial incentive, especially as the Depression worsened, to restrict their trade paper advertising budgets to the Quigley publications. The competing trade film industry papers that remained—in New York, Los Angeles, and the states in between—knew that they were at a significant disadvantage if they wanted to press on. Looking at it from the outside, at least, Quigley's monopoly plan should have worked.

Instead, the plan failed. The final chapter of this book explores why it failed and how a heterogeneous trade press came to flourish within the industry for the next four decades.

6

The Great Diffusion

Hollywood's Reporters, Exhibitor Backlash, and Quigley's
Failed Monopoly

In an internal memo from June 1932, *Motion Picture Herald* publisher Martin Quigley instructed his editor, Terry Ramsaye, to publish a testimonial from an independent producer in praise of the trade paper. "Because of circumstances attending the reorganization of our company a year-and-a-half ago, there was a natural suspicion in the minds of many people, including the Independents, that we were going to be all for the major companies and against everything else," wrote Quigley.[1] The memo was received by Ramsaye in their new offices in New York City.

The Quigley Publishing Company had left Chicago in 1931 after acquiring *Motion Picture News* and *Exhibitors Daily Review and Motion Pictures Today*. It was a move that made sense for reasons of economy—a New York base of operations was essential for *Motion Picture Daily*, and the proximity to the leading distribution executives was beneficial for the weekly *Motion Picture Herald*, too. But it only contributed to the perception that Quigley had turned his back on the independent exhibitors of the Heartland, the struggling managers and owners who had once pledged loyalty to a "'Herald Only' Club."

Recognizing the perception problems, Quigley told Ramsaye, "It is important that we should do everything possible to establish ourselves as an all-industry paper."[2] Quigley and Ramsaye (along with the editors of *Motion Picture Daily* and *Hollywood Herald*) tried to find ways to make themselves valuable to the entire industry, publishing detailed reports on market conditions, labor relations, and production schedules. If judged strictly by the quality of what they published week after week, they were succeeding. *Motion Picture Herald* was a model for the application of industrial journalism practices toward the film industry. Even the typography, printing, and paper stock were of superior quality, boasted Quigley Publications' general manager, Colvin W. Brown.[3]

Yet none of this was enough. Technical mastery and typographical excellence ultimately mattered far less to key constituents of the *Herald*'s readers than what they perceived as the paper's true allegiances. Over the next year, Quigley would watch his subscriptions plummet, a former employee challenge him with a rival publication, and his Hollywood paper go out of business. In 1932, Quigley took out a $50,000 loan from ERPI—AT&T's licensing arm for its sound technologies—to keep his operations going. It was a secretive arrangement that proved embarrassing when the news became public a few years later during a Federal Communications Commission (FCC) investigation.[4] Despite having the backing of the major studios and AT&T's patent pool, it was clear by the end of 1933 that Quigley's attempted monopoly and vision of an "all-industry paper" had failed.

Why did Quigley fail? And what does his failure tell us about the business cultures and attitudes within the film industry? To answer these questions, we need to look closely at the publications that successfully competed against Quigley's well-capitalized machine. *Variety* and *Hollywood Reporter* were the most important of these challengers, and as a result, I will give them the most attention. But *Showmen's Round Table* and *Boxoffice* also played important roles in the undoing of Quigley's grand plans, as did the money and support of workers within sectors across the film industry. By exploring (first) *Variety*, (second) the LA production community, and (third) the exhibitor community and rival papers pitched to them, we can see how the combination of tenacious, opportunistic publishers and the cultures of industry workers resulted in the formation of a Hollywood trade press that did not adhere to the rules or plan that Quigley and the Motion Picture Producers and Distributors of America (MPPDA) had agreed upon.

Before analyzing those trade papers, though, we need to analyze the environment in which they published and competed. "In light of the current depression," "on account of the depression," and "despite the depression" were frequently used phrases across all of the industry's publications.[5] The Great Depression was also boldly invoked in the advertisements within the papers. Paramount promised exhibitors booking its pictures that "Your Box Office Depression ends."[6] MGM went a step further in its 1932 campaign, "The Hell with Depression!," which featured cartoon illustrations of Leo the Lion enthusiastically dancing, and, in another ad, punching a man wearing a tuxedo and top hat (fig. 28). "GOOD pictures sock depression RIGHT on the schnozzola!," emphasized the latter ad, taking the hardsell approach with lots of text, product details, and even another illustration. This larger and more prominent illustration imagined a young boy talking with his grandfather in the year 1972. "Grandpa, what did you do during the Great Depression? Were you licked too?" asked the boy. "No, my lad," responds Grandpa. "I played Metro-Goldwyn-Mayer Pictures." This imaginary exchange reveals one way in which the Great Depression was already being memorialized as it played out in real time. The film industry's workers and the American people were living through something historic, and they knew it.

FIGURE 28. "Merrily We Roll Along!" [MGM advertisement], *Film Daily,* April 13, 1932, 3, https://lantern.mediahist.org/catalog/filmdailyvolume55859newy_0887.

THE DEPRESSION AND THE MOVIES

"The motion picture business is neither depression-proof nor fool-proof," observed Abram F. Myers in the pages of *Film Daily* and *The Film Daily Year Book* at the dawn of 1932.[7] The occasion was reflections from industry leaders on the past year, and Myers, the chairman of the Allied States Association and longtime opponent of vertical integration, was not in any mood to pull his punches. Indeed, no sector of American life was truly depression-proof by 1932. Unlike its relatively fast bounce-backs from previous financial panics, the United States was now two full years into this depression, and the conditions were only worsening. The unemployment rate was more than 20 percent, hitting African American communities and working-class whites especially hard. People who had considered themselves middle class now worried about how they would get by; those who always had worried about how they would get by and who lacked safety nets were plunged into new depths of poverty.[8] Inexpensive forms of entertainment that were once considered depression-proof, like going to the movies, increasingly became perceived as a luxury, one more thing that needed to be rationed.[9]

Within this context, the nation's film exhibition sector experienced tremendous losses and closures.[10] Film historian Kathryn Fuller-Seeley emphasizes that small-town theaters were hit especially hard; she estimates that "by 1932, about 8,000 of the nation's 23,000 movie theaters were closed. Densely populated urban areas of the East Coast and West Coast experienced a relatively minor theater closure rate of from 7 percent to 20 percent, but the Midwest, Plains, South, and northern New England lost from 22 percent to 47.7 percent of all their movie houses."[11] Small-town theaters fought to stay afloat by offering reduced price admissions, double-features, and "dish night" promotions (which were eventually surpassed by "bank night" cash prize drawings).[12] These practices were regarded with disdain by the major distributors and frequently critiqued in the pages of *Motion Picture Herald* for the ways they seemed to devalue the core products of the industry and, in the case of double features, keep children up too late at night.[13] But the promotions clicked with Depression-era audiences, and they brought warm bodies and much-needed revenue into theaters on nights that they might otherwise sit empty. To inexpensively book the content needed for a dish night, bank night, or the second half of a double bill, exhibitors turned to the Poverty Row producer-distributors, such as Monogram, Tiffany, and Astor.[14] These Poverty Row companies, in turn, became the best advertising customers of *Boxoffice, Showmen's Round Table,* and the other exhibitor papers of the 1930s that wound up providing Martin Quigley with unanticipated competition.

The same theaters that the major companies resented for running double features and dish nights had their own long list of grievances coming back toward them. Independent exhibitors complained about block booking, high rental fees, and an abundance of pictures that they regarded as too "urban"—a term that could mean something either too racy and risqué or too highbrow and sophisticated—for the tastes of their audiences.[15] As we will see, these exhibitors looked for trade papers that would keep them informed, give them forums to discuss problems and solutions, and forcefully represent their interests. They also found a champion in the abovementioned Abram F. Myers, who as a former Federal Trade Commissioner understood how to lobby the government into greater investigation and oversight into antitrust practices within the film industry.[16]

The Depression's effects, of course, extended to theaters located in major American cities, too. Theater ownership proved to be financially disastrous for some of the industry's biggest corporations. In January 1933, Paramount-Publix and RKO both entered receivership, the result of a depressed box office and the huge debt burdens that both corporations had taken on in their massive theater acquisitions of the late 1920s. As Tino Balio notes, "Paramount's bankruptcy was the second largest the country had ever known and one of the most complicated."[17] In the weeks following the announcements, Paramount took out full-page advertisements in several trade papers to emphasize that its subsidiaries, Paramount Productions Inc. and Paramount Pictures Distributing Corp. were "NOT in receivership. They will continue to produce and distribute quality motion pictures under the same management and personnel as before."[18] Yet the power structure had changed. Paramount's Adolph Zukor, who had long been regarded as the film industry's human embodiment of unrestrained expansion and monopoly, was no longer in charge of the corporation he had built. William Fox and Universal's Carl Laemmle also lost control owing to major financial restructurings of their companies.[19] Ironically, just as the nation's Prohibition laws were ending, a more sober and cautious approach to the corporate management of the major film corporations was taking hold.

The RKO and Paramount bankruptcies were both announced during the period now widely viewed as the lowest point of the entire Great Depression—the four months between the November 8, 1932, election of Franklin Delano Roosevelt to the presidency and his inauguration on March 4, 1933.[20] Outgoing president Herbert Hoover resisted helping Roosevelt implement the bold policies on which he had campaigned and beaten the incumbent. A stressed financial sector became even more uncertain, and the general public worried about the solvency of local banks and the security of their savings accounts. Although thousands of American banks had already closed during the Depression, a new wave of bank runs—with customers withdrawing their money from banks en masse—created an all-out crisis in February 1933 that threatened to decimate the institutions that remained.[21] Roosevelt famously addressed the panic in his inaugural address, declaring that "the only thing we have to fear is fear itself." Yet words alone were not enough. Within days of taking the Oval Office, Roosevelt declared a banking holiday, closing all banks temporarily to try to avoid their permanent collapse.[22]

The March 1933 bank holiday proved a pivotal moment in Hollywood history, particularly in the relationship between studios and their creative workers. In response to the bank holiday, the studios implemented 50 percent salary cuts to most of their production workers. The studios claimed that the cuts were a temporary necessity resulting from the tightened credit situation and a shortage of cash to meet payroll obligations.[23] But as banks reopened and the salary cuts remained in place, Hollywood's writers, actors, and other creatives came to believe they had been duped. They felt that the studios had cynically and opportunistically used the bank crisis to cut salaries and increase corporate profits, all at the expense of people who actually made the movies that audiences paid their hard-earned money to see. Galvanized, writers organized and formed the Screen Writers Guild in April 1933.[24] Actors followed soon after with the Screen Actors Guild.[25] All of these groups read the local trade papers closely, looking for voices in the press to affirm their perspectives and call out the greed of their opponents.

Somehow, in the midst of so much upheaval, these studios and their workers managed to produce some of the most spectacular and memorable movies ever made. Depression audiences were temporarily transported watching *King Kong* (1933) climb the Empire State Building, Fred Astaire and Ginger Rogers dance in *Top Hat*'s (1935) art-deco Venice, and Clark Gable lead a *Mutiny on the Bounty* against Charles Laughton's Captain Bligh. The high-energy, show-must-go-on spirit of the Warner Bros. backstage musicals *42nd Street* (1932) and *Gold Diggers of 1933* (1933), featuring a mix of new and seasoned chorus girls, presented the enduring American dream of upward mobility alongside a jaded knowingness that *life ain't fair, kid*. The real showstoppers always came at the end: Busby Berkeley's kaleidoscopic musical numbers, using massive sets, high camera angles, dozens of dancers, and intricate editing to transform the cast into plastic abstractions.

The style, energy, and ambition dramatized and embodied in the backstage musical found their way into showbusiness journalism, too. The film industry's trade papers found new ways to compete, and the ones that survived lasted for decades to follow. Mirroring the plots and aesthetics of backstage musicals, the first battles waged in the *Motion Picture Herald* era would be over matters of speed, money, and style.

VARIETY STAYS IN THE PIX SHEET BIZ

Martin Quigley hated *Variety*. It's easy to see why. The paper had scooped him on the giant story of 1930 that belonged to him: the creation and adoption of a new Production Code. And this was just one of many ways that *Variety* thumbed its nose at Quigley and his publications. *Variety* played by its own rules, always trying to have it both ways: *Variety* was a relentless scorekeeper of how the studios, theaters, and other trade papers were doing, yet it refused to have its own circulation audited. As a result of *Variety*'s keeping its numbers a secret, an exasperated Quigley estimated "that the cost per page per thousand units of trade circulation in VARIETY is as high as $100," compared to a rate of $15 per page for *Motion Picture Herald*.[26] Why did the studios not see the error of their ways?

Quigley was infuriated when he saw traces of *Variety* slang seeping into his own publications. When he read through one of the first issues of *Motion Picture Herald* in January 1931, Quigley fired off a lengthy memo to his staff, warning them not "to attempt any imitation of the style of 'Variety' by the unbridled use of corrupted

English words and resort to cheap and near-obscene slang expressions which are decidedly more representative of the carnival racket and variety show business than the motion picture industry." Quigley highlighted several specific offenses:

> From page 8, Jan. 17 issue: "One of the gravest bulls, and most expensive ones at that, pulled daily etc. etc." Cheap language for publication. We don't want it.
>
> From page 12, same issue: "An 'Examiner' reviewer was aired" etc. etc. Some more stuff we don't want.
>
> From caption on box, page 50: "Up in the Big Dough". Not printable English.
>
> Personal talent on the stage may not be any more properly referred to as "flesh and blood" entertainment than as "liver and kidney" entertainment. The word "flesh" as descriptive of a form of entertainment is prohibited.
>
> Keep "sex" out of headlines.[27]

These objections to "flesh" and "sex" demonstrated the strong degree to which morality and propriety loomed large for Quigley in the language used in his publications.

The memo and its chiding also revealed that *Motion Picture Herald*'s editor, Terry Ramsaye, was still getting acclimated to his new boss. Ramsaye's writing in *A Million and One Nights* (1926), his book about cinema's early history, brought a playful quality to the stories he told, and he had championed the use of film slang early in his career. In 1916, for example, Ramsaye, then the director of publicity for the Mutual Film Corporation, sent postcards to exhibitors and journalists proposing that the industry consider using *pix* as a substitute for the word *movies*.[28] He was largely unsuccessful, however, and *pix* was used infrequently in the trade press until 1928, when *Variety* took it up.[29] Now, Quigley was making it clear that such slang had no place in the pages of *Motion Picture Herald*. Ramsaye seems to have adapted quickly, publicly excising instances of the very slang word that he had championed fifteen years earlier, even as he privately filed away clippings and notes that he found interesting into what he labeled as his "dope files."[30]

If style and language served as markers of difference between *Variety* and *Motion Picture Herald*, then speed and breadth of box-office reporting became a common objective—an obsession, even—on which both papers competed directly. The major metropolitan houses were seen as bellwethers for how a film would perform across the nation's other major markets. The grosses also functioned as a form of industry scorekeeping, tracking the comparative performances of movies, studios, and theaters.[31] In its efforts to be as timely and comprehensive as possible, *Variety* generated weekly estimates based on information it said it received about Friday's performances—noting, for example, that Columbia's *Criminal Code* (1931) "jacked business up to $14,000" at LA's Pantages (a Fox-owned theater), while RKO's *Royal Bed* (1931) had "no names to lure; weak and may get $3,000" at Minneapolis's Seventh Street Theatre (an Orpheum house that had become part of RKO).[32] Not to be outdone, *Motion Picture Herald* published several pages of "Theatre Receipts" near the middle of most issues. *Herald* distinguished its coverage by including markets that *Variety* typically ignored, like Charlotte, Providence, and Des Moines.[33]

In the March 1931 issue of *Harrison's Reports*, editor P. S. Harrison lampooned this competition, referring to it as the "'Variety'-'Herald' Farce-Comedy." Harrison highlighted discrepancies in the figures they reported for the same films and theaters, refusing to give the upper hand to either publication. Harrison argued that the managers "do not give out receipt figures to either paper, and that both papers are forced to guess such receipts in order to pretend that they are giving their readers a real service."[34] Harrison was minimizing the networks of sources that *Variety* publisher Sime Silverman and Quigley had both cultivated and that did, in fact, deliver authentic information. Ultimately, however, the race became a draw. Both papers continued to gather and publish box-office information as quickly as they could, with Quigley using the frequency of the *Motion Picture Daily* as an added weapon in the battle.

On one important and measurable front, however, *Motion Picture Herald* took the clear lead. As chronicled in the previous chapter, Quigley had financed the acquisition of *Motion Picture News* and *Exhibitors Daily Review and Motion Pictures Today* through persuading the major film corporations to sign large five-year advertising contracts with Quigley Publications. The chief rationale was "substantial savings to the motion picture advertisers by eliminating duplication in advertising efforts," with Quigley estimating that each studio would save $25,000 to $40,000 per year.[35] The plan worked like gangbusters for Quigley. In the first two years of *Motion Picture Herald*, Quigley saw the number of advertising pages in his weekly trade paper increase substantially, from a median of 22.75 advertising pages in 1930 (the year preceding the new arrangement) to 55 pages in 1931 and 44 pages in 1932.[36] Meanwhile, *Variety* watched the number of film-related advertising pages drop from 18.75 pages in a typical issue in 1930, to 14 pages in 1931, to 9.25 pages in 1932.[37] To make matters worse, the other chief entertainment forms that *Variety* covered—vaudeville and "legit" theater—had been hit even harder than the movies. Two-thirds of Broadway theaters were dark in 1932, and *Variety* sold a mere 3.25 pages of non-film-related advertising per issue that year.[38] "Depression cutting deep into biz," reported *Variety* on its Times Square entertainment page, a statement equally true about the paper itself.[39]

Sime Silverman needed cash to keep his paper afloat. To try to raise money quickly, *Variety* lowered its subscription price from $10 per year to $6 per year (with additional promotional discounts for subscribers who signed up for multiple years).[40] *Variety*'s new rate was still double the $3 yearly subscription cost of *Motion Picture Herald*, but the price drop appears to have been calculated to create a sense of urgency for readers to subscribe or renew, paying up front for subscriptions that would last up to three years and expand the paper's advertising reach. The subscription drive alone did not raise enough money, though, and Sime Silverman took on substantial debt—so much so that, by the end of 1931, the bank refused to continue lending to him.

Deep in debt and unable to borrow more money, Silverman called in a favor from Joseph Kennedy. The godfather of RKO and father of a future president contractually agreed to become the guarantor of Silverman's bank loans.[41] If Silverman defaulted, the bank could debit the money owed from Kennedy's account (a scenario that happened in April 1933 to the tune of $11,944).[42] The structure of the deal was classic Kennedy.[43] He was able to put in relatively little of his own money yet achieve a substantial result: saving *Variety*, a paper that had helped him achieve success in the film industry, through extending access to an ongoing credit facility.[44] But if this deal feels completely congruent with what we know about Kennedy, then it is equally incongruent with much of the lore that has been passed down over the years about Sime Silverman. In Hugh Kent's influential 1926 *American Mercury* essay, Kent celebrated more than simply *Variety*'s language. He praised the paper's independence—its refusal to follow in the footsteps of the *Clipper* and enter into financial entanglements with captains of industry that might compromise the paper's editorial integrity.[45] During the Great Depression and a time of need, however, Silverman accepted financial help from Joseph Kennedy to keep the lights on.

Sime Silverman's greatest accomplishment may ultimately have been in grooming a deeply loyal and hardworking staff who believed in *Variety*'s mission with an almost religious fervor. During the early 1930s, Silverman experienced a severe decline in health. As he took a step back, his lieutenants stepped up. Their contributions, even much more than Kennedy's credit line, proved vital for *Variety*'s continued existence. In 1931, Sime's son, Sid Silverman, took over much of the publishing responsibilities and shrewdly decided to enhance *Variety*'s coverage of radio, a strategic decision that paid off later that decade.[46] Meanwhile, managing the day-to-day operations of *Variety* fell largely to editor Abel Green and manager Harold Erichs. "Abel was the star, but Harold signed the checks," writes Peter Besas, who emphasizes the financial discipline that Erichs imposed on the paper during the Depression.[47] When Sime Silverman died, on September 22, 1933, he left seven hundred stock shares to his wife and son, and the remaining three hundred were split among Green, Erichs, and six other loyal staffers. Together, they took ownership of the paper in every sense of the word.[48]

Sime Silverman spent the final months of his life in 1933 living in Southern California. He had moved for his health, with doctors recommending the warm, dry climate. While living in the region, Silverman met frequently with Arthur Ungar, who had opened *Variety*'s LA office in the mid-1920s and had been selected to edit the company's new LA-based paper, *Daily Variety*. The new paper debuted on September 6, 1933, less than three weeks before Silverman passed away.[49] In *Daily Variety*'s first issue, Arthur Ungar promised a paper that would deliver "the news of the show business" without "vanity publicity" and without any attempt to "tell those in the show business how to conduct their business."[50] This was followed a few weeks later by a full-page self-advertisement for *Daily Variety*: "NOT A TRADE PAPER PRINTING TRADE VIEWS but A NEWSPAPER PRINTING TRADE NEWS."[51]

For readers today, these might sound just like any other journalistic platitudes—a commitment to objectivity, news gathering, and editorial judgment. Readers in the Hollywood of 1933, however, would have recognized Ungar's words and the advertisement for exactly what they were: attacks on the movie colony's most popular publication, the paper that had outmaneuvered Martin Quigley's *Hollywood Herald*, provoked several libel lawsuits, and even stolen *Variety*'s own news.

THE RISE OF *HOLLYWOOD REPORTER*

"We have never at any time been 100% in the good graces of the majority of the production and distributing companies," reflected W. R. "Billy" Wilkerson about the early history of his trade paper, the *Hollywood Reporter*.[52] It was an understatement from a publisher who had been banned from more than one studio lot. The occasion for Wilkerson's musings was court, a familiar setting for a publisher who was also frequently accused of libel and other transgressions.[53] In this particular case, Wilkerson was trying to avoid paying the taxes that the government said he owed. His defense was becoming a popular one among Hollywood personnel: deductions for homes, clothes, and luxury items were all necessary in an industry in which business and social life were inseparable.[54] Although Wilkerson was not able to persuade the Board of Tax Appeals on the merits of his case, there is no doubt that Wilkerson's power and success emerged from his effectiveness at operating within Hollywood's social circles and culture. Even when a studio would officially bar the *Hollywood Reporter*, Wilkerson was always able to find people who worked within it to leak news, buy ads, and even lend him money (fig. 29).

The legacy of Billy Wilkerson is complex, with his shameful role in the postwar blacklist (which primary sources substantiate) and his possible involvement in organized crime (for which there are not primary sources to substantiate).[55] W. R. Wilkerson III has recently addressed these aspects of his father's life in *Hollywood Godfather*, and I am grateful for the biographical details, character traits, and personal memories that he has shared.[56] For the purposes of this chapter, I will focus on the trade paper's first few years and Wilkerson's activities that I have been able to document using primary sources. By turning to correspondences that were saved in the manuscript collections of Hollywood personnel, along with documentation generated through lawsuits and old copies of the trade paper itself, we can identify the strategies and tactics that differentiated the *Hollywood Reporter* from its competitors and appealed to the sensibilities of Hollywood's creative community.

The *Hollywood Reporter* was audacious from the start. But it was not immediately combative or incendiary. The early issues, published daily and generally running four pages, looked a great deal like *Film Daily* in their makeup, with short news items pertaining to all branches of the film industry. The most detailed and valuable reporting went into tracking the production schedules of the studios—snapshots of how many pictures each studio was making, and which stages of the production

FIGURE 29. Two of Hollywood's behind-the-scenes power brokers: *Hollywood Reporter* founder, W. R. Wilkerson (left), and influential attorney Edwin J. Loeb pictured together at the Eighth Academy Awards Banquet in 1935. Photograph courtesy of the Motion Picture Academy of Arts and Sciences, Margaret Herrick Library.

process those pictures were in, at a given moment.[57] The *Hollywood Reporter* also devoted considerable attention and energy to the review of new pictures, an area of interest to exhibitor readers (who might book and play the pictures) and Hollywood creative workers (who liked to keep tabs on one another's films and note whose work stood out within a particular production). To compete with other trade papers based on speed of reviews and capitalize on its Southern California location, Wilkerson tried to embed *Hollywood Reporter* agents within the preview screenings that took place throughout the region.[58]

Two of the *Hollywood Reporter*'s signature columns were included in the paper's first issue. The first and most famous, "Trade Views," was Billy Wilkerson's platform for addressing the industry. He would later use it to taunt and attack his perceived enemies, but in the early issues, he spoke more generally on matters related to advertising, distribution, production budgets, and picture quality.[59] Wilkerson knew something about all these topics, but he projected the confidence and authority of the world's foremost expert—a self-assuredness (or narcissism, in the eyes of his critics) that would only grow over the next three decades. The second of the *Hollywood Reporter*'s signature columns was the gossipy "The Low Down," penned by Edith Wilkerson, who was married to Billy at the time.[60] Edith Wilkerson had a knack for using playful language to hook readers and keep them interested—even when there wasn't much to report. "At a hey-hey party the other evening in Hollywood, a movie star found himself with several 'impromptu' dinner guests on hand, and an undersupply of food," revealed Edith Wilkerson in one such "Low Down" column. She generally refrained from identifying people by name in the column, instead dishing on "a well known actor" or "a certain studio executive of the valley." She frequently employed a two-sentence joke structure of setup and punchline: "We hear that a certain 'popular' young writer is about to be presented with deportation papers. This does not exactly come under the heading of 'Bad News' to anyone who worked on the same lot with him."[61] Between "Trade Views" and "The Low Down," Billy and Edith Wilkerson set the tone for the *Hollywood Reporter*—a publication that was both playful and forceful, breezy and authoritative.

While gossip, reviews, and industry prognostications were plentiful in early *Hollywood Reporter* issues, pages of advertising were not. Especially after the *Reporter* entered its second full month of publication in October 1930, the advertisements that provided the profit center for any trade paper became relatively scarce. The major film corporations were opting not to buy ads, a practice in keeping with their overall approach to earlier LA trade papers, such as *Camera!*, *Film Mercury*, and *Film Spectator*. But some of these companies were going a step further: warning their employees against purchasing ads. Billy Wilkerson later reflected: "We will get along very well with a studio for months and months, then because we happen to print a true story of something that happened on their lot or reviewed one of their pictures that they thought was good, but our reviewers didn't, would bar us off the lot and suggest that their employees refuse to advertise with us."[62] While these sorts of anecdotes about studio access might sound apocryphal or like the stuff of lore, contemporaneous evidence and sources back them up.

The problems with access appear to have begun within months of the trade paper's debut. In a March 1931 letter to Edwin Loeb, Billy Wilkerson pleaded with the influential Hollywood attorney to help him gain access to the studio lots. Some of the studios, Wilkerson protested, were barring *Hollywood Reporter* staff but permitting entrance to New York trade papers. In his letter, Wilkerson emphasized that the reason he wanted to be on the lots was about advertising, not newsgathering. He framed his request around "soliciting the writers on the lots" to buy ads in a forthcoming special "Writer's Number" issue. Wilkerson promised that *Hollywood Reporter* would use "disgression" in its sales techniques and avoid interrupting people who were busy at work. "We will not use high pressure methods in getting writers to sign for space AND THERE IS NO RETALIATORY EXPRESSIONS if a writer denies our request for advertising assistance," Wilkerson assured Loeb. The attorney may have read this, considered Wilkerson's reputation, and wondered if the publisher doth protest too much.[63] The *Hollywood Reporter* managed to expand its advertising business in the months and years that followed, but the matters of studio access and ad sales to creative workers continued to loom large.

Wilkerson also needed help with the news-gathering functions of his young paper. He cunningly found a solution in the three thousand miles that separated New York from Los Angeles. Many members of the Hollywood creative community loved *Variety*, but they didn't appreciate how long they had to wait for it. The Silvermans' LA subscribers waited at least three days longer for each new issue than their New York City counterparts, as trains hauled their copies cross-country. Thanks to the telegraph and telephone, however, information could travel much faster than paper. Billy Wilkerson capitalized on this advantage. When the new week's issue of *Variety* came hot off the press each Tuesday morning, a *Hollywood Reporter* correspondent was among the first to devour it. The correspondent would then relay—via phone or telegram—all the important film news back to the *Hollywood Reporter* home office, which repackaged the information into Wednesday's daily paper, sometimes saving a few items for Thursday as well. Wilkerson never attributed the source of this news, which after he was done with it, had become old news by the time *Variety* reached the West Coast on Friday.

In February 1932, *Variety* sued *Hollywood Reporter*, demanding an injunction and alleging that Wilkerson had been stealing its news for months.[64] Suspicious that they were getting scooped on their own news, *Variety* had set up a sting operation, publishing a deliberately fake news item to see if it cropped up in the pages of *Hollywood Reporter*. Sure enough, it did.[65] The fictitious news item concerned an executive's return to the Fox studio, a far more bland plagiarism trap than the time, in 1908, when *Variety* caught the *New York Dramatic Mirror* copying its vaudeville reviews by inventing a new comedy act called "The Undertaker" and waiting for a slightly altered review to pop up in the competitor's paper.[66] The *Dramatic Mirror* episode became a favorite and often repeated story in *Variety*'s self-lore, most likely because of the way it turned the tables on the more established and snooty *Dramatic Mirror*, with the added flourish of naming the takedown "The Undertaker."[67] In contrast, *Variety* and the *Hollywood Reporter* seldom rehashed the news-copying incident, perhaps because the particular lawsuit fizzled (no injunction was awarded) or because the rivalry would escalate, over time, to much greater heights.

THE HERALD LAYS AN EGG IN HOLLYWOOD

As Billy Wilkerson's *Hollywood Reporter* fought in the mud to obtain news, advertising, and attention, Martin Quigley's *Hollywood Herald* seemed to have everything going for it. The major studios had committed to purchase advertising, aiding with the single biggest challenge to a trade paper's financial health. On the newsgathering side, Quigley had a reporting network in place that he could use, with correspondents in LA and most other major cities. And not to be over-looked, one of the industry's most respected trade paper editors and thought leaders, William A. Johnston, had agreed to serve as the *Hollywood Herald*'s editor. Yet Quigley's daily LA paper never caught on. *Hollywood Herald* lived for an undistinguished twenty-six months (June 1931 to August 1933) before shutting down and fading into obscurity.[68] Few film historians have ever heard of this paper, and Martin S. Quigley never mentions *Hollywood Herald* in his book about his father's career.[69] What went wrong?

There was more than one cause for *Hollywood Herald*'s failure. Because of the lack of primary sources addressing the paper and the publication's rarity (most of the issues are lost), some causes are easier to identify than others. One cause—and likely a symptom of larger problems—was a lack of steady leadership. William A. Johnston lasted as editor for a mere three months.[70] The circumstances surrounding his departure are unclear. Was his style a mismatch for the LA creative community? For Quigley Publications? For both? Johnston stayed active in the film industry, working in studio publicity and story departments, but he never again enjoyed the influence he held during the 1910s and 1920s.[71] Johnston's successor was Leo Meehan, who had earlier served as *Hollywood Herald*'s general manager (and, before that, worked as a producer and director).[72] But Meehan, too, would ultimately leave. In March 1933, Wid Gunning, formerly of *Wid's Daily* and *Wid's Weekly* and an on-again, off-again screenwriter, took over as the paper's editor.[73] Even Wid, though, could not make the venture successful; *Hollywood Herald* folded just a few months later.[74] The rapid turnover of editors clearly hurt *Hollywood Herald* in its efforts to compete locally against the *Hollywood Reporter*, *Film Spectator*, and *Film Mercury*—all publications with strong, consistent leadership.

On a broader level, Quigley had underestimated the difficulty of the entire enterprise. He was launching a new publication into the already saturated marketplace of LA-based film industry trade papers. In addition to the *Hollywood Reporter*, Quigley was competing with Tamar Lane's *Film Mercury*, Jack Josephs's *Inside Facts of Stage and Screen*, and Welford Beaton's *Film Spectator*—which, perhaps because of the heightened regional competition, changed its title to *Hollywood Spectator*.[75] The format Quigley had chosen—a daily paper rather than a weekly—placed additional pressures on the news-gathering and ad-selling operations. By the spring of 1932, less than a full year into its existence, *Hollywood Herald* slowed down its publication frequency and became a weekly.[76] And the timing of the entire initiative meant that Quigley and his revolving door of editors were trying to sell subscription and advertisements during the height of the Great Depression.

Yet Quigley had misjudged something even more fundamental. He did not understand Hollywood culture. He could never fully wrap his mind around—or come to accept and embrace—what made the movie colonists tick. The editorial pages that I have been able to read in extant copies of *Hollywood Herald* are models of tone deafness, excruciatingly out of touch with the lives, desires, and tastes of Hollywood's creative community. Just as he did in *Motion Picture Herald* and *Motion Picture Daily*, Quigley insisted on including his own editorials in the pages of *Hollywood Herald*. Firmly taking the side of producers over creative laborers, Martin Quigley excoriated his readers for the "high salary and excessive cost evils which threaten the industry" and declared that "the production colony must adjust itself to a changed order."[77] To Hollywood's production community, Quigley was a mouthpiece for corporate interests, blaming the industry's problems on labor and speaking to them in a condescending way. To make matters worse, the paper's attempts at gossip in its "Talk of Hollywood" section were always boring and flat. Why would any actor, screenwriter, or craftsperson want to subscribe or purchase an ad in this paper? Quigley loathed *Film Spectator* and *Variety*, and he made sure *Hollywood Herald* did not replicate *Spectator*'s prolabor stance or *Variety*'s playful style and juicy gossip. The result was a Hollywood paper that he was proud of but that no one in Hollywood actually wanted.

A defining moment for both *Hollywood Herald* and its biggest competitor, the *Hollywood Reporter*, occurred in March and April of 1933 when the studios implemented 50 percent salary cuts in response to the national bank holiday.[78] *Hollywood Herald*'s newly installed editor, Wid Gunning, offered his thoughts in an editorial entitled "Your Time Is Coming. Don't Rock the Boat!," which veered between empty platitudes ("Don't be blue. Be happy. This country is going places now.") and demands that laborers fall into line and do as they are told ("Right now every film worker in Hollywood should 'play ball' with the big companies until the present emergency is over.").[79] Quigley and Gunning had adopted the exact opposite strategy that Welford Beaton utilized six years earlier, when, during an industry-wide salary dispute, Beaton forcefully took the side of labor, and *Film Spectator* rocketed in popularity. For a paper that was already struggling to find traction, this stance may have been *Hollywood Herald*'s mortal blow.

Billy Wilkerson, however, used the salary cut to engage the *Hollywood Reporter*'s base of readers and deepen divisions between the LA production community and New York corporate executives. In addressing the national bank holiday, Wilkerson initially adopted a unifying tone, noting that a shared sacrifice was required by all for the good of the industry and country. As the weeks went on, however, and as it became clear that some studios (most infamously, Warner Bros.) were not going to restore full salaries, Wilkerson went on the attack. He praised Hollywood creatives and criticized their corporate overlords who "in their arrogance [have] shown that they are stupid. They have underestimated the intelligence, the brains of their employees."[80] He called out MGM and Warner Bros. for being greedy,[81] and he celebrated production executive Darryl F. Zanuck's decision to leave Warner Bros. when the company's president, Harry Warner, reneged on a promise to restore salaries.[82] Wilkerson also directed a great deal of column space toward bashing Will Hays, the MPPDA head and longtime ally of Martin Quigley.[83]

Hollywood's screenwriters and actors, who were organizing during this period to form their own unions, had found the trade paper that they wanted to read. They rewarded *Hollywood Reporter* with their subscriptions, advertisements, and news tips. A few years later during a legal dispute over his taxes, Wilkerson recounted his memories of the period in an effort to explain large income fluctuations. "When [the studios] declared a 50% salary cut for eight weeks we fought it and lost all of the $190,000.00 advertising business we had from the major studios," recalled Wilkerson. "We were barred out of the studios, but we had the support of the writers, directors, and technicians. Otherwise, we would have been forced out of business."[84] Wilkerson claimed that this episode solidified the studios' view of *Hollywood Reporter* during this period as the "labor paper" (a designation that just slightly more than a decade later would have been unthinkable, as Wilkerson weaponized his column into an instrument for blacklisting suspected communists and ruining careers). But much like he demonstrated during the blacklist era, Wilkerson showed his power through a willingness to call out and publicly shame specific groups and individuals. He named names.

In his combative "Trade Views" columns from the spring of 1933, Wilkerson carefully delineated between insiders and outsiders, between Hollywood's authentic, hardworking, and knowledgeable production community and the ignorant, lazy East Coast corporate officers who tightly controlled the purse strings.[85] "Well, the New York execs have come and gone," wrote Wilkerson in one such column, noting that "if they accomplish twice as much on their next trip six months hence, as they did this time, the result of those efforts will still total nothing."[86] Meanwhile, Wilkerson generally spared the high-paid production executives who worked in Southern California (and with whom he frequently socialized) from his blistering criticisms. In these ways, the *Hollywood Reporter* helped to produce and reiterate the film industry's production culture and community boundaries. Working actors, writers, directors, craftspeople, top-tier agents, and studio producers were all members of the authentic Hollywood production community. Outside of these velvet ropes stood exhibitors, distribution exchange managers, and New York corporate officers—all part of the same industry but not the true filmmaking community. Also on the outside, looking in, were the many aspiring actors, writers, and Hollywood wannabes. All of these constituencies included subscribers and readers of the *Hollywood Reporter*, but not all of them belonged to the community, as it was constituted and reproduced by Wilkerson.[87]

Wilkerson's relationship with MGM's central producer, Irving Thalberg, provides a particularly interesting example of how behind-the-scenes arrangements influenced the *Hollywood Reporter*'s content, financial health, and community gatekeeping. Thalberg was an outstanding producer of movies, but he was also a brilliant producer of his own self-image—Hollywood's wunderkind who had the magic touch and understood every component of the filmmaking process.[88] During the period of fall 1932 to summer 1933, Thalberg became especially self-conscious about his perception within the industry. His fragile health was widely known. More embarrassing, MGM's heads on the East Coast (Nick Schenck) and West Coast (Louis B. Mayer) had conspired during his recovery from illness to effectively demote Thalberg, relieving him of the duty of supervising all MGM productions and, instead, making him one of several unit producers on the studio lot (alongside Mayer's talented son-in-law and former RKO executive, David O. Selznick).[89] Rumors swirled that Thalberg might soon leave MGM altogether.[90] Within this context, Wilkerson and Thalberg developed a mutually beneficial alliance. Thalberg supplied Wilkerson with news and likely tipped him off about the test screenings for MGM films—a practice that Thalberg was famous for embracing and reviews of which helped to distinguish the *Hollywood Reporter* against its competitors. In a private letter, Wilkerson thanked the producer for "the font of information you furnish me on each and every visit we have."[91] For his part, Wilkerson made sure that Thalberg stayed in the news and his columns in a manner that Thalberg approved, noting, for example, the producer's "great health" and how he "respects artists" in February 1933.[92]

But the relationship did not end there. During the same period in April 1933 when Wilkerson publicly attacked MGM's New York executives for their greediness, he privately asked Thalberg for a big favor: "Would you be inclined to make me a loan of $4,000 or $5,000 . . . with my personal IOU your only security?" Wilkerson closed his letter with two promises: he would pay the money back within twelve to fourteen months, and "nobody will ever know this letter is written and certainly no one will ever know of this transaction."[93] Both promises were broken. Wilkerson never paid back the $4,000 loan. In fact, three years later, he borrowed an additional $2,500 from Thalberg. The reason we today know about these clandestine loans, the reason the original letter was saved for posterity, is that they became part of an accounting of the Thalberg estate after the producer's untimely death in September 1936.[94] By that point, ironically, Wilkerson was in a dispute with the Screenwriters Guild, and rumors swirled among Hollywood creatives that "L. B. Mayer owns a controlling interest of all 'Wilkerson' enterprises such as Reporter, Vendome, and Trocadero."[95]

Shortly after receiving Thalberg's loan in spring 1933, and as the "Trade Views" column continued needling East Coast executives, Wilkerson opened his first restaurant—the abovementioned Vendome. In one of the early ads for Vendome, Wilkerson emphasized the restaurant's Sunset Boulevard location and its proximity to the Writer's Club, a clear message to the constituency whose support he had cultivated through his columns on the salary cuts (see fig. 30). The opening of Vendome marked a turning point in the history of Hollywood trade papers. By creating a lunch restaurant (which also served as an imported food store), Wilkerson was taking the cultural functions of a show-business trade paper and grafting them onto a physical space. As Wilkerson later reflected in a court deposition, "The restaurants were built to help the newspapers. When the Vendome was built

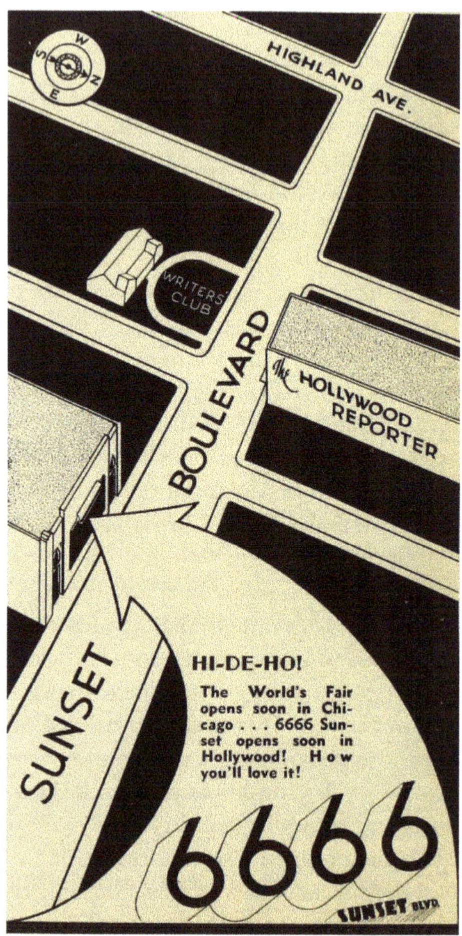

FIGURE 30. Advertisement for Vendome—promoted for its address, 6666 Sunset Blvd., and its proximity to the Writers Club—in the trade paper published by Vendome's owner, W. R. Wilkerson. *Source:* "6666 Sunset Blvd." [Advertisement], *Hollywood Reporter,* April 24, 1933, https://lantern .mediahist.org/catalog /hollywoodreporte1215wilk_0692.

we had difficulty getting into the studios and I wanted an attractive place where people could come so I could get news and help my advertising. The Vendome accomplished that purpose over a period of five or six years. Almost everybody in the motion picture business that wasn't exactly working that day was at the Vendome for lunch. The result was that my men could go there and collect news that they could not otherwise get."[96]

Wilkerson's critics accused him of selling overpriced lunches at the Vendome in exchange for brief mentions in *Hollywood Reporter*.[97] Indeed, this was core to Vendome's *raison d'être*. The restaurant simultaneously brought in successful Hollywood creatives who Wilkerson could no longer access on the studio lots, along with ambitious aspiring writers, actors, and directors who would do almost anything for a studio contract. For those trying to break into show business or move up in the pecking order, a lunch they could hardly afford meant the chance of getting written up in *Hollywood Reporter* and getting closer to their dreams. Show business trade papers had long profited from selling ads to aspiring stars; Wilkerson continued selling those ads but now included fine cheeses and cured meats on the menu.

Acting as good maître d's, Wilkerson's Vendome staff gave preferential treatment to the more established and powerful Hollywood figures who came in for lunch. Their presence and patronage increased the prestige value of the restaurant for Wilkerson and everyone who walked through the door. Wilkerson was surely exaggerating when he claimed to be serving lunch for "almost everybody in the motion picture business that wasn't exactly working that day," but his phrasing was emblematic of a show business culture in which work and leisure, in which the commercial and the personal, were intimately bound up. Additionally, this blending of work and social life echoes Tom Kemper's research into the emergence of talent agents in 1930s Hollywood. Kemper conceives of "Hollywood as a business world embedded within a social network" and calls on film historians to draw on the field of economic sociology, which studies "how markets remain deeply and internally structured as social systems."[98] Wilkerson understood that Hollywood operated as a social network, and he created both a newspaper for that network to follow one another and physical spaces for that network to convene.

In contrast, Martin Quigley had no aptitude or appetite for this side of Hollywood society and culture. Despite declaring that *Hollywood Herald* would be "*the* daily journal of the motion picture's creative community," Quigley and his string of short-lived *Hollywood Herald* editors were always on the outside of that community looking in, like reporters in the Polo Grounds' press box trying to yell down at the players on the field. In fairness to Quigley and his editors, they were hardly alone in their failure during this period. *Inside Facts of Stage and Screen* closed shop in 1931.[99] *Film Mercury*'s editor, Tamar Lane, claimed to seldom mingle "socially with the film colony," preferring to maintain the sort of boundaries that Wilkerson trampled over.[100] He suspended the publication of *Film Mercury* in 1931. Although it began intermittently publishing again two years later, *Film Mercury* was never the same force it had once been.[101] Tamar Lane's vision was for Hollywood to devote more resources to the production of artistically ambitious films to be distributed into specialized theaters patronized by intelligent, adult audiences. In the context of widespread theater closures, this vision seemed more far-fetched than ever before.

In October 1931, Lane took a job at RKO as a story consultant and editor. And, on the side, he worked on writing a story of his own. Published in 1932, *Hey Diddle Diddle* was Lane's satire of the stupidity and greed that ruled Hollywood. Largely forgotten today, especially compared to Nathaniel West's *Day of the Locust* (1939) or Budd Schulberg's *What Makes Sammy Run* (1941), Lane's novel takes readers through the inner workings of a large film company. Perhaps not surprisingly, trade papers play a prominent role in the book. A team of studio executives select their next season of movie projects by spreading out a trade paper, looking at the advertisements, and imitating what they see their competitors doing.[102] A sleazy distribution sales manager charges $35,000 to his expense account while traveling the country to rig votes for an exhibitor paper's contest about the public's favorite stars.[103] Later, the studio's production chief boasts: "The trade papers we can depend on—they've got to give us good reviews. One paper is just as good as another for quoting to exhibitors."[104] But if Lane believed this last part, he was wrong. American exhibitors were reading their trade papers with a critical eye, and they did not regard the publications as equally trustworthy.

EXHIBITOR RESISTANCE AND READING ALTERNATIVES

As Quigley faltered in his attempts to replace *Hollywood Reporter* with *Hollywood Herald* as the premiere trade paper of the Los Angeles production community, the publisher encountered resistance from an even more important constituency: exhibitors. During the late 1910s and most of the 1920s, independent exhibitors had trusted Quigley's *Exhibitors Herald* as a staunch advocate for their interests. As we saw in the previous chapter, however, that sense of loyalty shifted during the transition to sound and the three years that led up to the formation of *Motion Picture News*. Independent exhibitors increasingly perceived Quigley as a sellout, a mouthpiece for the studios and the Hays Office. One year before the launch of *Motion Picture Herald*, P. S. Harrison went so far as to say that "Martin Quigley has forgotten that the independent exhibitors exist."[105] Harrison's readers would have found evidence to support this claim in *Motion Picture Herald*'s pages. The "What the Picture Did for Me" section, especially popular among small-town theater managers, had been phased out in 1930, just as the Depression was setting in. And *Motion Picture Herald*'s masthead had made two symbolically important changes from *Exhibitors Herald World*: the paper was now published in New York, not Chicago, and the word *Exhibitor* was nowhere to be found in the title. The days of the "'Herald Only' Club" were over. Many independent exhibitors looked toward other papers for their sources for news, community, and an affirmation of their grievances.

The most acrimonious fight for the loyalty of exhibitor readers emerged from within *Motion Picture Herald*'s own ranks. When Quigley acquired *Motion Picture News* in 1930, one of its biggest assets was the "Managers Round Table" section, edited by Chick Lewis. But whereas *Motion Picture News'* William A. Johnston had given Lewis free rein on the section's content, style, and length, *Motion Picture Herald* publisher Martin Quigley and editor Terry Ramsaye insisted that "Managers Round Table" conform to their editorial guidelines. Lewis bristled under the increased scrutiny and control. In December 1931, he fired off an angry memo to Quigley: "After four years, during which time I have never published a single item which proved embarrassing to the publication, I feel fairly competent to judge what is best for the department and those who read it. I cannot possibly agree to anything but a free hand and unless you can convince Mr. Ramsaye that such a course is best all around, I will have to withdraw from the publication immediately."[106] Just over a year later, the break finally happened. Quigley claimed he fired Lewis. But in a maneuver that feels straight out of a Hollywood movie, Chick Lewis pulled a *you can't fire me, I quit*, insisting that he voluntarily resigned. One fact neither party disputed was that Lewis did not stay idle for long. In May 1933, just two months after his exit from *Motion Picture Herald*, Chick Lewis debuted his slim new trade paper—*Showmen's Round Table*.[107]

In launching *Showmen's Round Table*, Lewis capitalized on the goodwill he had earned among exhibitors from editing the "Manager's Round Table" and the long-simmering suspicions that Quigley was in the pockets of the major studios. Lewis called *Showmen's Round Table* "the Foremost Independent Trade Paper of the Industry," emphasizing that it was "Unbiased, Honest and Truthful in Its Editorial Policy and a Proved Record for Fearlessness," clearly attempting to contrast his new paper against the *Herald*.[108] Lewis received letters of support from exhibitors along the East Coast. "I and my gang in this part of the country are for you 100%," wrote the owner of the Maryland Theatre, who added that "the Managers' Round Table Club is a Chick Lewis organization and not a Motion Picture Herald proposition." The theater owner closed by saying: "If you are going back into publication work I feel confident in saying that 10,000 showmen will be with you."[109] The actual number was far less, but the threat and embarrassment were great enough for Quigley to file a lawsuit, alleging that Lewis acted with "the intent and purpose to deceive the buyers and readers" of *Motion Picture Herald* by prominently displaying "Round Table" in his new paper's title.[110]

Quigley's lawsuit succeeded only superficially. In response to the claims of consumer deception, Chick Lewis dropped "Round Table" from the title and rebranded the publication as *Showmen's Trade Review*. He continued to publish his paper for the next two decades, offering his readers wisecracks, marketing gimmicks, and a sense of belonging to a community of savvy, independent showmen. Setting up his offices on 42nd Street, Lewis brought a wisecracking New York sensibility to his paper, the Bugs Bunny to *Herald*'s Elmer Fudd. His readers, mostly concentrated in the mid-Atlantic region, could page through and find sections such as "The Product Check-Up!," "Advance Dope," and "Box Office Slant."[111] As these section titles suggest, Lewis took a more freewheeling and playful approach to language than most other exhibitor papers. He was also looser with his sense of screen propriety than the prudish Quigley and Harrison. Lewis openly reflected on a picture's "sex appeal" and exploitation opportunities geared toward promoting a film's steamy lure.

Showmen's Round Table / Showmen's Trade Review found its affinity with independent exhibitors who occupied the middle ranks of the exhibition sector. A neighborhood theater owner in Baltimore, for example, or a theater manager located on a Main Street in eastern New Jersey was likely to be a loyal Chick Lewis reader. They viewed themselves as underdogs compared to the downtown movie palaces and studio-affiliated theaters. Yet they also viewed themselves as superior (bigger, better, more modern) than small-town and rural movie houses located out in the sticks. These midrank theaters needed an edge to compete and stay relevant; Chick Lewis supplied them with tips and techniques, and he made them feel seen and appreciated in the process.

Chick Lewis's best advertising customers were the Poverty Row studios, such as Monogram, Astor, and, later, Republic. The Poverty Row studios did not own their own theaters, and the major film corporations generally would not give them screen space in their prestigious downtown houses, so they needed the bookings of *Showmen's* midtier exhibitors to stay in business. And because Poverty Row pictures generally lacked major star power, the studios depended more on genre, an exciting title, and other exploitation angles to sell them—all of which fell squarely within Chick Lewis's wheelhouse. Lewis thanked his advertisers with the traditional quid pro quo of news and editorial attention. As a result, Monogram's slate of pictures made front-page news in a 1934 issue in which the studio bought two advertising pages.[112] Although the title changed to *Showmen's Trade Review*, the overall structure continued: the paper was a mutually beneficial enterprise for midtier exhibitors, Poverty Row studios, and editor-publisher Chick Lewis.

Another mid-Atlantic trade paper—one more militant than *Showmen's Round Table*—emerged in 1934 to challenge the power structure of the major film companies, affiliated theater chain, and *Motion Picture Herald*. In its debut issue, *Independent Exhibitors Film Bulletin* called for a "Revolt in the Industry!" and announced itself as the official organ of the Independent Exhibitors' Protective Association (IEPA), which was supportive of Abram F. Myers's Allied States Association and fought against what it considered to be unfair trade practices, ranging from block booking to the showing of movies in churches, taprooms, and other "non-theatrical" venues (fig. 31). *Independent Exhibitors Film Bulletin* claimed to speak up for all independent exhibitors who no longer wanted to be "the doormat of the industry," but it was published in Philadelphia, and the advertisements taken out by local vendors and states'-rights distributors suggest that it was primarily consumed by exhibitors in eastern Pennsylvania, New Jersey, Delaware, and Maryland (one issue referenced one thousand readers).[113] *Independent Exhibitors Film Bulletin's* chief target was the larger trade organization it was "revolting against," the Motion Picture Theater Owners of America (MPTOA), which it viewed as a corrupt instrument for the benefit of the major film corporations and theater chains.[114] But *Independent Exhibitors Film Bulletin* also took aim at *Motion Picture Herald*, which it perceived as a mouthpiece for the MPTOA and major companies.[115]

As Martin Quigley struggled for the attention of mid-Atlantic exhibitors against *Showmen's Round Table* and *Independent Exhibitors Film Bulletin*, he also faced competition for readers and advertising dollars from increasingly powerful regional exhibitor papers. Quigley himself had started as the editor of a regional

INDEPENDENT EXHIBITORS

FILM BULLETIN

VOL. 1 No. 1   TUESDAY, SEPTEMBER 11, 1934   PRICE 10 CENTS

Revolt in the Industry!

Much is heard these days about the Tories of the business world—those gentlemen of wealth who oppose all progress and change for fear it might cut into their hoard. For them the plight of the many means nothing. Theirs is the gospel of "Privileges for the Few". Destitution to them is the problem of charity not social justice.

Just as in Colonial times the Tories were the big boys who stuck by the King and opposed the American Revolution, so to-day the Tories of the trade are those exhibitors who are sticking with the producers and their chain theatres and opposing the attempts of the independent exhibitors to organize.

But to-day, when we think of the Revolution, we remember, not the Tories who played safe and stuck by the King, but the "Independents" of that time, who left their bloody footprints on the snows of Valley Forge. Similarly, in the years to come, when the independent movement throughout the industry is firmly established, the exhibitors will honor, not the Tories of the M. P. T. O. who, subsidized by the producers, tried to destroy the independent movement for selfish reasons of their own or because they were too timid to fight. Rather will they remember that hardy little band of pioneers who, in the face of the most discouraging obstacles, carried on to success.

The independent exhibitor, to-day, is the doormat of the industry. The spectacle of 13,000 exhibitors waiting fearfully each season to learn what new impossible demands the eight major film companies will impose upon them is not a pretty one to behold. If these 13,000 theatre men ever learned their true strength they would sweep the eight major monopolists with their $10,000 weekly star salaries and their fancy bonuses for executives into the Pacific. And the industry would carry on and be a lot healthier.

The blame for the disorganized state of the independents can be placed squarely on the shoulders of the M. P. T. O. Tories. Playing the game of the producers, these M. P. T. O. Tories maintain a pseudo-exhibitor organization in each territory with a skeleton membership in which predominate producer - owned theatres. And the most discouraging feature of all is to see a number of really estimable independent exhibitors in the M. P. T. O. permitting themselves to be used as a respectable front for the producers and their chain theatres in the plan to keep the independent strength scattered. BUT THE HEIGHT OF SOMETHING OR OTHER IS THE FACT THAT CERTAIN OF THESE EXHIBITORS ACTUALLY PAY DUES INTO AN ORGANIZATION OF THEIR BUSINESS ENEMIES — THE PRODUCER-OWNED THEATRES WHOSE CLEAR PURPOSE IS TO ELIMINATE ALL INDEPENDENT COMPETITION BY ONE MEANS OR ANOTHER!

Every independent theatre owner in this zone must make his choice. Will he join the I. E. P. A.—a group of grimly determined Vigilantes organized to battle for the independent's rights? Or will he support an organization of producers and chain theatres?

FIGURE 31. *Independent Exhibitors Film Bulletin* declared a "Revolt in the Industry!" in its first issue and provided another source of competition against Martin Quigley's *Motion Picture Herald*. *Source:* "Revolt in the Industry!," *Independent Exhibitors Film Bulletin*, Sept. 11, 1934, 1, https://lantern.mediahist.org/catalog/filmbulletin193401film_0001.

trade paper, growing *Exhibitors Herald* from a trade paper for the community of Chicago exchanges into one of the leading nationals. A handful of the regional trade papers that were his peers during the mid to late 1910s remained active throughout the 1930s. One of the very first regionals, *Amusements*, continued to publish from Minneapolis and serve exhibitors in the northwestern region of the US. Meanwhile, that paper's founding editor, Tom Hamlin, had relocated permanently to New York City, where, starting in 1923, he edited and published *Film Curb*. A short, weekly trade sheet, *Film Curb* primarily held interest for exhibitors, exchanges, and executives in New York, although it appears to have enjoyed some additional reach across the country (Hamlin self-reported the circulation in 1935 as seven thousand, although he declined to have that figure audited). Meanwhile, in Toronto, Ray Lewis continued to advocate for Canada to obtain greater sovereignty over its screens, both in the pages of *Canadian Moving Picture Digest* and in her work aiding the White Commission's 1929 antitrust investigation into Paramount's Famous Players Canadian Corporation.[116] She was a close reader of *Motion Picture Herald*, and she wrote to Quigley and Ramsaye to let them know when they veered too far north of their lane and reported something inaccurate about Canada's film market.[117]

Two other regional papers—*The Exhibitor* and the *Reel Journal*—underwent dramatic expansions in the early 1930s. *The Exhibitor* had served the greater Philadelphia film community reliably since its 1917 founding by David Barrist. In 1928, however, the paper changed hands when it was acquired by Jay Emanuel, a local film industry insider who was elected as MPTOA treasurer that same year. Emanuel had a background in both exhibition and distribution, having previously worked as a theater manager, distribution sales agent, and exchange operator.[118] Leveraging his professional contacts in the region, Emanuel expanded *The Exhibitor* into, in his words, "the Pride of the East Coast!," with three different editions for Washington, DC; New York State; and, of course, Philadelphia. By 1932, *The Exhibitor* could claim to deliver the "Home Town Trade Papers of 4600 Showmen!"[119] But not everyone in Emanuel's hometown appreciated his work. His active role in the MPTOA and support of the organization's polices earned him the enmity of many independents in these regions, some of whom broke away to form the IEPA and *Independent Exhibitors Film Bulletin*.[120] Yet the IEPA did not seem to permanently damage Emanuel or his brand; subscriptions and advertising sales for the Philadelphia Exhibitor trended upward across the second half of the 1930s.[121]

Yet even Jay Emanuel's expansion of *The Exhibitor* paled in comparison to transformation and growth of Ben Shlyen's *Reel Journal*. Founded in Kansas City in 1920, the *Reel Journal* had been a model of film row friendliness, reporting on the community activities of Kansas City's exchanges and the theaters they served, including updates on how the local industry's bowling league was doing. But Shlyen's ambitions extended beyond the theaters and exchanges of Kansas and Missouri. Beginning in the mid-1920s, Shlyen embarked on a campaign to acquire as many regional trade papers as possible. A new company name was needed for this venture, and in 1926, Reel Journal Publishing Company rebranded itself as Associated Publications. The name and idea may sound familiar to readers. As we saw in chapter 3, Tom Hamlin had created a network of regional trade papers just a few years earlier called the Associated Film Press. Both Hamlin and Shlyen no doubt hoped the name "associated" would evoke positive affinities in the minds of readers and advertisers with the Associated Press, which had been syndicating news content to newspapers across the world since the mid-nineteenth century. Yet a key difference separated Shlyen's Associated Publications from Hamlin's Associated Film Press: ownership. Whereas Hamlin had served as a New York–based advertising representative for regional trade papers, Shlyen's strategy was to acquire regional trade papers outright, as well as create and publish new papers for adjacent territories in which he sought to compete.

In August 1927, Associated Publications took a big leap forward, announcing it had expanded into seven regional papers, spanning seventeen contiguous states fanning outward from Shlyen's Kansas City.[122] The *Reel Journal* was now joined by two trade papers that Shlyen acquired—Omaha's *Movie Age* and Detroit's *Michigan Film Review*—as well as four new papers that he created: *Film Trade Topics* (Denver and Salt Lake City territory), *Exhibitors' Tribune* (Oklahoma and Memphis), *Motion Picture Digest* (Chicago and Indianapolis), and *Ohio Showman* (Cleveland and Cincinnati). Like today's media conglomerates that own local newspapers scattered across the country, Associated Publications operated by pushing out national news, editorial, and advertising content across all of its newspapers. Initially, Shlyen believed that the sense of local flavor would be a selling point for readers and advertisers. In an ad that ran in *Film Daily*, Associated Publications emphasized "7 DISTINCTIVE PUBLICATIONS. Each the HOME Paper in its Home Region."[123] Despite the fact that the same printing press in Kansas City published *Film Trade Topics* and *Ohio Showman* every week, each paper was given its own title, logo, and cover design. "National in Scope. Local in Service" was the Associated Publications slogan.[124]

During the peak Depression years of the early 1930s, however, Associated Publications adjusted its strategy and changed its branding. Efficiency became more important, local distinctiveness less so. These changes emerged out of Shlyen's ambition to expand the reach of his regional papers to cover all of the US (and eventually Canada). In 1931, he started a new regional paper, *Boxoffice*, to compete against *The Exhibitor* in the East Coast exchange cities of New York, Philadelphia, and Washington, DC.[125] In starting *Boxoffice*, Associated Publications created a single regional trade paper to cover markets that, in the estimation of Jay Emanuel and *The Exhibitor*, were sufficiently distinctive to publish three different editions. This was telling of what was to follow: the replacement of "regions," rooted in exchange hubs, with broader map areas that divided the country into "sectional editions."

TABLE 2. *Boxoffice* Regional Editions and Predecessor Journals

Boxoffice Region	States Encompassed	Previous Titles Absorbed into Boxoffice
New England	Massachusetts, Rhode Island, Connecticut, New Hampshire, Vermont, Maine	*New England Film News* (Boston)
Eastern	New York, New Jersey, Delaware, Maryland, Virginia, Pennsylvania (East), Washington, DC	—
Southern	Texas, Oklahoma, Arkansas, Tennessee, Louisiana, Alabama, Mississippi, Georgia, Florida, North Carolina, South Carolina	*Motion Picture Times* (Dallas), *Weekly Film Review* (Atlanta), *Exhibitors Tribune* (Memphis)
Mideast	Michigan, Ohio, Kentucky, West Virginia, Pennsylvania (West)	*Exhibitors Forum* (Pittsburgh), *Ohio Showman* (Cleveland), *Michigan Film Review* (Detroit)
Central	Illinois, Wisconsin, Indiana, Upper Michigan, Missouri (East)	*Motion Picture Digest* (Chicago)
Midwest	Missouri (West), Kansas, Iowa, Nebraska, North Dakota, South Dakota, Minnesota	*Reel Journal* (Kansas City), *Movie Age* (Omaha/ Minneapolis)
Western	California, Oregon, Washington, Montana, Wyoming, Arizona, New Mexico, Colorado	*Film Trade Topics* (San Francisco)

SOURCES: Ben Shlyen, "The Last Word," *Reel Journal,* June 16, 1931, 18; Audit Bureau of Circulations, "Auditor's Report: Boxoffice. Report for the Twelve Months Ending June 30, 1939," Sept. 1939, Alliance for Audited Media, Arlington Heights, IL, microfilm.

The full rebranding of Associated Publications' papers took place in 1933. The *Reel Journal, Film Trade Topics, Michigan Film Review,* and the other Associated Publications regional titles were phased out. Shlyen replaced them all with *Boxoffice*: "the National Film Weekly, published in seven sectional editions."[126] The seven sections covered New England, Eastern, Southern, Mideast, Central, Midwest, and Western. Advertisers could purchase space nationally for all seven editions of *Boxoffice* or by single edition.[127] As table 2 shows, Associated Publications collapsed previous distinctions among regions, bringing multiple exchange cities into the same fold.[128] A side-by-side comparison of different regional editions of *Boxoffice* allows us to reverse engineer how the paper was prepared and published. The earliest date for which I have been able to locate multiple sectional editions of *Boxoffice* is January 12, 1935. The Midwest and New England sectional editions both ran exactly forty-eight pages that week (longer than usual because the issues included the "Modern Screen and Its Furnishings" equipment section, *Boxoffice*'s counterpart to *Motion Picture Herald*'s "Better Theatres" and, before that, *Motion Picture News*' "Accessory News" sections). The cover page of both sectional editions featured an advertisement for Monogram's *Women Must Dress* (1935). In the

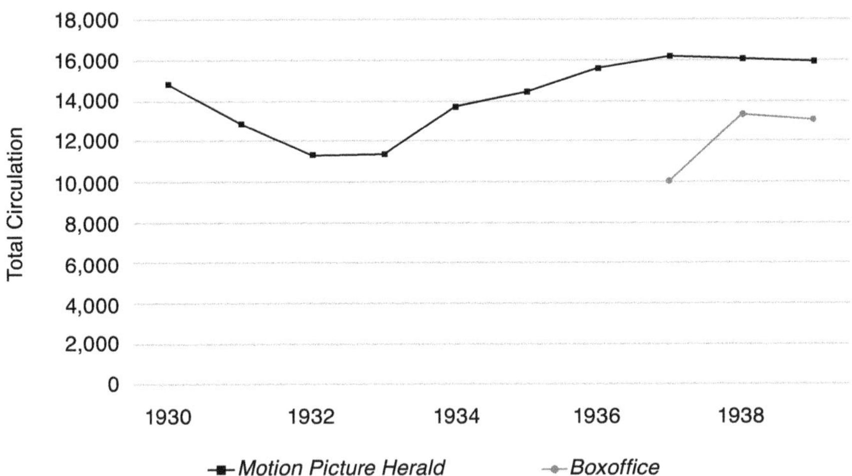

FIGURE 32. 1930s Audited Circulations: *Motion Picture Herald* vs. *Boxoffice*. The earliest audited circulation data for Plaintiff Complaint, undated, at 4, Quigley Publishing Company v. Showmen's Round Table and Charles E. Lewis, US District Court for the Southern District of New York, Equity Case Files, RG 21, E 76–321; Audit Bureau of Circulations, "Auditor's Report: Motion Picture Herald. Report for the Twelve Months Ending June 30, 1936," Sept. 1936. Alliance for Audited Media, Arlington Heights, IL, microfilm.

very front and back of both editions, an exhibitor reader could find a few pages of local news items, announcements, and advertisements. Almost everything in the middle, however, was identical. The same news, reviews, editorials, and advertisements—all laid out in the same style and printed on the same press—filled the bulk of the magazine. In total, forty out of the forty-eight pages of these two *Boxoffice* sectional editions were the exact same that week in 1935, whether you received the paper in Bangor, Maine, or Topeka, Kansas.[129] From a publishing standpoint, then, *Boxoffice* was a model of paper efficiency—cheaper to produce on a per-unit basis and more profitable than either a strictly regional trade paper or a more elaborate national weekly, like *Motion Picture Herald*.

A spirit of cheerful efficiency also characterized the paper's editorial style and much of its appeal to exhibitor readers. Ben Shlyen did not have the ego of William A. Johnston or Martin Quigley. His priority was building a successful trade paper, not being a thought leader whose editorial comments would echo across the nation. He spoke adamantly against tax increases and other government policies that he thought would place hardships on the industry; but, generally, his editorials took a soft touch, siding with his exhibitor readers without demonizing the major film corporations with whom they so often fought (and who purchased ads in his paper). Sometimes, he spun the formula around, agreeing with the studios on a small point, then explaining why they were wrong about a bigger point. When a federal judge ruled in 1935 that the studios' prohibitions against double features were illegal, for example, Shlyen responded by praising the decision on the basis of helping exhibitors compete and survive. "We hold no brief for double features; personally we don't like them," began Shlyen, distancing *Boxoffice* from the controversial practice. "But too many exhibitors have told us they would be out of business, if it were not for their double bills, to call it a 'destructive' policy. It seems to be a matter for each individual to decide for himself—to sell the kind of merchandise that his clientele will buy tickets to see and to put it before their eyes in a form that is appealing and profitable." Shlyen called for "clean competition of the 'live-and-let-live' type [that] will enable many darkened theatres to be lighted again."[130] *Boxoffice* spoke to these exhibitor readers, who valued its straightforward style, clarity, and brevity. As more darkened theaters lit up again, the paper's subscriptions soared (fig. 32).

MOTION PICTURE HERALD—A SUCCESS IN FAILURE

Martin Quigley's consolidation plan for the film industry's trade press had failed. *Hollywood Herald* was shuttered. Quigley looked on bitterly as *Motion Picture Herald*'s paid circulation declined from 16,108 in December 1930 to 14,811 in December 1931 to 12,860 in 1932 to 11,292 in December 1933.[131] While much of this decline was caused by the Depression marketplace pushing exhibitors out of business, it was also a sign that many exhibitors who remained had found new trade papers to read—alternatives to *Motion Picture Herald* that they preferred and more closely identified with. In response to the plummeting subscriptions and widespread perception that he had sold out to the studios, Quigley reinstated the "What the Picture Did for Me" department in 1933 as a consistent three- to four-page section in every issue. Small-town exhibitors greeted the section's return enthusiastically, and, as Kathryn Fuller-Seeley has shown, they used "What the Picture Did for Me" reviews as a forum to share experiences and try to communicate to producers about the types of movies they did and didn't want.[132] The change appears to have helped, and *Herald*'s circulation increased to 13,703 in December 1934 and 14,438 in December 1935.[133] The *Herald* won back readers by returning to its roots.

That Quigley failed in his goal to dominate trade publishing for the motion picture industry does not mean that *Motion Picture Herald* was a failure as a trade paper. In fact, many exhibitors of the time, as well as film historians decades later, found enormous value in the paper's comprehensive news coverage, reviews, and special issues that took deep dives into different corners of the industry. Quigley's archives contain several folders of testimonials, letters and telegrams from producers and exhibitors around the world—London, Amsterdam, Calcutta, Nebraska—thanking him and congratulating him on such a wonderful paper.[134] And, as Quigley Publications' general manager, Colvin W. Brown, liked to remind people, *Motion Picture Herald*'s typography and paper quality stood far above its peers.[135] Yet none of this was enough to convince the film industry that it should concentrate its advertisements, readership, and loyalty into Martin Quigley's publications.

In 1938, Martin Quigley took years of pent-up frustration and expressed it in a memorandum. "Quigley Publications invested upward of $600,000 and promised the business a trade press which would do credit to any industry. Those promises have been fulfilled," he stated emphatically. He then continued:

> It was possible for these publications to attain the degree of excellency which they have attained largely because the industry concentrated its advertising in their pages. As business improved, within and without the industry, appropriations became larger and more widely diffused. Today appropriations have contracted, but the diffusion has continued, resulting in a reduction in the volume of advertising which went into these publications under the original distribution of appropriations.
>
> Continuation of this diffusion can, and unless corrected will, destroy that value which the motion picture industry has created in an outstanding trade press.[136]

From a rational perspective, Quigley could not understand why the larger industry enabled this diffusion of advertising spending. On a cost-per-thousand basis of authentic industry readers, the Audit Bureau of Circulation data showed that *Motion Picture Herald*'s per-page cost of $15.00 was a bargain compared to *Boxoffice* ($24.04), the *Philadelphia Exhibitor* ($38.45), and *Variety* (potentially more than $100). *Motion Picture Herald* even beat out the leading journals of the restaurant industry ($16.58), plumbing market ($17.81), hospital field ($18.12), and hotel field ($22.12). Plus, *Motion Picture Herald* was far more professional in its presentation than other magazines that claimed to serve the film industry. "Advertising is the right arm of the sales machine," remarked Quigley. "It is not a sales practice to cover his territory, regularly or periodically, with inexperienced men, or ill-informed men, or men shabbily attired with questionable reputations and manners, merely because they need a job. Advertising can, and should be bought, on the same basis of value and the same tests of character that prevail in the employment of salesmen."[137] Yet this is exactly what had happened. Dressed in their shabby suits—metaphorically and perhaps literally—*Variety, Hollywood Reporter, Showmen's Round Table, Independent Exhibitors Film Bulletin, The Exhibitor*, and *Boxoffice* had swooped in and spoiled Quigley's plans. A decade after his 1927 acquisition of *Moving Picture World*, Quigley had as many competitors as he had ever had.

A major bright spot was emerging, though, for Quigley and his legacy. As we saw in the previous chapter, Quigley had initially been disappointed by the film producers' lack of compliance to the Production Code that he had helped formulate in late 1929 and early 1930. But thanks to the pressure campaign of the Legion of Decency that Quigley and Joseph Breen stage-managed in 1933 and 1934, major gains had been achieved in the Code's enforcement. The key turning point came in June 1934 with the establishment of the Production Code Administration (PCA), headed by Breen, and the elimination of the jury of producers (which had been a major obstacle for the Code's earlier enforcement).[138] With the strong-willed Breen at the helm of the PCA, the system finally worked as Quigley had hoped. Immoral and salacious material was addressed at the script stage, then revisited again when the finished picture went up for Code approval.[139] Without the PCA's approval, a picture could not be distributed by the major film companies. It was a policy that also applied to older films; dozens of films in the studios' libraries were recut or blocked from re-release.[140] Quigley was pleased by what he perceived as improvements in film quality and the public's regard for the motion picture industry. He saw this as his greatest achievement, and he was ready to publicly take the credit he thought he was due.

Quigley's first major steps in writing his role into the history of the Production Code occurred in April 1935 with the help of his allies. In a speech to British film producers about the Code's history, Will Hays introduced Quigley, the event's main speaker, as having "played a leading part" in the development of the Code.[141] A few months later, the twentieth anniversary issue of *Exhibitors Herald* contained a six-page celebratory biography that described the Code as "conceived and directed by Martin Quigley."[142] *Motion Picture Herald*'s Terry Ramsaye wrote the biography, and he also wrote a blurb in praise of Quigley's 1937 book, *Decency in Motion Pictures.* In the book, Quigley laid out his philosophy for the Code in greater detail than in any other single publication, and he discussed the involvement of Hays and Father Daniel Lord.[143] But lest anyone forget Quigley's starring role in the formation of the Code, Ramsaye explained in his blurb: "These pages from the hand of Martin Quigley have been set down with a characteristic modesty, but also with the very considerable authority of the man who first conceived the need and the growing necessity for the Production Code with which to-day the organized motion picture industry aligns, and seeks to align, its wares with American mores and the civilized standards of a wider world—the man, too, who brought the Code into being and put through its acceptance, against many obstacles."[144]

With Ramsaye, Hays, and others writing his contributions to the Production Code into the historical record, Quigley could remain modest in his self-presentation and focus his efforts on making the case for the Code's necessity and relevance. He continued to perform this work for the rest of his career.

Quigley also continued playing a mediating role between the film industry and the Catholic Church. If the artifacts we choose to keep are representative of what we value most, it was Quigley's communications with Catholic leaders, speeches to Catholic organizations, and his role in formulating and supporting the Code that he felt proudest of and came to see as his legacy. The majority of documents preserved in the Martin J. Quigley Papers at the Georgetown University Library speak to these aspects of his career. In contrast, only a small part of the collection directly emerges from the more ordinary, day-to-day operations of his five-decade career as an editor and publisher. Quigley came to accept that he would be one of many trade paper publishers for the film industry and not even the leader, at that. But he was singular among his peers in his role in aligning Hollywood film content with Catholic morality.

CONCLUSION

Martin Quigley's attempt to create an "all-industry paper" and produce a network of publications addressing a united film industry ran into an intractable problem: no spirit of all-industry unity existed. Instead, the early 1930s witnessed further fracturing of different constituencies. The West Coast production community demanded gossip, taste judgments, and a social forum that could not be serviced by a single trade paper, especially not one that took the side of management over workers. The prolabor magazine *New Theatre* speculated that "Quigley tried to break into Hollywood with a daily and sank $175,000 in the venture. It failed because it was recognized as a company union organ."[145] Quigley had major corporate backers to fund this and other initiatives. But *Variety* and the *Hollywood Reporter* also made it through the Depression with the support of wealthy patrons (Joseph Kennedy and Irving Thalberg, respectively) from within the industry.

Meanwhile, independent exhibitors continued to favor a partisan, explicitly pro-exhibitor press over the conciliatory model championed by Quigley. *Motion Picture Herald*'s calls for fair dealing across industry branches rang hollow for the majority of participants, who lacked the market power and scale of the handful of vertically integrated studios. We should also remember that show business was (and remains) a porous, aspirational industry in which new actors, writers, producers, exhibitors, and even trade publishers were continually trying to insert themselves and advance their status. Debates over what the industry was, what it should be, and what defined its culture were played out in print, week after week, in the 1930s trades.

Among so much turmoil, however, new structures of stability emerged. Remarkably, most of the trade papers that stayed afloat until 1934 (or began publishing in the early 1930s) stayed in business for two or three more decades, including *Film Daily, Showmen's Trade Review, Harrison's Reports, The Exhibitor, Independent Exhibitors Film Bulletin,* and, from Quigley Publications, *Motion Picture Herald* and *Motion Picture Daily*. This was a "diffused" stability, to use Quigley's term. But this web of competing trade papers outlasted many other industrial structures, including the vertically integrated studios, resistance to licensing A-level pictures to television, and the Production Code Administration. Four publications—*Daily Variety, Variety,* the *Hollywood Reporter,* and *Boxoffice*—survived much longer, and they remain active to this day, largely as digital publications.

For Quigley, the great diffusion was disappointing and frustrating. But for film and media historians, it is something to be celebrated as a triumph. We should recognize the millions of pages published by the American film industry's trade press as among Hollywood's greatest productions. Much like Hollywood films of the same era, these papers are complex productions; celebrating the heterogeneity of the papers does not mean reading them uncritically. But the film industry's trade papers include a diversity of voices, perspectives, and expressions of language that you don't find in the trades covering other, frequently bigger, American industries. They did more than write the rough draft of film history; they helped make that history, too.

Epilogue

Do the Hollywood trades still hold relevance in the 2020s? By some measurements, there has been more transformative change in the entertainment industry's trade papers over the last fifteen years (between my first entering the talent agency mailroom and the year 2020) than in the seventy years from 1935 (when this book concludes) to 2005. Much like the fate of many American newspapers, *Variety* and the *Hollywood Reporter* were hit hard by the combination of the digital revolution and the recession of 2007–8.[1] Many industry workers dropped their subscriptions, which had increased in price dramatically over the preceding decades. The daily print editions of the *Hollywood Reporter* and *Daily Variety* that I had once loaded onto a mail cart were phased out completely in favor of digital services with a weekly print component.[2]

One of the major change agents during this period was Nikki Finke. Finke's blog, *Deadline Hollywood Daily*, followed the same growth trajectory as *Film Spectator* in 1927 and the *Hollywood Reporter* in 1933: a young publication that skyrocketed in circulation by siding with creatives during a dispute with management. In 2007, the Writers Guild of America (WGA) went on strike against the major film and television studios over profit participation in the online environment, as well as other grievances. During the strike, WGA members and their allies generally perceived *Daily Variety* and the *Hollywood Reporter* as remaining beholden to the major companies that purchased advertising. But the WGA members found their Welford Beaton-esque champion in Nikki Finke, a seasoned entertainment journalist who unapologetically took their side, reported dispatches from the front lines, and called out studio executives as greedy and incompetent.[3] *Deadline Hollywood Daily* became the industry's essential trade sheet, and the strike dealt a blow to *Variety*'s and the *Hollywood Reporter*'s reputations in the creative community. In 2009, Penske Media purchased *Deadline Hollywood* from Finke for $14 million.[4] Three years later, for $25 million, Penske Media acquired *Variety*, which had lost further ground to Finke by putting its web content behind a paywall.[5] In Penske's calculations, *Variety*'s seasoned personnel, physical assets, subscription lists, and reputation—developed over 107 years—were all worth just $11 million more than a website launched in 2006.

The changes in exhibitor-oriented trade papers have been equally profound, if less dramatic, than the transformations of *Variety* and the *Hollywood Reporter*. Beginning in the 1970s, the rise of multiplexes and consolidation among theater chains squeezed out the majority of US independent exhibitors, who had been core readership constituencies of *Motion Picture Herald, The Exhibitor, Showmen's Trade Review*, and *Independent Exhibitor Film Bulletin*.[6] The only 1930s exhibitor trade paper to survive into the multiplex era was *Boxoffice*, which continues to be published today as a monthly and in digital form. In 2007, *Boxoffice* absorbed *In Focus*, a publication of the National Association of Theater Owners (NATO), and *Boxoffice Pro* now serves as NATO's "official magazine."[7] It is a consolidated publication for a highly consolidated exhibition marketplace.

Despite the many changes and challenges, there are signs that the major entertainment trade papers have found their footing again in the digital era. The *Hollywood Reporter* remains an important source for industry information, and its editor-at-large, Kim Masters, commands a large following on Twitter and her weekly podcast and radio show, "The Business." Meanwhile, Nikki Finke, the catalyst for so much digital change, has taken a step back from her leadership role. In an acrimonious split in 2013, Finke left *Deadline Hollywood*, allegedly frustrated by the resources and attention that Penske Media was putting into *Variety* rather than her website.[8] In the time since then, she has operated a website for fiction about the Hollywood industry, but she no longer occupies the position of power, influence, and fear that she held during and immediately after the WGA strike.[9]

Over the past five years, *Variety* has been the most successful entertainment trade paper at learning from its missteps and leveraging its brand for the online environment. The paywall is gone, at least for most of *Variety*'s content. Gone, too, is the showbiz slanguage that had been a hallmark of the paper since the 1920s. In the world of search engine optimization and online advertising, it is better business to print "Disney" than "Mouse House," better to refer to a "president" than a "prexy." Yet even without slanguage playing a gatekeeping function, *Variety* finds other ways to keep score, report news, share gossip, and retain its thought leadership role within the industry. My email inbox receives updates every day with *Variety*'s latest film reviews, breaking news stories, and the occasional provocative opinion piece. All of this, like most of *Variety*'s content, is now free to the end-user and supported by ad revenue. The trade generates additional revenue by putting on splashy events and selling a premium service, VIP+, which aggregates market data and contains other exclusive content. *Variety* has also ventured into the media production business. Like the *Hollywood Reporter*, it produces awards season web videos—roundtable discussions, one-on-one actor interviews—that feature big-name talent, who willingly lend their services for free in exchange for stirring up Oscars, Emmys, and Golden Globes buzz.

After writing a first draft of this epilogue, I received an email from *Variety* alerting me of a new plot twist in the history of entertainment trade papers. In September 2020, the *Hollywood Reporter*'s parent company, Media Rights Capital, announced the formation of a joint venture with *Variety*'s and *Deadline*'s owner, Penske. The new venture, PMRC, is consolidating the operational costs, data services, and advertising power of a series of periodicals-turned-digital brands: *Billboard, Rolling Stone, Vibe, WWD, Variety*, and the *Hollywood Reporter*, as well as the born-digital *Deadline* and *Indiewire*.[10] Ironically, the rival trade papers that went to court over news stealing and fought bitterly over advertising dollars will now share much of the same digital infrastructure. PMRC's business strategy—consolidating operational expenses while seeking to leverage the uniqueness of each brand—is representative of a larger trend of online journalism mergers, which includes 2020's merger of *Vox* and *New York Magazine*, along with *HuffPost* and *BuzzFeed*.[11] Yet the particularly bleak conditions of the movie business during the COVID-19 pandemic may have accelerated this change. With the studios having slashed spending in 2020 and 2021 on awards campaigns and the marketing of theatrical releases, the trades are under particular pressure to cut costs and build their profit centers (hence the push toward more data services: the aggregating and selling of industry information and the data collected from online users).

What will come next? Honestly, I don't know. I don't think anyone else does either. But the uncertainty and anxiety about the future may bode well for the survival of the trades. Thought leadership takes on greater importance during periods of tumultuous change. When a community perceives itself as under attack, its members read the news closely both to stay informed and to have their feelings affirmed. And, in an even more competitive marketplace, the value of positive attention in the trades—a good review, inclusion on a list, an announcement of a new deal or promotion—can mean the world to industry workers trying to build careers in entertainment. Even though a young screenwriter or junior agent can announce something themselves on Twitter, there is validation that comes from making it "*Deadline* official," satisfaction from seeing one's name in *Variety* or the *Hollywood Reporter*. While publishing an entertainment trade paper would hardly be considered a risk-free enterprise today, it seems far less precarious than owning a chain of movie theaters, producing independent films, or making a living as a Broadway performer.

Ironically, the same digital technologies at the center of so many of contemporary Hollywood's and journalism's upheavals have allowed for broad access to the US film industry's earliest trade papers. The Media History Digital Library offers free online access to *Motion Picture News, Harrison's Reports, Film Mercury,* and most of the other publications discussed in this book. All it takes is a mouse click to toggle from a 1918 *Moving Picture World* article about the Spanish influenza and theater closings to a 2020 *Variety* think piece about the long-term consequences of the COVID-19 pandemic on audience behavior. Readers can jump between Franchon Royer's early 1920s *Camera!* editorials about women in Hollywood and *Deadline*'s late 2010s reporting on #MeToo and sexual assault allegations. As we identify changes and continuities across film history, we should take time to reflect on the sources that chronicle that history. These sources, whether print or digital, are more than vessels for the packing and conveying of information. They are voices of boosterism, criticism, opportunism, and outrage. They are complex coproductions between editorial independence and advertising-friendly environments. They are expressions of an industry seeking to define, maintain, and repair its identity and chart its future.

NOTES

INTRODUCTION

1. For more on the development of the Media History Digital Library and Lantern, see Eric Hoyt, "Building a Lantern and Keeping It Burning," in *Applied Media Studies*, ed. Kirsten Ostherr (New York: Routledge, 2017), 238–50.

2. Eric Hoyt, "Lenses for Lantern: Data Mining, Visualization, and Excavating Film History's Neglected Sources," *Film History* 26, no. 2 (Summer 2014): 146–68; Eric Hoyt, Kit Hughes, Derek Long, Kevin Ponto, and Anthony Tran, "Scaled Entity Search: A Method for Media Historiography and Response to Critiques of Big Humanities Data Research," *Proceedings of IEEE Conference on Big Data* (2014): 51–59, http://ieeexplore.ieee.org/xpl /articleDetails.jsp?arnumber=7004453; Kit Hughes, Eric Hoyt, Derek Long, Kevin Ponto, and Anthony Tran, "Hacking Radio History's Data: Station Call Letter, Digitized Magazines, and Scaled Entity Search," *Media Industries Journal* 2, no. 2 (2015): n.p., www.mediaindus triesjournal.org/index.php/mij/article/view/128/182; Eric Hoyt, Derek Long, Anthony Tran, and Kit Hughes, "*Variety*'s Transformations: Digitizing and Analyzing a Canonical Trade Paper," *Film History* 27, no. 4 (2015): 76–105; Derek Long, Eric Hoyt, Anthony Tran, Kevin Ponto, and Kit Hughes, "Who's Trending in 1910s American Cinema? Exploring ECHO and MHDL at Scale with Arclight," *Moving Image* 16, no. 1: (2016): 57–81.

3. See especially the work of scholars collected in two recent edited anthologies: Lies Van de Vijver and Daniel Biltereyst, eds., *Mapping Movie Magazines: Digitization, Periodicals and Cinema History* (Cham, Switzerland: Springer Nature and Palgrave Macmillan, 2020); and Tamar Jeffers McDonald and Lies Lackman, eds., *Star Attractions: Twentieth-Century Movie Magazines and Global Fandom* (Iowa City: University of Iowa Press, 2019).

4. For more on new cinema history, see Daniel Biltereyst, Richard Maltby, and Philippe Meers, eds., *The Routledge Companion to New Cinema History* (New York: Routledge, 2019).

5. Eric Smoodin, "The History of Film History," in *Looking Past the Screen: Case Studies in American Film History*, ed. Jon Lewis and Eric Smoodin (Durham, NC: Duke University Press, 2007), 2.

6. For exemplary works of media industry studies, see Timothy Havens, Amanda D. Lotz, and Serra Tinic, "Critical Media Industry Studies: A Research Approach," *Communication, Culture & Critique* 2 (2009): 234–53; Jennifer Holt and Alisa Perren, eds., *Media Industries: History, Theory, and Method* (Malden, MA: Wiley-Blackwell, 2009); and Derek Johnson, *Media Franchising: Creative License and Collaboration in the Culture Industries* (New York: New York University Press, 2013).

7. Tino Balio, *Grand Design: Hollywood as a Modern Business Enterprise* (Berkeley: University of California Press, 1993); Douglas Gomery, *The Hollywood Studio System: A History* (London: British Film Institute, 2005); David Bordwell, Janet Staiger, and Kristin Thompson, *The Classical Hollywood Cinema: Film Style & Mode of Production to 1960* (New York: Columbia University Press, 1985); Richard B. Jewell, *The Golden Age of Cinema: Hollywood, 1929–1945* (Malden, MA: Blackwell, 2007); Thomas Schatz, *Boom and Bust: The American Cinema in the 1940s* (New York: Charles Scribner's Sons, 1997).

8. Kia Afra, *The Hollywood Trust: Trade Associations and the Rise of the Studio System* (Lanham, MD: Rowman & Littlefield, 2016), 159–268; Erin Hill, *Never Done: A History of Women's Work in Media Production* (New Brunswick, NJ: Rutgers University Press, 2018); Peter Labuza, "When a Handshake Meant Something: Lawyers, Deal Making, and the Emergence of New Hollywood" (PhD diss., University of Southern California, 2020); Derek Long, "Reprogramming the Movies: Distribution Strategy and Production Planning in the Early Studio System, 1915–1924" (PhD diss., University of Wisconsin–Madison, 2017); Luci Marzola, "Engineering Hollywood: Technology, Technicians, and the Building of the Studio System, 1915–1930" (PhD diss., University of Southern California, 2016); Paul Monticone, "For the Maintenance of the System: Institutional and Cultural Change within the Motion Picture Producers and Distributors of America, 1922–1945" (PhD diss., University of Texas–Austin, 2019); Miriam Petty, *Stealing the Show: African American Performers and Audiences in 1930s Hollywood* (Berkeley: University of California Press, 2016); Chris Yogerst, *Hollywood Hates Hitler! Jew-Baiting, Anti-Nazism, and the Senate Investigation into Warmongering in Motion Pictures* (Jackson: University Press of Mississippi, 2020).

9. Michael Schudson, *Discovering the News: A Social History of American Newspapers* (New York: Basic Books, 1978); Gerald J. Baldasty, *The Commercialization of News in the Nineteenth Century* (Madison: University of Wisconsin Press, 1992); Carolyn Marvin, *When Old Technologies Were New: Thinking about Electric Communication in the Late Nineteenth Century* (New York: Oxford University Press, 1988).

10. Richard Abel, *Menus for Movieland: Newspapers and the Emergence of American Film Culture, 1913–1916* (Berkeley: University of California Press, 2015); Anna Everett, *Returning the Gaze: A Genealogy of Black Film Criticism, 1909–1949* (Durham, NC: Duke University Press, 2001); Paul Moore, "Advance Newspaper Publicity for the Vitascope and Cinema's Mass Reading Public," in *A Companion to Early Cinema*, ed. André Gaudreault, Nicolas Dulac, and Santiago Hidalgo (Malden, MA: Blackwell, 2012), 381–97; Jan Olsson, *Los Angeles before Hollywood: Journalism and American Film Culture, 1905 to 1915* (Stockholm: National Library of Sweden, 2008).

11. Kathryn H. Fuller, *At the Picture Show: Small-Town Audiences and the Creation of Movie Fan Culture* (Charlottesville: University Press of Virginia, 2001); Anthony Slide,

Inside the Hollywood Fan Magazine (Jackson: University Press of Mississippi, 2010); McDonald and Lackman, *Star Attractions.*

12. Anthony Slide, ed., *International Film, Radio, and Television Journals* (Westport, CT: Greenwood Press, 1985).

13. Peter Besas, *Inside "Variety": The Story of the Bible of Show Business, 1905–1987* (Madrid: Ars Millenii, 2000); Dayton Stoddart, *Lord Broadway: Variety's Sime* (New York: Wilfred Funk, 1941).

14. Martin S. Quigley, *Martin J. Quigley and the Glory Days of American Film, 1915–1965* (Groton, MA: Quigley Publishing, 2006).

15. W. R. Wilkerson III, *Hollywood Godfather: The Life and Crimes of Billy Wilkerson* (Chicago: Chicago Review Press, 2018).

16. James W. Carey, "A Cultural Approach to Communication," in *Communication as Culture: Essays on Media and Society* (New York: Routledge, 1988), 13–36, 20, 21.

17. Carey, "Cultural Approach to Communication," 23.

18. John Thornton Caldwell, *Production Culture: Industrial Reflexivity and Critical Practice in Film and Television* (Durham, NC: Duke University Press, 2008), 15.

19. Caldwell, 2.

20. Benedict Anderson, *Imagined Communities: Reflections on the Origin and Spread of Nationalism*, rev. ed. (London: Verso, 1991), 46, 6.

21. Gregory A. Waller, "Search and Re-search: Digital Print Archives and the History of Multi-sited Cinema," in *The Arclight Guidebook to Media History and the Digital Humanities*, ed. Charles R. Acland and Eric Hoyt (Falmer, East Sussex: REFRAME/Project Arclight, 2016), 4564, open access download at https://projectarclight.org/book/.

22. We first shared these results in Hoyt, Long, Tran, and Hughes, "*Variety*'s Transformations."

23. Horace M. Swetland, *Industrial Publishing* (New York: New York Business Publishers Association, 1923), 4, 9; W. H. Ukers, "Standards of Practice of the Business Press," in *Lectures in the Forum in Industrial Journalism at the New York University, Season of 1915* (New York: Advertising & Selling Magazine, 1915), 104, https://archive.org/details /lecturesinforumioonewyrich.

24. Swetland, *Industrial Publishing*, 9.

25. For more on the boundaries between insiders and outsiders, see Carolyn Marvin's analysis of late nineteenth-century electrical journals in Marvin, *When Old Technologies Were New*, 1532.

26. Julien Elfenbein, *Business Journalism: Its Function and Future* (New York: Harper and Brothers, 1945), 300.

27. David Nasaw, *Going Out: The Rise and Fall of Public Amusements* (Cambridge, MA: Harvard University Press, 1999), 4.

28. Nasaw, 29.

29. Benjamin McArthur, *Actors and American Culture, 1880–1920* (Iowa City: University of Iowa Press, 2000), 7.

30. McArthur, 9.

31. McArthur, 214.

32. Arthur Frank Wertheim, *Vaudeville Wars: How the Keith-Albee and Orpheum Circuits Controlled the Big-Time and Its Performers* (New York: Palgrave Macmillan, 2006), 30.

33. Wertheim, 18–19.

34. Robert C. Allen, *Vaudeville and Film, 1895–1915: A Study in Media Interaction* (New York: Arno, 1980), 203–5.

35. [Editorial], *Variety*, Dec. 16, 1905, 3, https://lantern.mediahist.org/catalog/variety01 -1905-12_0002.

36. "Benjamin Franklin Keith," *New York Clipper*, July 14, 1906, 554, https://lantern .mediahist.org/catalog/clipper54-1906-07_0029.

37. [Editorial], *Variety*, June 9, 1906, 3, https://lantern.mediahist.org/catalog/variety03 -1906-06_0026.

38. "Why the Vaudeville Artists of America Should Organize," *Variety*, June 2, 1906, 4, https://lantern.mediahist.org/catalog/variety03-1906-06_0003.

39. Charles Musser, *The Emergence of Cinema: The American Screen to 1907* (New York: Scribner's, 1991).

40. Eileen Bowser, *The Transformation of Cinema, 1907–1915* (New York: Scribner's, 1991).

41. "To Our Readers," *Views and Films Index*, April 25, 1906, 1.

42. F. H. Richardson, "Lessons for Operators," *Moving Picture World*, July 18, 1908, 44, http://lantern.mediahist.org/catalog/movingor03chal_0052.

43. "Moving Picture News," *Moving Picture News*, Jan. 7, 1911, 22, http://lantern.mediahist .org/catalog/movingpicturenew04unse_0030; see also Alan Gevinson, "Motion Picture News," in *International Film, Radio, and Television Journals*, ed. Anthony Slide (Westport, CT: Greenwood Press, 1985), 243.

44. The account of the *Hollywood Reporter*'s early history from the fortieth anniversary issue was reprinted in Tichi Wilkerson and Marcia Borie, preface to *"The Hollywood Reporter": The Golden Years*, ed. Tichi Wilkerson and Marcia Borie (New York: Arlington House, 1986), 5.

1. REMAKING FILM JOURNALISM IN THE MID-1910S

1. Data collected through sampling six issues per year, selected through use of a random number generator. Data only collected for the even years (e.g., 1908, 1910, 1912), and no data available for 1908 and 1910 runs of *Moving Picture News* (as it was originally titled). Thank you to Derek Long for his assistance and diligence in collecting the data, as well as for helping me more precisely understand feature film production and distribution in the 1910s (topics explored in his forthcoming dissertation).

2. In 1909, four trade papers covered the film industry, and five theatrical trade papers gave film at least some discussion. In 1915, there were six trade papers focused on film, and five theatrical trade papers addressed the medium. Put another way, the number of film-oriented trade papers had increased by 50 percent during those eight years, and the number of theatrical trade papers addressing the medium had actually decreased by 17 percent. But size matters. From 1908 to 1916, the size of a typical issue of *Moving Picture World* had increased 890 percent, from 20 pages in 1908 to 178 pages in 1916.

3. In January 1917, *Motography* acknowledged its dearth of advertising compared to *Motion Picture News* and *Moving Picture World*, reasoning that its Chicago location, "Reader's First" policy, and lack of self-promotion were to blame. "While we have advertised MO-TOGRAPHY to exhibitors, we have never advertised MOTOGRAPHY to advertisers. We have worked hard and kept quiet—too quiet. Our press-agenting has all been for other

people." "New Conditions for the Film Papers," *Motography*, Jan. 13, 1917, 67, https://lantern .mediahist.org/catalog/motography17elec_0081.

4. Kia Afra, "Hollywood's Trade Organizations: How Competition and Collaboration Forged a Vertically-Integrated Oligopoly, 1915–1928" (PhD diss., Brown University, 2011), 98.

5. For more on Rothafel and his self-promotional strategies, see Ross Melnick, *American Showman: Samuel "Roxy" Rothafel and the Birth of the Entertainment Industry* (New York: Columbia University Press, 2012).

6. William A. Johnston, "Board of Trade Declares War on Enemies," *Motion Picture News*, Oct. 2, 1915, 45, https://lantern.mediahist.org/catalog/motionpicturenew121unse _1709.

7. Eileen Bowser, *The Transformation of Cinema, 1907–1915* (New York: Scribner, 1990), 33; Robert Anderson, "The Motion Picture Patents Company: A Reevaluation," in *The American Film Industry*, ed. Tino Balio, rev. ed. (Madison: University of Wisconsin Press, 1985), 146.

8. Scott Curtis, "A House Divided: The MPPC in Transition," in *American Cinema's Transitional Era: Audiences, Institutions, Practices*, ed. Charlie Keil and Shelley Stamp (Berkeley: University of California Press, 2004), 239–64.

9. "Moving Picture News," *Moving Picture News*, Jan. 7, 1911, 22, https://lantern.media hist.org/catalog/movingpicturenew04unse_0030; Alan Gevinson, "Motion Picture News," in *International Film, Radio, and Television Journals*, ed. Anthony Slide (Westport, CT: Greenwood Press, 1985), 243.

10. The definition of what constituted a feature film changed during the 1910s, as did the methods used in distributing features. In the early 1910s, *feature* was a marketing term that could apply to a one- or two-reel film that an exhibitor included within its program. By 1915 and 1916, though, *feature* referred to longer, multireel films. This later definition involving length still persists today, and it is what I mean in this chapter when I refer to the rise of the feature film.

11. Ben Singer, "Feature Films, Variety Programs, and the Crisis of the Small Exhibitor," in *American Cinema's Transitional Era: Audiences, Institutions, Practices*, ed. Charlie Keil and Shelley Stamp (Berkeley: University of California Press, 2004), 80.

12. Michael J. Quinn, "Paramount and Early Feature Distribution: 1914–1921," *Film History* 11, no. 1 (1999): 100–101.

13. The exhibitor did not directly share this box-office gross with the distributor. The percentage split of box office was uncommon in the mid-1910s. But distributors reaped the benefits indirectly by asking exhibitors to enter contracts stipulating higher rental fees for feature programs.

14. Singer, "Feature Films," 89.

15. Singer, 89.

16. Laura Wittern-Keller, "Controlling Content: Governmental Censorship, the Production Code, and the Ratings System," in *Hollywood and the Law*, ed. Paul McDonald, Emily Carman, Eric Hoyt, and Philip Drake (London: Palgrave, 2015), 130–53.

17. Wittern-Keller, 133.

18. For more on the history and rhetoric of Sunday screening laws, see Lee Grieveson, *Policing Cinema: Movies and Censorship in Early-Twentieth-Century America* (Berkeley: University of California Press, 2004), 81–87.

19. William A. Johnston, "Board of Trade Declares War on Enemies of Industry," Motion Picture News, Oct. 2, 1915, 45, https://lantern.mediahist.org/catalog/motionpicture new121unse_1709.

20. Richard L. Stromgren, "The Moving Picture World of W. Stephen Bush," *Film History* 2, no. 1 (Winter 1988): 17–18.

21. W. Stephen Bush, "Peace with Honor," *Moving Picture World*, May 6, 1916, 941, https://lantern.mediahist.org/catalog/movpic28chal_0063.

22. W. Stephen Bush, "The Campaign for a Modern Sunday. III," *Moving Picture World*, March 9, 1912, 845, https://lantern.mediahist.org/catalog/movingpictureworl1 newy_0879.

23. "The Brightest Lights in the Theatrical Firmament Illuminate the Universal Program," *Moving Picture World*, Oct. 12, 1912, 107, https://lantern.mediahist.org/catalog /movinwor14chal_0125; "Universal Films—As Solid as a Rock," *Moving Picture World*, Nov. 30, 1912, 839, https://lantern.mediahist.org/catalog/movinwor14chal_0847.

24. Stromgren, "Moving Picture World of W. Stephen Bush," 20.

25. Paramount was the most prominent company to take this stance. "Two Groups in Industry Give Views on Censorship; Los Angeles Producers Back Board of Trade," *Motion Picture News*, Feb. 19, 1916, 975, https://lantern.mediahist.org/catalog/motionpicture new131unse_1139. See also Afra, "Hollywood's Trade Organizations," 101–2.

26. US Postal Commission, "Briefs and Points on Behalf [*sic*] Federation of Trade Press Associations in the United States," in *Hearings before the Postal Commission* (Washington, DC: Government Printing Office, 1907), 714, https://books.google.com /books?id=ThsvAAAAMAAJ.

27. Charles T. Root, "The History and Development of Economic Journalism," in *Lectures in the Forum in Industrial Journalism at the New York University, Season of 1915* (New York: Advertising & Selling Magazine, 1915), 21, https://archive.org/details/lecturesinfo rumiooonewyrich; "Report of Commission on Second-Class Mail Matter," in *United States Congressional Serial Set* 62 (Washington, DC: Government Printing Office, 1912), 54, https:// books.google.com/books?id=0Nw3AQAAIAAJ.

28. United States Postal Service, "Postage Rates for Periodicals: A Narrative History," June 2010, 3–4, https://about.usps.com/who-we-are/postal-history/periodicals-postage -history.pdf.

29. Kevin R. Kosar, "Postage Subsidies for Periodicals: History and Recent Developments" (Washington, DC: Congressional Research Service, 2009), 4, https://archive.org /details/PostageSubsidiesForPeriodicalsCRSReportR40162.

30. Kosar, 4.

31. Root, "History and Development of Economic Journalism," 21.

32. H. M. Swetland, "The Special Service of the Class Paper to an Industry," in *Lectures in the Forum in Industrial Journalism at the New York University, Season of 1915* (New York: Advertising & Selling Magazine, 1915), 68, https://archive.org/details /lecturesinforumiooonewyrich.

33. "Declaration of Trade Press Principles," quoted in W. H. Ukers, "Standards of Practice of the Business Press," in *Lectures in the Forum in Industrial Journalism at the New York University, Season of 1915* (New York: Advertising & Selling Magazine, 1915), 102, https:// archive.org/details/lecturesinforumiooonewyrich.

34. Simmons's lecture and lectures by seven other trade press leaders were published in book form, further defining and validating the field of "industrial journalism." See E. A. Simmons, "Business Press Opportunities," in *Lectures in the Forum in Industrial Journalism at the New York University, Season of 1915* (New York: Advertising & Selling Magazine, 1915), 46, https://archive.org/details/lecturesinforumioonewyrich.

35. "The Policy of This Paper," *Exhibitors' Times*, May 17, 1913, 1, https://lantern.media hist.org/catalog/exhibitorstimeso1wmaj_0009.

36. Thomas Bedding, "Right off the Reel," *Exhibitors' Times*, May 31, 1913, 3, https://lantern .mediahist.org/catalog/exhibitorstimeso1wmaj_0085; Thomas Bedding, "The Editor to His Readers," *Implet*, Jan. 20, 1912, 1, https://lantern.mediahist.org/catalog/impleto1bedd _0009; Thomas Bedding, "Right off the Reel," *Exhibitors' Times*, July 12, 1913, 3, https:// lantern.mediahist.org/catalog/exhibitorstimeso1wmaj_0281.

37. Bedding, "Editor to His Readers," 1, https://lantern.mediahist.org/catalog/implet o1bedd_0009.

38. See, e.g., Thomas Bedding, "Right off the Reel," *Exhibitors' Times*, July 12, 1913, 3, https://lantern.mediahist.org/catalog/exhibitorstimeso1wmaj_0281; and "The English Canon, the English Censor, and the English Cinema," *Exhibitors' Times*, July 26, 1913, 7, https:// lantern.mediahist.org/catalog/exhibitorstimeso1wmaj_0357.

39. "The Policy of This Paper," 1.

40. "Tess of the D'Urbervilles," *Exhibitors' Times*, June 21, 1913, 1, https://lantern.media hist.org/catalog/exhibitorstimeso1wmaj_0191.

41. "The Policy of This Paper," 1.

42. "'Motion' Pictures Not 'Moving' Pictures," *Moving Picture News*, Sept. 27, 1913, 17, https://lantern.mediahist.org/catalog/movingpicturenew81unse_0473.

43. Robert Grau, *The Theatre of Science: A Volume of Progress and Achievement in the Motion Picture Industry* (New York: Broadway Publishing, 1914), 248, https://lantern .mediahist.org/catalog/cu31924026115737_0423.

44. William Allen Johnston, "Advertising Is an Economy," *Motion Picture News*, Nov. 29, 1913, 17, https://lantern.mediahist.org/catalog/motionpicturenew82unse_0375.

45. Johnston, 17.

46. For more on the controversy that ensued, see "Which Two?," *Variety*, Dec. 14, 1917, 49, https://lantern.mediahist.org/catalog/variety49-1917-12_0104; and Leander Richardson to William A. Johnston (open letter), "One Trade Paper Enough," *Variety*, Dec. 28, 1917, 239, https://lantern.mediahist.org/catalog/variety49-1917-12_0400.

47. "Declaration of Trade Press Principles," in Ukers, "Standards of Practice," 102.

48. "Moving Picture News," *Moving Picture News*, Jan. 7, 1911, 22, https://lantern.media hist.org/catalog/movingpicturenew04unse_0030.

49. "The 'Why' of the Billboard's Popularity," *Billboard*, August 16, 1916, 11, https://lantern .mediahist.org/catalog/billboard28-1916-08_0154; "The Leading and Representative Publication of the Moving Picture Trade," *Moving Picture World*, Jan. 6, 1912, viii, https://lantern .mediahist.org/catalog/movingpicturewor11newy_0016; "Largest Prepaid Circulation in the Motion Picture Field," *Motography*, August 12, 1916, 1, https://lantern.mediahist.org /catalog/motography161elec_0385.

50. William A. Johnston, "Facts versus Statistics," *Motion Picture News*, Sept. 26, 1914, 17, https://lantern.mediahist.org/catalog/motionpicturenew101unse_0985; William A.

Johnston, "Circulation That Counts," *Motion Picture News*, Sept. 19, 1914, 17, https://lantern .mediahist.org/catalog/motionpicturenew101unse_0903.

51. "Declaration of Trade Press Principles," in Ukers, "Standards of Practice," 102.

52. *Motion Picture News*, Sept. 26, 1914, [Cover], https://lantern.mediahist.org/catalog /motionpicturenew101unse_0969.

53. William A. Johnston, "Accessory News," *Motion Picture News*, Nov. 14, 1914, 71, https://lantern.mediahist.org/catalog/motionpicturenew102unse_0489.

54. F. H. Richardson, "Lessons for Operators," *Moving Picture World*, July 18, 1908, 44, https://lantern.mediahist.org/catalog/movingor03chal_0052.

55. F. H. Richardson, *Motion Picture Handbook: A Guide for Managers and Operators of Motion Picture Theatres* (New York: Moving Picture World, 1910), vii, https://lantern .mediahist.org/catalog/motionpicturehanoorich_0005.

56. Ukers, "Standards of Practice," 101.

57. "Store Equipment Section of the Dry Goods Economist," *Dry Goods Economist*, Nov. 25, 1911, 67, https://babel.hathitrust.org/cgi/pt?id=uiug.30112064273540&view=1up&s eq=265.

58. William A. Johnston, "A Trade Review," *Motion Picture News*, July 11, 1914, 27, https:// lantern.mediahist.org/catalog/motionpicturenew101unse_0027.

59. C. C. Cheadle, "Demand for Genuine Features in Springfield; Fakes Boycotted," *Motion Picture News*, July 11, 1914, 51, https://lantern.mediahist.org/catalog/motionpicture new101unse_0057; Roe S. Eastman, "Summer Hits Cincinnati Hard; Town Too 'Cheap' for Features," *Motion Picture News*, July 11, 1914, 50, https://lantern.mediahist.org/catalog /motionpicturenew101unse_0056.

60. William A. Johnston, "Motion Picture News Review of Film Trade Conditions in America," *Motion Picture News*, July 11, 1914, 29, https://lantern.mediahist.org/catalog /motionpicturenew101unse_0035.

61. William A. Johnston, "A Trade Review," *Motion Picture News*, July 11, 1914, 27, https:// lantern.mediahist.org/catalog/motionpicturenew101unse_0027.

62. Johnston, 27.

63. William A. Johnston, "The Structure of the Motion Picture Industry," *Annals of the American Academy of Political and Social Science* 128 (Nov. 1926): 24–25.

64. Grace Kingsley, "Universal City Opens," *Los Angeles Daily Times*, March 16, 1915, 4.

65. William A. Johnston, "What's the Matter?," *Motion Picture News*, Dec. 5, 1914, 21, https://lantern.mediahist.org/catalog/motionpicturenew102unse_0711.

66. William A. Johnston, "Getting Down to Brass Tacks," *Motion Picture News*, Nov. 28, 1914, 21, https://lantern.mediahist.org/catalog/motionpicturenew102unse_0611.

67. William A. Johnston, "Protect the Exhibitor," *Motion Picture News*, May 15, 1915, 31, https://lantern.mediahist.org/catalog/motionpicturenew112unse_0631.

68. William A. Johnston, "Murder in the First Degree," *Motion Picture News*, March 4, 1916, 1267, https://lantern.mediahist.org/catalog/motionpicturenew132unse_0055.

69. See, e.g., "Manufacturers' Synopses of Films," *Moving Picture News*, July 5, 1913, 29, https://lantern.mediahist.org/catalog/movingpicturenew81unse_0037.

70. Alan Gevinson, "Motion Picture News," in *International Film, Radio, and Television Journals*, ed. Anthony Slide (Westport, CT: Greenwood Press, 1985), 244.

71. "Wid's Independent Reviews of Features" [Advertisement], *Motion Picture News*, Jan. 29, 1916, 555, https://lantern.mediahist.org/catalog/motionpicturenew131unse_0551.

72. "Exhibitor's Film Review Service, Inc." [Advertisement], *Moving Picture World*, Nov. 6, 1915, 1205, https://lantern.mediahist.org/catalog/movinwor26chal_0159.

73. "A Reviewing Service Free from the Influence of Film Advertisers," *Harrison's Reports*, Jan. 5, 1935, 1, https://lantern.mediahist.org/catalog/harrisonsreports17harr_0005.

74. William A. Johnston, "Looking in on Us," *Motion Picture News*, May 20, 1916, 3060, https://lantern.mediahist.org/catalog/motionpicturenew133unse_0442.

75. Ukers, "Standards of Practice," 107.

76. Richardson to Johnston (open letter), "One Trade Paper Enough," 239.

77. These examples came from *Motion Picture News*, March 4, 1916, https://lantern.mediahist.org/catalog/motionpicturenew132unse_0007. In this example, Mutual and Essanay both had five full-page advertisements.

78. Caldwell calls *industrial critical practices* a "three-part concept [that] signifies trade methods and conventions involving interpretive schemes (the 'critical dimension') that are deployed within specific institutional contexts and relationships (the 'industrial' environment) when such activities are manifest during technical production tasks or professional interactions (labor and 'practice')." John Thornton Caldwell, *Production Culture: Industrial Reflexivity and Critical Practice in Film and Television* (Durham, NC: Duke University Press, 2008), 5–6.

79. W. Stephen Bush, "Looking Forward," *Exhibitor's Trade Review*, June 16, 1917, 91.

80. William A. Johnston, "Why the Board of Trade Is Representative," *Motion Picture News*, March 4, 1916, 1268, https://lantern.mediahist.org/catalog/motionpicturenew132unse_0056.

81. William A. Johnston, "That Action at Albany," *Motion Picture News*, March 25, 1916, 1723, https://lantern.mediahist.org/catalog/motionpicturenew132unse_0501.

82. William A. Johnston, "The Fat in the Fire," *Motion Picture News*, April 29, 1916, 2449, https://lantern.mediahist.org/catalog/motionpicturenew132unse_1275.

83. "Metro Withdraws from Motion Picture Board of Trade," *Motion Picture News*, April 29, 1916, 2501, https://lantern.mediahist.org/catalog/motionpicturenew132unse_1277; "Metro Quits Board of Trade," *Moving Picture World*, April 29, 1916, 779, https://lantern.mediahist.org/catalog/movwor28chal_0841.

84. Afra, "Hollywood's Trade Organizations," 129–32.

85. Johnston, "That Action at Albany," 1723.

86. "President Ochs Makes Statement," *Motography*, May 13, 1916, https://lantern.mediahist.org/catalog/motography152elec_0378. See also Afra, "Hollywood's Trade Organizations," 131.

87. Afra, "Hollywood's Trade Organizations," 157.

88. "Film Organization Needs Exhibitors," *Motography*, July 15, 1916, 121–22, https://lantern.mediahist.org/catalog/motography161elec_0141. See also Deron Overpeck, "Out of the Dark: American Film Exhibition, Political Action and Industrial Change, 1966–1986" (PhD diss., University of California, Los Angeles, 2007), 83–89.

89. W. Stephen Bush, "The National Association of the Motion Picture Industry," *Moving Picture World*, August 12, 1916, 1077, https://lantern.mediahist.org/catalog/mowor29chal_0231.

90. W. Stephen Bush, "Our Duty to Our Readers," *Moving Picture World*, August 12, 1916, 1077, https://lantern.mediahist.org/catalog/mowor29chal_0231.

91. William A. Johnston, "The Test That Tells," *Motion Picture News*, May 20, 1916, 3067, https://lantern.mediahist.org/catalog/motionpicturenew133unse_0449.

92. William A. Johnston, "Thanks!," *Motion Picture News*, April 29, 1916, 2500, https://lantern.mediahist.org/catalog/motionpicturenew132unse_1276.

93. William A. Johnston, "Other Trade Journals," *Motion Picture News*, May 27, 1916, 3249, https://lantern.mediahist.org/catalog/motionpicturenew133unse_0625.

94. Swetland, "Special Service of the Class Paper," 68–69.

95. "More Libel Suiting," *Variety*, March 2, 1917, 24, https://lantern.mediahist.org/catalog/variety46-1917-03_0023.

2. TRADE PAPERS AT WAR

1. "Ochs Used League Presidency for His Own Gain, Is Charge," *Variety*, Oct. 27, 1916, 22, https://lantern.mediahist.org/catalog/variety44-1916-10_0173.

2. "Stormy Scenes at Ochs Hearing," *Moving Picture World*, Dec. 2, 1916, 1304, https://lantern.mediahist.org/catalog/movingpicturewor30newy_1436.

3. "Stormy Scenes at Ochs Hearing."

4. "Ochs Committee Gets Cold Feet," *Moving Picture World*, Dec. 16, 1916, 1622, https://lantern.mediahist.org/catalog/movingpicturewor30newy_1768.

5. "Charges against Ochs Filed by Exhibitors and Publishers," *Wid's Daily*, July 9, 1918, 1, https://lantern.mediahist.org/catalog/filmdailyvolume556newy_0005.

6. "More Libel Suiting," *Variety*, March 2, 1917, 24, https://lantern.mediahist.org/catalog/variety46-1917-03_0023.

7. "Announcement to Exhibitors," *Exhibitor's Trade Review*, Dec. 9, 1916, 16.

8. "Our Answer to the Anvil Chorus," *Exhibitor's Trade Review*, Dec. 9, 1916, 15.

9. "An Ally in Spite of Himself," *Motion Picture News*, Nov. 4, 1916, 2812, https://lantern.mediahist.org/catalog/motionpicturenew14moti_4_0074.

10. Roscellus S. Guernsey, "When a Libel Is Not a Libel," *Yale Law Journal* 20, no. 1 (1910), 37, http://www.jstor.org/stable/785040.

11. Lee A. Ochs (*Exhibitor's Trade Review*) to Members of the National Association of the Motion Picture Industry, Dec. 26, 1916, Aitken Collection, Box 13, WHS.

12. N. W. Ayer & Son, *N. W. Ayer & Son's American Newspaper Annual and Directory* (Philadelphia): 1900–1930, 1935, 1940, 1945, 1955, 1960. The editions I used are located at the Wisconsin Historical Society. Several editions of the Ayer Annuals are also available online at HathiTrust, http://catalog.hathitrust.org/Record/006110092.

13. W. Stephen Bush, "Special Announcement to All Exhibitors of Motion Pictures," *Exhibitor's Trade Review*, Dec. 16, 1916, 97.

14. "'Trade Review' Sold?," *Variety*, March 15, 1918, 46, https://lantern.mediahist.org/catalog/variety50-1918-03_0151.

15. "Lee Ochs' Trial Is a Thrilling Affair," *Motion Picture News*, Dec. 2, 1916, 3452, https://lantern.mediahist.org/catalog/motionpicturenew14moti_4_0716.

16. William A. Johnston, "An Exhibitor's Dream of a League from Which He Would Derive Some Benefit," *Motion Picture News*, Dec. 23, 1916, 3982, https://lantern.mediahist.org/catalog/motionpicturenew14moti_4_1240.

17. "We Would Like for Christmas," *Motion Picture News*, Dec. 30, 1916, 4173, https://lantern.mediahist.org/catalog/motionpicturenew14moti_4_1433; "Our Candidate Is Mr. Trigger," *Motion Picture News*, Dec. 30, 1916, 4174, https://lantern.mediahist.org/catalog/motionpicturenew14moti_4_1434.

18. "We Resolve," *Motion Picture News*, Dec. 30, 1916, 4173, https://lantern.mediahist.org/catalog/motionpicturenew14moti_4_1433.

19. The "Dear Old Frank" was Frank Rembusch, a prominent Indiana exhibitor. "Sweet William and Dear Old Frank," *Exhibitor's Trade Review*, Jan. 27, 1917, 533.

20. "Motion Picture Exhibitors League of America vs. William A. Johnston," *Exhibitor's Trade Review*, Feb. 3, 1917, 533.

21. "Amended Complaint," April 11, 1917, 7, William A. Johnston v. Exhibitors Trade Review (1917), Case no. 5810–1917, NYCC.

22. George Chauncey, *Gay New York: Gender, Urban Culture, and the Making of the Gay Male World, 1890–1940* (New York: Basic Books, 1995), 47–63.

23. "Serving It with Speed and Ginger," *Motion Picture News*, June 15, 1918, 3533, https://lantern.mediahist.org/catalog/motionpicturenew172unse_1601; "Merritt Crawford, UA Publicity Man, Dies," *Motion Picture Herald*, August 18, 1945, 58, https://lantern.mediahist.org/catalog/motionpictureher160unse_0514.

24. "Sidelights on the Costume Ball at Madison Square," *Motion Picture News*, March 4, 1916, 1270, https://lantern.mediahist.org/catalog/motionpicturenew132unse_0058.

25. "Wanted—$50,000," *Exhibitor's Trade Review*, Feb. 24, 1917, 806.

26. "Editor Johnston Sues Some More," *Exhibitor's Trade Review*, March 10, 1917, 947.

27. "As a Suer Johnston Is Some Suer: Now He Wants $25,000 from Lesley Mason, Managing Editor of 'Trade Review,'" *Exhibitor's Trade Review*, March 17, 1917, 1009.

28. "Memorandum in Opposition to Plaintiff's Motion for Judgment on the Pleadings," June 14, 1917, 13, William A. Johnston v. Exhibitors Trade Review (1917), Case no. 5810–1917, NYCC.

29. "Summary Judgment," June 15, 1917, William A. Johnston v. Exhibitors Trade Review (1917), Case no. 5810–1917, NYCC

30. "Notice of Appeal," July 9, 1917, William A. Johnston v. Exhibitors Trade Review (1917), Case no. 5810–1917, NYCC.

31. Lee A. Ochs, "Clean House!," *Exhibitor's Trade Review*, Jan. 27, 1917, 534.

32. R. H. Cochrane, "Statement," Jan. 19(?), 1917, Aitken Collection, Box 13, WHS.

33. "President Ochs vs. Universal Company," *Moving Picture World*, Feb. 3, 1917, 663, https://lantern.mediahist.org/catalog/moviwor31chal_0077; "Universal-Ochs Argument," *Billboard*, Feb. 3, 1917, 51, https://lantern.mediahist.org/catalog/billboard29-1917-02_0062; "League Slams Universal at Albany Convention," *New York Clipper*, Jan. 31, 1917, 33, https://lantern.mediahist.org/catalog/Clipper64-1917-01_0176; "That Ochs-Universal Feud," *Variety*, Feb. 2, 1917, 16, https://lantern.mediahist.org/catalog/variety45-1917-02_0015.

34. William A. Johnston, "Time for House Cleaning," *Motion Picture News*, Feb. 10, 1917, https://lantern.mediahist.org/catalog/motionpicturenew15moti_1_0869.

35. W. Stephen Bush, "No Waste Here," *Exhibitor's Trade Review*, Feb. 24, 1917, 805.

36. "A Serious Menace to the Whole Trade," *Exhibitor's Trade Review*, Feb. 10, 1917, 674.

37. Merritt Crawford, "Warfare Below the Belt," *Exhibitor's Trade Review*, March 17, 1917, 1008.

38. J. Ray Murray, "Ochs' High-Handed Methods Disrupt League," *Exhibitors Herald*, August 4, 1917, 9, https://lantern.mediahist.org/catalog/exhibitorsherald05exhi_0267.

39. Deron Overpeck, "Out of the Dark: American Film Exhibition, Political Action and Industrial Change, 1966–1986" (PhD diss., University of California, Los Angeles, 2007), 83–86.

40. "'Trade Review' Cutting Down," *Variety*, March 1, 1918, 46, https://lantern.mediahist .org/catalog/variety50-1918-03_0045; "Bush Out of Review," *Variety*, March 8, 1918, 45, https://lantern.mediahist.org/catalog/variety50-1918-03_0098.

41. "Lee A. Ochs Resigns as Trade Review Head," *Exhibitors Herald*, April 27, 1918, 23, https://lantern.mediahist.org/catalog/exhibitorsherald06exhi_0807.

42. "'Trade Review' Sold?," *Variety*, March 15, 1918, 46, https://lantern.mediahist.org /catalog/variety50-1918-03_0151.

43. Horace M. Swetland, *Industrial Publishing* (New York: New York Business Publishers Associations, 1923).

44. "Trade Review Sold to Press Syndicate," *Exhibitors Herald*, Jan. 31, 1920, 45, https:// lantern.mediahist.org/catalog/exhibitorsherald10exhi_0521.

45. Leslie Midkiff DeBauche, *Reel Patriotism: The Movies and World War I* (Madison: University of Wisconsin Press, 1997), 116, 118.

46. "Exhibitors Protest Lightness Nights," *Moving Picture World*, Jan. 5, 1918, 120, https://lantern.mediahist.org/catalog/movingpicturewor35newy_0138; "Liberty Loan Night Is Now a Fact," *Moving Picture World*, March 23, 1918, 1633, https://lantern.mediahist.org /catalog/movingpicturewor35newy_1767.

47. Kia Afra, "Hollywood's Trade Organizations: How Competition and Collaboration Forged a Vertically-Integrated Oligopoly, 1915–1928" (PhD diss., Brown University, 2011), 152–55.

48. Kia Afra, "'Seventeen Happy Days' in Hollywood: Selig Polyscope's Promotional Campaign for the Movie Special of July 1915," *Film History* 22, no. 2 (2010): 212, 217; "Film Industry Feels Pinch of War Tax Nov. 1," *Exhibitors Herald*, Oct. 27, 1917, 15, https://lantern .mediahist.org/catalog/exhibitorsherald05exhi_0855.

49. "How Exhibitors Are Handling Tax Detailed in Reports to 'Herald,'" *Exhibitors Herald*, Dec. 1, 1917, 15, https://lantern.mediahist.org/catalog/exhibitorsherald05exhi_1079.

50. For more on this history, see Eric Hoyt, "Asset or Liability? Hollywood and Tax Law," in *Hollywood and the Law*, ed. Paul McDonald, Emily Carman, Eric Hoyt, and Philip Drake (London: BFI/Palgrave, 2015), 183–208.

51. For a detailed account of this history, see John M. Barry, *The Great Influenza: The Story of the Deadliest Pandemic in History* (New York: Penguin, 2005).

52. "Portland Exchanges Report Decrease," *Moving Picture World*, Feb. 8, 1919, 783, https://lantern.mediahist.org/catalog/movingwor39chal_0813.

53. "Many St. Louis Houses Are Reopening," *Moving Picture World*, March 8, 1919, 1367, https://lantern.mediahist.org/catalog/movwor39chal_0257; "Death of Mrs. C. E. Almy," *Moving Picture World*, March 8, 1919, 1370, https://lantern.mediahist.org/catalog/movwor 39chal_0260.

54. W. Stephen Bush, "Abuses of the Deposit System," *Moving Picture World*, Sept. 16, 1916, 1805, https://lantern.mediahist.org/catalog/movurewor29chal_0407; "Triangle Steps Out Bravely," *Motion Picture News*, April 28, 1917, 2632, https://lantern.mediahist.org /catalog/motionpicturenew153unse_0582; "Abolishing the Advance Deposit System," *Motography*, July 7, 1917, 12, https://lantern.mediahist.org/catalog/motography18elec_0018;

Martin Quigley, "Credit Protection Due Distributors," *Exhibitors Herald*, Feb. 16, 1918, 11, https://lantern.mediahist.org/catalog/exhibitorsherald06exhi_0327.

55. "Facts and Comments," *Moving Picture World*, March 18, 1916, 1797, https://lantern.mediahist.org/catalog/movingpicturewor27newy_1923; S. A. de Waltoff, "Program or Open Booking: Practical Exhibitor Points Out Advantages of First Plan—Blames Latter Method for Small Profits," *Moving Picture World*, May 5, 1917, 785, https://lantern.mediahist.org/catalog/movingpicturewor32newy_0869; Sam Spedon, "'Open Booking'—What Is It?," *Moving Picture World*, August 18, 1917, 1052, https://lantern.mediahist.org/catalog/mowor33chal_0402; "Facts and Comments," *Moving Picture World*, Sept. 15, 1917, 1661, https://lantern.mediahist.org/catalog/movpict33chal_0463.

Motion Picture News ran a three-part series in October 1916 to highlight a dearth of viewpoints and perspectives on open booking versus its predecessor, program booking: "Editorial," *Motion Picture News*, Oct. 14, 1916, 2346, https://lantern.mediahist.org/catalog/motionpicturenew14moti_3_1070; "Open Booking or the Program—Which?—I," *Motion Picture News*, Oct. 14, 1916, 2351, https://lantern.mediahist.org/catalog/motionpicturenew14moti_3_1075; "Open Booking or the Program—Which?—II," *Motion Picture News*, Oct. 21, 1916, 2515, https://lantern.mediahist.org/catalog/motionpicturenew14moti_3_1239; "Open Booking or the Program—Which?—III," *Motion Picture News*, Oct. 28, 1916, 2655, https://lantern.mediahist.org/catalog/motionpicturenew14moti_3_1661.

See also Hiram Abrams, "Hiram Abrams States the Case for Program Booking: An Attack on the Principles of Open Booking," *Motion Picture News*, March 10, 1917, 1528, https://lantern.mediahist.org/catalog/motionpicturenew152unse_0238; "Calls Uniformity Trade Solution," *Motography*, March 25, 1916, 699, https://lantern.mediahist.org/catalog/motography151elec_0758; "Combine Seeks Industry Control, Says A.E.A.," *Exhibitors Herald*, Sept. 1, 1917, 13, https://lantern.mediahist.org/catalog/exhibitorsherald05exhi_0463.

56. Thank you to Derek Long for helping me understand the complex history of film distribution during the 1910s and 1920s and correcting many errors I would have otherwise made. Long explores these issues in depth in Derek Long, "Reprogramming the Movies: Distribution Strategy and Production Planning in the Early Studio System, 1915–1924" (PhD diss., University of Wisconsin–Madison, 2017).

57. "Prominent Film Folk," *Wid's Daily*, July 22, 1918, 3, https://lantern.mediahist.org/catalog/filmdailyvolume556newy_0105.

58. Cecile B. Horowitz, "Film Daily," in *International Film, Radio, and Television Journals*, ed. Anthony Slide (Westport, CT: Greenwood Press, 1985), 121–23; Douglas Gomery, *The Coming of Sound: A History* (New York: Routledge, 2005), xiv.

59. Alan Gevinson, "Motion Picture News," in *International Film, Radio, and Television Journals*, ed. Anthony Slide (Westport, CT: Greenwood Press, 1985), 245.

60. Richard Abel, *Menus for Movieland: Newspapers and the Emergence of American Film Culture, 1913–1916* (Berkeley: University of California Press, 2015).

61. Robert Grau, *The Theatre of Science: A Volume of Progress and Achievement in the Motion Picture Industry* (New York: Broadway Publishing, 1914), 251, https://lantern.mediahist.org/catalog/cu31924026115737_0423.

62. "'Reviews' by Exhibitors," *Motography*, Oct. 7, 1916, 802, https://lantern.mediahist.org/catalog/motography162elec_0014.

63. "What the Picture Did for Me," *Motography*, Oct. 14, 1916, 855, https://lantern.mediahist.org/catalog/motography162elec_0071.

64. "How Did That Picture Go at Your Theatre?," *Exhibitor's Trade Review*, June 9, 1917, 37.

65. "We Started It!," *Motography*, Sept. 22, 1917, 608, https://lantern.mediahist.org/catalog/motography18elec_0638.

66. For more on the later history of the "What the Picture Did for Me" department, see Kathryn Fuller-Seeley, "'What the Picture Did for Me': Small Town Exhibitors' Strategies for Surviving the Great Depression," in *Hollywood in the Neighborhood: Historical Case Studies of Local Moviegoing*, ed. Kathryn Fuller-Seeley (Berkeley: University of California Press, 2008): 186–207.

67. "Variety's Daily Bulletin," *Variety*, Dec. 13, 1916, 1, https://lantern.mediahist.org/catalog/variety45-1916-12_0125.

68. Arthur Frank Wertheim, *Vaudeville Wars: How the Keith-Albee and Orpheum Circuits Controlled the Big-Time and Its Performers* (New York: Palgrave Macmillan, 2006).

69. Editorial, *Variety*, Dec. 16, 1905, 3, https://lantern.mediahist.org/catalog/variety01-1905-12_0002.

70. "Benjamin Franklin Keith," *New York Clipper*, July 14, 1906, 554, https://lantern.mediahist.org/catalog/clipper54-1906-07_0029.

71. Editorial, *Variety*, June 9, 1906, 3, https://lantern.mediahist.org/catalog/variety03-1906-06_0026.

72. "Why the Vaudeville Artists of America Should Organize," *Variety*, June 2, 1906, 4, https://lantern.mediahist.org/catalog/variety03-1906-06_0003.

73. Wertheim, *Vaudeville Wars*, 106–7.

74. Editorial, *Variety*, Dec. 23, 1905, 3, https://lantern.mediahist.org/catalog/variety01-1905-12_0018.

75. Wertheim, *Vaudeville Wars*, 186–93.

76. Editorial, *Variety*, Jan. 14, 1911, 7, https://lantern.mediahist.org/catalog/variety21-1911-01_0046.

77. "Variety Is 'Blacklisted' by United Booking Offices," *Variety*, March 7, 1913, 1, https://lantern.mediahist.org/catalog/variety30-1913-03_0002; "English Act Canceled by United Booking Offices through Advertising in Variety," *Variety*, March 28, 1913, 1, https://lantern.mediahist.org/catalog/variety30-1913-03_0126.

78. "United Booking Offices and 'Variety' Again Friendly," *Variety*, August 28, 1914, 1, https://lantern.mediahist.org/catalog/variety35-1914-08_0102.

79. Editorial, *Variety*, Nov. 28, 1913, 9, https://lantern.mediahist.org/catalog/variety32-1913-11_0120.

80. Wertheim, *Vaudeville Wars*, 170–75.

81. "Mountford Back in Harness for Aggressive Campaign," *Variety*, Oct. 22, 1915, 4, https://lantern.mediahist.org/catalog/variety40-1915-10_0139; Harry Mountford, "Can They Come Back?," *Variety*, Oct. 22, 1915, 13, https://lantern.mediahist.org/catalog/variety40-1915-10_0148.

82. "Managers Are Still Barring Rat Acts," *New York Clipper*, Nov. 8, 1916, 7, https://lantern.mediahist.org/catalog/Clipper64-1916-11_0042.

83. Wertheim, *Vaudeville Wars*, 229.

84. *Billboard*, e.g., called Mountford the "Prince of Sophists." See "When Facts Give Out Why Worry?," *Billboard*, Feb. 3, 1917, 6, https://lantern.mediahist.org/catalog/billboard29-1917-02_0005.

85. Editorial, *Variety*, Dec. 29, 1916, 9, https://lantern.mediahist.org/catalog/variety45-1916-12_0346.

86. "The Funny Side," *Variety*, March 23, 1917, 9, https://lantern.mediahist.org/catalog/variety46-1917-03_0204.

87. "Complaint," May 23, 1917, 3, Edward Clark v. Variety, Inc. (1917), Case no. 22121–1917, NYCC.

88. "Eddie Clark Feels 'Damaged,'" *Variety*, June 2, 1917, 6, https://lantern.mediahist.org/catalog/variety47-1917-06_0005; "Complaint (Second Action)," June 25, 1917, 1, Edward Clark v. Variety, Inc. (1917), Case no. 22121–1917, NYCC.

89. "Complaint (Second Action)," July 3, 1917, Edward Clark v. Variety, Inc. (1917), Case no. 22121–1917, NYCC.

90. "Answer to Complaint (Second Action)," August 20, 1917, Edward Clark v. Variety, Inc. (1917), Case no. 22121–1917, NYCC.

91. "Settlement Agreement," Jan. 30, 1920, 1, Edward Clark v. Variety, Inc. (1917), Case no. 22121–1917, NYCC.

92. "Clark Suits Settled," *Variety*, Feb. 6, 1920, 4, https://lantern.mediahist.org/catalog/variety57-1920-02_0002.

93. Federal Trade Commission v. Vaudeville Managers' Protective Association et al., Complaint, May 7, 1918, 5, Docket no. 128, FTC Docketed Case Files, RG 122, Box 69, NARA-CP.

94. Wertheim, *Vaudeville Wars*, 234, 235.

95. Robert C. Allen, "Vaudeville and Film, 1895–1915: A Study in Media Interaction" (PhD diss., University of Iowa, 1977), 316.

96. Universal to Mr. Cobe (Unity Film Company), Jan. 26, 1917, Aitken Collection, Box 13, WHS. *Exhibitor's Trade Review* later reprinted this same letter in "A Serious Menace to the Whole Trade," *Exhibitor's Trade Review*, Feb. 10, 1917, 674.

97. Quoted in Leander Richardson to William A. Johnston (open letter), "One Trade Paper Enough," *Variety*, Dec. 28, 1917, 239, https://lantern.mediahist.org/catalog/variety49-1917-12_0400.

98. "Which Two?," *Variety*, Dec. 14, 1917, 49, https://lantern.mediahist.org/catalog/variety49-1917-12_0104.

99. Richardson to Johnston, "One Trade Paper Enough," https://lantern.mediahist.org/catalog/variety49-1917-12_0400

100. "Pictures in Front," *Variety*, May 5, 1926, 3, https://lantern.mediahist.org/catalog/variety82-1926-05_0002.

101. "Incorporations," *Variety*, April 5, 1917, 37, https://lantern.mediahist.org/catalog/variety50-1918-04_0046.

3. THE INDEPENDENT EXHIBITOR'S PAL: LOCALIZING, SPECIALIZING, AND EXPANDING THE EXHIBITOR PAPER

1. Joan Baer, "The Boxoffice Story," *Boxoffice*, Jan. 2010 (reprinted from July 20, 1970), 19–21.

2. Ben Singer, "Feature Films, Variety Programs, and the Crisis of the Small Exhibitor," in *American Cinema's Transitional Era: Audiences, Institutions, Practices*, ed. Charlie Keil and Shelley Stamp (Berkeley: University of California Press, 2004), 89.

3. John Joseph Phelan, *Motion Pictures as a Phase of Commercial Amusement in Toledo, Ohio* (Toledo, OH: Little Book Press, 1919), 236–37, http://www.archive.org/details/motion picturesaoophelgoog.

4. P. S. Harrison, "Let Us Not Forget," *Harrison's Reports*, Sept. 4, 1920, 1; P. S. Harrison, "An Open Letter to Mr. J. D. Williams, General Manager First National," *Harrison's Reports*, Sept. 11, 1920, 1; P. S. Harrison, "Analysis of the First National Franchise," *Harrison's Reports*, Sept. 18, 1920.

5. Kuhn Loeb Report on Paramount Publix, Dec. 20, 1934, 52–55, Vertical File Collection, 21, AMPAS.

6. For a discussion of exhibitors expressing concern over Paramount acquiring theaters, see Martin J. Quigley, "Independence or—Disaster!," *Exhibitors Herald*, June 12, 1920, 33.

7. For a detailed study of distribution practices during this period, see Derek Long, "Reprogramming the Movies: Distribution Strategy and Production Planning in the Early Studio System, 1915–1924" (PhD diss., University of Wisconsin–Madison, 2017). Long points out that distribution practices varied greatly across the studios. The trend during the early 1920s was toward block booking, but it came in different forms and in fits and starts.

8. Richard Maltby, "The Standard Exhibition Contract and the Unwritten History of the Classical Hollywood Cinema," *Film History* 25, no. 1–2 (2013): 143.

9. FTC v. Famous Players-Lasky Corporation et al. 11 FTC Dec. 187 (1927).

10. For an in-depth account of Thomas Watson's exhibition practices, see Davis Resha, "Strategies for Survival: The Little Exhibitor in the 1920s," *Quarterly Review of Film and Video* 29, no. 1 (2012): 12–23.

11. Metro Pictures Service to Thomas J. Watson, Dec. 15, 1920, Thomas J. Watson Papers, Metro Picture Service 1920–1925, box 9, folder 6, MSS 820, Wisconsin Historical Society.

12. Pathé Exchange Branch Manager to Thomas J. Watson, May 24, 1921, Thomas J. Watson Papers, box 9, folder 6, MSS 820, Wisconsin Historical Society.

13. Thomas J. Watson to Chicago Board of Trade, June 26, 1922, Thomas J. Watson Papers, Chicago Film Board of Trade, 1922–1930, box 11, folder 17, MSS 820, Wisconsin Historical Society.

14. The extent of Watson's potential membership and participation in the Ku Klux Klan is unclear. His possessions, however—accessioned and arranged by the Wisconsin Historical Society—contain Ku Klux Klan publications, including a pamphlet titled *First Lesson in the Science and Art of Klankraft*. Thomas J. Watson Papers, "KKK memorabilia, 1920, undated," box 13, folder 11, MSS 820, Wisconsin Historical Society.

15. "Five Hundred Attend F.I.L.M. Field Day," *Exhibitors Herald*, August 20, 1921, 36, https://lantern.mediahist.org/catalog/exhibitorsherald13exhi_0658.

16. Howard T. Lewis, *Motion Picture Industry* (New York: D. Van Norstrand, 1933), 264, https://lantern.mediahist.org/catalog/motionpictureindoohowa_0286.

17. Howard McClellan, "Arbitration Working Successfully," *Exhibitor's Trade Review*, Feb. 4, 1922, 658–59.

18. Kia Afra, *The Hollywood Trust: Trade Associations and the Rise of the Studio System* (Lanham, MD: Rowman & Littlefield, 2016), 159–201.

19. Maltby, "Standard Exhibition Contract," 145.

20. JoAnne Yates, *Control through Communication: The Rise of System in American Management* (Baltimore: Johns Hopkins University Press, 1993), 45–56, 65–77.

21. Colvin W. Brown (General Manager of Quigley Publications), "A Promise and a Performance," ca. 1935, Martin J. Quigley Papers, box 3, folder 17, Georgetown University Library.

22. Afra, *The Hollywood Trust*, 113–14.

23. For an excellent history of exhibitor organizations, see Deron Overpeck, "Out of the Dark: American Film Exhibition, Political Action and Industrial Change, 1966–1986" (PhD diss., University of California, Los Angeles, 2007).

24. *N. W. Ayer & Son's American Newspaper Annual and Directory*, 1914–24, WHS.

25. *Amusements: The Motion Picture Exhibitors Weekly Trade Journal*, August 10, 1916. AMPAS.

26. "Fore!," *Film Daily*, June 24, 1923, 12, https://lantern.mediahist.org/catalog/filmdaily 2324newy_1194.

27. Sime Silverman, "Inside Stuff—Pictures," *Variety*, May 15, 1929, 55, https://lantern .mediahist.org/catalog/variety95-1929-05_0206; Sime Silverman, "Inside Stuff—Pictures," *Variety*, June 12, 1929, 53, https://lantern.mediahist.org/catalog/variety95-1929-06_0116.

28. Jessica L. Whitehead, Louis Pelletier, and Paul S. Moore, "'The Girl Friend in Canada': Ray Lewis and *Canadian Moving Picture Digest* (1915–1957)," in *Mapping Movie Magazines: Digitization, Periodicals and Cinema History*, ed. Lies Van de Vijver and Daniel Biltereyst (Cham, Switzerland: Springer Nature and Palgrave Macmillan, 2020), 130.

29. Whitehead, Pelletier, and Moore, 130.

30. "A Welcome to New England," *The Exhibitor*, March 15, 1939, 3.

31. "Motion Picture Journal in Experienced Hands," *Motion Picture News*, Jan. 24, 1920, 1031, https://lantern.mediahist.org/catalog/motionpicturenew21moti_1_0725.

32. "Twelve Great Regionals" [Advertisement for Associated Film Press], *Wid's Daily*, Dec. 9, 1920, 3, https://lantern.mediahist.org/catalog/filmdailyvolume11314newy_1309.

33. "The Fourteen Points of Successful Advertising" [Advertisement for Associated Film Press], *Moving Picture World*, May 14, 1921, 178, http://lantern.mediahist.org/catalog /movpicwor501movi_0238.

34. "Tom Hamlin Resigns," *Moving Picture World*, Jan. 20, 1923, 223, https://lantern .mediahist.org/catalog/movpicwor60movi_0189.

35. Quoted in Baer, "The Boxoffice Story," 21.

36. "Collingswood Theatre, Collingswood, N.J. Opening with Fitting Ceremony," *The Exhibitor*, Oct. 15, 1920, 26.

37. Gregory A. Waller, "Imagining and Promoting the Small-Town Theater," *Cinema Journal* 44, no. 3 (2005): 15–16.

38. "From Newsboy to Exhibitor," *Motion Picture Weekly*, Nov. 1, 1919, 12, AMPAS.

39. Michael M. Gore (open letter), *Motion Picture Weekly*, Nov. 1, 1919, 12, AMPAS.

40. "Demand a Removal," *Wid's Daily*, May 4, 1920, 1, https://lantern.mediahist.org /catalog/filmdailyvolume11112newy_0959.

41. "The 21st Exchange," *Wid's Daily*, Jan. 11, 1921, 6, https://lantern.mediahist.org/catalog /filmdailyvolume11516newy_0106.

42. P. S. Harrison, "Are Your Film Contracts Just So Many Scraps of Paper?," *Harrison's Reports*, Dec. 6, 1919, 1.

43. "A Radical Step in Review Service," *Motion Picture News*, March 16, 1918, 1542, https://lantern.mediahist.org/catalog/motionpicturenew171unse_1582.

44. "Exhibitor to Exhibitor," *Motion Picture News*, March 23, 1918, 1542, https://lantern.mediahist.org/catalog/motionpicturenew171unse_1743.

45. "Radical Step," *Motion Picture News*, 1542, https://lantern.mediahist.org/catalog/motionpicturenew171unse_1582.

46. "Exhibitor to Exhibitor Review Service," *Motion Picture News*, May 18, 1918, 2956, https://lantern.mediahist.org/catalog/motionpicturenew172unse_1022; "Radical Step," *Motion Picture News*, 1542, http://lantern.mediahist.org/catalog/motionpicturenew171unse_1582.

47. P. S. Harrison, review of "The Desired Woman," *Motion Picture News*, March 23, 1918, 1720, https://lantern.mediahist.org/catalog/motionpicturenew171unse_1760.

48. P. S. Harrison, review of "Broken Blossoms," *Harrison's Reports*, July 19, 1919, 11.

49. P. S. Harrison, review of "'Anne of Green Gables' with Mary Miles Minter," *Harrison's Reports*, Nov. 22, 1919, 2.

50. P. S. Harrison, review of "Selfish Yates," *Motion Picture News*, May 18, 1918, 2956, https://lantern.mediahist.org/catalog/motionpicturenew172unse_1022.

51. P. S. Harrison, "To All Exhibitors," *Harrison's Reports*, July 5, 1919, 1.

52. Harrison, 1.

53. "To All Exhibitors: Harrison's Reviews by Mail" [Advertisement], *Motion Picture News*, July 12, 1919, 466, https://lantern.mediahist.org/catalog/motionpicturenew201unse_0230; "Harrison Starts Well on Review Project," *Motion Picture News*, July 19, 1919, 719, https://lantern.mediahist.org/catalog/motionpicturenew201unse_0491.

54. See, e.g., P. S. Harrison, "Organize!," *Harrison's Reports*, Sept. 13, 1919, 1; P. S. Harrison, "Organize in Self Defense," *Harrison's Reports*, Sept. 20, 1919, 1; P. S. Harrison, "Now Is the Time to Organize," *Harrison's Reports*, Sept. 27, 1919, 1.

55. P. S. Harrison, "Organize, or Censorship Is Inevitable," *Harrison's Reports*, Nov. 8, 1919, 1.

56. Letters, *Harrison's Reports*, March 12, 1921, 44.

57. D. Richard Baer calls attention to these disputes in his preface to *Harrison's Reports and Film Reviews*, vol. 1, *1919–1922* (Hollywood: Hollywood Film Archive, 1991), iv. For the relevant editorials, see P. S. Harrison, "Vitagraph," *Harrison's Reports*, Dec. 4, 1920, 1; P. S. Harrison, "The Vitagraph Company of America Reverses Their Policy," *Harrison's Reports*, Jan. 15, 1921, 1; and P. S. Harrison, "To Every Subscriber," *Harrison's Reports*, March 13, 1920, 1.

58. Harrison, "To Every Subscriber," 1.

59. Harrison, "Vitagraph Company of America," 1.

60. P. S. Harrison, "The Matter between Fred Warren and This Service Has Been Settled," *Harrison's Reports*, Dec. 4, 1920, 1; Harrison, "Vitagraph Company of America," 1.

61. Harrison, "Is the Game Worth the Struggle?," *Harrison's Reports*, April 30, 1921, 1.

62. Quoted in P. S. Harrison, "Letters You Should Read and Digest," *Harrison's Reports*, May 28, 1921.

63. P. S. Harrison, "Bananas and Pictures," *Harrison's Reports*, April 16, 1932, 61, https://lantern.mediahist.org/catalog/harrisonsreportsooharr_7_0073.

64. D. Richard Baer, preface to *Harrison's Reports and Film Reviews*, 1:iv.

65. Martin J. Quigley, "About Cancelled Bookings," *Exhibitors Film Exchange*, August 28, 1915, 18.

66. *Exhibitors Film Exchange*, June 24, 1915, 14. Masthead for vol. 1, no. 1.

67. *Exhibitors Film Exchange*, July 22 1915, 14. Masthead for vol. 1, no. 5.

68. Martin S. Quigley, *Martin J. Quigley and the Glory Days of American Film, 1915–1965* (Groton, MA: Quigley Publishing, 2006), 10–13.

69. Martin S. Quigley, 10–13.

70. Martin J. Quigley, "'Film Play' and 'Movies,'" *Exhibitors Herald*, Nov. 20, 1915, 10; Martin J. Quigley, "Substituting 'Film Play' for 'Movies,'" *Exhibitors Herald*, Dec. 11, 1915, 10.

71. Martin J. Quigley, "A Cure for Censorship," *Exhibitors Herald*, Oct. 28, 1916, 13.

72. Martin J. Quigley, "About Cancelled Bookings," 18.

73. Martin J. Quigley, "Ochs Fails to Make Good on Charges," *Exhibitors Herald*, Dec. 2, 1916, 11.

74. J. Ray Murray, "Ochs' High-Handed Methods Disrupt League," *Exhibitors Herald*, August 4, 1917, 9, https://lantern.mediahist.org/catalog/exhibitorsherald05exhi_0267. See also Overpeck, "Out of the Dark," 83–86.

75. Martin J. Quigley, "The Convention: A Lesson to Autocrats," *Exhibitors Herald*, August 4, 1917, 7, https://lantern.mediahist.org/catalog/exhibitorsherald05exhi_0265.

76. Martin J. Quigley, 7, https://lantern.mediahist.org/catalog/exhibitorsherald05exhi_0265.

77. For a discussion of the publication's shift from weekly to monthly, and from the title *Nickelodeon* to *Motography*, see *Motography*, "Motography's Salutatory," April 11, 1911, 3, https://lantern.mediahist.org/catalog/motography56elec_0013.

78. "New Conditions for the Film Papers," *Motography*, Jan. 13, 1917, 67, https://lantern.mediahist.org/catalog/motography17elec_0081.

79. "Enter—an Innovation in Reviewing," *Motography*, April 20, 1918, 754, https://lantern.mediahist.org/catalog/motography19elec_0830.

80. Self-Advertisement, *Exhibitors Herald and Motography*, Sept. 21, 1918, 10, https://lantern.mediahist.org/catalog/exhibitorsherald07exhi_0686.

81. Martin S. Quigley, *Martin J. Quigley*, 7.

82. Self-Advertisement, *Exhibitors Herald*, Oct. 27, 1923, 22, https://lantern.mediahist.org/catalog/exhibitorsherald17exhi_0446.

83. For more on the opening of the Capitol Theatre, see Ross Melnick, *American Showman: Samuel "Roxy" Rothafel and the Birth of the Entertainment Industry* (New York: Columbia University Press, 2012), 184–90.

84. Martin J. Quigley, "To the Industry," *Exhibitors Herald*, June 12, 1920, 31.

85. Motion Picture Theatre Owners of America, "To the Exhibitors of America," *Exhibitors Herald*, June 26, 1920, 41.

86. "Voice of Industry Commends 'Exhibitors Herald,'" *Exhibitors Herald*, June 26, 1920, 39.

87. "IN THE EXHBITORS' FIGHT FOR INDEPENDENCE—WHERE DO YOU STAND?" (Self-Advertisement), *Exhibitors Herald*, June 26, 1920, 37.

88. Self-Advertisement, *Exhibitors Herald*, April 30, 1921, 17, https://lantern.mediahist.org/catalog/exhibitorsherald12exhi_0_0423.

89. Self-Advertisement, *Exhibitors Herald*, Dec. 17, 1921, 37, https://lantern.mediahist.org/catalog/exhibitorsherald13exhi_0_1217.

90. Martin J. Quigley, "Mr. Johnson Accepts—But . . . ," *Exhibitors Herald*, Jan. 14, 1922, 37, https://lantern.mediahist.org/catalog/exhibitorsherald14exhi_0235.

91. The Audit Bureau of Circulations performed audits of *Moving Picture World* and *Motion Picture News* in 1921 and for *Exhibitors Herald* starting in 1923. I am grateful to the

staff of the Alliance for Audited Media, the ABC's successor organization, for granting me access to its historic auditor reports on microfilm.

92. George Rea to *Exhibitors Herald, Exhibitors Herald*, May 26, 1923, 69, https://lantern .mediahist.org/catalog/exhibitorsherald16exhi_0_0869.

93. C. M. Hartman, quoted in "'Herald Only' Club Gains Six; Veteran and Newcomer Give Reasons for Joining," *Exhibitors Herald*, March 29, 1924, 63, https://lantern.mediahist .org/catalog/exhibitorsherald18exhi_0_0073.

94. "'Herald Only' Club Roster," *Exhibitors Herald*, Dec. 8, 1923, 62, https://lantern .mediahist.org/catalog/exhibitorsherald17exhi_1162.

95. "Nebraska Leads in Club Roll Call; Ohio Second," *Exhibitors Herald*, Dec. 8, 1923, 63, https://lantern.mediahist.org/catalog/exhibitorsherald17exhi_1163.

96. Kathryn Fuller-Seeley, "'What the Picture Did for Me': Small-Town Exhibitors' Strategies for Surviving the Great Depression," in *Hollywood in the Neighborhood: Historical Case Studies of Local Moviegoing*, ed. Kathryn Fuller-Seeley (Berkeley: University of California Press, 2008), 186–207.

97. For more on the digital methods used to produce this analysis, see Eric Hoyt, "Arclights and Zoom Lenses: Searching for Influential Exhibitors in Film History's Big Data," in *The Routledge Companion to New Cinema History*, ed. Daniel Biltereyst, Richard Maltby, and Philippe Meers (New York: Routledge, 2019), 83–95.

98. Philip Rand, "In 'Follywood' with Philip Rand," *Exhibitors Herald*, Dec. 29, 1923, 62, http://lantern.mediahist.org/catalog/exhibitorsherald18exhi_0091.

99. Martin J. Quigley, "Better Theatres," *Exhibitors Herald*, May 26, 1923, III, http://lantern .mediahist.org/catalog/exhibitorsherald16exhi_0_0889.

100. P. S. Harrison, "The 'Variety'-'Herald' Farce-Comedy," *Harrison's Reports*, March 14, 1931, 44, https://lantern.mediahist.org/catalog/harrisonsreportsooharr_6_0052.

4. COASTLANDER READING: THE CULTURES AND TRADE PAPERS OF 1920S LOS ANGELES

1. Franchon Royer, "Pictures and the Girl Question," *Camera!*, April 16, 1921, 3, https:// lantern.mediahist.org/catalog/camera04unse_0007.

2. Denise McKenna, "The Photoplay or the Pickaxe: Extras, Gender, and Labour in Early Hollywood," *Film History* 23, no. 1 (2011): 5–19.

3. Lisle Foote, "Fanchon Royer," in *Women Film Pioneers Project*, ed. Jane Gaines, Radha Vatsal, and Monica Dall'Asta, Center for Digital Research and Scholarship (New York: Columbia University Libraries, 2013), https://wfpp.cdrs.columbia.edu/pioneer/fanchon -royer/.

4. For more on the early relationship between cinema and Los Angeles, see Jan Olsson, *Los Angeles before Hollywood: Journalism and American Film Culture, 1905 to 1915* (Stockholm: National Library of Sweden, 2008); and Leo Braudy, *The Hollywood Sign: Fantasy and Reality of an American Icon* (New Haven, CT: Yale University Press, 2011).

5. Alan Gevinson, "Motion Picture News," in *International Film, Radio, and Television Journals*, ed. Anthony Slide (Westport, CT: Greenwood Press, 1985), 245.

6. "Studio Directory," *Motion Picture News*, Oct. 21, 1916, 18, https://lantern.mediahist .org/catalog/motionpicturestuoomoti_0028.

7. Johnston added that "newspaper editors, studio managers, employment agencies, libraries and professional clubs and societies will find it equally indispensable." But Johnston's main emphasis remained on the *Directory*'s utility for exhibitors. "Studio Directory," *Motion Picture News*, Oct. 21, 1916.

8. "Studio Directory," *Motion Picture News*, April 12, 1917, 38, https://lantern.mediahist .org/catalog/moctuoomoti_0058.

9. Federal Trade Commission v. Vaudeville Managers' Protective Association et al., Complaint, May 7, 1918, 5, Docket no. 128, FTC Docketed Case Files, RG 122, Box 69, NARA-CP. For more on this history and related conflicts, see Arthur Frank Wertheim, *Vaudeville Wars: How the Keith-Albee and Orpheum Circuits Controlled the Big-Time and Its Performers* (New York: Palgrave Macmillan, 2006), 234.

10. Entry for "Cannon, Raymond," in Early Cinema History Online (ECHO), a database built using the credits information previously published as *The American Film-Index*, https://echo.commarts.wisc.edu/items/browse?tags=Cannon%2C+Raymond+%28cast+member%29.

11. See, e.g., "The Pulse of the Studio," *Camera!*, April 13, 1919, 8, https://lantern.media hist.org/catalog/camera1919losa_0034; and "Where to Sell Your Scenarios," *Camera!*, April 13, 1919, 13, https://lantern.mediahist.org/catalog/camera1919losa_0039.

12. "Another Social Break," *Camera!*, May 1, 1920, 5, https://lantern.mediahist.org/catalog /camera03unse_0055.

13. "In Regard to the Income Tax," *Camera!*, May 8, 1920, 5, https://lantern.mediahist .org/catalog/camera03unse_0079.

14. Royer, "The Censors Differentiate," *Camera!*, Dec. 3, 1921, https://lantern.mediahist .org/catalog/camera04unse_0797.

15. Foote, "Fanchon Royer."

16. Royer, "Pictures and the Girl Question."

17. Peter Lester, "Why I Am Ashamed of the Movies: Editorial Policy, Early Hollywood, and the Case of *Camera!*," *Moving Image* 18, no. 1 (Spring 2018), 53–54.

18. Lester, 58.

19. "They May Not Always Agree—But They Do Read Wid's" [advertisement], *Wid's Weekly*, Oct. 6, 1923, 2, https://lantern.mediahist.org/catalog/widsweekly192301wids_0002.

20. Tamar Lane, *What's Wrong with the Movies?* (Los Angeles: Waverly, 1923), 13.

21. Lea Jacobs, *The Decline of Sentiment: American Film in the 1920s* (Berkeley: University of California Press, 2008), 1–78.

22. Tamar Lane, "Are the Movies Art or Entertainment?," *Film Mercury*, May 22, 1925, 3.

23. Anabel Lane, "Anabel Lane Says," *Film Mercury*, July 29, 1927, 15, https://lantern .mediahist.org/catalog/filmmercury1926100merc_0209; see also "Mr. Mencken Pays Tribute to the Film Mercury," *Film Mercury*, Dec. 17, 1926, 3, https://lantern.mediahist.org/catalog /filmmercury1926100merc_0177.

24. Lane, *What's Wrong with the Movies?*, 12.

25. For more on *Close Up*, see James Donald, Anne Friedberg, and Laura Marcus, *Close Up (1927–1933): Cinema and Modernism* (Princeton, NJ: Princeton University Press, 1998).

26. Advertisement for *Film Mercury*, *Close Up*, June 1928, n.p., https://lantern.media hist.org/catalog/closeup02macp_0714.

27. For more on the Little Cinema Movement, see Anne Morey, "Early Art Cinema in the U.S.: Symon Gould and the Little Cinema Movement of the 1920s," in *Going to the Movies: Hollywood and the Social Experience of the Cinema*, ed. Richard Maltby, Melvyn Stokes, and Robert C. Allen (Exeter: University of Exeter Press, 2008), 235–47.

28. David E. James, *The Most Typical Avant-Garde: History and Geography of Minor Cinemas in Los Angeles* (Berkeley: University of California Press, 2005), 22.

29. See, e.g., "Warner Brothers Seeking Chain for Films and Shows," *Inside Facts of Stage and Screen*, Jan. 11, 1930, 1, https://lantern.mediahist.org/catalog/insidefacts11-1930-01-11_0000.

30. Allan Dunn, "Paul Kohner: Is He Another Thalberg?," *Motion Picture Review*, Dec. 1926, 8, https://lantern.mediahist.org/catalog/motionpicturerevoomoti_0008.

31. See, e.g., *Hollywood Topics*, Jan. 22, 1927, 1, https://lantern.mediahist.org/catalog/hollywoodtopicsoo1holl_0243.

32. See, e.g., "FLESH AND THE DEVIL Is a CLARENCE BROWN PRODUCTION" [advertisement], *Hollywood Topics*, Jan. 8, 1927, 39, https://lantern.mediahist.org/catalog/hollywoodtopicsoo1holl_0201; "Clarence Brown Names Staff," *Hollywood Topics*, Jan. 15, 1927, 10, https://lantern.mediahist.org/catalog/hollywoodtopicsoo1holl_0220; "Clarence Brown to Direct Super-Feature," *Hollywood Topics*, Jan. 22, 1927, 8, https://lantern.mediahist.org/catalog/hollywoodtopicsoo1holl_0250; I. W. Irving, review of "Flesh and the Devil," *Hollywood Topics*, Jan. 29, 1927, 12, https://lantern.mediahist.org/catalog/hollywoodtopicsoo1holl_0286.

33. For an insightful examination of this Tinseltown icon, see Braudy, *The Hollywood Sign*.

34. Hollywood Knolls [advertisement], *Hollywood Topics*, Nov. 3, 1926, https://lantern.mediahist.org/catalog/hollywoodtopicsoo1holl_0070.

35. Denise McKenna and Charlie Keil, "Mirrors of Hollywood: Strategies of Self-Representation," paper presented at the Society for Cinema and Media Studies Conference, Chicago, March 24, 2017.

36. Phil M. Roe, "At the World's Crossroads," *Moving Picture World*, Feb. 26, 1927, 629, https://lantern.mediahist.org/catalog/movingpicturewor84janf_0685.

37. "Belle Bennett Faints after Goldwyn Row," *Hollywood Vagabond*, Feb. 10, 1927, 1, https://lantern.mediahist.org/catalog/hollywoodvagabono1vaga_0007.

38. Welford Beaton, "Close-Ups Spoil a Good Picture," *Film Spectator*, Feb. 19, 1927, 11, https://lantern.mediahist.org/catalog/filmspectator1920ofilm_0027.

39. Welford Beaton, "Poor Material to Inspire a Staff," *Film Spectator*, Feb. 5, 1927, 15, https://lantern.mediahist.org/catalog/filmspectator1920ofilm_0012.

40. Welford Beaton, "Writers and Actors Should Be Organized," *Film Spectator*, July 23, 1927, 3, https://lantern.mediahist.org/catalog/filmspectator1920ofilm_0099.

41. Welford Beaton, "How Not to Make a Picture," *Film Spectator*, June 25, 1927, 5, https://lantern.mediahist.org/catalog/filmspectator1920ofilm_0081.

42. Welford Beaton, "Some Day Will Be Much Better," *Film Spectator*, June 25, 1927, 5, https://lantern.mediahist.org/catalog/filmspectator1920ofilm_0081.

43. Beaton, "Writers and Actors Should Be Organized."

44. Welford Beaton, "Academy Becomes Tool of Producers," *Film Spectator*, August 20, 1927, 3, https://lantern.mediahist.org/catalog/filmspectator1920ofilm_0147.

45. Welford Beaton, "Spectator Celebrates Its Second Birthday," *Film Spectator*, March 3, 1928, 3, https://lantern.mediahist.org/catalog/filmspectatorvol56welf_0013.

46. Beaton, 3.

47. Peter Besas, *Inside "Variety": The Story of the Bible of Show Business, 1905–1987* (Madrid: Ars Millenii, 2000), 105.

48. Besas, 106–7.

49. Hugh Kent, "Variety," *American Mercury*, Dec. 1926, 462–66, 462.

50. Kent, 465.

51. For more on the methodology employed here and a more detailed analysis of the findings, see Eric Hoyt, Derek Long, Anthony Tran, and Kit Hughes, "*Variety*'s Transformations: Digitizing and Analyzing a Canonical Trade Paper," *Film History* 27, no. 4 (2015): 76–105.

52. David Wilton, "Journo's Boffo Lingo: The Slang of *Daily Variety*," *Verbatim: The Language Quarterly* 30, no. 1 (Spring 2005): 2.

53. "'Dramatic Mirror' as a Monthly," *Variety*, Feb. 10, 1922, 11, https://lantern.mediahist.org/catalog/variety65-1922-02_0058.

54. "Variety and 'Clipper,'" *Variety*, July 19, 1923, 11, https://lantern.mediahist.org/catalog/variety71-1923-07_0098.

55. For more on the founding of *American Mercury* and Mencken and Nathan's partnership, see Vincent Fitzpatrick, "THE AMERICAN MERCURY," *Menckeniana*, no. 123 (1992): 1–6, www.jstor.org/stable/26483894; and Marion Elizabeth Rodgers, *Mencken: The American Iconoclast* (Oxford: Oxford University Press, 2005), 256–70, https://books.google.com/books?id=F60762CfNPQC.

56. For more on the methodology employed here and a more detailed analysis of the findings, see Hoyt et al., "*Variety*'s Transformations."

57. Besas, *Inside "Variety,"* 187; see also Dayton Stoddart, *Lord Broadway*: Variety's *Sime* (New York: Wilfred Funk, 1941), 129.

58. "Variety's Los Angeles Office. Arthur Ungar in Charge," *Variety*, March 18, 1925, 56, https://lantern.mediahist.org/catalog/variety78-1925-03_0183. *Variety*'s *Clipper* acquisition is discussed in "Variety and 'Clipper,'" 11, https://lantern.mediahist.org/catalog/variety71-1923-07_0098. Ungar later served as the editor of the Los Angeles–based *Daily Variety* from the paper's 1933 inception until his death in 1950.

59. George Jeremiah Hoffman, "The Reminiscences of Jerry Hoffman" (Oral History), American Film Institute / Louis B. Mayer Oral History Collection, Part 1 (1977), TIB/P26.

60. "Pictures in Front," *Variety*, May 5, 1926, 3, https://lantern.mediahist.org/catalog/variety82-1926-05_0002.

61. "'American Mercury' Gives Space on Why 'Variety' Is So Terrible," *Variety*, Dec. 1, 1926, 4, https://lantern.mediahist.org/catalog/variety85-1926-12_0003.

62. "Why Should You Advertise in Variety?," *Variety*, Dec. 1, 1926, 35, https://lantern.mediahist.org/catalog/variety85-1926-12_0038.

63. Martin Quigley, "Memorandum on Trade Advertising," undated [probably 1935], Martin J. Quigley Papers, box 3, folder 17, Georgetown University Library.

64. See, e.g., "Inside Stuff on Pictures," *Variety*, April 20, 1927, 23, https://lantern.mediahist.org/catalog/variety86-1927-04_0076; "Inside Stuff on Pictures," *Variety*, August 3, 1927, 7, https://lantern.mediahist.org/catalog/variety87-1927-08_0014; and "Film Trade Paper's

Editor's Method Soliciting Advertising from Acts," *Variety*, June 27, 1928, 5, https://lantern .mediahist.org/catalog/variety91-1928-06_0196.

65. "Picture Critics' Score," *Variety*, Sept. 14, 1927, 1, 10, https://lantern.mediahist.org /catalog/variety87-1927-09_0064.

66. Donald Crafton, *The Talkies: American Cinema's Transition to Sound, 1926–1931* (New York: Charles Scribner's Sons, 1997), 19–61; Ross Melnick, "Station R-O-X-Y: Roxy and the Radio," *Film History* 17, no. 2/3 (Jan. 1, 2005): 217–33.

67. As Richard Jewell discusses, this deal was especially noteworthy considering that in 1928, Kennedy had gotten RCA general manager David Sarnoff to overpay for Film Booking Offices of America and Keith-Albee-Orpheum, corporations in which Kennedy owned a large stake and which became the basis for RKO. Richard B. Jewell, *RKO Radio Pictures: A Titan Is Born* (Berkeley: University of California Press, 2012), 31–32. For a specific example of the favorable coverage Kennedy received, see "Kennedy Working Out Pathe Problem, without F.B.O. Going in Murdock Deal," *Variety*, Feb. 15, 1928, 4, https://lantern.mediahist .org/catalog/variety90-1928-02_0131.

5. CHICAGO TAKES NEW YORK: THE CONSOLIDATION OF THE NATIONALS

1. Tino Balio, *MGM* (New York: Routledge, 2018), 17–28.

2. Martin J. Quigley, "The Consolidated Publication!," *Exhibitors Herald and Moving Picture World*, Jan. 7, 1928, 20, https://lantern.mediahist.org/catalog/exhibitorsherald 90unse_0028.

3. "Radio Corp. in Combine with FBO," *Exhibitors Herald and Moving Picture World*, Jan. 7, 1928, 21, https://lantern.mediahist.org/catalog/exhibitorsherald90unse_0029.

4. Cari Beauchamp, *Joseph P. Kennedy Presents: His Hollywood Years* (New York: Alfred A. Knopf, 2009), 211–21.

5. Will Hays to Martin Quigley, published in *Exhibitors Herald and Moving Picture World*, Jan. 7, 1928, 22, https://lantern.mediahist.org/catalog/exhibitorsherald90unse_0030.

6. Martin J. Quigley to Will Hays, "Subject: Motion Picture Trade Papers and Advertising," Jan. 11, 1928, Martin J. Quigley Papers, box 1, folder 6, Georgetown University Library.

7. "T.O.C.C. Moves to Offer Cooperation for Booking Bill," *Exhibitors Herald and Moving Picture World*, Jan. 7, 1928, 35, https://lantern.mediahist.org/catalog/exhibitorsherald 90unse_0043; "Columbus," *Exhibitors Herald and Moving Picture World*, Jan. 7, 1928, 46, https://lantern.mediahist.org/catalog/exhibitorsherald90unse_0054.

8. "Lines Form for Senate Battle over Bill to Bar Block Booking," *Exhibitors Herald and Moving Picture World*, Jan. 21, 1928, https://lantern.mediahist.org/catalog/exhibitorsherald 90unse_0193.

9. Richard Maltby, "The Production Code and the Hays Office," in *Grand Design: Hollywood as a Modern Business Enterprise, 1930–1939*, by Tino Balio (Berkeley: University of California Press, 1993), 43–45.

10. Michael J. Quinn, "Paramount and Early Feature Distribution: 1914–1921," *Film History* 11, no. 1 (1999): 100–101.

11. For discussions of the different studios during this period, see Richard Koszarski, *An Evening's Entertainment: The Age of the Silent Picture, 1915–1928* (Berkeley: University of

California Press, 1990), 69–94; and Douglas Gomery, *The Hollywood Studio System: A History* (London: British Film Institute, 2005), 7–70.

12. Kia Afra, *The Hollywood Trust: Trade Associations and the Rise of the Studio System* (Lanham, MD: Rowman & Littlefield, 2016), 159–268.

13. Luci Marzola, "Engineering Hollywood: Technology, Technicians, and the Building of the Studio System, 1915–1930" (PhD diss., University of Southern California, 2016).

14. Derek Long, "Reprogramming the Movies: Distribution Strategy and Production Planning in the Early Studio System, 1915–1924" (PhD diss., University of Wisconsin–Madison, 2017), 245.

15. William Paul, *When Movies Were Theater: Architecture, Exhibition, and the Evolution of American Film* (New York: Columbia University Press, 2016), 155. Paul writes: "By the late 1920s, a bifurcation in exhibition systematically reflected a preexisting bifurcation in production." To illustrate his points, Paul turns to trade paper advertising in *Motion Picture News* in the mid to late 1920s and finds that "studio ads of a season's production slate would generally highlight 'specials' that were intended for pre-release engagement" at large downtown theaters. In other words, the site of exhibition was meant to communicate to audiences and other exhibitors the type of picture it would be.

16. Tino Balio, introduction to *Grand Design: Hollywood as a Modern Business Enterprise, 1930–1939* (Berkeley: University of California Press, 1993), 7; Gomery, *The Hollywood Studio System*, 71–80.

17. Douglas Gomery, *The Coming of Sound: A History* (New York: Routledge, 2005), 23–26.

18. Janet Wasko, *Movies and Money: Financing the American Film Industry* (Norwood, NJ: Ablex, 1982), 47.

19. William A. Johnston, "Man Power and Money," *Motion Picture News*, Jan. 9, 1926, 151, https://lantern.mediahist.org/catalog/motionpic33moti_0155.

20. L. W. Boynton, "Motion Pictures and Finance," *Wall Street Journal*, May 13, 1924, 3; L. W. Boynton, "Movie Industry Adopting Budget," *Wall Street Journal*, May 14, 1924, 3; L. W. Boynton, "Key to Success of Film Industry," *Wall Street Journal*, May 15, 1924, 3.

21. For more on the Triangle frauds, see Eric Hoyt, *Hollywood Vault: Film Libraries before Home Video* (Berkeley: University of California Press, 2014), 25–49.

22. Richard B. Jewell, *RKO Radio Pictures: A Titan Is Born* (Berkeley: University of California Press, 2012), 9.

23. Beauchamp, *Joseph P. Kennedy Presents*, 36.

24. "Foreign Service," *Film Daily*, April 7, 1929, 12, https://lantern.mediahist.org/catalog/filmdaily4748newy_0874.

25. "Seven Midwestern Regional Papers Welded Together," *Motion Picture News*, August 26, 1927, 580, https://lantern.mediahist.org/catalog/motion36moti_0696; "Regional Papers Combine; Gross Circulation 9,000," *Variety*, August 31, 1927, 9, https://lantern.mediahist.org/catalog/variety87-1927-08_0304/.

26. Anne Kail, "Moving Picture World," in *International Film, Radio, and Television Journals*, ed. Anthony Slide (Westport, CT: Greenwood Press, 1985), 243.

27. Appeal of Chalmers Publishing Co. to United States Board of Tax Appeals, Docket no. 839, 1 B.T.A. 629 (1925); 1925 BTA LEXIS 2847 (1925).

28. "'World'–'Exhib. Herald' Merger by Purchase," *Variety*, Jan. 4, 1928, 10. https://lantern.mediahist.org/catalog/variety89-1928-01_0009.

29. Laura Isabel Serna, "Cine-Mundial" (see Description under "Book/Volume Details"), *Lantern*, 2013, https://lantern.mediahist.org/catalog/cinemundial13unse_1068.

30. *N. W. Ayer & Son's American Newspaper Annual and Directory*, Library of Congress Digital Collections, https://lccn.loc.gov/sn91012092.

31. F. H. Richardson, "Lessons for Operators," *Moving Picture World*, July 18, 1908, 44, https://lantern.mediahist.org/catalog/movingpro3chal_0052.

32. F. H. Richardson, *Motion Picture Handbook: A Guide for Managers and Operators of Motion Picture Theatres* (New York: Moving Picture World, 1910), vii, https://lantern.mediahist.org/catalog/motionpicturehanoorich_0005.

33. F. H. Richardson, *Richardson's Handbook of Projection: The Blue Book of Projection*, 5th ed. (New York: Chalmers, 1927), https://archive.org/details/richardsonshandbo2fhri/page/n5.

34. Horace M. Swetland, *Industrial Publishing* (New York: New York Business Publishers Association, 1923).

35. New York Supreme Court, Special Term, Part III, pp. 91–110, James M. Davis v. Adelbert B. Swetland et al. (1928), Case no. 1824–1928, NYCC.

36. Davis v. Swetland et al., Supreme Court of New York, Appellate Division First Department, 228 A.D. 759; 239 N.Y.S. 816; 1930 N.Y. App. Div. LEXIS 12930.

37. "Swetland Upheld in Sale of His Trade Paper," *Variety*, Feb. 19, 1930, https://lantern.mediahist.org/catalog/variety98-1930-02_0146.

38. Audit Bureau of Circulations, "Auditor's Report: Exhibitor's Trade Review. Report for the Twelve Months Ending Dec. 31, 1924," April 1925, Alliance for Audited Media, Arlington Heights, IL, microfilm.

39. Alan Gevinson, "Exhibitor's Trade Review," in *International Film, Radio, and Television Journals*, ed. Anthony Slide (Westport, CT: Greenwood Press, 1985), 96.

40. "Arthur James Acquires Exhibitors Daily Review," *Exhibitors Herald and Moving Picture World*, Oct. 13, 1928, 22, https://lantern.mediahist.org/catalog/exhibitorsherald93quig_0104.

41. Arthur James, "Block Booking Now Stands as the Really Great Evil," *Motion Pictures Today*, Nov. 25, 1925, 1, AMPAS.

42. Arthur James, "Grief Ahead for Famous Players: Investigator Delves into Workings of Zukor," *Motion Pictures Today*, Nov. 7, 1925, 7, AMPAS.

43. Arthur James, "GIVE HIM A CHANCE!," *Motion Pictures Today*, Nov. 7, 1925, 7, AMPAS.

44. Arthur James, "Leadership, Courage, Confidence, Power!," *Motion Pictures Today and Exhibitors Daily Review*, Jan. 6, 1930, 1, https://lantern.mediahist.org/catalog/exhibitorsdailyr27unse_0017.

45. Arthur James to C. C. Pettijohn, July 9, 1929, MPPDA Digital Archives, http://mppda.flinders.edu.au.

46. James's earlier editorials tended to Arthur James, "Face the Enemy and Fight!," *Moving Picture World*, Jan. 29, 1921, https://lantern.mediahist.org/catalog/movpicwor482movi_0043.

47. "The Important Twelve," in *Film Year Book 1922–1923*, ed. Joseph Dannenberg (New York: Wid's Films and Film Folks, 1923), 267, https://lantern.mediahist.org/catalog/filmyearb1922192223newy_0283.

48. "A Booking Guide to All Pictures" (self-advertisement), *Motion Picture News*, Nov. 26, 1921, 2790, https://lantern.mediahist.org/catalog/motionpicturenew24moti_7_0444;

Raymond E. Gallagher, ed., *Motion Picture News Booking Guide* (New York: Motion Picture News, 1922), https://archive.org/stream/motionpicturenewoomoti_11.

49. "Trade Hails Publication Merger as Greatest Step to Progress," *Exhibitors Herald and Moving Picture World*, Jan. 7, 1928, 21, https://lantern.mediahist.org/catalog/exhibitor sheraldgounse_0029.

50. Johnston, "Man Power and Money," 151, https://lantern.mediahist.org/catalog /motionpic33moti_0155.

51. William A. Johnston, "Wall Street," *Motion Picture News*, Jan. 23, 1926, 359, https:// lantern.mediahist.org/catalog/motionpic33moti_0363.

52. "Former Publishers Ask Angus Co. Proxies," *New York Times*, April 14, 1932, 31.

53. Deposition of Charles E. Lewis, April 14, 1934, p. 2, Quigley Publishing Company v. Showmen's Round Table and Charles E. Lewis, US District Court for the Southern District of New York, Equity Case Files, RG 21, E 76–321.

54. Oscar Cooper to Charles E. Lewis, April 26, 1928, included as Exhibit 29 in Quigley Publishing Company v. Showmen's Round Table and Charles E. Lewis, US District Court for the Southern District of New York, Equity Case Files, RG 21, E 76–321.

55. Joan Baer, "The Boxoffice Story," *Boxoffice*, Jan. 2010, 21–31 (reprinted from July 20, 1970 issue).

56. Deposition of Charles E. Lewis, 3.

57. William A. Johnston, "An Announcement," *Motion Picture News*, Sept. 14, 1929, 973, http://lantern.mediahist.org/catalog/motionnew4omoti_0987.

58. P. S. Harrison, "Mr. Quigley!," *Harrison's Reports*, Jan. 25, 1930, 16, http://lantern .mediahist.org/catalog/harrisonsreportsooharr_4_0018.

59. Martin J. Quigley, "The Consolidated Publication!," *Exhibitors Herald and Moving Picture World*, Jan. 7, 1928, 1, http://lantern.mediahist.org/catalog/exhibitorsherald-d9ounse_0028.

60. Quigley, 1.

61. W. E. Mason to Martin J. Quigley, Dec. 21, 1930, 3, Martin J. Quigley Papers, box 3, folder 16, Georgetown University Library.

62. "Literati," *Variety*, July 11, 1928, 18, https://lantern.mediahist.org/catalog/variety91 -1928-07_0089.

63. Martin J. Quigley, "Brookhart Bill Fades," *Exhibitors Herald and Moving Picture World*, March 10, 1928, 22, http://lantern.mediahist.org/catalog/exhibitorsherald 9ounse_0856.

64. Martin J. Quigley, "The Brookhart Bill," *Exhibitors Herald and Moving Picture World*, Feb. 11, 1928, 16, http://lantern.mediahist.org/catalog/exhibitorsheraldgounse_0498.

65. "Text of C. C. Pettijohn Opinion Calls Brookhart Measure Unfair," *Exhibitors Herald and Moving Picture World*, Feb. 25, 1928, 24–25, https://lantern.mediahist.org/catalog /exhibitorsheraldgounse_0716.

66. "Lines Form for Senate Battle over Bill to Bar Block Booking," *Exhibitors Herald and Moving Picture World*, Jan. 21, 1928, 31, https://lantern.mediahist.org/catalog/exhibitorsherald 9ounse_0193.

67. A. E. Hancock, review of "Angel of Broadway," *Exhibitors Herald and Moving Picture World*, March 3, 1928, 63, https://lantern.mediahist.org/catalog/exhibitorsherald 9ounse_0827.

68. Martin J. Quigley, "The Name Hunt," *Exhibitors Herald World*, Jan. 5, 1929, 20, https://lantern.mediahist.org/catalog/exhibitorsherald94quig_0028.

69. J. C. Jenkins, "J. C. Jenkins—His Colyum," *Exhibitors Herald World*, Jan. 5, 1929, 61, https://lantern.mediahist.org/catalog/exhibitorsherald94quig_0068.

70. Jenkins, 61.

71. Kathryn Fuller-Seeley, "'What the Picture Did for Me': Small-Town Exhibitors' Strategies for Surviving the Great Depression," in *Hollywood in the Neighborhood: Historical Case Studies of Local Moviegoing*, ed. Kathryn Fuller-Seeley (Berkeley: University of California Press, 2008), 187.

72. Harrison, "Mr. Quigley!," 16, https://lantern.mediahist.org/catalog/harrisonsreport sooharr_4_0018; P. S. Harrison, "Why the Worry?," *Harrison's Reports*, May 30, 1930, 88, http://lantern.mediahist.org/catalog/harrisonsreportsooharr_4_0102.

73. Martin J. Quigley, "Hoosier Assault," *Exhibitors Herald and Moving Picture World*, March 31, 1928, 20, https://lantern.mediahist.org/catalog/exhibitorsherald90unse_1120.

74. Frank Rembusch to Martin Quigley, March 31, 1928, MPPDA Digital Archives, http://mppda.flinders.edu.au.

75. Frank Rembusch to Martin Quigley, undated [probably March or April 1928], MPPDA Digital Archives, http://mppda.flinders.edu.au.

76. Abram F. Myers, "To All Affiliated and Cooperative Bodies," Sept. 28, 1929, MPPDA Digital Archives, http://mppda.flinders.edu.au.

77. "Revolt in the Industry!," *Independent Exhibitors Film Bulletin*, Sept. 11, 1934, 1, https://lantern.mediahist.org/catalog/filmbulletin193401film_0001.

78. Maltby, "The Production Code," 46.

79. Maltby, 46.

80. Stephen Vaughn, "Morality and Entertainment: The Origins of the Motion Picture Production Code," *Journal of American History* 77, no. 1 (June 1990): 44.

81. Maltby, "The Production Code," 47.

82. Vaughn, "Morality and Entertainment," 49.

83. Daniel Lord to Martin Quigley, Jan. 2, 1930, Martin J. Quigley Papers, box 1, folder 18, Georgetown University Library; Martin Quigley to Daniel Lord, Jan. 3, 1930, Martin J. Quigley Papers, box 1, folder 18, Georgetown University Library.

84. Maltby, "The Production Code," 46.

85. "Reporter's Transcript of the Proceedings at Conference," Feb. 10, 1930, MPPDA Digital Archives, http://mppda.flinders.edu.au.

86. Maltby, "The Production Code," 46.

87. Vaughn, "Morality and Entertainment," 56.

88. "A Code Regulating Production of Motion Pictures," *Exhibitors Herald World*, April 5, 1930, 12, https://lantern.mediahist.org/catalog/exhibitorsherald99unse_0022.

89. "Picture 'Don'ts' for '30," *Variety*, Feb. 19, 1930, 9, https://lantern.mediahist.org/catalog /variety98-1930-02_0144.

90. Martin J. Quigley to Daniel Lord, March 6, 1930, Martin J. Quigley Papers, box 1, folder 18, Georgetown University Library.

91. Will H. Hays to Daniel Lord, Feb. 26, 1930, Martin J. Quigley Papers, box 1, folder 18, Georgetown University Library.

92. Quigley to Lord, March 6, 1930.

93. Martin Quigley to Will Hays, March 6, 1931, MPAA-PCA Records, *Millie* (RKO, 1931), AMPAS.

94. Joseph L. Breen to Martin J. Quigley, May 1, 1932, Martin J. Quigley Papers, box 1, folder 3, Georgetown University Library.

95. Wasko, *Movies and Money*, 50–52.

96. "Former Publishers Ask Angus Co. Proxies," *New York Times*, April 14, 1932, 31.

97. W. E. Mason to Martin J. Quigley, Dec. 21, 1930, 3, Martin J. Quigley Papers, box 3, folder 16, Georgetown University Library.

98. Martin J. Quigley to Adolph Zukor, Oct. 15, 1930, Martin J. Quigley Papers, box 3, folder 16, Georgetown University Library.

99. Jack Wilson to Carl Milliken, May 10, 1929, MPPDA Digital Archives, http://mppda .flinders.edu.au.

100. Tamar Lane responded to Martin Quigley's editorial, "Pictures Are Not Art but Entertainment" in Tamar Lane, "Are the Movies Art or Entertainment?," *Film Mercury*, May 22, 1925, 3. Lane also skewered "What the Picture Did for Me" exhibitor reviews as ignorant in Tamar Lane, *What's Wrong with the Movies?* (Los Angeles: Waverly, 1923), 109–23.

101. Martin Quigley, Announcement, *Motion Picture Daily*, Dec. 22, 1930, 1, https:// lantern.mediahist.org/catalog/exhibitorsdailyr28unse_0805; Obituary: Maurice "Red" Kann, *Boxoffice*, May 17, 1952, AMPAS clipping files.

102. Masthead, *Motion Picture Herald* ("Better Theatres" section), April 11, 1931, 6, https://lantern.mediahist.org/catalog/motionpictureher103unse_0196.

103. Obituary: Terry Ramsaye, *Variety*, August 25, 1954, 63, https://lantern.mediahist .org/catalog/variety195-1954-08_0264.

104. "A Century of Cinema Literature: The 'Film History' Survey," *Film History* 10, no. 4 (1998): 429–47.

105. James R. Quirk, "The Romantic History: From Edison to Hays, 1887–1925," *Photoplay*, March 1925, 68, https://lantern.mediahist.org/catalog/pho28chic_0334.

106. Terry Ramsaye, *A Million and One Nights: A History of the Motion Picture* (New York: Simon and Schuster, 1926).

107. Martin J. Quigley, "Next Week: Motion Picture Herald," *Exhibitors Herald World*, Dec. 27, 1930, 6, https://lantern.mediahist.org/catalog/exibitorsheraldw10unse_0_1146.

108. Martin J. Quigley, "To the Industry," *Exhibitors Herald*, June 12, 1920, 31.

109. "It has been generally reported that the merger was largely brought about through the friendly offices and assurance of co-operation of the Hays Organization, though this has been strenuously denied by the interested parties. It will remain to be seen just how 'independent' the new publications will be and how ready to say a needed word at times in the exhibitor's behalf," wrote P. S. Harrison in "The Trade-Press Merger," *Harrison's Reports*, Jan. 10, 1931, 8, https://lantern.mediahist.org/catalog/harrisonsreports00harr_6_0012.

110. Daniel A. Lord to Martin J. Quigley, Dec. 28, 1930, Martin J. Quigley Papers, box 1, folder 18, Georgetown University Library.

6. THE GREAT DIFFUSION: HOLLYWOOD'S REPORTERS, EXHIBITOR BACKLASH, AND QUIGLEY'S FAILED MONOPOLY

1. Martin J. Quigley to Terry Ramsaye, June 27, 1932, Martin J. Quigley Papers, box 3, folder 32, Georgetown University Library.

2. Quigley to Ramsaye, June 27, 1932.

3. Colvin W. Brown (General Manager of Quigley Publications), "A Promise and a Performance," ca. 1935, Martin J. Quigley Papers, box 3, folder 17, Georgetown University Library.

4. Merritt Crawford, "Observing the Motion Picture Industry," *Independent Exhibitors Film Bulletin*, April 1, 1936, 4, 10, https://lantern.mediahist.org/catalog/filmbulletin 193502film_0262; *Variety*, "AT&T's Financing of Films Disclosed," April 1, 1936, 4, https://lantern.mediahist.org/catalog/variety122-1936-04_0003.

5. See, e.g., "Indes [*sic*] Rushing in as Slump Re-opens Field," *Inside Facts of Stage and Screen*, Jan. 31, 1931, 1, https://lantern.mediahist.org/catalog/insidefacts13-1931-01-31_0000.

6. Paramount Pictures advertisement, *Motion Picture Herald*, Jan. 16, 1932, 16, https://lantern.mediahist.org/catalog/motionpictureher106unse_0225.

7. Abraham F. Myers, quoted in "Words and Wisdom, from Within and Without," *Film Daily*, Jan. 8, 1932, 8, https://lantern.mediahist.org/catalog/filmdailyvolume 55859newy_0050; see also Abram F. Myers in *The Film Daily Year Book of 1932*, 55, https://lantern.mediahist.org/catalog/filmdailyyearbooo0film_2_0083.

8. José A. Tapia Granados and Ana V. Diez Roux, "Life and Death during the Great Depression," *Proceedings of the National Academy of Sciences* 106, no. 41 (Oct. 13, 2009): 17290–95, www.pnas.org/cgi/doi/10.1073/pnas.0904491106; Susan Estabrook Kennedy, *The Banking Crisis of 1933* (Lexington: University Press of Kentucky, 1973).

9. Kathryn Fuller-Seeley, "Dish Night at the Movies: Exhibitors and Female Audiences during the Great Depression," in *Looking Past the Screen: Case Studies in American Film History and Method*, ed. Jon Lewis and Eric Smoodin (Durham, NC: Duke University Press, 2007), 246–49.

10. Jesse Steiner, *Research Memorandum on Recreation in the Depression* (New York: Social Science Research Council, 1937).

11. Kathryn Fuller-Seeley, "'What the Picture Did for Me': Small-Town Exhibitors' Strategies for Surviving the Great Depression," in *Hollywood in the Neighborhood: Historical Case Studies of Local Moviegoing*, ed. Kathryn Fuller-Seeley (Berkeley: University of California Press, 2008), 197.

12. Fuller-Seeley, "Dish Night at the Movies."

13. See, e.g., "Spreading of Double Feature Alarms Leaders of Industry," *Motion Picture Herald*, Nov. 14, 1931, 9, https://lantern.mediahist.org/catalog/motionpictureher 105unse_0569.

14. Fuller-Seeley, "Dish Night at the Movies," 255; Tino Balio, *Grand Design: Hollywood as a Modern Business Enterprise, 1930–1939* (Berkeley: University of California Press, 1995), 29.

15. Fuller-Seeley, "'What the Picture Did for Me,'" 197.

16. Kia Afra, *The Hollywood Trust: Trade Associations and the Rise of the Studio System* (Lanham, MD: Rowman & Littlefield, 2016), 249–51; Giuliana Muscio, *Hollywood's New Deal* (Philadelphia: Temple University Press, 1997), 105–42.

17. Balio, *Grand Design*, 16.

18. "A Statement to the Motion Picture Industry" [Paramount advertisement], *Hollywood Reporter*, Jan. 27, 1933, 3, https://lantern.mediahist.org/catalog/hollywoodreporte 1215wilk_0145; "A Statement to the Motion Picture Industry" [Paramount advertisement], *Variety*, Jan. 31, 1933, 20, https://lantern.mediahist.org/catalog/variety109-1933-01_0301.

19. Balio, *Grand Design*, 16–17.

20. Morris Dickstein, *Dancing in the Dark: A Cultural History of the Great Depression* (New York: Norton, 2009), 223.

21. Barrie A. Wigmore, "Was the Bank Holiday of 1933 Caused by a Run on the Dollar?," *Journal of Economic History* 47, no. 3 (Sept. 1987): 739–55; Charles W. Calomiris and Joseph R. Mason, "Fundamentals, Panics, and Bank Distress during the Depression," *American Economic Review* 93, no. 5 (Dec. 2003): 1615–47.

22. Kennedy, *Banking Crisis of 1933*.

23. For more on this period and formation of the Screen Writers Guild, see Miranda J. Banks, *The Writers: A History of American Screenwriters and Their Guild* (New Brunswick, NJ: Rutgers University Press, 2015), 27–32; and Catherine L. Fisk, *Writing for Hire: Unions, Hollywood, and Madison Avenue* (Cambridge, MA: Harvard University Press, 2016), 58–63.

24. Danae Clark, *Negotiating Hollywood: The Cultural Politics of Actors' Labor* (Minneapolis: University of Minnesota Press, 1995), 42–81; Balio, *Grand Design*, 15.

25. Balio, *Grand Design*, 19.

26. Martin J. Quigley, "Memorandum on Trade Advertising," ca. 1935, Martin J. Quigley Papers, box 3, folder 17, Georgetown University Library.

27. Martin J. Quigley to Editorial Staff, January 19, 1931, Martin J. Quigley Papers, box 3, folder 17, Georgetown University Library.

28. "'Split Reel' Notes for Theater Men," *Motography*, Dec. 23, 1916, 1367, http://lantern.mediahist.org/catalog/motography162elec_0624.

29. For more on this, see Eric Hoyt, Derek Long, Anthony Tran, and Kit Hughes, "*Variety*'s Transformations: Digitizing and Analyzing a Canonical Trade Paper," *Film History* 27, no. 4 (2015): 89.

30. As Georgetown University Library's finding aid for the Terry Ramsaye papers notes, "the Dope File Series, the largest series in the collection, was Ramsaye's own collection of 'dope,' or information, on particular individuals or subjects." "Dope File, 1898–1951," Georgetown University Archival Resources, Georgetown University Library, https://findingaids.library.georgetown.edu/repositories/15/archival_objects/1297239.

31. *Variety*, for example, published monthly reports of comparative grosses across cities, theaters, and pictures. See "Comparative Grosses for January," *Variety*, Feb. 4, 1931, 26, https://lantern.mediahist.org/catalog/variety101-1931-02_0025.

32. "L.A. Grosses" and "Minn. Grosses," *Variety*, Feb. 11, 1931, 24, https://lantern.mediahist.org/catalog/variety101-1931-02_0111.

33. "Theatre Receipts," *Motion Picture Herald*, April 25, 1931, 61–65, https://lantern.mediahist.org/catalog/motionpictureher103unse_0515.

34. P. S. Harrison, "The 'Variety'-'Herald' Farce-Comedy," *Harrison's Reports*, March 14, 1931, 44, https://lantern.mediahist.org/catalog/harrisonsreports00harr_6_0052.

35. Martin J. Quigley to Adolph Zukor, Oct. 15, 1930, Martin J. Quigley Papers, box 3, folder 16, Georgetown University Library.

36. What a typical or representative issue looked like during this period was harder to determine than for other eras that were sampled. The 1931 and 1932 totals would be lower if the sample excluded issues that had either Better Theatres sections or lengthy promotional inserts from the studios. For example, the May 28, 1932, issue of *Motion Picture Herald* carried a massive fifty-six-page insert for Fox studios. Excluding such issues from the sample,

however, would present larger methodological challenges, since the content analysis shows that distributors spread their advertising expenditures unevenly across the entire film season. All of this is to say that the exact median numbers should be read with a grain of salt, but the overall trend line of increased advertising in 1931 and 1932 compared to 1930 is indisputable.

37. This quantitative content analysis of *Variety* was first shared in Hoyt, Long, Tran, and Hughes, "*Variety*'s Transformations."

38. Hoyt, Long, Tran, and Hughes, "*Variety*'s Transformations"; Steiner, *Research Memorandum*, 94; Balio, *Grand Design*, 14.

39. "2-for-1 Splicings," *Variety*, Nov. 29, 1932, 57, https://lantern.mediahist.org/catalog/variety108-1932-11_0298.

40. *Variety* subscription advertisement, *Variety*, Feb. 4, 1931, 41, https://lantern.mediahist.org/catalog/variety101-1931-02_0040.

41. "Guaranty of Account," Dec. 9, 1931, Joseph P. Kennedy Personal Papers, Series 3.6.4, Business and Finance: Investments and Finances, Subject Files, Golder Title: "Sime Silverman Estate, 1931–1936," John F. Kennedy Presidential Library and Museum.

42. Joseph P. Kennedy to Redmond & Co., April 26, 1933, Joseph P. Kennedy Personal Papers, Series 3.6.4, Business and Finance: Investments and Finances, Subject Files, Golder Title: "Sime Silverman Estate, 1931–1936," John F. Kennedy Presidential Library and Museum.

43. Cari Beauchamp, *Joseph P. Kennedy Presents: His Hollywood Years* (New York: Alfred A. Knopf, 2009), 36.

44. Beauchamp, 301.

45. Hugh Kent, "Variety," *American Mercury*, Dec. 1926, 462–66.

46. During the early period that Sid Silverman took the paper's helm, *Variety*'s coverage of radio dramatically increased—from only 0.54 pages in 1930 to 2.67 pages in 1931 to 3.79 pages in 1932 to 6.25 pages in 1933 to 9.875 pages in 1934. See also Dayton Stoddart, *Lord Broadway: Variety's Sime* (New York: Wilfred Funk, 1941), 346, 357; Peter Besas, *Inside "Variety": The Story of the Bible of Show Business, 1905–1987* (Madrid: Ars Millenii, 2000), 231–37; and Hoyt, Long, Tran, and Hughes, "*Variety*'s Transformations."

47. Besas, *Inside "Variety*," 213–15.

48. Besas, 213.

49. Besas, 201–6.

50. Arthur Ungar, "Your Business and Ours," *Daily Variety*, Sept. 6, 1933, 2.

51. [Self-advertisement], *Daily Variety*, Oct. 27, 1933, 7.

52. Wilkerson Daily Corporation, Ltd. v. Commissioner of Internal Revenue, 1938, Testimony of William R. Wilkerson in Transcript of the Record, at 97, Ninth Circuit Court of Appeals, case no. 9864, box 3714, NARA-SF.

53. In 1936, six libel suits were pending against Wilkerson Daily Corporation, with $600,000 in damages demanded against it, according to Wilkerson Daily Corporation, Ltd. v. Commissioner of Internal Revenue, United States Board of Tax Appeals, 42 B.T.A. 1266, 1268 (1940).

54. For more on disputes over tax deductions in Hollywood during this period, see Eric Hoyt, "Hollywood and the Income Tax, 1929–1955," *Film History* 22, no. 1 (2010): 5–20.

55. Billy Wilkerson used the pages of the *Hollywood Reporter* to champion the blacklist and call out suspected communists. See, e.g., "A Vote for Joe Stalin," *Hollywood*

Reporter, July 26, 1949, 1; "The Writers' 'Authority,'" *Hollywood Reporter*, August 23, 1946, 1; W. R. Wilkerson, "The $600 Question?," *Hollywood Reporter*, August 27, 1946, 1. Regarding organized crime, W. R. Wilkerson III alleges that Billy Wilkerson helped mastermind an extortion ring within the Hollywood film industry. See W. R. Wilkerson III, *Hollywood Godfather: The Life and Crimes of Billy Wilkerson* (Chicago: Chicago Review Press, 2018), 90–95, 157–63.

56. Wilkerson, *Hollywood Godfather*.

57. "Big Studios Average Well Up on Their Production Schedules," *Hollywood Reporter Daily*, Sept. 25, 1930, 3.

58. "Metro-Pathe-Warner Show New Pictures," *Hollywood Reporter Daily*, Sept. 8, 1930, 5; "Par.-Warner-Radio Show Pictures in Preview Form," *Hollywood Reporter Daily*, Sept. 22, 1930, 4.

59. W. R. Wilkerson, "Trade Views," *Hollywood Reporter Daily*, Sept. 9, Sept. 12, Sept. 22, 1930, 1.

60. Wilkerson, *Hollywood Godfather*, 96–102.

61. Edith Wilkerson, "The Low Down," *Hollywood Reporter Daily*, Sept. 25, Sept. 5, Sept. 15, 1930, 2.

62. Wilkerson Daily Corporation, Ltd. v. Commissioner of Internal Revenue, 1938, Testimony of William R. Wilkerson in Transcript of the Record, at 97, Ninth Circuit Court of Appeals, case no. 9864, box 3714, NARA-SF.

63. W. R. Wilkerson to Edwin Loeb, March 1, 1931, Edwin Loeb Correspondence Collection, File 2-f115, AMPAS.

64. Variety, Inc. v. Wilkerson Daily Corp., "Complaint: Action for Injunction and Damages," Feb. 17, 1932, Case no. 335493, Los Angeles County Superior Court Record Center.

65. "Variety Charges Hollywood Daily with Stealing Its News Each Wk," *Variety*, Jan. 5, 1932, https://lantern.mediahist.org/catalog/variety105-1932-01_0001.

66. See "The Thieving 'Dramatic Mirror' Caught Red-Handed with the Goods," *Variety*, May 23, 1908, 5, https://lantern.mediahist.org/catalog/variety10-1908-05_0114.

67. Stoddart, *Lord Broadway*, 126.

68. "Plans Daily Film Paper: Martin Quigley to Launch The Hollywood Herald June 8," *New York Times*, May 26, 1931, 33; "Hollywood," *Variety*, August 29, 1933, 51, https://lantern .mediahist.org/catalog/variety111-1933-08_0290.

69. See Martin S. Quigley, *Martin J. Quigley and the Glory Days of American Film, 1915–1965* (Groton, MA: Quigley Publishing, 2006).

70. Warren Stokes, "This Week in Hollywood," *Motion Picture Times*, Sept. 1, 1931, 12, https://lantern.mediahist.org/catalog/motionpicturetim00asso_0292.

71. Johnston's later career is mentioned in a news item about a car accident; see "Ill in Pix," *Daily Variety*, Sept. 27, 1944, 13.

72. "Plans Daily Film Paper," *New York Times*, May 26, 1931, 33.

73. "Meehan Resigns," *Variety*, March 7, 1933, 47. https://lantern.mediahist.org/catalog /variety109-1933-03_0046.

74. "Hollywood," 51, https://lantern.mediahist.org/catalog/variety111-1933-08_0290.

75. Beaton had changed the title to *Hollywood Spectator* by the June 20, 1931, issue https://lantern.mediahist.org/catalog/hollywoodspectatooholl_0001.

76. "Coast 'Herald' as Weekly," *Film Daily*, April 3, 1932, 2, https://lantern.mediahist .org/catalog/filmdailyvolume55859newy_0804.

77. Martin Quigley, Editorial, *Hollywood Herald*, June 25, 1932, 7, AMPAS.

78. For more on this episode, see Balio, *Grand Design*, 15.

79. Wid Gunning, "Your Time Is Coming. Don't Rock the Boat!" *Hollywood Herald*, March 11, 1933, 3, AMPAS.

80. W. R. Wilkerson, "Trade Views," *Hollywood Reporter*, April 18, 1933, 1, https://lantern .mediahist.org/catalog/hollywoodreporte1215wilk_0665.

81. W. R. Wilkerson, "Trade Views," *Hollywood Reporter*, April 4, 1933, 1, http://lantern .mediahist.org/catalog/hollywoodreporte1215wilk_0593.

82. "Presenting Mr. Zanuck," *Hollywood Reporter*, April 24, 1933, 4, https://lantern .mediahist.org/catalog/hollywoodreporte1215wilk_0693.

83. W. R. Wilkerson, "My Dear Mr. Hays," *Hollywood Reporter*, April 10, 1933, 1, https:// lantern.mediahist.org/catalog/hollywoodreporte1215wilk_0617; W. R. Wilkerson, "Trade Views," *Hollywood Reporter*, April 26, 1933, 1, https://lantern.mediahist.org/catalog/holly woodreporte1215wilk_0749; W. R. Wilkerson, "Trade Views," *Hollywood Reporter*, April 19, 1933, 1, http://lantern.mediahist.org/catalog/hollywoodreporte1215wilk_0669.

84. Wilkerson Daily Corporation, Ltd. v. Commissioner of Internal Revenue, 1938, Testimony of William R. Wilkerson in Transcript of the Record, at 98, Ninth Circuit Court of Appeals, case no. 9864, box 3714, NARA-SF.

85. W. R. Wilkerson, "Trade Views," *Hollywood Reporter*, May 11, 1933, https://lantern .mediahist.org/catalog/hollywoodreporte1215wilk_0825.

86. W. R. Wilkerson, "Trade Views," *Hollywood Reporter*, April 27, 1933, 1, http://lantern .mediahist.org/catalog/hollywoodreporte1215wilk_0753.

87. Leo C. Rosten called attention to the *Hollywood Reporter*'s role in the production and reflection of Hollywood culture in his famous sociological study, *Hollywood: The Movie Colony, the Movie Makers* (New York: Harcourt, Brace, 1941), 115, 146, 149, 212.

88. Bob Thomas, *Thalberg: Life and Legend* (Beverly Hills, CA: New Millennium Press, 2020, reprint of 1969 volume), 189–91.

89. Thomas, 212–16.

90. "The Rumor Market," *Hollywood Reporter*, June 15, 1933, 1, https://lantern.mediahist .org/catalog/hollywoodreporte1215wilk_1055.

91. W. R. Wilkerson to Irving Thalberg, undated, Thalberg and Shearer Collection, file no. 1-f.2, "Correspondence" folder, AMPAS.

92. W. R. Wilkerson, "Trade Views," *Hollywood Reporter*, Feb. 25, 1933, https://lantern .mediahist.org/catalog/hollywoodreporte1215wilk_0327; W. R. Wilkerson, "Trade Views," Feb. 16, 1933, 1, https://lantern.mediahist.org/catalog/hollywoodreporte1215wilk_0283.

93. W. R. Wilkerson to Irving Thalberg, undated, Thalberg and Shearer Collection, file no. 1-f.2, "Correspondence" folder, AMPAS.

94. Robert M. Vandegrift to E. M. Kennedy, "Re: Trust No. 50556," Dec. 8, 1936, Thalberg and Shearer Collection, file no. 1-f.2, "Correspondence" folder, AMPAS.

95. In 1936, James Wong Howe wrote from London to his partner, Sanora Babb, "Very interesting to read about the fight between writers and producers. Told Mr. Howard about Reporter, Trocadero, and Vendome having boycotted, and he said that they should, and that 'Wilkerson' the owner is a bad boy for sticking [up] for the producers. The reason for that is because L. B. Mayer owns a controlling interest of all 'Wilkerson' enterprises such as Reporter, Vendome, and Trocadero." James Wong Howe to Sanora Babb, May 14, 1936, James Wong Howe Collection, folder 224a, AMPAS.

96. Wilkerson Daily Corporation, Ltd. v. Commissioner of Internal Revenue, 1938, Testimony of William R. Wilkerson in Transcript of the Record, at 112–13, Ninth Circuit Court of Appeals, case no. 9864, box 3714, NARA-SF.

97. S. F. Van Buren, "The Trade Paper Racket," *New Theatre*, May 1936, 32.

98. Tom Kemper, *Hidden Talent: The Emergence of Hollywood Agents* (Berkeley: University of California Press, 2009), ix, x.

99. "Josephs Opens Agency," *Variety*, Sept. 22, 1931, 6, https://lantern.mediahist.org /catalog/variety103-1931-09_0253.

100. Tamar Lane, "In Explanation," *Film Mercury*, April 23, 1926, 1, https://lantern .mediahist.org/catalog/filmmercury1926100merc_0015.

101. The history of *Film Mercury* after 1931 is difficult to fully pin down. *Variety* referred to *Film Mercury* as "extinct" in 1932 ("Hollywood Again," *Variety*, June 14, 1932, 47, https://lantern.mediahist.org/catalog/variety106-1932-06_0110). The New York Public Library's catalog record indicates it "suspended publication, Oct. 23, 1931," then resumed again on Nov. 8, 1933, for a handful of issues (NYPL, "Film Mercury," http://catalog.nypl .org/record=b15192815~S1). *Film Mercury* appears into the 1940s in the list of trade papers included in some industry annuals ("Trade Journals," *Kinematograph Year Book 1945*, 1945, 19, https://lantern.mediahist.org/catalog/kinematographyea32unse_0025. But the extent of *Film Mercury*'s actual activity during that later period is unclear.

102. Tamar Lane, *Hey Diddle Diddle* (New York: Adelphia, 1932), 40.

103. Lane, 75.

104. Lane, 117.

105. P. S. Harrison, "Mr. Quigley!," *Harrison's Reports*, Jan. 25, 1930, 16, http://lantern .mediahist.org/catalog/harrisonsreportsooharr_4_0018.

106. Charles E. Lewis to Martin Quigley, Dec. 17, 1931, "Exhibit 12," Quigley Publishing Company v. Showmen's Round Table and Charles E. Lewis, US District Court for the Southern District of New York, Equity Case Files, RG 21, E 76–321.

107. Deposition of Charles E. Lewis, April 14, 1934, at 2, Quigley Publishing Company v. Showmen's Round Table and Charles E. Lewis, US District Court for the Southern District of New York, Equity Case Files, RG 21, E 76–321.

108. "Mr. Exhibitor" [self-advertisement], *Showmen's Round Table*, April 17, 1934, 4.

109. FMB (owner of the Maryland Theatre) to Chick Lewis, March 30, 1933, "Exhibit 4," Quigley Publishing Company v. Showmen's Round Table and Charles E. Lewis, US District Court for the Southern District of New York, Equity Case Files, RG 21, E 76–321.

110. Plaintiff Complaint, undated, at 7, Quigley Publishing Company v. Showmen's Round Table and Charles E. Lewis, US District Court for the Southern District of New York, Equity Case Files, RG 21, E 76–321.

111. These sections all appear in *Showmen's Round Table*, April 17, 1934, 4.

112. "Monogram Bookings Set Record, Convention Told," *Showmen's Round Table*, April 17, 1934, 2; *Manhattan Love Song* [advertisement], *Showmen's Round Table*, April 17, 1934, 2.

113. "Thanks," *Independent Exhibitors Film Bulletin*, April 17, 1935, 1, https://lantern .mediahist.org/catalog/filmbulletin193401film_0231.

114. "Revolt in the Industry!," *Independent Exhibitors Film Bulletin*, Sept. 11, 1934, 1, https://lantern.mediahist.org/catalog/filmbulletin193401film_0001.

115. "Block Booking 'Scare,'" *Independent Exhibitors Film Bulletin*, April 10, 1935, 3, https://lantern.mediahist.org/catalog/filmbulletin193401film_0223; "The M.P. Herald Goes

on New 'Red' Rampage," *Independent Exhibitors Film Bulletin*, August 28, 1935, 7, https://lantern.mediahist.org/catalog/filmbulletin19340ifilm_0431.

116. Jessica L. Whitehead, Louis Pelletier, and Paul S. Moore, "'The Girl Friend in Canada': Ray Lewis and *Canadian Moving Picture Digest* (1915–1957)," in *Mapping Movie Magazines: Digitization, Periodicals and Cinema History*, ed. Lies Van de Vijver and Daniel Biltereyst (Cham, Switzerland: Springer Nature and Palgrave Macmillan, 2020), 137.

117. Whitehead, Pelletier, and Moore, 133.

118. "Jay Emanuel Rites in Phila. Tomorrow," *Film TV Daily*, June 5, 1969, AMPAS clippings file.

119. "The Pride of the East Coast!" [Advertisement], *New York State Exhibitor*, Dec. 25, 1925, 27, http://lantern.mediahist.org/catalog/newyorkstateexhi04eman_0663.

120. Jeanette Willensky to Editor, "A Reply to a 'Sneer,'" *Independent Exhibitors Film Bulletin*, July 24, 1935, 6, https://lantern.mediahist.org/catalog/filmbulletin19340ifilm_0378.

121. Audit Bureau of Circulations, "Auditor's Report: The Philadelphia Exhibitor. Report for the Twelve Months Ending June 30, 1936," Sept. 1936, Alliance for Audited Media, Arlington Heights, IL, microfilm; Audit Bureau of Circulations, "Auditor's Report: The Philadelphia Exhibitor. Report for the Twelve Months Ending March 9, 1939," June 1939, Alliance for Audited Media, Arlington Heights, IL, microfilm.

122. "Seven Midwestern Regional Papers Welded Together," *Motion Picture News*, August 26, 1927, 580, https://lantern.mediahist.org/catalog/motion36moti_0696; "Regional Papers Combine; Gross Circulation 9,000," *Variety*, August 31, 1927, 9, https://lantern.mediahist.org/catalog/variety87-1927-08_0304.

123. "An Advertisement to Advertisers: Announcing Associated Publications," *Film Daily*, August 16, 1927, 11, https://lantern.mediahist.org/catalog/filmdaily4142newy_0405.

124. *Reel Journal*, June 16, 1931, cover and p. 18.

125. Frank Leyendecker, "The Boxoffice Story!," *Boxoffice*, July 12, 1965, 33.

126. Masthead, *Boxoffice* (Southern edition), Feb. 23, 1935, 7. The number would grow to eight sectional editions by 1939—see Masthead, *Boxoffice* (national edition), July 1, 1939, 3.

127. Audit Bureau of Circulations, "Auditor's Report: Boxoffice. Report for the Twelve Months Ending June 30, 1939," Sept. 1939. Alliance for Audited Media, Arlington Heights, IL, microfilm.

128. Audit Bureau of Circulations, "Auditor's Report: Boxoffice. Report for the Twelve Months Ending June 30, 1939," Sept. 1939. Alliance for Audited Media, Arlington Heights, IL, microfilm.

129. *Boxoffice* (New England edition), Jan. 12, 1935, https://archive.org/details/newengboxoffice1935chicrich,

130. Ben Shlyen, "The Right to Live," *Boxoffice* (Western edition), Feb. 16, 1935, 7.

131. Plaintiff Complaint, undated, at 4, Quigley Publishing Company v. Showmen's Round Table and Charles E. Lewis, US District Court for the Southern District of New York, Equity Case Files, RG 21, E 76–321; Audit Bureau of Circulations, "Auditor's Report: *Motion Picture Herald*, Report for the Twelve Months Ending June 30, 1936," Sept. 1936, Alliance for Audited Media, Arlington Heights, IL, microfilm.

132. Fuller-Seeley, "'What the Picture Did for Me,'" 188.

133. Audit Bureau of Circulations, "Auditor's Report: *Motion Picture Herald*. Report for the Twelve Months Ending June 30, 1937," August 1937, Alliance for Audited Media, Arlington Heights, IL, microfilm.

134. Alexander Korda to Martin Quigley, June 16, 1932, Martin J. Quigley Papers, box 3, folder 22, Georgetown University Library; N. V. Cinema Royal to *Motion Picture Herald*, April 20, 1933, Martin J. Quigley Papers, box 3, folder 22, Georgetown University Library; Otto Stadermann to *Motion Picture Herald*, Martin J. Quigley Papers, box 3, folder 26, August 9, 1934; Das & Bhowmik to *Motion Picture Herald*, Oct. 1, 1934, Martin J. Quigley Papers, box 3, folder 26, Georgetown University Library.

135. Colvin W. Brown (General Manager of Quigley Publications), "A Promise and a Performance," ca. 1935, Martin J. Quigley Papers, box 3, folder 17, Georgetown University Library.

136. Martin J. Quigley, "Memorandum on Trade Advertising," ca. 1935, Martin J. Quigley Papers, box 3, folder 17, Georgetown University Library.

137. Martin J. Quigley, "Memorandum on Trade Advertising," ca. 1935, Martin J. Quigley Papers, box 3, folder 17, Georgetown University Library.

138. Richard Maltby, "The Production Code and the Hays Office," in *Grand Design: Hollywood as a Modern Business Enterprise*, by Tino Balio (Berkeley: University of California Press, 1996), 59–61.

139. For an engaging study of Breen's working methods in the PCA, see Thomas Doherty, *Hollywood's Censor: Joseph I. Breen and the Production Code Administration* (New York: Columbia University Press, 2007).

140. Eric Hoyt, *Hollywood Vault: Film Libraries before Home Video* (Berkeley: University of California Press, 2014), 90–91.

141. "London to Hear about American Code," *Motion Picture Herald*, April 20, 1935, 25, https://lantern.mediahist.org/catalog/motionpictureher118iunse_0751; "Hays Representative," *Philadelphia Exhibitor*, May 1, 1935, 35, https://lantern.mediahist.org/catalog/philadelphiaexhi17jaye_0399.

142. Terry Ramsaye, "Twenty Years A-Growing: The Story of Martin Quigley in Motion Picture Journalism," *Motion Picture Herald*, Sept. 28, 1935, 27, https://lantern.mediahist.org/catalog/motionpictureher120iunse_0311.

143. Martin Quigley, *Decency in Motion Pictures* (New York: Macmillan, 1937), 50–52.

144. Advertisement for *Decency in Motion Pictures, Motion Picture Herald*, Feb. 27, 1937, 75, https://lantern.mediahist.org/catalog/motionpictureher126unse_0975.

145. S. F. Van Buren, "The Trade Paper Racket," *New Theatre*, May 1936, 16.

EPILOGUE

1. Patrick Goldstein, "The Big Picture: Variety's Future Looks Bleak," *Los Angeles Times*, July 19, 2012, www.latimes.com/entertainment/movies/la-xpm-2012-jul-19-la-et-mn-big-picture-variety-20120719-story.html.

2. National Public Radio, "Not Doing So 'Boffo,' 'Daily Variety' Drops Print Edition," *Morning Edition*, March 23, 2013, www.npr.org/2013/03/22/174965500/not-doing-so-boffo-daily-variety-drops-print-edition.

3. Brian Stelter, "Alternative Journalist's Web Site Is Scrutinized for Writers' Strike News," *New York Times*, Nov. 26, 2007, https://www.nytimes.com/2007/11/26/business/media/26variety.html.

4. Aly Weisman, "Nikki Finke Wants Deadline Hollywood Blog Back from Penske Media," *Business Insider*, Sept. 6, 2013, https://www.businessinsider.com/nikki-finke-wants-deadline-back-from-penske-media-2013-9.

5. Joe Flint, "Meet Variety's New Boss," *Los Angeles Times*, Oct. 10, 2012, www.latimes.com/entertainment/la-xpm-2012-oct-10-la-et-ct-morningfix-20121010-story.html.

6. For more on this history, see Douglas Gomery, *Shared Pleasures: A History of Movie Presentation in the United States* (Madison: University of Wisconsin Press, 1992); and Charles R. Acland, *Screen Traffic: Movies, Multiplexes, and Global Culture* (Durham, NC: Duke University Press, 2003).

7. "*Boxoffice* Magazine and the National Association of Theatre Owners (NATO) Ink Pact," *Boxoffice Pro* (press release), Nov. 30, 2006, www.natoonline.org/wp-content/uploads/2013/07/bx_nato_final.pdf.

8. Weisman, "Nikki Finke."

9. Nikki Finke's fiction website is called Hollywood Dementia, https://hollywooddementia.com/. See also Ravi Somaiya, "Nikki Finke, Feared Hollywood Reporter, Turns to Fiction," *New York Times*, May 29, 2015, www.nytimes.com/2015/05/30/business/media/feared-hollywood-reporter-turns-to-fiction.html.

10. Anousha Sakoui, "Penske Media and MRC Form Joint Venture Combining Control of Hollywood, Music Titles," *Los Angeles Times*, Sept. 23, 2020, https://www.latimes.com/entertainment-arts/business/story/2020-09-23/penske-media-mrc-hollywood-reporter-variety-billboard-rolling-stone-vibe.

11. Edmund Lee and Tiffany Hsu, "BuzzFeed to Acquire HuffPost from Verizon Media," *New York Times*, Nov. 19, 2020, www.nytimes.com/2020/11/19/business/media/buzzfeed-huffpost.html.

BIBLIOGRAPHY

ARCHIVES

Academy of Motion Picture Arts and Sciences (AMPAS)
Alliance for Audited Media
Georgetown University Library
John F. Kennedy Presidential Library and Museum
Los Angeles County Superior Court Record Center
National Archives and Record Administration, College Park (NARA-CP)
National Archives and Record Administration, San Francisco (NARA-SF)
New York County Clerk Records Center (NYCC)
Wisconsin Historical Society, Madison (WHS)

PUBLISHED COURT DECISIONS AND LAWS

Appeal of Chalmers Publishing Co. to United States Board of Tax Appeals, docket no. 839, 1 B.T.A. 629 (1925). LEXIS 2847.

Davis v. Swetland et al., Supreme Court of New York, Appellate Division First Department, 228 A.D. 759; 239 N.Y.S. 816; 1930 N.Y. App. Div. LEXIS 12930.

FTC v. Famous Players-Lasky Corporation et al. 11 FTC Dec. 187 (1927).

Quigley Publishing Company v. Showmen's Round Table and Charles E. Lewis, US District Court for the Southern District of New York, Equity Case Files, RG 21, E 76–321.

Wilkerson Daily Corporation, Ltd. v. Commissioner of Internal Revenue, United States Board of Tax Appeals, 42 B.T.A. 1266 (1940).

BOOKS, JOURNAL ARTICLES, DISSERTATIONS, AND REPORTS

"A Century of Cinema Literature: The 'Film History' Survey." *Film History* 10, no. 4 (1998): 429–47. www.jstor.org/stable/3815190.

Abel, Richard. *Menus for Movieland: Newspapers and the Emergence of American Film Culture, 1913–1916*. Berkeley: University of California Press, 2015.

———. *The Red Rooster Scare: Making Cinema American, 1900–1910*. Berkeley: University of California Press, 1999.

Acland, Charles R. *Screen Traffic: Movies, Multiplexes, and Global Culture*. Durham, NC: Duke University Press, 2003.

Afra, Kia. "Hollywood's Trade Organizations: How Competition and Collaboration Forged a Vertically-Integrated Oligopoly, 1915–1928." PhD diss., Brown University, 2011.

———. *The Hollywood Trust: Trade Associations and the Rise of the Studio System*. Lanham, MD: Rowman & Littlefield, 2016.

Allen, Robert C. "Vaudeville and Film, 1895–1915: A Study in Media Interaction." PhD diss., University of Iowa, 1977.

———. *Vaudeville and Film, 1895–1915: A Study in Media Interaction*. New York: Arno, 1980.

Anderson, Benedict. *Imagined Communities: Reflections on the Origin and Spread of Nationalism*. Rev. ed. London: Verso, 1991.

Anderson, Robert. "The Motion Picture Patents Company: A Reevaluation." In *The American Film Industry*, edited by Tino Balio, rev. ed., 133–52. Madison: University of Wisconsin Press, 1985.

Baer, D. Richard. Preface to *Harrison's Reports and Film Reviews*. Vol. 1, *1919–1922*. Hollywood: Hollywood Film Archive, 1991.

Baldasty, Gerald J. *The Commercialization of News in the Nineteenth Century*. Madison: University of Wisconsin Press, 1992.

Barry, John M. *The Great Influenza: The Story of the Deadliest Pandemic in History*. New York: Penguin, 2005.

Balio, Tino. *Grand Design: Hollywood as a Modern Business Enterprise, 1930–1939*. Berkeley: University of California Press, 1993.

———. *MGM*. New York: Routledge, 2018.

Banks, Miranda J. *The Writers: A History of American Screenwriters and Their Guild*. New Brunswick, NJ: Rutgers University Press, 2015.

Beauchamp, Cari. *Joseph P. Kennedy Presents: His Hollywood Years*. New York: Alfred A. Knopf, 2009.

Besas, Peter. *Inside "Variety": The Story of the Bible of Show Business, 1905–1987*. Madrid: Ars Millenii, 2000.

Biltereyst, Daniel, Richard Maltby, and Philippe Meers, eds. *The Routledge Companion to New Cinema History*. New York: Routledge, 2019.

Bordwell, David, Janet Staiger, and Kristin Thompson. *The Classical Hollywood Cinema: Film Style & Mode of Production to 1960*. New York: Columbia University Press, 1985.

Bowser, Eileen. *The Transformation of Cinema, 1907–1915*. New York: Scribner, 1990.

Braudy, Leo. *The Hollywood Sign: Fantasy and Reality of an American Icon*. New Haven, CT: Yale University Press, 2011.

Caldwell, John Thornton. *Production Culture: Industrial Reflexivity and Critical Practice in Film and Television*. Durham, NC: Duke University Press, 2008.

Calomiris, Charles W., and Joseph R. Mason. "Fundamentals, Panics, and Bank Distress during the Depression." *American Economic Review* 93, no. 5 (Dec. 2003): 1615–47.

Carey, James W. *Communication as Culture: Essays on Media and Society*. New York: Routledge, 1988.

———. "A Cultural Approach to Communication." In Carey, *Communication as Culture*, 13–36.

Chauncey, George. *Gay New York: Gender, Urban Culture, and the Making of the Gay Male World, 1890–1940*. New York: Basic Books, 1995.

Clark, Danae. *Negotiating Hollywood: The Cultural Politics of Actors' Labor*. Minneapolis: University of Minnesota Press, 1995.

Crafton, Donald. *The Talkies: American Cinema's Transition to Sound, 1926–1931*. New York: Charles Scribner's Sons, 1997.

Curtis, Scott. "A House Divided: The MPPC in Transition." In *American Cinema's Transitional Era: Audiences, Institutions, Practices*, edited by Charlie Keil and Shelley Stamp, 239–64. Berkeley: University of California Press, 2004.

DeBauche, Leslie Midkiff. *Reel Patriotism: The Movies and World War I*. Madison: University of Wisconsin Press, 1997.

Dickstein, Morris. *Dancing in the Dark: A Cultural History of the Great Depression*. New York: Norton, 2009.

Doherty, Thomas. *Hollywood's Censor: Joseph I. Breen and the Production Code Administration*. New York: Columbia University Press, 2007.

Elfenbein, Julien. *Business Journalism: Its Function and Future*. New York: Harper & Brothers, 1945.

Everett, Anna. *Returning the Gaze: A Genealogy of Black Film Criticism, 1909–1949*. Durham, NC: Duke University Press, 2001.

Fisk, Catherine L. *Writing for Hire: Unions, Hollywood, and Madison Avenue*. Cambridge, MA: Harvard University Press, 2016.

Fitzpatrick, Vincent. "THE AMERICAN MERCURY." *Menckeniana*, no. 123 (1992): 1–6. www.jstor.org/stable/26483894.

Foote, Lisle. "Fanchon Royer." In *Women Film Pioneers Project*, edited by Jane Gaines, Radha Vatsal, and Monica Dall'Asta. Center for Digital Research and Scholarship. New York: Columbia University Libraries, 2013. https://wfpp.cdrs.columbia.edu/pioneer/fanchon-royer/.

Fuller, Kathryn H. *At the Picture Show: Small-Town Audiences and the Creation of Movie Fan Culture*. Charlottesville: University Press of Virginia, 2001.

Fuller-Seeley, Kathryn. "Dish Night at the Movies: Exhibitors and Female Audiences during the Great Depression." In *Looking Past the Screen: Case Studies in American Film History and Method*, edited by Jon Lewis and Eric Smoodin, 246–75. Durham, NC: Duke University Press, 2007.

———. "'What the Picture Did for Me': Small Town Exhibitors' Strategies for Surviving the Great Depression." In *Hollywood in the Neighborhood: Historical Case Studies of Local Moviegoing*, edited by Kathryn Fuller-Seeley, 186–207. Berkeley: University of California Press, 2008.

Gevinson, Alan "Motion Picture News." In Slide, *International Film*, 242–46.

Gomery, Douglas. *The Coming of Sound: A History*. New York: Routledge, 2005.

———. *The Hollywood Studio System: A History*. London: British Film Institute, 2005.

————. *Shared Pleasures: A History of Movie Presentation in the United States.* Madison: University of Wisconsin Press, 1992.

Grau, Robert. *The Theatre of Science: A Volume of Progress and Achievement in the Motion Picture Industry.* New York: Broadway Publishing, 1914. http://lantern.mediahist.org /catalog/cu31924026115737_0423.

Gray, Tim. *"Variety": An Illustrated History of the World from the Most Important Magazine in Hollywood.* New York: Rizzoli, 2012.

Grieveson, Lee. *Policing Cinema: Movies and Censorship in Early-Twentieth-Century America.* Berkeley: University of California Press, 2004.

Guernsey, Roscellus S. "When a Libel Is Not a Libel." *Yale Law Journal* 20, no. 1 (1910): 37. www.jstor.org/stable/785040.

Havens, Timothy, Amanda D. Lotz, and Serra Tinic. "Critical Media Industry Studies: A Research Approach." *Communication, Culture & Critique* 2 (2009): 234–53.

Hill, Erin. *Never Done: A History of Women's Work in Media Production.* New Brunswick, NJ: Rutgers University Press, 2018.

Hoffman, George Jeremiah. "The Reminiscences of Jerry Hoffman" (Oral History). American Film Institute / Louis B. Mayer Oral History Collection, Part 1 (1977), TIB/P26.

Holt, Jennifer, and Alisa Perren, eds. *Media Industries: History, Theory, and Method.* Malden, MA: Wiley-Blackwell, 2009.

Horowitz, Cecile B. "Film Daily." In Slide, *International Film,* 121–24.

Hoyt, Eric. "Arclights and Zoom Lenses: Searching for Influential Exhibitors in Film History's Big Data." In *The Routledge Companion to New Cinema History,* edited by Daniel Biltereyst, Richard Maltby, and Philippe Meers, 83–95. New York: Routledge, 2019.

————. "Asset or Liability? Hollywood and Tax Law." In *Hollywood and the Law,* edited by Paul McDonald, Emily Carman, Eric Hoyt, and Philip Drake, 183–208. London: BFI/ Palgrave, 2015.

————. "Building a Lantern and Keeping It Burning." In *Applied Media Studies,* edited by Kirsten Ostherr, 238–50. New York: Routledge, 2017.

————. "Dossier: Technology and the Trade Press: Exhibitors, Technology, and Industrial Journalism in the 1910s and 1920s." *Velvet Light Trap* 76 (2015): 49–53.

————. *Hollywood Vault: Film Libraries before Home Video.* Berkeley: University of California Press, 2014.

————. "Lenses for Lantern: Data Mining, Visualization, and Excavating Film History's Neglected Sources." *Film History* 26, no. 2 (2014): 146–68.

Hoyt, Eric, Kit Hughes, Derek Long, Kevin Ponto, and Anthony Tran. "Scaled Entity Search: A Method for Media Historiography and Response to Critiques of Big Humanities Data Research." *Proceedings of IEEE Conference on Big Data* (2014): 51–59. http://ieeexplore .ieee.org/xpl/articleDetails.jsp?arnumber=7004453.

Hoyt, Eric, Derek Long, Anthony Tran, and Kit Hughes. "*Variety*'s Transformations: Digitizing and Analyzing a Canonical Trade Paper." *Film History* 27, no. 4 (2015): 76–105.

Hughes, Kit, Eric Hoyt, Derek Long, Kevin Ponto, and Anthony Tran. "Hacking Radio History's Data: Station Call Letter, Digitized Magazines, and Scaled Entity Search." *Media Industries Journal* 2, no. 2 (2015): n.p. www.mediaindustriesjournal.org/index.php/mij /article/view/128/182.

"The Important Twelve." In *Film Year Book, 1922–1923*, edited by Joseph Dannenberg, 267. New York: Wid's Films and Film Folks, 1923. https://lantern.mediahist.org/catalog/film yearb1922192223newy_0283.

Jacobs, Lea. *The Decline of Sentiment: American Film in the 1920s*. Berkeley: University of California Press, 2008.

James, David E. *The Most Typical Avant-Garde: History and Geography of Minor Cinemas in Los Angeles*. Berkeley: University of California Press, 2005.

Jewell, Richard B. *The Golden Age of Cinema: Hollywood, 1929–1945*. Malden, MA: Blackwell, 2007.

———. *RKO Radio Pictures: A Titan Is Born*. Berkeley: University of California Press, 2012.

Johnson, Derek. *Media Franchising: Creative License and Collaboration in the Culture Industries*. New York: New York University Press, 2013.

Johnston, William A. "The Structure of the Motion Picture Industry." *Annals of the American Academy of Political and Social Science* 128 (Nov. 1926): 24–25.

Kail, Anne. "Moving Picture World." In Slide, *International Film*, 262–66.

Kemper, Tom. *Hidden Talent: The Emergence of Hollywood Agents*. Berkeley: University of California Press, 2009.

Kennedy, Susan Estabrook. *The Banking Crisis of 1933*. Lexington: University Press of Kentucky, 1973.

Kosar, Kevin R. "Postage Subsidies for Periodicals: History and Recent Developments." Washington, DC: Congressional Research Service, 2009. https://archive.org/details /PostageSubsidiesForPeriodicalsCRSReportR40162.

Koszarski, Richard. *An Evening's Entertainment: The Age of the Silent Feature Picture, 1915–1928*. Berkeley: University of California Press, 1990.

Labuza, Peter. "When a Handshake Meant Something: Lawyers, Deal Making, and the Emergence of New Hollywood." PhD diss., University of Southern California, 2020.

Lane, Tamar. *Hey Diddle Diddle*. New York: Adelphia, 1932.

———. *What's Wrong with the Movies?* Los Angeles: Waverly, 2013.

Lester, Peter. "Why I Am Ashamed of the Movies: Editorial Policy, Early Hollywood, and the Case of *Camera!*" *Moving Image* 18, no. 1 (Spring 2018): 48–66.

Lewis, Howard T. *The Motion Picture Industry*. New York: D. Van Norstrand, 1933. http:// lantern.mediahist.org/catalog/motionpictureindoohowa_0286.

Long, Derek. "Reprogramming the Movies: Distribution Strategy and Production Planning in the Early Studio System, 1915–1924." PhD diss., University of Wisconsin-Madison, 2017.

Long, Derek, Eric Hoyt, Anthony Tran, Kevin Ponto, and Kit Hughes. "Who's Trending in 1910s American Cinema? Exploring ECHO and MHDL at Scale with Arclight." *Moving Image* 16, no. 1 (2016): 57–81.

Maltby, Richard. "The Production Code and the Hays Office." In *Grand Design: Hollywood as a Modern Business Enterprise*, by Tino Balio, 37–72. Berkeley: University of California Press, 1993.

Marvin, Carolyn. *When Old Technologies Were New: Thinking about Electric Communication in the Late Nineteenth Century*. New York: Oxford University Press, 1988.

Marzola, Luci. "Engineering Hollywood: Technology, Technicians, and the Building of the Studio System, 1915–1930." PhD diss., University of Southern California, 2016.

McArthur, Benjamin. *Actors and American Culture, 1880–1920*. Iowa City: University of Iowa Press, 2000.

McDonald, Tamar Jeffers, and Lies Lackman, eds. *Star Attractions: Twentieth-Century Movie Magazines and Global Fandom*. Iowa City: University of Iowa Press, 2019.

McKenna, Denise. "The Photoplay or the Pickaxe: Extras, Gender, and Labour in Early Hollywood." *Film History* 23, no. 1 (2011): 5–19.

McKenna, Denise, and Charlie Keil. "Mirrors of Hollywood: Strategies of Self-Representation." Paper presented at the Society for Cinema and Media Studies Conference, Chicago, March 24, 2017.

Melnick, Ross. *American Showman: Samuel "Roxy" Rothafel and the Birth of the Entertainment Industry*. New York: Columbia University Press, 2012.

———. "Station R-O-X-Y: Roxy and the Radio." *Film History* 17, no. 2/3 (Jan. 1, 2005): 217–33.

Monticone, Paul. "For the Maintenance of the System: Institutional and Cultural Change within the Motion Picture Producers and Distributors of America, 1922–1945." PhD diss., University of Texas, Austin, 2019.

Moore, Paul. "Advance Newspaper Publicity for the Vitascope and Cinema's Mass Reading Public." In *A Companion to Early Cinema*, edited by André Gaudreault, Nicolas Dulac, and Santiago Hidalgo, 381–97. Malden, MA: Blackwell, 2012.

Morey, Anne. "Early Art Cinema in the U.S.: Symon Gould and the Little Cinema Movement of the 1920s." In *Going to the Movies: Hollywood and the Social Experience of the Cinema*, edited by Richard Maltby, Melvyn Stokes, and Robert C. Allen, 235–47. Exeter: University of Exeter Press, 2008.

Muscio, Giuliana. *Hollywood's New Deal*. Philadelphia: Temple University Press, 1997.

Musser, Charles. *The Emergence of Cinema: The American Screen to 1907*. New York: Scribner's, 1991.

Nasaw, David. *Going Out: The Rise and Fall of Public Amusements*. Cambridge, MA: Harvard University Press, 1999.

N. W. Ayer & Son's American Newspaper Annual and Directory. Library of Congress Digital Collections. https://lccn.loc.gov/sn91012092.

Olsson, Jan. *Los Angeles before Hollywood: Journalism and American Film Culture, 1905 to 1915*. Stockholm: National Library of Sweden, 2008.

Overpeck, Deron. "Out of the Dark: American Film Exhibition, Political Action and Industrial Change, 1966–1986." PhD diss., University of California, Los Angeles, 2007.

Petty, Miriam. *Stealing the Show: African American Performers and Audiences in 1930s Hollywood*. Berkeley: University of California Press, 2016.

Phelan, John Joseph. *Motion Pictures as a Phase of Commercial Amusement in Toledo, Ohio*. Toledo, OH: Little Book Press, 1919. www.archive.org/details/motionpicturesaoophelgoog.

Quigley, Martin [J.]. *Decency in Motion Pictures*. New York: Macmillan, 1937.

Quigley, Martin S. *Martin J. Quigley and the Glory Days of American Film, 1915–1965*. Groton, MA: Quigley Publishing, 2006.

Quinn, Michael J. "Paramount and Early Feature Distribution: 1914–1921." *Film History* 11, no. 1 (1999): 98–113.

Ramsaye, Terry. *A Million and One Nights: A History of the Motion Picture*. New York: Simon and Schuster, 1926.

"Report of Commission on Second-Class Mail Matter." *United States Congressional Serial Set* 62:53–148. Washington, DC: Government Printing Office, 1912. https://books.google.com/books?id=oNw3AQAAIAAJ.

Resha, Davis. "Strategies for Survival: The Little Exhibitor in the 1920s." *Quarterly Review of Film and Video* 29, no. 1 (2012): 12–23.

Richardson, F. H. *Motion Picture Handbook: A Guide for Managers and Operators of Motion Picture Theatres.* New York: Moving Picture World, 1910. http://lantern.mediahist.org/catalog/motionpicturehanoorich_0005.

———. *Richardson's Handbook of Projection: The Blue Book of Projection.* 5th ed. New York: Chalmers Publishing, 1927. https://archive.org/details/richardsonshandbo2fhri/page/n5.

Rodgers, Marion Elizabeth. *Mencken: The American Iconoclast.* Oxford: Oxford University Press, 2005. https://books.google.com/books?id=F60762CfNPQC.

Root, Charles T. "The History and Development of Economic Journalism." In *Lectures in the Forum in Industrial Journalism at the New York University, Season of 1915,* 9–27. New York: Advertising & Selling Magazine, 1915. https://archive.org/details/lecturesinforumioonewyrich.

Rosten, Leo C. *Hollywood: The Movie Colony, the Movie Makers.* New York: Harcourt, Brace, 1941.

Schatz, Thomas. *Boom and Bust: The American Cinema in the 1940s.* New York: Charles Scribner's Sons, 1997.

Schudson, Michael. *Discovering the News: A Social History of American Newspapers.* New York: Basic Books, 1978.

Serna, Laura Isabel. "Cine-Mundial" (Description). In *Lantern,* 2013, https://lantern.mediahist.org/catalog/cinemundial13unse_1068.

Simmons, E. A. "Business Press Opportunities." In *Lectures in the Forum in Industrial Journalism at the New York University, Season of 1915,* 28–46. New York: Advertising & Selling Magazine, 1915. https://archive.org/details/lecturesinforumioonewyrich.

Singer, Ben. "Feature Films, Variety Programs, and the Crisis of the Small Exhibitor." In *American Cinema's Transitional Era: Audiences, Institutions, Practices,* edited by Charlie Keil and Shelley Stamp, 76–100. Berkeley: University of California Press, 2004.

Slide, Anthony. *Inside the Hollywood Fan Magazine.* Jackson: University Press of Mississippi, 2010.

———, ed. *International Film, Radio, and Television Journals.* Westport, CT: Greenwood Press, 1985.

Smoodin, Eric. "The History of Film History." In *Looking Past the Screen: Case Studies in American Film History and Method,* edited by Jon Lewis and Eric Smoodin, 1–34. Durham, NC: Duke University Press, 2007.

Steiner, Jesse. *Research Memorandum on Recreation in the Depression.* New York: Social Science Research Council, 1937.

Stoddart, Dayton. *Lord Broadway: Variety's Sime.* New York: Wilfred Funk, 1941.

Stromgren, Richard L. "The Moving Picture World of W. Stephen Bush." *Film History* 2, no. 1 (Winter 1988): 13–22.

Swetland, Horace M. *Industrial Publishing.* New York: New York Business Publishers Association, 1923.

———. "The Special Service of the Class Paper to an Industry." In *Lectures in the Forum in Industrial Journalism at the New York University, Season of 1915*, 59–70. New York: Advertising & Selling Magazine, 1915. https://archive.org/details/lecturesinforumioonewyrich.

Tapia Granados, José A., and Ana V. Diez Roux. "Life and Death during the Great Depression." *Proceedings of the National Academy of Sciences* 106, no. 41 (Oct. 13, 2009): 17290–95. www.pnas.orgcgidoi10.1073pnas.0904491106.

Thomas, Bob. *Thalberg: Life and Legend*. Beverly Hills, CA: New Millennium Press, 2020. Reprint of 1969 volume.

Ukers, W. H. "Standards of Practice of the Business Press." In *Lectures in the Forum in Industrial Journalism at the New York University, Season of 1915*, 97–113. New York: Advertising & Selling Magazine, 1915. https://archive.org/details/lecturesinforumioonewyrich.

United States Postal Service. "Postage Rates for Periodicals: A Narrative History." June 2010. https://about.usps.com/who-we-are/postal-history/periodicals-postage-history.pdf.

US Postal Commission. "Briefs and Points on Behalf, Federation of Trade Press Associations in the United States." In *Hearings before the Postal Commission*. Washington, DC: Government Printing Office, 1907. https://books.google.com/books?id=ThsvAAAAMAAJ.

Van de Vijver, Lies, and Daniel Biltereyst, eds. *Mapping Movie Magazines: Digitization, Periodicals and Cinema History*. Cham, Switzerland: Springer Nature and Palgrave Macmillan, 2020.

Vaughn, Stephen. "Morality and Entertainment: The Origins of the Motion Picture Production Code." *Journal of American History* 77, no. 1 (June 1990): 39–65.

Waller, Gregory A. "Imagining and Promoting the Small-Town Theater." *Cinema Journal* 44, no. 3 (2005): 3–19.

———. "Projecting the Promise of 16mm, 1935–1945." In *Useful Cinema*, edited by Charles R. Acland and Haidee Wasson, 125–48. Durham, NC: Duke University Press, 2011.

———. "Search and Re-search: Digital Print Archives and the History of Multi-sited Cinema." In *The Arclight Guidebook to Media History and the Digital Humanities*, edited by Charles R. Acland and Eric Hoyt. Falmer, East Sussex: REFRAME/Project Arclight, 2016. https://projectarclight.org/book/.

Wasko, Janet. *Movies and Money: Financing the American Film Industry*. Norwood, NJ: Ablex, 1982.

Wertheim, Arthur Frank. *Vaudeville Wars: How the Keith-Albee and Orpheum Circuits Controlled the Big-Time and Its Performers*. New York: Palgrave Macmillan, 2006.

Whitehead, Jessica, Louis Pelletier, and Paul S. Moore. "'The Girl Friend in Canada': Ray Lewis and *Canadian Moving Picture Digest* (1915–1957)." In *Mapping Movie Magazines: Digitization, Periodicals and Cinema History*, edited by Lies Van de Vijver and Daniel Biltereyst, 127–52. Cham, Switzerland: Springer Nature and Palgrave Macmillan, 2020.

Wigmore, Barrie A. "Was the Bank Holiday of 1933 Caused by a Run on the Dollar?" *Journal of Economic History* 47, no. 3 (Sept. 1987): 739–55.

Wilkerson, Tichi, and Marcia Borie. Preface to *"The Hollywood Reporter": The Golden Years*, edited by Tichi Wilkerson and Marcia Borie. New York: Arlington House, 1986.

Wilkerson, W. R., III. *Hollywood Godfather: The Life and Crimes of Billy Wilkerson*. Chicago: Chicago Review Press, 2018.

Wilton, David. "Journo's Boffo Lingo: The Slang of *Daily Variety*," *Verbatim: The Language Quarterly* 30, no. 1 (Spring 2005): 2–6.

Wittern-Keller, Laura. "Controlling Content: Governmental Censorship, the Production Code, and the Ratings System." In *Hollywood and the Law*, edited by Paul McDonald, Emily Carman, Eric Hoyt, and Philip Drake, 130–53. London: Palgrave, 2015.

Yates, JoAnne. Control through Communication: The Rise of System in American Management. Baltimore: Johns Hopkins University Press, 1993.

Yogerst, Chris. *Hollywood Hates Hitler! Jew-Baiting, Anti-Nazism, and the Senate Investigation into Warmongering in Motion Pictures.* Jackson: University Press of Mississippi, 2020.

FILM AND ENTERTAINMENT INDUSTRY TRADE PAPERS

Accessory News
Allied Amusements Bulletin
American Cinematographer
Amusements
Billboard
Boxoffice
Camera!
Canadian Moving Picture Digest
Cine-Mundial
Close Up
Daily Film Renter (London)
Daily Variety
Deadline Hollywood
Die Lichtbild-Bühne (Berlin)
The Exhibitor
Exhibitors Daily Review and Motion Pictures Today
Exhibitor's Film Review Service
Exhibitors Herald (previously *Exhibitors Film Exchange*)
Exhibitors Herald and Moving Picture World
Exhibitors' Journal
Exhibitors' Times
Exhibitor's Trade Review
Exhibitors' Tribune
Film Curb
Film Daily
Film Mercury
Film Spectator (later *Hollywood Spectator*)
Film Trade Topics
Film Views and Index
Greater Amusements
Harrison's Reports
Hollywood Filmograph
Hollywood Herald
Hollywood Reporter

Hollywood Topics
Hollywood Vagabond
The Implet
Independent Exhibitors Film Bulletin
Inside Facts of Stage and Screen
International Photographer
International Projectionist
Interstate Film News
Journal of the Society of Motion Picture Engineers
La Cinématographie française (Paris)
Michigan Film Review
Morning Telegraph
Motion Picture Bulletin
Motion Picture Daily
Motion Picture Digest
Motion Picture Herald
Motion Picture Journal (Dallas, TX)
Motion Picture Journal (New York)
Motion Picture News
Motion Picture Review
Motion Picture Weekly
Motion Pictures Today
Motion Pictures Today and Exhibitors Daily Review
Motography
Movie Age
Moving Picture Bulletin
Moving Picture News
Moving Picture World
New England Exhibitor
New Theatre
New York Clipper
New York Dramatic Mirror
New York Morning Telegraph
New York State Exhibitor
Nickelodeon
Ohio Showman
Oklahoma Film News
Pacific Coast Independent Exhibitor
Philadelphia Exhibitor
Reel Facts
Reel Journal
Rocky Mountain Screen News
Screencraft
Showmen's Trade Review (previously *Showmen's Round Table*)
Southern Picture News

Tullar's Weekly
Universal Weekly
Variety
Views and Films Index
Weekly Film Review
Wid's Daily
Wid's Weekly

NEWSPAPERS AND MAGAZINES

Los Angeles Times
New York Times
Saturday Evening Post
Wall Street Journal

INDEX

Founded in 1893,
UNIVERSITY OF CALIFORNIA PRESS
publishes bold, progressive books and journals
on topics in the arts, humanities, social sciences,
and natural sciences—with a focus on social
justice issues—that inspire thought and action
among readers worldwide.

The UC PRESS FOUNDATION
raises funds to uphold the press's vital role
as an independent, nonprofit publisher, and
receives philanthropic support from a wide
range of individuals and institutions—and from
committed readers like you. To learn more, visit
ucpress.edu/supportus.